HISTORY OF
THE COMMUNIST PARTY
OF USSR

Rudolf Schlesinger

HISTORY OF THE COMMUNIST PARTY OF USSR

PAST AND PRESENT

South Asia Books

SOUTH ASIA BOOKS

Box 502

COLUMBIA
MISSOURI 65201

© ORIENT LONGMAN LIMITED, CALCUTTA, 1977

ISBN 0-88386—921-7

Printed in India at
SREEBHUMI MUDRANIKA
77 Lenin Sarani, Calcutta 700013

PREFACE

ORGANISED bodies of active revolutionaries have played their part in all major revolutions. The Russian revolution, and those which have followed its example, present some novelty in that the organization of the revolutionary vanguard has turned into the institutional framework of the new polity. Events following Stalin's death have confirmed this thesis. Whatever conclusions as to the supposed necessity of an individual leader of predominant authority may be drawn from these events (in my opinion, the observation period is still far too short for generalisations on that issue), it is obvious that individual leadership can play its part only within the party framework. During the foreseeable future, changes in Soviet society will proceed through that framework just as foreseeable changes in British society will proceed through the parliamentary framework. It is the purpose of this book to show how the Party framework has grown and how its functions have developed. It may also help in understanding the reasons for the development of the Communist Party as a permanent institutional framework, while so many other revolutions ended in military dictatorship and/or restoration. Political and economic history is relevant to our investigation only as the background for the Party's development. It is not my intention to offer an alternative to the existing studies in these fields. Least of all is it my intention to go into the *chronique scandaleuse* of the Russian revolutionary movement, or even into the personal conflicts between the communist leaders except in so far as these are relevant to an appreciation of the social forces which shaped and changed the party institution.

Our study is orientated towards an understanding of the present. Some readers may hence ask why I have reached so far back to the pre-Marxist origins of the Russian revolutionary movement. I believe, however, that there is a continuity in the main purpose which that movement had to fulfil, even though it was not always conscious of its historical function and though there could be no continuity in its organisational bodies. Even the acceptance of continuity of traditions was broken (at certain times, the Bolsheviks accepted the inheritance of their predecessors—of course, with necessary criticisms—at others the very concept of 'one stream' (*ediny potok*) was denounced as an ideological deviation). Yet the problem of turning a backward peasant country into a modern industrial society based upon socialist principles dominated the Russian revolution. It began in the days when the young revolutionary intellectuals tried to express socialist ideas through the village community and has continued up to our times when the *kolkhoz* was freed from the tribute it had to pay in order to help industrialization and compete with the socialist state industry. Without a study of the earlier periods it is not possible to appreciate either the current Western treatment of Soviet developments in terms of an *elite* which becomes effective by the dynamics of its own internal conflicts rather than by its dependence on the mass-processes of the time, or the recent Soviet tendency to describe present tasks in terms of a 'return to Lenin'. The relative attention devoted to the various stages in party history in this study is bound to differ from that in western studies, dominated as they are by the Trotsky-Stalin feud, or by the consolidation of Stalin's dictatorship as the supposedly central event in the development of Soviet communism.

Since this book is not intended as a history of the USSR, general problems of Russian history and even the non-Bolshevik trends within the Russian revolutionary movement are touched upon (preferably by reference to the original sources rather than by argument with other historians) only in so far as I felt it necessary for the study of the party as a political institution. There is little sense in a description of 'rules' without reference to the problems in tackling which they were applied or in giving data about the party's social structure without asking what the party members actually did. The question of where to draw the line without making this book either far too long, or too dry, cannot be answered in an abstract way. Every solution found is bound to provoke criticism, even justified ones. An author afraid even of justified criticism should keep clear of complicated subjects.

In describing the sources on which this book is based, a distinction should be made between the general political framework and the party's internal life, as seen not just from the top but also, as far as possible, from the standpoint of the rank and file. As regards the first, conditions have thoroughly changed since, when writing the first draft of this book, I had to rely on the writings of the three outstanding leaders—Lenin, Stalin and Trotsky—plus the proceedings of the Party Congresses (even these are not easily accessible in Britain) for the bulk of the available material. By now, the work of my colleagues has turned the period up to 1926—where, for the moment, Carr's History of the USSR ends—into an ordinary 'period' of contemporary history, distinct from others mainly in that every gap in information on Soviet politics is regarded as the appearance of a sinister 'iron curtain' even by people who regard the secrecy of British Cabinet records and the inaccessibility of pre-1914 archives as most natural. Since the Twentieth Party Congress, Soviet source publications and, at least for the pre-1922 period, also the original work of Soviet historians have created conditions which are not less favourable than those existing for the student of other political movements. From about 1929 onwards, however, the descriptive type of evidence does not only dry up but is even replaced by a mythology which in recent Soviet publications is being pruned of its worst excesses. Thus such evidence as we have on the later part of the Stalin period is mainly indirect, based on legislation, on the character of party interventions in the ideological fields, etc. This does not allow for definite statements about the organizational channels through which the trends thus described found expression.

For the last, still current, period we have again much evidence on details of organizational life, in particular if we supplement the dry statements of the Central Committee's house journal (now *Fartiinaya zhizn*) and of organizational handbooks, by the fairly frank description of actual life given since the 'thaw' by Soviet authors. About events at the top we still do not know more than the majority group of the Central Committee deems fit to publish, e.g. formal submission of outvoted minorities appears to be the condition for the more civilized treatment which they receive in the post-Stalin era. But since the secrecy on basic economic data has been lifted, and major reforms are now prepared by open discussion with some scope for dissenting opinion, it is possible to guess what the disputes even within the party leadership actually were about and which social pressures find expression in the party framework. It is these processes with which we, as distinct from those who regard power struggle between individuals as the most interesting subject of history, are concerned.

The first text of this book was prepared in the years 1959-61, and published, in 1962, in an Italian translation by Elena Spagnol Vaccari and Danilo Montaldi, under the title *Il partito Communista nell URRS,* by Giangiacomo Feltrinelli, Milano. For the present publication, in English, the text has been thoroughly revised, in particular in the last chapter, and brought up to date up to the Twenty-third Party Congress in spring 1966.

Invereoch, Kilmun by Dunoon   RUDOLF SCHLESINGER
Argyll
August 30, 1966

CONTENTS

CHAPTER I

FROM THE CIRCLE TO THE PARTY

(a) THE YOUNG INTELLECTUALS AND THE PEASANTRY

FROM the emancipation of the serfs to the October revolution the growth of capitalism in Russia was accompanied by a succession of revolutionary organisations. These were rooted in the traditions of the prolonged struggle against serfdom. In some respects, the insurrection of the Decembrists in 1825 may be regarded as the last of the military conspiracies through which young army officers, members of the nobility, tried to shape their country's fate. At the same time it marked the culmination of the impact made by the liberal ideas of revolutionary France upon Russian youth. Decades later Herzen described the *Te Deum* sung in the Moscow Kremlin on the occasion of the execution of the Decembrists as one of the formative influences of his youth. But the circles of the thirties in which Stankevich, Bakunin, Belinsky, Herzen, Ogarev and Passek learnt about contemporary German philosophy and Fourier and St. Simon reflected a stage of western intellectual development which went beyond the ideas even of the left-wing of the Decembrists. Ogarev later remembered the sacred promise which three young friends—Herzen, Passek and himself—made to each other :

> We three—we children of the Decembrists,
> And apprentices of the New World,
> Apprentices of Fourier and Saint Simon,
> We swore that we would devote all our lives,
> To the people and to the cause of its emancipation,
> That we would lay foundation stones of socialism.

The promise was kept. Young Russians differed from Western undergraduates of those days, not so much in their romantic dreams as in that circumstances drove them to transform the dreams of their youth into reality.

Herzen developed the idea that a purely political revolution was no longer possible as early as June 1843,[1] i.e. at about the same time as it found expression in Marx's most important pre-Marxist writing, *Introduction to a Critique of the Hegelian Philosophy of Law*. The idea was 'in the air' but it is relevant to note that the air breathed by the most advanced Russians was not much inferior to that of post-Hegelian Germany. The emigration of Russian progressives to the West played its part in the transfer of western radical concepts to Russia. The frequently alleged anticipation of some Bolshevik ideas by Bakunin, Nechayev and Tkachev, if submitted to a critical analysis, shows that certain concepts of conspiracy, as developed by the Blanquists in France and received by the anarchist wing of the International, had their application in the Russian underground. Still there was no clear distinction between cosmopolitan revolutionary adventure, as represented most prominently by Bakunin, and the idea of the exiles as helpers of the revolutionary movement at home (nor could it be elaborated as long as the movement inside Russia was negligible). Herzen came nearest to it, but only by the following generation of revolutionaries was it firmly established. The borderline between the pre-history and the history of the Russian revolutionary movement was passed when the emancipation of the peasants opened a fundamental cleavage. It was between those who wished to get rid of the obsolete forms of serfdom in a way which left the vested interests unaffected (the aspirations of the right-wing of the Decembrists had not gone beyond such a 'Prussian' solution) and those who regarded peasant emancipation as revolution involving the foundations of Russian society.

Using the impact made by Russia's defeat in the Crimean War upon the upper strata of Russian society, Herzen started abroad the publication of his *Polarnaya zvezda* (The Polar Star—intentionally, the title of one of the abortive publications of the Decembrists was resumed) and of his more famous *Kolokol* (*The Bell*, 1857-67). For a time, *Kolokol's* circulation rose to two to three thousand copies and reached the highest strata of the Russian government. Within Russia, there arose a new generation of revolutionaries, whose outstanding leaders were Chernyshevski and Dobrolyubov. As distinct from the earlier period, it was not the young aristocrat revolting against his surroundings but the young intellectual from a lower-middle-class home (the *raznochinets*) who became the predominant figure in the circles. At first, the new trend found expression in open publications, thinly veiled as concerned with mere literary criticism. In 1861, however, its sympathisers published three issues of *Velikoruss,* the first important underground periodical in the history of the Russian revolutionary movement. About forty persons are known to have participated in this work, 600 copies of which were distributed at the universities and in the army.[2] Chernyshevski, soon supported by Herzen, initiated the organisation *Zemlya i volya* (Land and Liberty—the two slogans proclaimed in a programmatic article of Ogarev, published in *Kolokol*). At least on his part, it was conceived as a centralised underground organisation preparing for decisive struggle. Publication of Manifestos formed the organisation's main activity. One of the first of these,[3] written at the time of the revolts of the disappointed peasants which followed the publication of the Emancipation Manifesto, warned against premature insurrections, yet invited the peasants to prepare for the struggle which would be organised and coordinated by the revolutionary organisation. Such evidence of the programme discussed in the groups of *Zemlya i volya* as we possess[4] points to a platform of consistent democracy and to nationalisation of the land as well as of the basic industries, the land being distributed amongst the peasants for their use in communities (there is, however, no such one-sided emphasis on the village community as in later Narodnik publications). The need for a popular revolution, led by the revolutionary party, was clearly accepted.

The real strength of the organisation *Zemlya i volya* is still a matter of controversy. Soviet versions of an organised body with a Central Committee, represented by the *Kolokol* group abroad, may have been inspired by retrojection of the conditions existing in the later stages of the revolutionary movement.[5] But it should be kept in mind that only modern Soviet publica-

tions are based upon archive materials, as distinct from the work
of exiles who relied mostly upon declarations made by defendants on trial with an obvious desire to avoid involving
comrades still at large.[5] From recent publications[6] we get the
picture of an organisation functioning fairly well as late as the
first half of 1863, i.e. after the re-organisation caused by the
arrest of Chernyshevski and his closest friends. It formed a
federation of circles under local committees, each based, for
security reasons, on groups of five, the members of which knew
only each other. Local branches, of unequal strength, existed in
Petersburg, Moscow, Kazan, Saratov (where Chernyshevski's
personal influence still was felt), Vologda, Nizhny-Novgorod,
Astrakhan, Tver, Tula, Vladimir, Kursk, Poltava and possibly
Perm. Apart from these there existed a military organisation.
Zemlya i volya's total strength appears to have reached only a
few hundred, most of them students and army officers, but its
connecions appear to have reached even fairly high into the
bureaucracy.

These data reflect more than a confusion in the minds of
participants as well as of prosecutors, of active participants and
mere sympathisers, but the old *Zemlya i volya* evidently equalled
its successor[7] in numerical strength—though, of course, not in
experience and efficiency. It formed a landmark in the history
of the Russian revolutionary movement, not because of its
immediate effects (in March 1864 it had to dissolve itself due to
persecuion) but because of the new type of revolutionary produced in its ranks, and even more in its hopes as manifested in
Chernyshevski's novel *What is to be Done*? written in prison.
The outlook of the revolutionary circles, at home and abroad,
was changed by the predominance of the serious type of *raznochinets* boy (or girl) who had to work hard for his study, held
firm convictions and detested the Bohemian's as well as the wealthy
benefactor's way of life. Neither Bakunin nor Herzen was a
suitable model for the generation who shaped their lives in
Rakhmatov's image. Although for a long time the *raznochintsy*
remained predominant in the circles, the lack of social barriers
between them and the self-educaed workers enabled the latter's
influx, first as isolated individuals and later as a stratum of

increasing importance, though not predominant before the 1905 revolution.

The breakdown of the first attempt at a revolutionary appeal to the masses caused the young intellectuals to search for a new orientation. One way was suggested by Pisarev's advice to acquire concrete knowledge of the sciences as a means to be useful to society, thereby anticipating something for which Russia would be ready seventy years later when, in consequence of the efforts of intellectuals who had spent their life in revolution, she had found her modern social structure. Kropotkin's memoirs illustrate the impact made by Pisarev upon the young intellectuals (particularly, the girls) who reacted to the decay of the old-Russian society by a desire for an active and creative life. The obstacles put by Tsarism in the way of even their non-political intellectual ambitions, however, during the following years drove them into the revolutionary movement. Nor could Pisarev's replacement of the dialectics of Chernyshevski and Dobrolyubov by mechanical materialism of the contemporary western pattern entirely satisfy young Russia's intellectual needs.

Disappointed at the reaction which followed the 'spring' of reforms other groups of young intellectuals resorted to terrorism. Ishutin's circle (active in 1865-6) came to an end after a member had made an attempt on Alexander II's life. In 1868-9 it was followed by Nechayev's attempt to organise a centralised conspiracy from amongst the undergraduates of St. Petersburg (it achieved literary fame by Dostoyevski's use of it, in *The Possessed,* as a caricature of the revolutionary movement). Nechayev's concept of definite timetables for revolutionary actions suggests closer affinity with Blanqui's concept of revolutionary dictatorship to be established by coups of well-organised *elites* than with anarchism. With the latter the group was associated mainly by Nechayev's connections with Bakunin, established during his stay abroad. The extent to which each of the two, i.e. Blanqui and Bakunin, contributed to Nechayev's famous Rules for a Revolutionary's Attitude to Himself is controversial[8] but hardly relevant for our present investigation. A large share of Bakunin's would simply prove that the latter, like so many other anarchists, was incapable of carrying through his worship of mass-spontaneity to all its implications and hence supplemented it by conspiracy in its most adventurous forms, as supplied by a Russian adventurer who pursued conspiracy for conspiracy's sake. Nevski and other followers of Pokrovski emphasise the *formal* analogies existing between Nechayev's concepts of conspiracy and the later activities of *Narodnaya volya* (the idea of finding in Nechayev an intellectual ancestor of Lenin was left to modern anti-Communist authors). *Narodnaya volya,* however, had a clear political programme and would never have recruited members with lies about a non-existing mass-organisation, not to speak of murders committed merely for the sake of enforcing the members' obedience to the Leader. The application of terrorism, under Russian conditions, for the purpose of enforcing the granting of a liberal constitution was a tactical error subject to correction. The use of terrorism as a means of the self-assertion of personalities who described themselves as revolutionary leaders would have led to fascism. In the history of the international labour movement the Nechayev episode survives mainly by Marx's use of it to demonstrate the implications of Bakunin's policies. Amongst the young revolutionary intellectuals of Russia it led to the a-politicism and purely educational approach of the Chaikovski circle,[9] formed in 1869.

In 1872 the Chaikovski circle had ramifications in Moscow, Kiev and Odessa[10] (another circle had been formed by Dolgushintsev in Moscow in 1871). It established in Petersburg a number of workers' educational circles[11] the impact of which was felt in the subsequent movement. In many places there existed other, less known, but fairly similar circles of undergraduates. Readings would include the writings of Chernyshevski, Dobrolyubov, Pisarev, Tkachev, Bakunin, Marx and Lassalle. Ways and means would be discussed to carry the acquired knowledge to the people, and to link the circle with similar ones (as a rule, police agents would thus get their opportunity to enter the circle, and to bring it to a speedy end.) Yet the very confinement of the movement to a small stratum of young intellectuals, connected by close personal contacts and friendship, ensured regeneration after the periodical catastrophes. This held good as long as the revolutionary climate in the *intelligentsia* persisted and the tasks were restricted to what the average young intellectual with socialist sympathies could appreciate. Whenever one circle was dispersed by the police, the survivors and new entrants to the universities would form another.

Being mainly educational in character, the circles had hardly to take decisions other than the (very responsible) one about the admission of new members. As Rules and majority decisions were unknown (and would have been regarded as contradicting the principle of personal freedom and responsibility), all decisions had to be taken unanimously. In the minority's readiness eventually to vote with the majority, not under any statutory obligation but by free conviction, participants would find the first realization of Rousseau's ideal of social relationships.[12] Links with the progressive movement abroad were secured and maintained by the intellectuals' predominance in the Russian revolutionary movement and by the exclusion of women from the Russian universities, which forced girls with academic ambitions to study abroad. When the Russian government, afraid of the intellectual climate prevailing amongst the Russian students in Zurich, forced them to return home, it gave the Russian circles a powerful injection of people with very definite views about the need to propagate socialist propaganda 'amongst the people', as suggested already by Herzen to the students expelled from Petersburg university.[13]

At that stage, what hence was to be known as the *Narodnik* (Populist) movement found a powerful spokesman in Peter Lavrov. Having in 1862 joined *Zemlya i volya*,[14] after his arrest, exile and escape abroad he witnessed the struggle of the Paris Commune and joined the International. In 1873, co-operating with the Chaikovski circle, and later with the Central Committee of the new *Zemlya i volya,* he established a periodical and two years later another, both under the title *Vpered* (Forward). These were the first *emigre* publications which, as distinct from *Kolokol,* had well-established organisational links within Russia. Lavrov's notorious eclecticism enabled very different views to find expression in his publications and thus to make their impact upon the Russian underground.

Pisarev had taught the young intellectuals that they should

develop their personalities and be useful to society by acquiring knowledge. Lavrov added that society needed the intellectuals mainly as an active minority which would prevent social stagnation. Professional knowledge was useful if it helped to promote the necessary changes in social structure. Unless widely disseminated, a man's talents or knowledge, by themselves, could not serve the cause of progress even though he did everything in his power.[15] Thinking minorities could be the motors of progress only if they succeeded in implanting their ideas in the minds of the majority.

Lavrov rejected a purely political revolution as it would replace only one form of oppression by another. Yet he emphasised that his opposition to states applied only to the existing ones, i.e. feudal and *bourgeois* ones. His warning against artificial play with insurrections—not unjustified in view of the existing Blanquist influences—was accompanied by his advice to prepare the soil by propaganda for the revolution so that it would succeed when produced 'by the course of the historical events and by the actions of the Government'.[16] In later political terms he should be described as a supporter of the 'theory of spontaneity' rather than as an anarchist. In the Russian conditions of those days where even mere propaganda presupposed careful conspiracy and penetration tactics,[17] an approach such as that of Lavrov's would not delay even the organisational development of the revolutionary movement.

For the time being, the movement of the young intellectuals in Russia developed a demand for practical action rather than for theoretical fare. In 1873 the members of the circles decided to 'go amongst the people'. Some makeshift organisations in the localities, supported by well-wishing members of the gentry, supplied passports, money, peasants' dress, cared for apprenticing the propagandists in some craft by which they might earn their living in the village. But there was nothing even resembling a central committee, nor was it necessary as only peaceful propaganda was intended. The further course of events would be left to the enlightened peasants. Lavrov had conceived the settlement of the revolutionary intellectuals in the villages as a long-term preparation of *nuclei* of the socialist movement which eventually would lead to the political organisation of the dispersed peasantry.[18] The prevailing idealisation of the peasants' revolutionary potentialities promoted sanguine expectations. These were disappointed within a few months when a thousand of the propagandists were arrested without resistance on the part of the peasants (there were in fact some cases of denunciation by the peasants—hardly avoidable though they were in a young revolutionary movement—and these were particularly disappointing). Of the original 770 defendants, eventually 193 were brought to trial. A considerable number of them had died in prison during the preliminary investigation.[19] The only propagandist result of the enterprise was the impact upon the educated strata of society by the powerful speeches of the main defendants.

The young intellectuals reacted to the failure by dropping the purely educational approach. The elaborate socialist programme of the eventual transition from the *mir* to a collectivist order of society, was replaced, for the time being, by the propaganda of more elementary popular demands (hence the name *Narodniki*—Populists). The replacement of the intellectuals and workers was envisaged. The Lavrovists opposed this transition to propaganda of topical slogans ('agitation' in later terms). For the time being, they were unpopular amongst the young intellectuals as their Marxism was interpreted as escape from work 'amongst the people', i.e. the peasants.[20] Yet the very idea of the peasants' predominant role in the coming revolution defeated the intention of putting the revolutionary movement on a broader basis. Even the skilled workers found access to the peasantry difficult.[21] Only one isolated attempt was made at that time in the direction where the future of the Russian revolution lay. In 1874 an 'All-Russian Social-Revolutionary organisation' was formed by a group of girls, former students of Zurich university, together with Moscow factory workers trained in the circles (Moscow had been chosen in order to avoid the strict police supervision of students returned from abroad which was current in Petersburg). The former students entered the ranks of the manufacturers as workers. A journal *Rabotnik* (The Worker) was printed abroad on the group's behalf. Notwithstanding the prevailing anarchist ideology, the logic of the situation enforced the use of everyday problems arising in the workers' lives as a bridge to the discussion of basic issues. This was similar to Lenin's later propaganda regarding the Factory By-Laws.[22] After initial success, the group's activities were interrupted by the arrest of its members. It became famous by the trial of 'the fifty' in which the weaver Alexeyev, thanking the young intellectuals who were helping the workers to become conscious of their tasks, proclaimed that for their emancipation the workers must rely only upon themselves. 'The day will come when the muscular arm of the millions of working people will be raised, and the yoke of despotism, protected by its bayonets, will fall in ashes'. The statement was eventually repeated in the programme of Russian Social Democracy, but Dan[23] may be right in doubting whether Alexeyev and his co-defendants were conscious of the fact that their statements contradicted the accepted Narodnik ideology.

For the moment, the discrepancy between the partial success of 'the fifty' and the complete failure of the attempt to go amongst the peasants could not overcome the prejudices about the latter's predominant role in the coming revolution (in which 'the fifty' had shared). Yet even so moderate a programme as 'the emancipation of the *mir* from bureaucratic supervision' could not be realised without a centralized conspiratorial organisation. In 1876 the surviving members of the Chaikovski circle, together with the representatives of the circles of Moscow, Kharkov and Rostov, founded the first revolutionary party in Russia. In honour of the attempts of the early 'sixties' it was again called *Zemlya i volya*. From 1878 it succeeded in publishing (under the same name) the first underground periodical regularly printed in Russia. As the organisation was intended to include only experienced revolutionaries, it was numerically weak, with a nucleus of 61 members ; 150 more were organised in students' and workers' circles.[24] In the programme some tribute was paid to the need for organising all strata of the population capable of revolutionary action, including the industrial workers and the army, but the only real attempt at mass-propaganda was the organisation, in 1877-78, of a second levy of young intellectuals going to the villages. This time systematic action was intended. The young intellectuals were not disguised as peasants but settled as teachers, midwives etc. for prolonged professional work in which they might win the peasants' confidence. The areas of settlement were selected according to their propensity for revolutionary action (in assessing this, romantic tribute was paid to the memory of the peasant insurrections of the seventeenth and eighteenth centuries; slightly more realistic was the attention devoted to religious dissent as a traditional force of opposition). Very few of the propagandists, however, stayed in the villages longer than a year or two. This was due to disappointment with the results of the propaganda as much as to police persecution.

Workers trained in a study group organised by intellectuals of Lavrovian sympathies (who opposed the anarchist wing of the *Narodniks*) started in Odessa, in 1873, a 'savings-group for mutual aid'. It served as a substitute for a trade union (the formation of which, of course, was prohibited) and organised two minor strikes. Out of it in 1875 grew the South Russian Workers' Union. This had about sixty active members organised in six factory groups, and another 150-200 organised sympathisers (probationers in later party terminology) from amongst whom its members were recruited. Eventually it extended its activities to Kharkov and Rostov-on-Don, where an affiliated organisation developed as a Workers' Library, to distribute prohibited publications. Its underground printing press issued a number of pamphlets. Elaborate Rules, clearly influenced by those of the Geneva section of the International,[25] contained the Union's political platform. It was established in order to prepare the struggle against the existing economic and political order. Recognition of the workers' rights could be secured only by a violent revolution which, naturally, presupposed the workers' unity and consciousness of their conditions. In a letter to its North Russian brother organisation the South Russian Workers' Union emphasised the importance of political freedom as a first step towards the socialist transformation of society.

In 1878 the North Russian Workers' Union was established after some strikes in Petersburg textile mills. These strikes had been supported, and to some extent even organised, by members of the circles, and a demonstration organised by *Zemlya i volya* in January 1878 on the occasion of the funeral of some workers killed in a factory explosion had strengthened the workers' confidence. Obnorski, a worker who after preparatory study in the circles and participation in the formation of the Union at Odessa had spent some years abroad, was one of the organisers. Solidarity with western Social Democracy was explicitly expressed in the Rules, which were adopted in two meetings of the members held in December 1878 and printed in the underground press of *Zemlya i volya*.[26] Axelrod, the editor of the Union's paper, approved the political demands of the Eisenach programme only as a means of demonstrating to the workers the injustice of the existing order[27] but in the Rules political freedom was described as a precondition to the solution of the social question. The immediate programme opened with the demands for freedom of speech, of the press and of association. The usual Narodnik phraseology about the village community was still in use. The *mir*'s concepts of Justice were described as the foundation of the society to come ; the factories were to be transferred to Producers' Associations of the workers analogous to the *mir*. But the transformation of society was expected to originate from the activities of 'the workers' estate', as it was called in Lassallean phraseology. No. 4 of the journal *Zemlya i volya,* which was issued in February 1879, had two articles by Klements and Plekhanov, dealing with the Unions' activities. Klements criticised the programme because of the inclusion of positive demands for political freedom as allegedly contradicting the social revolutionary approach, for its failure to discuss 'propaganda by facts', and for the insufficient attention devoted to practical problems of conspiracy.[28] Plekhanov realised, on the basis of the experience of the Petersburg strikes but still within accepted *Narodnik* ideology, the importance of the industrial working class which now imposed itself upon the intellectual revolutionaries 'in spite of their *a priori* theoretical assumptions' of the peasant character of the coming revolution.[29] In Plekhanov's view the (intellectual) revolutionaries' main error consisted in their treatment of the industrial workers as raw material from which individual personalities should be recruited[30] instead of as a group whose struggle for its own common interests brings the basic class-antagonisms to the fore. It was the duty of the revolutionary intellectuals to organise the masses for the struggle, through the struggle and during the struggle. The education of outstanding personalities from amongst the workers was only a means to make them more efficient mass-agitators. Already in this pre-Marxist stage of the Russian labour movement the problem of 'agitation vs. propaganda'[31] arose out of necessity. It was involved in conditions where class-consciousness had to be brought to the workers 'from outside',[32] as distinct from a spontaneous trade-unionist movement which required only 'agitation' for its immediate demands.

Plekhanov paid tribute to *Narodnik* traditions by his conception of the workers as the elite of the peasants, closely connected with their brethren in the village, sharing their aspirations and ideas, as distinct from the West European workers who were divorced from the village. By dispersing into the villages, the urban workers prepared the soil for the coming peasant insurrection which, however, might be suppressed unless the central government itself was paralysed by an insurrection at the seat of power. Statements such as those just quoted would eventually need quite a lot of 'turning upside down' in order to forecast the course of the Russian revolution correctly. But there is no reason to assume that the course of the Russian labour movement (with help from its intellectual sympathisers) need have been less an organic process than was in Germany the replacement of Lassalleanism by Marxism as the predominant ideology of the labour movement. Nor was there anything specifically Russian in the wave of anarchist and even terrorist ideologies and activities which answered the increasingly brutal repression of the growing labour movement by the ruling classes. Such were the birthpangs not only of the labour movement of the Romanic countries and of the USA but even of Central European Social Democracy, which in the late 'seventies and early 'eighties went through the hardest period of repression. In their reply to Klements' criticism,[33] the leaders of the North Russian Workers' Union remained firm on the decisive issue that political freedom would create the conditions for a social revolution. They realised, however, their failure duly to recognise peasant problem as equally important as the emancipation of the workers. This failure was said to be due to the influence of their urban environment and of western socialist programmes. When the Union's reply was published in April 1879, the majority of *Zemlya i volya* was itself turning to politics. Aptekman[34] soon realised that the workers' reply to the terrorist trend had been superior to that given by himself and his friends, who clung to a political propaganda for the glorified village-community to come.

The North Russian Workers' Union had two hundred members and about the same number of probationers (these needed recommendations by two existing members in order to be admitted to full membership : this arrangement has continued in the Communist party to the present day). In its appeals to the workers it described itself as an elite offering advice and leadership. Suitable arrangements were made for the security of its underground activities. Its activities, however, ended within a year, partly as a result of arrests and partly because in times other than those of actual strikes the educated workers proved incapable of preserving contacts with their more backward fellow-workers.[35] The frustration arising out of this was as much instrumental as the propaganda of the *Narodnik* intellectuals in leading some of the most active members of the Union to political terrorism. A strange sort of class-consciousness developed within the Union which was subservient to the dominant trend in the intellectuals' circles. Thus Khalturin, one of its first leaders, joined the *Narodnaya volya* with the declaration that Alexander II should be assassinated by a worker ; otherwise Tsarism would not take the workers seriously.

Meanwhile, the *Narodnik* intelligentsia had turned from socialist propaganda to an effort at bringing about political change by terrorist means. Disappointment with the failure of the second attempt at settling in the villages had coincided with the sharp anti-Government turn in public opinion caused by Russia's diplomatic defeat at the Berlin Congress, when the gains of the military victories of 1877-78 were taken away. The *Narodnik* intellectuals, being the only organised opposition group, were thus offered a fruitful line of operation.[36] The average bourgeois liberal would be in stronger sympathy with a young intellectual who had killed a brutal and corrupt police officer than he would be if that intellectual had had to go into hiding for having incited workers to strike. Such external factors were bound to influence the young intellectuals' reactions to the failure of the propaganda in the villages, though the connection was recognised only by a few.

With the exception of the Nechayev-Tkachev interlude, the Russian revolutionary movement had been strictly propagandist. It was in no way pacifist but the violence which it accepted was the violence of the armed peasants who would follow Pugachev's footsteps. Bakuninism, though never the predominant ideology of the movement, had sufficient influence to exclude the concept of a centralised insurrection. When faced with a wave of mass-movements, the power of the established regime would dissipate and the way would be open to the village community, embracing a hundred million people of different nationalities joined in a free federation. The revolutionaries' activities were intended to make the masses conscious of their future tasks. The revolution, and the reconstruction which was to follow, was to be left to the enlightened people's initiative.

But the Tsarist regime was not inclined to wait till peaceful propaganda would result in mass insurrection. It struck early and struck hard in a way which is familiar to those who have witnessed the resistance movements during the last war. The revolutionary groups had to defend themselves against police spies sent into their ranks. The indignation caused by police brutalities against defenceless prisoners created an atmosphere in which retaliation by the revolver (followed by an impressive stand in court and, presumably, by death on the gallows, heroically borne), was sure to evoke sympathies even amongst ordinary liberals and to bring the regime's brutalities into the open, thereby limiting them insofar as it could be influenced by public opinion.[37] In January 1878, Vera Zasulich—who was never a supporter of terrorism and who soon became a leader of the anti-terrorist trend within the Russian revolutionary movement—shot at the Governor of the City of St. Petersburg in protest against the corporal punishment to which he had subjected a political prisoner. She was acquitted by the jury; the verdict was acclaimed by public opinion but the result was that all political trials were removed from the jurisdiction of juries. A series of similar terrorist actions followed. As the victims were despised by public opinion at least moral success would crown the terrorists' self-sacrifice. The intellectual leaders of *Zemlya i volya* warned against the imagined potentialities of terrorism. The editorial of the first issue of their periodical—written by Kravchinski who had just killed the Chief of the Gendarmes—described the terrorists as a mere protecting squad which covered the party's essential activity which was propaganda amongst the people. Terrorism was not a means of social emancipation nor even of overthrowing the existing order : 'Against a class only a class can make an insurrection'.[38] Comparisons with later communist publications may appear inviting but it should be kept in mind that Narodniks, as distinct from modern communist parties working under comparable circumstances, had no mass-basis nor theoretical convictions enabling young revolutionaries to prefer patient and prolonged preparatory work to heroic self-sacrifice. They had, on the other hand, a centralised underground organisation which was capable of carrying out efficient terrorism. Its very possibilities carried them away from the theoretical tenets to which their party still paid lip-service.

The organisation *Zemlya i volya* consisted of five different bodies with special functions : the central committee (called Administration) which was now elected by majority vote and took its decision by majority vote ; then three groups carrying out propaganda amongst the intellectuals, workers and peasants (the last-mentioned forming by far the largest part of the whole organisation); and the 'Disorganisation Group' which was concerned only with violent activities[39] such as liberation of imprisoned comrades, liquidation of traitors (which it carried out on its own responsibility without even the Administration having any say) and whatever else it found necessary 'for the protection of the movement'. In theory, political decisions rested with the Party Council (Soviet) which was formed by the Administration together with the members permanently residing in Petersburg. In practice, it was quite easy for the Disorganisation Group (i.e. for the active terrorist) to produce a situation where the government's reactions to their activities would force the party to proceed on their way. As early as spring 1878 its aspirations were illustrated by its assumption of the description 'Executive Committee', which was later used by the leading body of *Narodnaya volya*.[40] The intellectual climate of the underground changed in their favour when the village propagandists, disappointed by the failure of the second move 'amongst the people' began to realise that political freedom was a necessity. Political freedom could not be achieved in Tsarist Russia except by revolutionary action. While the masses, in particular the peasants, remained silent, the increasing list of successful terrorist actions against individual representatives of the Tsarist regime showed the possible course of such action.

In spring 1879 the Administration received from the provinces some declarations of party members willing to kill the Tsar. One of the applicants, Solovyev, was chosen as the most suitable because he did not belong to a national minority. The village propagandists who formed the majority of the Party Council protested. Sharp arguments resulted in the compromise that not the party 'as such' but 'those of its members who felt this necessary' (i.e. the terrorist section amongst the leaders) might support the attempt.[41] Within a few weeks Solovyev paid with his life : but while Alexander II was left with two more years to live from one attempt to the next, Solovyev's sponsors had dealt a deadly blow to the ideology of the *Narodnik* movement. Capital punishments, new terrorist acts and new repressions followed each other at short intervals. The memory of the martyrs strengthened the hand of those who described their way as the only correct one. The party's official journal now described political murder as 'the actual realisation of the revolution'. Those who still believed in mass propaganda were driven so far on the defensive that they described the action to be taken against the landlords as 'agrarian terror' (possibly of the Irish pattern).[42]

Opposition to the swing towards terrorist action was still strong enough for a Congress to be called (at Voronezh, June 24, 1879). On its eve the supporters of terrorism held a factional conference at Lipetsk, to constitute themselves as the Executive Committee of the Social Revolutionary Party, to adopt Rules and to elect the officials of the organisation which would carry out terrorism

2

even if the Congress of *Zemlya i volya* should disown it. This conference appears superfluous if it is kept in mind that fourteen of the twenty-five delegates of the Voronezh Congress participated in the Lipetsk meeting,[43] but the terrorists had realised that their policy could not be carried out by an organisation which included members who questioned its very legitimacy. Though some of the terrorists temporised at the Voronezh Congress so that the appearance of unity might be preserved, their leader, Zhelyabov, frankly stated that, for the time being, the class struggle should be replaced by 'political action'—which was mainly conceived at the killing of Tsars and Ministers. In Zhelyabov's opinion, political freedom was valuable as a means for the peasants to get education and to organise themselves. Due to the liberal's weakness, freedom had to be conquered by the terrorists. (Speaking to Axelrod, however, Zhelyabov rejected 'factory terror'—which presumably meant strikes—because it would alienate liberal opinion).[44] A compromise which allowed terrorists as well as propagandists to proceed with their respective activities lasted just a month. In view of the unbridgeable conflict a parting of the ways was agreed upon. Neither side should use the title *Zemlya i volya* and the assets were to be divided. Both groups pledged mutual support and many of those members who felt like supporting terrorism were transferred from the anti-terrorist to the terrorist party. Polemics were confined to the friendliest of tones.

The terrorists, supported by some young intellectuals, reconstituted the party as *Narodnaya volya* (People's Freedom).[45] The dissenters, led by Plekhanov and Vera Zasulich but supported by a mere minority even of the village propagandists, organised the group *Cherny peredel* (Redistribution—of land—without Compensation; this formula eventually provided the agrarian programme of the October revolution). Efforts at reviving the settlements of revolutionaries in the countryside failed. Even the supporters of *Cherny peredel* refused to leave the town and nearly all the existing settlements dissolved within those years.[46] The group recognised the industrial workers as nearly equal to and potentially perhaps even more important than the peasants. By working in the factories as well as in the villages, the revolutionaries would improve the prospects of revolution both before and after industrialisation.[47] Yet Plekhanov had to explain to his friends his connections with the North Russian Workers' Union by arguments such as that 'the workers, too, are peasants'. Eventually this effect was defeated by Khalturin's decision to join the terrorists.[48] After the failure of their efforts at winning mass backing in the countryside and town alike the leaders of *Cherny peredel,* driven into exile, had to took for theoretical re-orientation.

Meanwhile, *Narodnaya volya* attracted nearly all the active forces of the *Narodnik* movement. In this programme due tribute was paid to socialistic and anarchic principles but its immediate activities were concentrated upon the preparation of an armed insurrection against the government, the triumph of which was to be followed by the convocation of the Constituent Assembly. Collaboration with the liberals was desired. In theory, there was an elaborate programme of revolution : by the properly timed annihilation of ten to fifteen leading persons and by subsequent mass-demonstrations of factory workers the existing regime should be paralysed to such an extent that the revolutionary party might seize power and establish its dictatorship, pending the convocation of a Constituent Assembly. Provision was made for political propaganda 'amongst the people' and in the army also. In fact, however, activities were restricted to the recruitment to its own ranks of active revolutionaries from amongst the workers (who were thus offered an apparently more promising alternative to the difficulties involved in factory propaganda) and oppositional army officers. For reasons of secrecy, propaganda by revolutionary officers amongst the private soldiers was explicitly prohibited by the Rules of *Narodnaya volya*'s military organisation, and left to the local workers' circles. The military organisation had contacts with about 200 officers, mostly junior ones whose mood corresponded to that of the young intelligentsia (some generals were however said to have been sympathisers). Although these elements thought more in terms of an armed coup than of terrorism their potentialities were obviously restricted by their numerical weakness.[49]

In early February 1881 the chances of insurrection were discussed at a meeting of the Executive Committee with repre-

sentatives of the provincial organisations. It became clear that
the necessary forces were not available but the only conclusion
drawn was the decision to concentrate on the assassination of the
Tsar, as the only action which could succeed. On the eve of the
appointed date, March 1, the organisation was paralysed by
arrests. Only by superhuman efforts the survivors ensured the
success of an operation which, in the circumstances, could be no
more than a spectacular protest against Tsarism. Even supposing
that the Tsar's assassination had resulted in the triumph of a
court clique sympathising with the liberals, it would have been
a success similar to that sought by the moderate wing of the
Decembrists fifty-six years before. Only the *Narodovoltsy's* defeat
enabled them to go down in history as ancestors of those who
strove for the realisation of their original socialist ideas rather
than as somewhat romantic forerunners of the Kadet party of later
Tsarist Russia.

Yet the very logic of aiming at quick results which doomed
Narodnaya volya to failure, notwithstanding its anarchist starting-
point, produced the model of an organisation of 'professional
revolutionaries'. During his trial in 1881 Zhelyabov stated that
the decision of 1878-9 in favour of violent revolution was necessitated by repressive measures of the government which prevented
peaceful propaganda. As soon as civic freedoms were granted
all underground organisations would come to an end. In principle,
work could proceed on every socialist's own responsibility. Even
the centralised organisation of *Narodnaya volya* was asserted to
have consisted of 'autonomous circles acting according to a
central plan for a common aim'. A man giving his last message
to the future before proceeding to the gallows was likely to speak
more about what the organisation of revolutionaries should be like
than about what it actually was. This was not the hour to tackle
the eventual problems of 'democratic centralism' even if Zhelyabov
had grasped them (they would have appeared to him, with his
anarchist background, more difficult than to his Bolshevik
successors to whom subordination of the minority to majority
decisions was quite acceptable). Within the framework of
Narodnik ideology, as long as spiritual freedom was preserved
in the 'autonomous circles' it did not perhaps matter so much

whether they could have their say in deciding upon actions which might endanger their lives. Yet there was amongst the leaders a real feeling of responsibility for those led. In his last message, A. V. Mikhailov warned against sending fairly young people to action and death before they had had the opportunity to develop all their spiritual energies.[50] This statement may have been influenced by the weakness of a few members who, after arrest, betrayed their comrades and thus turned a few individual arrests into practical destruction of the whole Executive Committee. It may be read as self-criticism for failure to husband resources, made by an organiser who could not think in terms other than those of terrorist tactics. He failed to see that their very adoption had been the wildest waste of human resources in the whole history of the revolutionary movement, not because it called for human sacrifices (there can be no revolution without readiness for sacrifice) but because it asked for sacrifices where failure led to a political breakdown.

As distinct from the earlier organisations of the Russian revolutionary intelligentsia, *Narodnaya volya* was an elite organisation. Its members—never more than five hundred—had up to a decade's experience in revolutionary activities since the days of the Chaikovski circle or at least the 'Going amongst the People'. The Executive Committee which had appointed itself at the Lipetsk Conference did not claim to represent anyone except themselves. It acted as a collective (twenty-eight persons participated during the period before March 1, 1881, but not at the same time). The Dispatching Commission of three members never did exceed its functions as a technical agency. Central groups in the localities, which directed the activities of the circles, were established by members of the Executive Committee or its agents. These had autonomy in local affairs and also the right to kill traitors and officials up to the rank of Provincial Governor but were prohibited from entering on behalf of the party into agreements with other political groups, or starting an insurrection. Their representatives might be invited to party conferences but had only consultative voice in determining the party's policies. Ultimate decisions remained with the Executive Committee only. New Members of the Executive Committee and of the central groups could be admitted by qualified majorities (in the central military circle an unanimous ballot was required). Their property belonged to the party and they had no right to withdraw from the organisation before the revolution had succeeded (leave, even of indefinite duration, might however, be granted.) Members of the lower military circles—and presumably of the other lower circles, too—were allowed to leave the party, on the obvious condition that they kept confidential all knowledge acquired during their membership.[51] The position of the central military organisation was unique in that it claimed for itself a decisive vote on issues involving changes in the party's programme and a consultative vote in framing current party policies or orders which had to be executed by the military organisation. As for other organisations, it evidently depended upon the Executive Committee's goodwill whether it would ask their advice. The danger of such rules in an organisation the leaving of which was regarded as treachery never did explode because the Executive Committee came to an end long before its defeat caused splits in the party.

Yet *Narodnaya volya* made some contribution to the eventual formation of its successor. In Petersburg, thirty intellectuals (at first directed by Zhelyabov himself) organised circles in the major factories, in which a total of 2-300 workers participated. In Moscow fifteen propagandists organised 30 circles with 120 organised workers. Similar circles were active in Odessa and Kiev. There were three types of circles : elementary, whose members received basic education (including reading and writing), which Russian workers lacked in those days ; secondary, where history and economics were studied (on the basis of Lassalle's writings and of the first volume of *Capital*); finally, a central group consisting of the most suitable workers who were put under the immediate guidance of the Executive Committee[52] with the intention of recruiting from the leading officials of the terrorist organisation. While *Narodnaya volya's* terrorist activities collapsed after March 1, 1881, the workers' (and also the military) circles continued to develop for another year or two. The feeling that no new attempt against a Tsar should be made before the foundations of mass insurrection were created, became predominant (special publications directed to workers and soldiers started, in fact, *after* the assassination of Alexander II). Some *Narodnik* publications of the following period showed a fair balance between economic and political-revolutionary struggle, emphasising the need for a transitional dictatorship of the working class and differing from Marxist concepts mainly by the vagueness—similar to the publication of *Cherny peredel*—with which the 'urban and rural' working-class was placed into one hypothetical unit.[53] Some later Social Democrats referred to the transition of their circles from the model of *Narodnaya volya* to Marxism as a continuous process.[54] To many revolutionaries in Russia (as distinct from those abroad where there was more opportunity and demand for theoretical clarification) the process may have appeared in that light. However, although the *Narodnik* movement realised that the workers were at least as important as the peasants, and that armed insurrection was preferable to the assassination of Tsars, it was not yet a Marxist movement.

(b) THE RECEPTION OF MARXISM

If Marxism in conceived *merely* as a system of economic and sociological theories, its reception must be said to have accompanied the growth of the Russian revolutionary movement. All its representatives, including Bakunin,[55] have tried to make its main documents accessible to Russians in order to use them as support for their specific point of view. In his Preface to the second edition of the German original, Marx quoted a Russian reviewer's discussion of his dialectic as full of understanding. Many years were to pass before anything similar could be said of any Western non-Marxist (and of most Western Marxists, too).

Nor would it be correct to date the recognition of the working-class as carrier of the socialist revolution from the declaration of September 25, 1883, in which the exiled leaders of the *Cherny peredel* group reconstituted themselves as the 'Emancipation of Labour' group. In his preface to the Russian edition of Count Thun's History of the Revolutionary Movement in Russia, Plekhanov stated that his group did not form its opinions 'from pieces of foreign theories' : 'we deduced them, consistently, *from our own revolutionary experience* as illuminated by the bright light of the Marxist theory.' We have seen that the realities of life had enforced recognition of the growing importance of the industrial working-class upon both the wings of the Russian revolutionary movement. It may be added that when the founders of the Emancipation of Labour group proclaimed their break with 'the old anarchist tendencies' this was more as a criticism of their own apolitical past than an objection to *Narodnaya volya* which had laid emphasis on politics. When the leaders of the new group dissociated themselves from the former belief that the village community (*mir*), if emancipated from the pressure of landlords and bureaucracy, could become the nucleus of a collectivist economy, they dropped a concept which was still upheld by Marx as one of the ways towards Russian socialism.[56]

As early as November 1877, i.e. *before* the growth of *Narodnaya volya*,[57] Marx, in his letter to the Editor of *Otechestvenniye zapiski* had pointed out the misinterpretation of some protests of his against Herzen's idealisation of the Russian village community. The Russian had searched for ways of the development of his country different from west European ones, the dynamics of which had been described in vol. I of *Capital*. Marx pointed to the deep respect and sympathy with which he had followed Chernyshevski's efforts to find a direct way from the village community to socialism though he doubted whether it might not soon be too late for Russia to avoid the fatal convulsions of the capitalist system. Nothing, Marx wrote, was further from his mind than to replace the study of the concrete conditions of every individual society by the proclamation of 'some general historico-philosophical theory the supreme virtue of which consists in its being supra-historical in character'. In the Preface to the Russian edition of the *Communist Manifesto* of 1882 (i.e. a few months after Marx's reply to Vera Zasulich) Marx and Engels stated that the evolution of the *mir* into socialism presupposed its being backed by a socialist industry. As they still assumed that revolution was imminent in Russia as well as in the West, they envisaged direct transition from the village community to socialism. The Russian democratic, anti-Tsarist revolution would coincide with a socialist revolution of the west European working-class. Even ten years later, Engels had no objection and no explanatory note to add to the publication, by Lavrov, of an interview given by him, in 1883, to a leading Narodnik in which the hope for a leading part played by Russia in the coming social transformation had been expressed.[58] By that time, however, his optimism regarding the speed of revolutionary developments in Russia as well as in the West had waned. As the west European proletariat had failed to create the framework in which Russia could develop on non-capitalist lines, she could satisfy her need for modern industries only in capitalist ways. Her way to a socialist future was to go through the sufferings of capitalist industrialisation. Yet Engels emphasised the much more catastrophic character that the expropriation of the lower-middle-classes was bound to assume in Russia in comparision with Western Europe, and the much quicker manner in which Russian capitalism was bound to approach its fall.[59]

We have dwelt a little on the views of the founders of Marxism in order to clarify what was implied in the reception of Marxism by the Russian socialists. It *did not* imply dropping the idea of involving the peasants in a revolution, and certainly not a delay in revolutionary prospects for very prolonged periods (although such conclusions eventually were drawn by some). It *did* imply, however, not only political struggle against the Tsarist regime (this was a novelty for *Cherny peredel,* though not for *Narodnaya volya*) but also, as the declaration of the Emancipation of Labour group put it 'the organisation of the Russian working-class in a special party with a definite social and political programme'. This was new from the standpoint of *all* the wings of the Narodnik movement, which as its name says, had been concerned with 'the people' as a whole.

Moreover, it did imply the acceptance of a new philosophy of history. The merit of the Emancipation of Labour group rests upon its struggle for the recognition, against strong emotional resistance in the circles,[60] of disagreeable facts such as the need for a prolonged period of preparation before the industrial workers could turn into revolutionaries. Unless the Russians adopted the Marxist dialectics of history, they could not remain socialists while facing the prospect of a period of capitalist development. It was not only the ampler opportunity for theoretical study available to exiles, but also some intrinsic affinity that allowed the Russian Socialists to elaborate the philosophical aspects of Marxism, from Plekhanov's earliest works onwards, in a way far superior to even the best German Social Democrat writings (not to speak of the understanding of those writings by even the educated German trade union official or socialist M.P.). We should also note that Russian Social Democracy, even when rejecting *Narodnaya volya's* concepts of an insurrection carried out through a conspiracy, never for a moment dropped the prospect of violent revolution.[61] In *Our Disagreements* Plekhanov went to the length of stating that a socialist government, even if only a Provisional Government, would make a laughing-stock of itself if it failed to use its power for the establishment of a socialist system. This statement goes further than anything written by Lenin before 1906.

The literary Emancipation of Labour group could become effective only by influencing the underground circles. In the capital, since 1883 a succession of circles (most of them formed by students of the Technological Institute) followed each other after periodical routing by the police. The first of these circles, formed by Blagoyev, became important mainly because of the part eventually played by its leader in the formation of Bulgarian communism ;[62] the second, led by Tochinski, mainly because it sought the exclusion of the intellectuals.[63] In this it anticipated, rather crudely, the Economists' later opposition to the intellectuals' leadership. In fact, some of the workers were able to escape arrest when Tochinski's circle, after three years of work, was broken up by the police, and thus were available when the Union of Struggle for the Emancipation of the Working Class was formed. Tochinski's circle was followed by that of Brusnyev. When this, too, met with the usual fate some of the members who had escaped arrest together with some newcomers formed the circle which, under the nickname of 'the Old',[64] became famous as, since the autumn of 1893, it was joined by a young lawyer, V. I. Ulyanov (Lenin). The latter had in Fedoseyev's circle at Kazan University passed the transition stage from the Narodnik ideology to Marxism and later had been active in the Marxist circles of Samara. In 1894, 'the Old' was joined by another circle, headed by Yu. Martov who had come from Vilna. Little organisational progress had been made by then in the capital in comparison with the culmination of *Narodnaya volya's* activities. The number of workers' circles, twenty in Brusnyev's days, had not increased when numerous strikes started in 1894-95. But the movement had meanwhile spread to the Provinces. Yaroslavski's enumeration of towns where in the early 'nineties Social Democrat circle were active[65] showed that it was no longer a mere enumeration of university towns. In places such as Nizhny-Novgorod, Orekhovo-Zuyevo, Ivano-Voznesensk, Rostov-on-Don, Tula and Ekaterinoslav the influence of educated workers must already have been considerable.

Russia's industrial expansion was accompanied by a wave of strikes, involving as early as 1895 two per cent of all industrial workers. The Socialist circles had to consider ways of participation in the movement. In Vilna, there arose the issue of using the Jewish language for propaganda amongst the masses. Some of the workers, members of the circles, became afraid of the monopolisation of political leadership by the intellectuals. The workers' activities and outlook would then be restricted only to the narrow field of economic interests. In Petersburg, G. B. Krassin warned against the risk of losing cadres by arrests as soon as they were involved in factory conflicts—he was, however, supported only by a minority of 'the Old'. In Moscow the need for participation in economic conflicts was accepted as early as February 1894.[66] At the time of the Petersburg strikes there was still some collaboration (though not without reservations) between Narodnik and Social Democrat circles.[67] Lenin's booklet 'Explanation of the Law on (disciplinary) Fines to be Paid by Factory Workers', written in autumn 1895, and a questionnarie issued even later by the Union of the Struggle for the Emancipation of the Working Class as a guide to formulating economic demands, were still printed by the underground press of the Narodniks. Much later,[68] Krupskaya described the views of the Narodovoltsy as 'nearly identical with the views of Social Democracy'. Such facts should be kept in mind when considering the theoretical distinctions to which Lenin, shortly before, had devoted so much effort.

The origins of the coming cleavages lay in the occupation of the circles with industrial conflicts. It led to the decision taken by the 'the Old' in early 1894 to strengthen political leadership of the workers' circles by having them directly headed by the intellectuals. (Earlier, only the group leaders of the workers were instructed by the intellectuals so as to avoid the suspicions of the police.) In 1894 Kremer, a member of the Social Democrat group of Vilna, wrote a pamphlet 'On Agitation', to conclude the argument which had proceeded in the circles. Martov, who had edited the manuscript, brought it to St. Petersburg and read it in the circle of 'the Old'. The document accepted that the expansion possibilities of the educational-propagandist circles were exhausted while the workers fought their economic struggles in their own way without being influenced by the Social Democrats. It played an important part in inducing the circles to transfer their activities from the education of an *elite* ("propaganda" in the terminology of the revolutionary movement) to 'agitation'—i.e. in current English terminology to propaganda in favour of definite economic and political demands. The long-standing attempts to find at this stage the origins of the later differentiation between Bolsheviks and Mensheviks[69] appear to be exaggerated. The authors of the pamphlet clearly recognised the importance of the conquest of political power by the working-class and found that the workers' daily economic struggle made the workers conscious of that need. One-sided preoccupation with the daily struggle was rejected as equally mistaken as was one-sided study of long-term prospects.[70] Lenin (as well as Martov when writing his memoirs in 1922) recognised the merits and short-comings of the pamphlet. When writing to Plekhanov on the struggle against the 'economists' he noticed that, in particular in the early 'nineties, emphasis on economic struggle (as distinct from economism proper, which implied a replacement of political by economic struggle) had had its merits.[71] Later cleavages concerned the character of the political demands and tactics to be pursued. These however, could not become crystallised till the revolution of 1905 was at least in the preparatory stage.

Much of the conflict associated with the transition from 'propaganda' to 'agitation' date from a change in leadership which, though accidental, much affected the movement. In December 1895 the group of 'the Old' constituted itself for purposes of broader activities as the Union of Struggle for the Emancipation of the Working Class. But Lenin had been arrested a few days before ; a few days later Martov, too, was arrested. During the strike wave, the 'Young' joined the Union and carried out organisational changes which later, with some hindsight, were regarded as the beginning of the 'Economist' tendency. At the time of the formation of the Union, the Central Workers' Circle had been conceived as an auxiliary organ of its Central Organisation Group and of the three District Committee subordinated to it. This was useful because the workers' contacts with each other were less exposed to police supervision than their contacts with the intellectuals.[72] Now, representatives of the Central Workers' Circle were invited to join the Central Organisation Group. The Union's paper was to be written mainly by workers and express their thoughts (Lenin was indeed afraid lest this might cause neglect of revolutionary politics in favour of everyday economic issues). The 'Young' even drew up a project for a Workers' Relief Fund (i.e. an underground trade union) with an independent administration, the Union for the Emancipation of the Working Class serving as its auxiliary organ. In February 1897 Lenin and his friends met the 'Young' leaders of the Union, on the occasion of three days' leave which they had got from prison in order to straighten their personal affairs before their deportation to Siberia. There were sharp arguments.[73] For the moment, Lenin and his friends could prevent the publication of the controversial draft Rules for Workers' Relief Fund. A few months later, however, it was done. But, like so many other matters of those days, it remained on paper.

According to the Petersburg example, Unions of Struggle for the Emancipation of the Working Class were formed in Kiev, Ekaterinoslav and—on extremely weak foundations[74]— Moscow. In Vilna the *Bund* was organised on a regional basis (only after the First Party Congress did it raise its claim to the status of an autonomous organisation catering for Jewish workers all over Russia). In the summer of 1886 Krupskaya travelled to Kiev on behalf of the Petersburg committee as constituted after Lenin's and Martov's arrests but before 'the Young' had joined it. Perhaps because of the organisational and political difficulties of the Petersburg Union the initiative in convening a national Congress and establishing an all-Russian Social Democratic journal was passed to Kiev, and soon to Vilna. After an abortive effort made in spring 1897 by the Kiev organisation[75] on March 1-3, 1898 nine delegates of the four main Unions of Struggle for the Emancipation of the Working Class[76] met a Minsk to establish the Social Democrat Workers' Party of Russia.[77] (A narrow majority of the delegates had decided to exclude the word 'workers' from the party's title. It was, however, restored by the drafters of the Manifesto, to the astonishment of a member of the elected CC who saw it three years later in Siberia, and believed that his memory had misled him:[78] the incident illustrates the confusion surrounding the Congress.) The Congress reglement as drafted by Kremer (Vilna) provided for a representation of each organisation by two delegates, one intellectual and one worker (the Kiev workers' circle, however, elected one of the intellectuals attached to it). A group of intellectuals was commissioned to publish the Manifesto on behalf of the Congress (it was headed by Struve— a leading 'legal' Marxist who soon became one of the founders of the liberal party). The only explicit directive which it got was the demand for the inclusion of a statement that 'the RSDAP, as a fighting organisation, continues the work of *Narodnaya volya*'.[79] Struve and his colleagues are the authors of the famous declaration that 'on its own firm shoulders the Russian working class must and will achieve the conquest of political freedom' as the first step to the achievement of socialism, because 'the further to the east of Europe, the weaker, the more cowardly and mean appears the bourgeoisie'. This statement was not refuted by its author's participation in the foundation of the *bourgeois* Kadet party a few years later.

The Minsk Congress decided that the regional Unions for Struggle for the Emancipation of the Working Class were to regard themselves as committees of the new party and the Kiev periodical *Rabochaya gazeta* was adopted as its main organ. A Central Committee of three members—Radchonko from Petersburg, Kremer from the *Bund,* Eidelman from *Rabochaya gazeta*—was elected. The other delegates were told to regard themselves as candidate members of the CC who, if its members were arrested, should fill the gaps and convene the second Congress, which was expected to meet within six months and to be more representative than the first. In fact, however, not only two of the three members of the CC *but* all the delegates were arrested within a few months. The first Congress of Russian Social Democracy made no other than a declarative impact—except, perhaps, for the lesson that the constitution of a national party organisation was impossible before the local organisation problems had been solved.

(c) REVOLUTIONARY POLITICS *VERSUS* THE SECTIONAL CONCEPT OF THE LABOUR MOVEMENT

Even if freedom was restricted, the changes which we noticed in the organisation of the Unions for the Emancipation of the Working Class might have transformed these unions into embryonic trade-union centres. Such a development might have led to a split between those who would be satisfied with merely improving their material conditions and those who would fight for the overthrow of the Tsarist regime itself. In the actual conditions of Tsarist Russia, however, even the co-ordination of strikes was impossible without well-organised underground work. Lenin, from his Siberia exile, appealed to the young intellectuals whose collaboration was needed in order to close the gaps in the ranks of the underground organisation caused by arrests. His enumeration of the manifold tasks illustrates the outstanding organiser's ideas about the organisation of revolutionaries at the beginning of a new phase in the revolutionary movement. The organisation, Lenin wrote, needed 'legal agitators who can speak to the workers in such a way that they cannot be brought into court, restricting themselves to telling the A to be followed up, by other propagandists, by the B and C'. It needed 'distributors of books and leaflets, organisers of workers' circles and groups, correspondents from every factory who inform us upon what is happening there, people who follow up the spies and provocators, people who provide conspiratorial quarters, who transmit literature and all kinds of communications, people who collect money..agents amongst the intellectuals and the bureaucracy who have contact..with the workers' life and with the administration police, factory inspectors etc.' The organisation needed workers in maintaining communications with various towns of Russia and with other countries, or in learning the various methods of mimeographing and printing, storing publications, etc. etc. The more specialised the revolutionary's work, the greater the chance of his success in organising it, avoiding arrest and, even if the worst should happen, in preventing the police from following up his contacts. Then it is easier to replace the lost agents and members.

It is obvious that no specialisation such as desired by Lenin was on the cards. Most revolutionaries who wrote their memoirs even about better organised phases of the socialists' struggle report on their occupation with many tasks. Good specialists in revolutionary organisations, such as Pyatnitski or Stasova, did successively nearly every kind of underground work. Lenin made his appeal, not to support the Utopia of a giant underground bureaucracy but in order to encourage the young intellectuals to whom *Narodnaya volya* was a heroic memory, yet who might be deterred by the dullness of much of the work required.

We know (Lenin concluded) that such a specialisation is a very hard thing, hard because it demands maximum restraint and self-sacrifice, demands devotion of all one's efforts to some work which does not fall into the eyes, which is monotonous, excludes contacts with other comrades, subjects the revolutionary's whole life to a dry and strict regimentation. But only under such conditions did the coryphees of Russian revolutionary practice (i.e. the leaders of *Narodnaya volya*) succeed in carrying out the very greatest enterprises. . . .[80]

Lenin clearly differentiated his attitude from that of Narodniks such as Lavrov, who had interpreted Lenin's appeal to people from *all* social classes for the struggle against absolutism as a *de facto* acceptance of the Narodnik platform. It was true that the methods of Western European Social Democracy could not be applied to Russia but Lavrov was wrong when treating the necessary underground organisation as a conspiracy to overthrow the government (*zagovor*). It should lead the workers' struggles against both economic exploitation and the absolutist regime. It was for the future to decide whether the party would deliver the decisive stroke to absolutism by an insurrection, by a political mass-strike or some other form of attack.[81]

This concept of revolutionary tasks was immediately faced with an alternative—the 'trade unionist' one, as Lenin would soon describe it. In the first issue of the most influential of the Petersburg labour publications, *Rabochaya mysl* (October 1897) the existing socialist movement was denounced as 'a mere means for calming the contrite consciences of a penitent intelligentsia but alien to the worker himself' ; 'the desire never to forget the political ideal' was said to have obscured the economic basis of the movement. The struggle for economic interests, however, was the strongest not only because of the number of people who could understand it but also because of the degree of heroism with which ordinary people defended their right to existence. The workers should fight 'not for future generations but for themselves and their children'.

It should have been obvious that under Russian conditions, not only a political trade unionism but even separation of the workers from the intelligentsia was unattainable. If the Russian labour movement had confined itself to economic struggle and had dropped its claim to form a political party (together with the advanced strata of the intelligentsia), those workers who yearned for political freedom (i.e. for the very purpose of getting freedom of combination) would have had to join the groups of the Narodnik intelligentsia,[82] or even to support the *bourgeoisie* itself.

3

The latter alternative was straightforwardly advocated in a document published under the title *Credo* by a circle of intellectuals round Kuskova and Prokopovich.[83] With disregard for historical facts it was alleged that political freedom had been conquered in the West by the bourgeoisie without the participation of the workers. As the latter allegedly had an inherent tendency to pursue the line of least resistance, they rallied round the banner of revolutionary Marxism for struggle on the political plane, already opened up for them by the bourgeoisie. Enormous obstacles still prevented the participation of most workers in trade unions. Eventually, in the West, the opening or a broader field for trade unionism resulted in the replacement of the original, 'intolerant, negative and primitive Marxism' by a 'democratic Marxism' (of the Revisionist pattern) which *recognised* existing society. In Russia, however, the obstacles to political change were said to be insurmountable for the time being. Hence the workers' economic struggle, however difficult, represented that line of minor resistance which the labour movement was allegedly bound to follow. 'Talks about an independent political party of labour', the document said, 'are the mere result of the transfer of alien tasks and experiences to our soil'. The Russian Marxists' criticism of bourgeois-liberal tendencies in Russia expressed, the document said, a failure to understand that the Liberals' activities had opened, in the West, the field for the workers' political struggle. Hence the Russian Marxists, while supporting the workers' economic struggle, should also participate in the activities of the liberal bourgeoisie.

Kuskova and Prokopovich soon followed the consequences of this analysis and collaborated in the formation of what eventually was to become the Kadet (liberal) party, together with some 'legal Marxists' such as Struve who shortly before had explained why it was mistaken to expect Russia's political emancipation through her bourgeoisie.[84] However correct they may have been about the developments in Western Social Democracy, it was, in fact, *they* who transferred an alien concept to the Russian soil. Reference to the Russian bourgeoisie was totally at variance with Marx's emphasis on the fact that 'the emancipation of the workers can be the work only of the workers themselves'. The immediate reaction to the *Credo,* however, was conditioned by its break with all traditions of the Russian revolutionary movement. Writing a quarter of a century later, Balabanov said[85] that by the formation of *Iskra* the inherent continuity *(preyemstvennost)* of the Russian revolutionary movement, which had been interrupted by Economism, was restored. The memories of Khalturin, Perovskaya, Zhelyabov and many others helped to shape their country's future when they defeated those who had abused the 'penitent intelligentsia'.

On receipt of the *Credo* the socialists who shared Lenin's exile adopted a declaration of protest drafted by him.[86] The best-known party members of the older generation exiled to other places, including the later Menshevik leaders Martov, Potressov and Dan, joined immediately.[87] The *Credo* was denounced as the political suicide of Russian Social Democracy. With reference to the passage of the Party Manifesto which paid tribute to the preceding revolutionary movements it was demanded that the party should concentrate on the strengthening of its organisation and internal discipline and the development of the conspiratorial technique. Abroad, the Emancipation of Labour group referred to the exiles' protest in the declaration[88] in which it announced the resumption of its own publications. In 1898, the sympathisers of Economism had captured the organisation which had been recognised by the First Party Congress as the party's international representative.

Lenin's plan for building a homogeneous party was formulated immediately after the exiled Marxists' answer to the *Credo,* in his article *Our Next Task,* which was published only posthumously but already contained the basic concepts later elaborated in *What Is to be Done?* Social Democrat activities in Russia were said to suffer from the purely empirical approach of the local organisations : it should be replaced by the *general* work of one *party,* operating upon a common platform and jointly deciding problems of tactics and organisation. It was necessary to reconcile the autonomy of the local labour movement (which had been emphasised by the Minsk party congress) with the need for unity and centralisation.[89] Social Democracy, Lenin wrote, was not a mere servant of the labour movement but 'the combination of socialism with the labour movement.... its task is to carry definite socialist ideals into the spontaneous labour movement'.[89] The new party needed to assimilate the experiences of the west European labour movement and of the preceding revolutionary parties (including again, 'the old masters of the revolutionary and conspiratorial technique') as well as of the spontaneous Russian labour movement. But how could a revolutionary party avoid transformation into a conspiratorial group which would try to force upon the workers some 'plan' of attack elaborated behind their back ? Lenin found the answer in the establishment of a party periodical, closely connected with the local organisations. It would reflect their experiences and, by enabling real discussions, arrive at joint concepts and methods of work. Without such an organ, the party was organised merely on paper (this was a clear hint at the abortive attempt, at the Minsk Congress, to create a national organisation). For the time be:ng, all Social Democrat efforts should be directed at creating such an organ.

When the exiled Socialists returned from Siberia, Lenin at a meeting in Pskov on April 1st, 1900, presented to them and also to the 'legal Marxists', the draft of the planned journal. Supported by those who opposed Economism and by the benevolent neutrality of the 'legal Marxists', he went with Y. O. Martov and A. N. Potressov to Switzerland and, not without some friction,[90] achieved the collaboration of Plekhanov and his friends. In December the first issue of *Iskra* (The Spark) was published, with a motto appealing to the Decembrists' traditions. Economism was already being defeated by bare facts : in February and March students' demonstrations spread from Moscow all over Russia ; in Kharkov, Moscow and Kiev the workers joined the students in the streets. As the prosperity of the late 'nineties gave way to depression, a new wave of strikes started, this time with a distinctly political flavour. When Lenin, in *Iskra* no. 4 (April 1901), reformulated the concepts of *Our Next Task* in an article *Where to Begin* he had to reproach the Petersburg 'Young' Socialists' periodical *Rabocheye delo,* which had previously sympathised with the Economists, for an over-enthusiastic interpretation of the situation and for a call for terrorist and insurrectionist activities. Conditions,

Lenin wrote, were not yet ripe for this : an organised party was needed to cope with the situation. A political journal should formulate a definite *plan* of organisation. The information collected for its purposes would allow the centre to arrive at a correct appreciation of the situation. Its agents and the organisational network needed for distribution would provide the links in the underground organisation, closely collaborating with the existing local committees.

When Lenin's article was read in Russia the movement had already passed the elementary stage. The May-day demonstration in 1901 at the St. Petersburg Obukhov works went to the length of active resistance against the police. Its suppression was followed by another wave of strikes in May and June. Before the year was over, workers and students demonstrated together in Nizhny-Novgorod, Kharkov and Ekaterinoslav. Those Social Democrat groups which had made the greatest concessions to Economism, the Jewish *Bund* and the 'Young' group which published the *Rabocheye delo*, now themselves urged the re-organisation of the party by a new Congress to replace the Central Committee arrested after the Minsk Congress. Such efforts may have been inspired by the fear lest delay result in an *Iskra*-controlled party Congress. Precisely for this reason Lenin wished for a delay. His position was strengthened by the fact that the sponsors organised the congress even though only a minority of the existing Social Democrat organisations[91] might be represented. When, in spring 1902, it assembled in Belostok the sponsors themselves had to agree that it could not be regarded as more than a preparatory conference which would elect a committee to prepare the Party Congress on more solid foundations.[92] At the same time the agents of *Iskra* established at least the basis of a real organisation. On 20th January 1902, sixteen of them, at Samara, elected a Russian Head Office of the *Iskra* organisation and decided to start a systematic struggle for the conquest of existing party organisations. If a party committee refused to recognise *Iskra* as its central organ, the agents should establish a parallel organisation.[93] Such as split occurred in Petersburg in June 1902, after the exit of the Economists in Odessa also. By the end of 1902, *Iskra* control of the majority of the party committees was established.[94] Martov may have been right when, writing in 1918, he ascribed the triumph of the 'political' tendency within Social Democracy to the impact made by the strike of the workers of the Rostov railway workshops in November 1902. Against the workers' hesitations the Social Democrat speakers had convinced them of the need for *political* demonstrations. For a week, freedom of meetings and public discussions was practically won. Bloody repression of the movement had only temporary success : half a year later mass-demonstrations took place in Rostov as well as in Baku and Tiflis.[95] This time the workers resisted the Cossacks' attacks. In July (new style) 1903, when the London Congress of Social Democracy was about to meet, general strikes started in Baku, Tiflis and Batum. Amongst the 44 Congress delegates—of 26 organisations, 20 of them within the country—who disposed of 51 votes, 27 delegates, with 33 votes, were supporters of *Iskra*.

A recently published document shows the organisation of the circles of the Rostov-on-Don Committee of the Iskrist Social Democrats, adopted in the summer of 1902, i.e. at a time when the workers' movement was already rising.[96] The circles form part of the party machinery. Their members are workers who have already received some systematic political education (presumably in circles for sympathisers) and are prepared to make sacrifices in the course of the struggle against the regime, such as imprisonment, loss of employment and separation from their families. For security reasons, circles should have no more than twelve members. Circles are organised by members of the Don Committee or by agents acting under their supervision. Admissions are checked by the organiser who is under an obligation to double-check every single recommendation. Arrivals from other places need the recommendation of their local revolutionary organisation. The circle elects its representative, if desired, by secret ballot. The Don Committee is entitled to suggest candidates for election and even to refuse the confirmation of those elected. The elected delegate represents the circle at the Committee and is responsible for the observation of the rules of conspiracy. (Where it is necessary, a finance officer and a librarian may also be elected.) The Committee, on its part, is represented at the circle by its 'propagandist' (presumably an intellectual) who may also be elected as the circle's delegate. Members of the circle may submit to the Don Committee, through the propagandist, any protests against elections of officials. The propagandist appears as the key figure in that system of dual representation. He leads the meetings (not less frequent than once a week) according to the programme of political education drawn up by the Committee but every member has the right to raise other interesting problems 'in the field of science and of revolutionary activities'. If the propagandist is absent, the circle meets under the representative's guidance and discusses suitable problems, or reads some books.

The members of the circles are obliged to conduct propaganda amongst the workers, not only of their factory but amongst all the proletarian elements with whom they come into contact, including peasants and soldiers. If necessary, they are entitled to start 'agitation' (i.e. to issue immediate slogans for industrial action). They have to fulfil all the tasks allotted to them by the Committee and to report to it, through the propagandist or the representative, their observations about the workers' feelings and demands (and also all arrests and house searches which come to their knowledge). They distribute party literature (distribution of pamphlets and manifestos not bearing the Committee's stamp is prohibited) and collect money from sympathisers. From their own income, they contribute 2 per cent for party needs. For these contributions, a receipt with the Committee's stamp is issued by the delegate who administers the funds. The enumeration of items of expenditure includes not only the purchase of literature but also such revolutionary activities as the printing of prohibited publications, the renting of secret quarters, support for arrested or unemployed comrades and their families, travel expenditure, etc. If we keep in mind that no circle can have more than twelve members, it is obvious that only successful collections amongst sympathetic workers might offer an opportunity 'to support other revolutionary organisations', i.e. to make contributions to the Don Committee's Provincial expenditure. Disciplinary power, including the right to reprimand and, in the most serious cases, to expel members, is exercised both by the circle and by the Don Committee, according to the character of the offence.

Apart from the fact, demonstrated by the strikes, that the *Iskrist* Don organisation was really rooted amongst the masses, we cannot say how much of the just quoted rules reflected more than organisers' plans. In any case, a comparison with Lenin's plans of 1897[97] shows that within half a decade the *Iskrists'* concepts of organisation had moved to a point which was fairly near to those of the organised Bolshevik party. No basic theories, however, yet arose in the average organiser's mind out of the practical needs of the struggle against Tsarism. Clarification emerged only gradually in the course of disputes which, at first, appeared to concern mere organisational methods and factional conflicts.

(d) BOLSHEVIKS AND MENSHEVIKS

Immediately after Lenin's organisation concepts had been sketched out in his article *Where to Begin,* they were elaborated as a platform for the conquest of leadership by the supporters of *Iskra,* in his pamphlet *What is to be Done?*[98] The pamphlet's main contribution to Marxist thought is found in the third chapter, in the opposition of 'Trade Union Politics and Social Democrat Politics'.

All the arguments for an independent party of labour current in the west assumed that industrial conflict needed, as its supplement, representation of labour's political interests. In this regard, only differences in straightforwardness divided the British labour movement from the 'orthodox' German Social Democrats. The latter demonstrated the usefulness of their party to sceptical trade unionists by the statement that all the fruits of decades of industrial struggle might be brought to naught by a single set of unopposed duties on foods.[99] To Lenin, however, the Economists' suggestion that 'the economic struggle *itself* should be given a political character' was the traditional *degradation* of Social Democratic politics to the level of trade union politics.[100] Class political consciousness does not deal merely with the relationships between workers and employers, or even between the workers and the government. It concerns 'the sphere of relationships between *all* the various classes and strata and the government'. Such consciousness can be brought to the workers *'only from without*, that is only outside of the economic struggle'.[101] It follows that, aside from the 'organisation of the workers', there must be an 'organisation of the revolutionaries' to lead the former ; 'it does not matter whether a student or a worker is capable of qualifying himself as a professional revolutionary.'[102] This last formulation is what Lenin[103] himself spoke of as use of provocative and simplified argument. Lenin saw 'the working-class as a champion of democracy'. Therefore it was important that as high a proportion of the professional revolutionaries as possible should be recruited from the workers. Nor did professional revolutionaries form more than a small minority even of the party officials in either faction at any time. But this was not the issue in *What is to be Done ?* What mattered to Lenin was whether the professional revolutionary, whatever his social origin, should become a leader of the broader workers' movement, or should he be degraded to the level of a trade union secretary.[104] The statement would have been clearly impossible unless the tradition of persons who engage in revolutionary activities as a vocation[105] had not been present since the Narodniks' days. Also it would have made little sense had it not generally been accepted that Russia, as distinct from the western European countries, needed a bourgeois-democratic revolution, the conditions of which could not be derived solely from those of the working-class.

In later disputes on the question whether Social Democrats or Communists could claim the Marxist inheritance it was asserted[106] that the Bolsheviks could claim continuity only with the Marx of the Communist Manifesto, (as distinct from later stages in his development) because of the similarity between the conditions to which the Manifesto owed its origin and those of revolutionary Russia. It is useless to argue about 'pure working-class socialism' because we have not seen it, and can never see it in isolation from the Russian and Chinese revolutions of the allegedly 'unorthodox' pattern. The topicality of bourgeois-democrat tasks in the context of an underdeveloped country is obvious, for the availability of 'professional revolutionaries' devoted to these tasks is conducive to the triumph of such socialist revolutions as are possible in the mid-twentieth century.

A considerable time was to elapse before the importance of the concepts developed in *What is to be Done?* was realised. In the West European communist parties it was appreciated only when the defeats of the first post-war period resulted in the reception of Leninism as opposed to the concepts of the left-wing of the Second International, from which those parties had developed. More than thirty years after the pamphlet was written Wilhelm Pieck described it as the Communist Manifesto of our century. It is not difficult to understand how the concept of the organised vanguard leading the working class to triumph must have impressed a former pupil of Rosa Luxemburg who had gone through the disappointments of the German revolution. Nor would I quarrel with an organiser to whom the message on what and how to organise has equal importance with the proclamation of world outlook. All through history there have been gospels and churches : no gospel has changed the world unless it inspired a church. Perhaps because this is the first time in history that a great change in man's relations to his world has been defined without resort to the supernatural, the *organisation* which co-ordinates his efforts and interprets the creed has been raised on a pedestal equal to the cause for which it stands. Even the philosopher will agree that man's answers to his basic questions have been determined not so much by the way in which these questions have been posed in general creeds (more often than not only summarising the general ideas current in their days), as by exegesis of such general statements in the practice of the communities applying them. The modern Communists' answers to problems such as the relations between subjective action and its objective limitations, between the individual and the community, between nation and class, at least in emphasis differ from those current not only in Marx's but even in Lenin's days. Part of the difference is due to the fact that the theory has fulfilled its task of re-shaping social relations. Problems look different in the middle from what they were bound to appear at the opening of the century. But part of the difference is certainly due to the specific characteristics of the tool which was brought into being by the author of *What is to be Done?*

It is remarkable that the historical importance of Lenin's analysis was not realised even by those who were soon to oppose it. All the external leaders of the Menshevist wing of the *Iskra* group approved of the pamphlet, and especially of the concept of Social Democrat politics as opposed to trade unionist politics.[107] They merely emphasised the polemical character of the pamphlet, as its author already had done.[103] Plekhanov withdrew his original approval of *What is to be Done?* as late as 1905. Lenin regarded this change as a mere adaptation to the changed constellations of intra-party struggle.[108] It is, indeed, difficult to overlook the foundations laid already in *What is to be Done?* for those practices of which the Mensheviks later complained as a 'state of siege within the party!'

In order to avoid the application of hindsight to the disputes within the *Iskra* camp we should remember that in those issues which split the Social Democrats and Communists, Mensheviks as well as Bolsheviks supported the position now associated with communism (precisely for this reason the Bolsheviks eventually carried the large majority of the Russian labour movement). At the Second Party Congress Lenin argued that a proletarian dictatorship was necessary because the Russian working-class might have to establish a minority government. The only disagreement with this statement came from Trotsky,[109] who eventually himself became a protagonist of dictatorship. Plekhanov followed up implications of Lenin's approach when he stated that every democratic principle, including universal suffrage, should be subordinated to the needs of the revolution. With special reference to Russian conditions he advocated measures such as the disenfranchisement of the exploiting classes, the prolongation of 'good' and dissolution of 'bad' parliaments.[110] The *Iskrists* applauded and only a few delegates near to the Economists hissed.

The phraseology current among the leading parties of the Second International was very radical. In Russia, as distinct from Germany, however, a revolution was a real possibility. Hence it was possible for the *Iskrists* to divide on practical issues of organisation. None of the later Mensheviks protested when Lenin, writing in September 1902 on *Iskra's* behalf a Letter to a Comrade on Our Organisational Tasks[111] elaborated the basic concepts. (His pursuit of these eventually caused the split). *Iskra* should be the party's ideological centre but the practical leadership should be entrusted to a Central Committee within Russia. The unity of these two centres should be secured, not only by their common programme but also by the election to both bodies of comrades working in complete unity. For reasons of conspiracy, every party member should be connected only with his committee. But the committees should be responsible for transmitting to the central bodies any communication of any party member (we have just learned how this principle was to be observed, on a smaller scale, by the Rostov-on-Don 'propagandist'). The ideological and practical leadership of the movement had to be centralised yet maximum decentralisation was needed for collecting information and carrying out the party's policies. It is clear that these requirements could be reconciled only within a community of people who agreed on all essentials and were prepared to defend the common views against any outsider. The *Iskra* group had been conceived by Lenin as that homogeneous nucleus within the loose conglomerate likely to be represented by any Social Democrat party. Moreover, the condition of Russia was complicated by her nationalities problem. The group split when some members refused to operate as a homogeneous bloc.[112]

During the first stage of the Second Party Congress the *Iskrist* delegates held a special caucus to prepare a common approach to the issues discussed at the full congress. The idea was to prevent the non-*Iskrist* delegates from carrying a majority on any important issue by splitting the *Iskrists*. At the very start of the Congress a conflict arose because J. M. Alexandrova, one of the two *Iskrist* members of the Organisational Committee which had prepared the congress, during the deliberations of that committee changed her former attitude and, together with its non-*Iskrist* members, voted for the admission to the Congress of F. Ryazanov, the representative of an uninfluential group which took an intermediate position between *Iskra* and the Economists : thus Ryazanov was admitted. Things got worse when the Organisation Committee demanded group discipline and attempted to prevent the lone 'firm' *Iskra* representative from explaining his point of view to the full congress. It was defeated by a majority and Alexandrova was rebuked by Martov as well as Lenin. But when, in the internal meeting of the *Iskra* caucus, Lenin omitted her name from the *Iskrist* proposals for the new Central Committee he was opposed by Martov and a minority of the *Iskrist* faction. This initial conflict on a trivial issue had brought to the open the question both of the Marxists' attitude to socialists who wavered between them and the Revisionists and of the definition of the group to which discipline was due. A few months later Martov saw the split in the party as originating from the conflict with the Organisation Committee. When Lenin found himself 'nearly isolated amongst the somewhat influential representatives of *Iskra*' (more precisely, amongst the persons with the old reputations) he appealed to the majority of the local *Iskra* organisers 'in order to base his system upon them'.[113] Martov himself believed that *Iskrism* had outlived its usefulness as a form of revolutionary Social Democracy since an all-embracing Social Democrat Party had become possible.[114]

Lenin took the opposite position : this was the substance of the famous dispute on Article One of the Rules. His confidential report does not mention any argument on this point in the private meetings of the *Iskra* supporters. He may have refrained from bringing before that body an issue in which he, though supported by a majority of the *Iskrist* delegates to the party congress, was opposed by a majority of the editors, and hence would have had to state that he regarded the editorial board as subordinate to a caucus within the party. However this may be, two different formulations of Article One were submitted to the Congress, both by members of the Editorial Board. Lenin proposed that only such persons should be recognised as party members who, apart from accepting the party programme and making contributions to the party funds, *participated in the work of one of the Party organisations*. In current conditions, this implied that they were sufficiently active and enjoyed sufficient confidence to be admitted into the ranks of the underground organisation. Martov, on the other hand, suggested only the requirement that a party member should *give the party regular*

personal support under the guidance of one of its organisations.
When Martov was reproached that his formulation would allow
every student who participated in a demonstration and every
worker who participated in a strike to describe himself as a Social
Democrat, he found no harm in this. The greater the number of
defendants in trials who described themselves as Social Democrats,
the more impressive would the party's strength appear. To
remove obvious objections against so loose a definition of membership, and this in an underground party, Martov noted that
the Rules conferred no rights upon party members (in the days
of the underground, committees renewed themselves by co-
option). Lenin replied that it would be better if workers would
declare in court that they were not members of the Social
Democrat party but thought its policies were right ; but great
harm would be done if the party had to bear the responsibility
for people whom it could not control. It was implied that the
party should be able to control the activities of its members.
Although the particular issue of Article One was ephemeral in
importance,[115] a basic principle was at stake. Should the right
to speak as a socialist stem from the consent of the active socialists only (and this in a country where being an active socialist
involved making serious sacrifices), or from the support of the
less decided, but more numerous, type of sympathiser ? The
second point of view, which was characteristic of the Revisionists
in Germany and is familiar to students of the British labour movement was put forward by Martov at the Second Congress.[116]
Certainly it had more attractions for a group likely to win the
sympathies of the liberal intelligentsia who had plenty of opportunities to speak out their minds. (In current conditions, most
of the spokesmen on either side were bound to be intellectuals
but amongst their immediate backers, the 'professional revolutionary' predominated on the Bolshevik, the left-wing member
of the professions on the Menshevik side).

Martov's formula, though supported by only nine of the
twenty-four *Iskrist* delegates was adopted at the full Congress
because of the non-*Iskrist* vote. The Economist Akimov stated
that both Lenin and Martov aimed at something which he disliked, namely a strong political party, and that he preferred that

formula which was least likely to achieve that aim.[117] The opportunity for Lenin's 'revenge'[118] came as soon as a majority of the opponents of *Iskra* had withdrawn from the Congress. The *Bundists* withdrew because the Congress rejected their demand both for an organisation of the party as a loose federation and for their recognition as the sole representatives of the Jewish proletariat, the Economists because the Congress demanded the dissolution of their separate organisation. On both these issues the Mensheviks, together with the Bolsheviks, had defended the Marxist framework. Yet they refused to face the fact that, within a setting of orthodox Marxists, Lenin's group formed a majority. The only concession which they were prepared to allow was the acceptance of one Leninist (he, too, sided with them in the following conflict) amongst three members of the Central Committee, and the re-election of the old Board of *Iskra,* which also had a two-thirds majority in their favour. Lenin, on his part, offered his opponents two out of five seats in the Central Committee and insisted on the reduction of the Editorial Board from six to three persons, i.e. the recognised party leaders. It was obvious that the election would go to Plekhanov, Lenin and Martov, amongst whom the latter was isolated on the issue of Article One of the Rules.[119] The negotiations failed and Lenin used his majority (hence the name Bolsheviks). Martov and his friends refused to accept their election and be relegated to the position of a minority. A few issues of *Iskra* were edited by Plekhanov and Lenin jointly but after the Mensheviks had gained a majority in the Congress of the League of Russian Socialists Abroad Plekhanov insisted on the return of all the old members of the Editorial Board who had failed to be elected at the Second Congress.

Lenin, who could not discourage the attempts to find a compromise and had apparently despaired of the possibility of carrying on *Iskra* without Plekhanov, 'in order to defend the position of the party majority moved into the Central Committee',[120] leaving *Iskra* to the Mensheviks with whom Plekhanov now collaborated. But the 'organisational guarantee of firm leadership', for the achievement of which Lenin had waged his struggle at the Congress, itself proved unreliable. When confronted with a hostile Editorial Board of the Central Organ, a majority of the Central Committee (CC) sought the co-option of Mensheviks and the removal of firm supporters of Lenin. Deserted by his own followers in the central bodies Lenin appeared defeated—at least in the eyes of the vociferous emigre circles. Indeed, with any leader of lesser stature, Bolshevism would have been defeated. The concept of action would have survived at best as a standard to be aimed at but not too energetically clung to, lest influential opinion abroad, and—last but not least—the workers' natural aversion to splits should shift the balance against the 'fanatics'.

But Lenin was not an average party leader. Nor was Russian Social Democracy an ordinary socialist party. Through *Iskra,* the traditions of the Russian revolutionary movement had inspired its cadres. For Russian underground workers, the concept of a centralised party, elsewhere the subject of lip-service, was a living force, whatever the *emigre* intellectuals with the great literary reputations had to say. In his letter to the members of the CC, of December 10, 1903, Lenin demanded a new Party Congress 'to settle accounts with the disorganisers'. The demand was rejected by a narrow majority but in February the first decision of a Russian party committee (that of Ekaterinoslav) in favour of immediate convention of the III Congress was adopted ; Petersburg, Moscow and the Caucasian Federation followed. In early August Lenin convened a conference of twenty-two Bolsheviks living abroad. Their appeal to convene the Congress, if necessary over the heads of the Central Committee, was soon supported by a majority of the party organisations in Russia.[121] The split was completed when the CC dissolved its South Russian *Buro* which had supported the demand for a new congress and the Bolsheviks opened a publishing house in order to start their own periodical *Vpered* (Forward). In November three regional conferences—for the North, the South and the Caucasus respectively—elected their delegates to a Board of the Committees and itself undertook to call the Congress. (The right of a majority of the party organisations to enforce the convention of the Congress even against a resisting CC has been since expressed in all Party Rules, up to the present day). In form, the struggle continued on the issue of the convocation of the Congress of a united party and the two factions continued to regard each other as such a party. The bitterest of Lenin's attacks[122] were directed, not so much against the opposite faction but against those ex-Bolsheviks who had attempted to appease it (the term Appeaser assumed from those days a most deprecatory meaning in the Bolshevik vocabulary). In substance, however, the split was accomplished. Temporary unification during the first revolution was no more than a coalition between two well-established organisations.

Lenin became the natural leader of those who accepted the Bolshevik tenets. He had no equal amongst them. None of the first-rank intellectual leaders, and in the next category only Bogdanov (who five years later parted ways) joined the Bolsheviks. Most of the practical organisers active in 1904 were younger men. With the exception of a few later Soviet diplomats such as Krassin and Litvinov, their names will be remembered mainly by the specialist who follows their contributions to the writing of party history. Of those who were to play leading parts after Lenin's death, in 1904 Kamenev and Rykov had just come to the foreground of party policies, Stalin was a young provincial organiser moving between underground work and prison (and only in the next year first seen at a national conference), Zinoviev a young intellectual serving his apprenticeship in the party, Trotsky one of the younger but most fanatic members of the Menshevik team (that year he wrote a number of anti-Leninist articles so sharp and unfair that they repelled even the Mensheviks and were remembered by the Old Bolsheviks whenever he collided with them). All members of the Bolshevik party rallying in the struggle after the Second Congress were Lenin's pupils. This fact accounts for the comparative ease with which he could lead the party.

Long before there was any question of a 'monolithic' centre of authority in a revolutionary state and its planned economics, the Bolshevik outlook was shaped by the struggle from which Bolshevism arose. To the Bolshevik the political scene did not appear as a spectrum of diverse shades of revolutionary opinion, from Economists and 'Social Revolutionary' successors of the Narodniks to the Bolsheviks themselves, all opposing Tsarism

4

though differing in their tactics and principles. To Lenin, the
major group in opposition, towards which the party had taken its
latest step in consolidation, was also its worst enemy : Marxism of
the early 'nineties was essentially anti-Narodnik, *Iskra* was essentially anti-Economist, Bolshevism was essentially anti-Menshevik.
The most dangerous opponent was he who within the party's ranks
prevented clarification by compromising with the object of
delimitation ; while the latter was an anti-Tsarist group with
which arrangements for joint action against the common enemy
might be made, the Appeaser within the party's own ranks was
merely harmful. Nuances of thought approaching the next group
on the Right had to be eliminated. As the broad principles were
common to all Marxist groups, the necessary delimitations had
to be found with accuracy.

As *What Is to be Done ?* had inspired the conquest of the
existing socialist organisations by the supporters of *Iskra, One
Step Forward, Two Steps Back* was written to rally the party
majority against the appeasing Central Committee and in favour
of reorganising the party independent of the Mensheviks. To
the outsider, the second of Lenin's organisational pamphlets is
bound to appear even more awkward than the first. The issue
whether the economic struggle plus its political supplements
would form a sufficient basis for the socialist movement is of
clearly general interest, however immersed in painstaking analysis
of diverse factions it appears to be in *What Is to be Done ?* But
One Step Forward, Two Steps Back centres on issues such as
whether, in the endless divisions of the Second Congress, one side
had accepted support from party members who were not inspired
by *Iskrist* principles, whether issues of principle were involved in
disputes about personalities, etc. etc. Precisely for this reason it
stands nearer to the realities of political life in which lofty ideas can
play no. part unless they also inspire definite decisions on the
details of party organisation. Having to justify the political
division of the young party, Lenin re-stated basic principles, as
evolved in the dispute on Article One. The important distinction was between those who belonged to, and those who merely
supported, the party of the working class. 'In its struggle for
power, the proletariat has no weapon other than organisation...it

will become an invincible force only when its ideological union by the principles of Marxism is strengthened by the material union of an organisation which fuses millions of toilers into an army of the working class'.[123]

NOTES AND REFERENCES

1. Dan *Proiskhozhdeniye bolshevizma* (The Origins of Bolshevism), New York, 1946 attempts to establish some link between the fact that Marx's critique of Proudhon, i.e. his decisive polemic against Utopian socialism published in those days, was known to some Russians, and the fact that some advanced members of the Petrashev group (a Left-wing discussion circle of intellectuals, famous through the barbaric treatment of its members, one of whom was Dostoyevski, by Nikolai I) described themselves, in their trial, as Communists, as distinct from the head of the group who professed Fourierism. The conclusion is not unwarranted as the description of any radical social reform group as 'Communist' was current in pre-1848 Central Europe.

2. Cf. N. N. Novikova's article in *Voprosy istorii*, 1957, No. 1.

3. To the Peasants under Private Lords (as distinct from the Crown Peasants who enjoyed more favourable conditions). Already before August 1861 it fell into the hands of a police agent and was never published (*History of the USSR,* vol. II, p. 459). Its basic ideas, however, were reflected in *Velikoruss.*

4. Cf. M. N. Nechkina's article in *Istoriya SSSR*, 1957, No. 1.

5. Cf. M. Nechkina in *Voprosy istorii* 1953, No. 7, Ya. I. Linkov, ibid. 1954, No. 3, S. A. Pokrovski, ibid. 1954, No. 9. These efforts, combined with a tendency to date the existence of the Russian underground organisation from even before 1861, appear to be contradicted by the political differences which—though surely as between comrades —were fairly expressed before 1860.

6. Occasionally defendants in political trials even succeeded in refuting witnesses who had turned traitors. Shelvunov caused the court-martial to leave open the authorship of the Manifesto To the Soldiers 'till the will of God will reveal it'. After the October Revolution, an unpublished part of Shelvunov's Memoirs could appear. In this he claimed the authorship of the manifesto for himself (and that of the Manifesto To the People for Chernyshevski). Cf. *Krasny arkhiv,* vol. III, 1923, pp. 229 ff.

7. See below, p. 16.

8. Memoirs of that period by Vera Zasulich, who joined the revolutionary movement in Nechayev's circle, and a critical article by L. Deich are published in vol. II of the collection *Gruppa osvobozh-*

deniya truda, Komitet po uvekovaniyu pamyati G. Plekhanova, Moscow, Gosizdat, 1924. See also Nevski, *Ocherki po istorii RKP,* Pt. I, Vol. I, Petrograd, 1923, p. 72.

9. Aptekman, *Obshchestvo zemlya i volya,* Petrograd, 1924, p. 68.

10. Ibid. p. 69 Stepnyak, another former member of that circle, mentions also Orel and Taganrog (*Podpolnaya Rossiya,* London, 1893, p. 10). In view of the loose organisational forms current at that time it depended very much on the participants' wishful thinking whether, say, a group of friends of a Petersburg undergraduate, meeting him when he came home, should be described as a ramification of the Petersburg circle at the local High School.

11. Cf. Kropotkin's *Memoirs* and S. H. Levin's article in *Katorga i ssylka,* No. 61 (1929).

12. Stepnyak, op. cit. p. 74.

13. Cf. E. Lampert, *Studies in Rebellion,* Routledge (London), 1957.

14. Cf. his biography in *Byloye,* February 1907, p. 258.

15. Quoted by Dan, op. cit. p. 76.

16. Cf. the programmatic article published in No. 1 of *Vpered,* excerpts of which are given by Aptekman, op. cit. pp. 123 ff.

17. These are well illustrated by young Perovskaya's activities, cf. ibid., pp. 70-1.

18. Cf. Dan, op. cit. p. 80. If successful, such permanent settlements would eventually have formed the *nuclei* of a peasants' party resembling the later Social Revolutionaries, but not the Social Democrats.

19. Nevski, op. cit. p. 85 ; L. Deich in *Gruppa osvobozhdeniya truda,* vol. IV, p. 65.

20. Aptekman (op. cit. pp. 182-84), however, believes that the Lavrovists' attitude led to the adoption of Social Democratic tenets by the platform of the North Russian Workers' Union.

21. V. Figner and I. Dzhabadari, quoted by Balabanov, *Ocherki po istorii rabochevo klassa v Rossii,* p. 306.

22. Cf. ibid. p. 305 (quotation from the memorial article for Betty Kaminskaya, one of those girl students, published in *Obshchina,* 1878, No. 8-9).

23. Op. cit. p. 116.

24. Aptekman, op. cit. p. 200.

25. Cf. B. Itenberg's paper in *Voprosy istorii,* 1951, No. 1 and Nevski, op. cit. p. 162.

26. Reprinted by Balabanov, op. cit. vol. III, pp. 317 ff., and in *Khrestomatiya,* vol. I, pp. 179 ff.

27. Cf. his article on German Social Democracy published in *Obshchina,* 1878, No. 2 partly reproduced by Balabanov, op. cit. vol. II, p. 320.

28. Cf. Nevski, op. cit. p. 170, Dan, op. cit. 180 ff., and Balabanov, *Ocherki po istorii rabochevo klassa v Rossii,* vol. II, pp. 32-5. Dan's suggestion that the dispute with Klements anticipated the later clea-

vages between Bolsheviks and Mensheviks on the organisational problem appears to me unjustified. First, the Union regarded itself as the underground nucleus of a trade union which, according to later Bolshevik teaching, would have to embrace workers with different political outlooks. Secondly, it was 'loose' only according to the standards of the *Narodniks* who were already turning towards terrorism but not according to the standards even of communist underground parties working in conditions other than the extreme ones, say of Hitlerism. See below, p. 24.

29. Large parts of these articles are reprinted by Balabanov, op. cit. vol. II, pp. 312, ff., and Aptekman, op. cit. pp. 353-55.

30. When Plekhanov wrote his article, the predominant purpose for which workers as 'individual personalities' were recruited was propaganda in the villages but the attitude hit also the recruitment of terrorists from amongst the workers.

31. See below, pp. 28, 29.

32. See below, Section (c).

33. Text in *Khrestomatiya*, pp. 183 ff. ; see also Dan, op. cit. p. 182.

34. Op. cit. p. 337.

35. *A fortiori*, the attempts of *zemlya i volya* to include some advanced workers, members of the circles, in the Going amongst the (peasant) People movement were doomed to failure. Cf. Dan, op. cit. pp. 184-85, Aptekman, op. cit. pp. 64-5.

36. Dan, op. cit. p. 131.

37. Comparisons with Hitlerism, against the brutalities of which the worst things which happened under Tsarism were child's play, are instructive. The *Reichstag* trial of December 1933 was the only public trial of revolutionaries under the Nazi regime ; and this occurred only because of a miscalculation on Goebbels' part of the length of servility and dishonesty to which the German judiciary would go when invited to sanction an obvious propaganda lie. Everyone, including the judges, knew that Dimitrov's accusers had themselves committed the crime for which the defendants were prosecuted, while the Russian revolutionaries had to defend the social and political necessity of actions the illegality of which could not be disputed. In spite of the much more favourable legal position of the defendants in the Leipzig trial, only one of them used the opportunity for an attack against the prosecuting government and this one was a Bulgarian, grown in the traditions of Chernyshevski and the Bolsheviks. There was no strong reaction of German public opinion to the disclosures (on the contrary, the immediate participants in the crime, so far as they died in the later internal disputes of Nazism, were regarded as martyrs of 'anti-Hitlerism', whatever this may mean). The only strong reactions to the trial outside the working class against which it was directed, came from liberals in the Western

countries who eventually opposed the 'appeasing' policies of their governments. Clearly, the suitability of a court as a platform of political propaganda does depend, not so much on the judicial soundness of the case but on the existence of a public which is prepared to put concepts of Justice (not necessarily in the legal sense) over recognition of the powers that be.

38. Cf. Aptekman, op. cit. p. 334.
39. Illegal activities not violent in character such as falsification of passports were supervised by the Administration.
40. Aptekman, op. cit. p. 327.
41. Cf. Serebryakov, *Obshchestvo Zemlya i Volya,* in *Materialy dlya istorii russkovo sotsialno-revolyutsionnovo dvizheniya,* London, vol. II. p. 51 ff. Serebryakov wrote in 1894 on the basis of the notes of (evidently anti-terrorist) participants in the meeting.
42. Aptekman, op. cit. pp. 326 ff., 357-58 and 369.
43. Cp. N. Morozov's reminiscences, published in *Byloye,* December, 1906.
44. Cf. Tikhomirov's record, reproduced by Levitski, *Partia Narodnaya Volya,* Moscow, 1928, pp. 67 and 70 ff.
45. Because of its more spectacular activities, *Narodnaya volya* has inspired a larger number of contemporary publications than any other branch of the early revolutionary movement in Russia. Cf. the bibliography published in *Katorga i ssylka,* No. 81 (1929).
46. Plekhanov, *Coll. Works* (Russian), vol. IV, p. 19.
47. Cf. the programmatic article published in No. 2 of the journal *Cherny peredel* (reprinted in parts by Balabanov, op. cit. vol. II, pp. 327-28).
48. Aptekman, op. cit. pp. 391 ff.
49. Cf. the documents reproduced by Balabanov, op. cit. p. 329, and Levitski, op. cit. pp. 13-4 and 125 ff.
50. *Narodnaya volya,* p. 257. The message originated nearly one year after the assassination of Alexander II and hence need not be regarded as characteristic of *Narodnaya volya*'s mood at the time of its strength.
51. *Narodnaya volya,* pp. 112 ff. ; Levitski, op. cit. pp. 92 ff.
52. Cf. Levitski in *Katorga i ssylka,* No. 62 (1930, No. 1) and op. cit. pp. 115 ff.
53. Cf. the announcement of the *Vestnik narodnoi voli,* 1883, No. 1, reproduced in *Narodnaya volya,* pp. 67-8.
54. L. Axelrod (Ortodox) in *Katorga i ssylka* 1930, No. 2, especially pp. 31 ff. where she speaks of her own and Leo Tishkojogistes' development in the Vilna circles.
55. Cf. *Perepiska,* pp. 47 and 57.
56. *Perepiska,* pp. 240 ff. Vera Zasulich's enquiry of March 1881, expresses abhorrence of the alternative that Russian Socialists would have to devote all their attention to the industrial working class whose ranks would be swelled by the disintegration of the *mir.* This would imply

a delay of the revolution for decades, if not for centuries till Russia was ripe for a revolution of the west European socialist pattern. From such a starting position Vera Zasulich was bound to become, in later terms, a Menshevik once she had recognised the importance of industrialisation as a condition of a socialist revolution. But Marx's draft replies to her enquiry (reprinted in *Marx-Engels Archiv*, vol. I, 1928) as well as attitude taken by him even years later (see below in the text) show that such an attitude of Zasulich in no way corresponded to that of the founders of Marxism. See also the following note.

57. This refutes the suggestion, frequently made by western authors with a desire to identify Marxism with some abstract scheme, that Marx's positive approach to the prospects of *mir* socialism was conditioned by a mere tactical desire to strengthen the Narodniks' opposition to Tsarism. Tactical desires, though of a different kind, may have caused Plekhanov to include Zasulich to treat Marx's reply to her enquiry as a secret—this was asserted by E. Yurevski, writing in *Sotsialisticheski vestnik*, April 1957, on the basis of alleged statements made by Plekhanov's widow. Since all those directly concerned have died it is impossible to check the correctness of such assertions. It may, however, be noticed that the present position of the Menshevik exiles allows for statements which would have been most impolitic thirty or forty years ago.

58. *Perepiska*, pp. 235 ff.

59. Ibid. pp. 136 and 144.

60. In *My Universities* Gorky gives a lively picture of such a discussion in a circle at Kazan : in all those arguments the advocates of obsolete tactics were supported by the memory of the fallen heroes. L. Axelrod (Ortodox) as quoted in note 54 above, states that as late as 1886-87 only a few of the members of the circles existing in Vilna supported Plekhanov. The majority fanatically defended the Narodnik tradition.

61. Even the defence of terrorism, as an occasional by-product of the mass-struggle, should not be regarded as a mere tactical concession made by Plekhanov to the emotional attitude of the revolutionary intelligentsia (though he himself described it in this way in a post-script to the 1905 edition of *Our Disagreements,* i.e. at a time of overt struggle against Bolshevism). Lenin regarded a general renunciation of terrorism as impossible for a revolutionary party though there were times when other tasks were more topical (*Sochineniya*, vol. IV, pp. 217-18). Dan, a Menshevik of long standing, even at the end of his life stated that the acceptance of terrorism as one means of action amongst others, needed no other explanation than that given in Plekhanov's *Our Disagreements,* namely the conditions of Tsarist Russia (op. cit. pp. 198-99).

62. Although the group had a mere twenty members (with no connections

outside St. Petersburg) it assumed the name 'Social Democratic Party'. Its draft programme is reprinted in *Khrestomatiya*, vol. I, pp. 257 ff. ; see also Lyadov, *Kak nachala skladyvatsya RKP*, pp. 44 ff. Plekhanov advised against publication ; not without ground, as the programme shows little progress beyond the concepts current already in the North Russian Workers' Union.

63. Cf. the materials published in *Krasnaya letopis*, No. 7 (1928).

64. Cf. Krupskaya's letter of 1930, published in *Istoricheski arkhiv* 1957, No. 2, p. 32, but also the note to Lenin's *Sochineniya*, 3rd ed. vol. IV, pp. 608-09.

65. Op. cit. (1926), vol. I, pp. 124-25. In Tula 50 and in Rostov-on-Don 150 workers are said to have been members of the circles active in 1894.

66. Yaroslavski, *History of the CPSU* (1926), vol. I, p. 128. Balabanov, op. cit. vol. III, pp. 535-37 ; Mitzkevich's article reprinted in *Khrestomatiya*, vol. I, p. 319. For the corresponding developments in Kiev cf. A. D. Polyak in *Katorga i ssylka*, No. 53 (1929).

67. Cf. Shelvunov's Memoirs, quoted by Nikitin, op. cit. p. 37.

68. *Tvorchestvo*, 1920, No. 7-10, reprinted in *Khrestomatiya*, vol. I, p. 326.

69. It is particularly evident in Nikitin's presentation. Popov (*Outline History of the C.P. of the Soviet Union*, vol. I, p. 48) and also Dan (op. cit. p. 245) were more cautious. They note the pamphlet's failure to mention the need for political organisation of the advanced sections of the working-class as an omission, *later* made use of by the Economists. It may, however, be mentioned that some of the worst instances of neglect of politics came on account of groups which never joined the 'Economist' camp but were strongly influenced by the pamphlet. Cf. Balabanov, op. cit. vol. III, p. 550.

70. *Istoriya RKP(b) v Dokumentakh*, vol. I (1926), pp. 41 ff. and 49 ff.

71. *Sochineniya*, vol. V, p. 348, *Kommunist*, 1956, No. 16, p. 16.

72. Nikitin, *Perviye rabochiye*, 1951, pp. 51-5.

73. The reminiscences of the participants are collected in note 87 to vol. IV of Lenin's Collected Works, 3rd edition.

74. Eidelman's article *Istorii voznikhoveniya RSDRP* published in *Proletarskaya revolyutsiya* 1921, No. 1 is reprinted in *Khrestomatiya* vol. 1 ; see also the police documents published in *Krasnaya letopis*, No. 7 (1929).

75. N. Nedasek (*Bolshevism v Revolyutsionnom dvizhenii*, Institute for the Study of the USSR, Munich 1956) thinks that the failure of this first attempt, contrasted with the comparative success of the Minsk Congress which was organised by the *Bund,* resulted from delaying tactics of the Vilna group which thus achieved control of the foundation congress of the RSDRP. The organisational arrangements made by the Congress, however, do not support this interpretation.

76. Three organisations known to the conveners of the Congress (Odessa,

Nikolayev and Kharkov) had not been invited as they were regarded
as not stable enough to avoid the risk of police infiltration.

77. The description of the new party as *Rossiiskaya* (of the Russian
empire) and not *Russkaya* (Russian) was intended as a proclamation
of its claim to represent all the nationalities of the Empire (the
Congress also demanded for them the right of self-determination).
This proclamation, important though it was in view of the Vilna
tendencies to transform the *Bund* from a regional Union into a
special party of the Jewish proletariat, should be read in connection
with the extreme autonomy granted to the constituting Unions. The
party as established in Minsk, if it at any time had become a functioning body, would have been a federation of regional Unions.

78. Eidelman, op. cit p. 383. See also Tuchanski, in *Istoriya RKP(b)
v Dokumentakh,* vol. I, p. 105. The Congress reglement has been
published in *Krasnaya letopis,* No. 7, pp. 390-91.
The available documentation on the I Congress is now collected in
the volume *Pervy S'ezd RSDRP : Dokumenty i materialy,* Gospolitizdat 1958 (this volume is intended to complete the republication of
the proceedings of the Party Congress now under way : as no protocols of the meetings of the first Congress were ever in existence
resort had to be made to the republication of memoirs of participants and individual documents).

79. Eidelman, op. cit. p. 387. Eidelman regards the passage of the Manifesto, which treats the struggle for the conquest of political freedom
as the element of continuity with 'the glorious fighters of the old
Narodnaya volya' as not quite successful a formulation of the idea
which the delegates had. It is, indeed, possible that the representatives of underground organisations were more conscious of the organisation problem than was the outsider Struve.

80. *Sochineniya,* vol. II, pp. 325-26.

81. Ibid. p. 318.

82. This alternative was shown, and rejected, by L. Axelrod, quoted by
Lenin, *Sochineniya,* vol. IV, pp. 160-61.

83. Text ibid. pp. 153 ff.

84. See above, pp. 30, 31.

85. Op. cit. vol. III, p. 553.

86. Dan, op. cit. p. 257.

87. Text reprinted as annex I to Lenin's *Sochineniya,* 3rd ed. vol. IV.

88. In appreciating such statements it should be kept in mind that the
local committees were responsible for large regions and made very
strong demands on the strict subordination of their branches to themselves (cf. Lyadov, op. cit. pp. 213-14). Lenin's struggle was directed
against the federal conception of the party rather than against autonomous decisions by local workers.

89. *Sochineniya,* vol. IV, p. 197. Lenin put the statement quoted from

Kautsky ('who, on his part, reproduced the basic concepts of the Communist Manifesto') in italics.

90. Cf. his notes 'How the Spark was nearly Extinguished', *Sochineniya*, vol. IV.

91. In his *History of the Workers' Movement in Russia*, published in 1907, Dan stated that, in 1901, there existed six Social Democrat unions of a regional character, and three isolated local groups.

92. Dan (op. cit. p. 265) as well as Ts. S. Zelikson-Bobrovskaya (*Vestnik akademii nauk*, 1950, No. 12, p. 16). Remember that the conference did not arrive at any important decisions; this contradicts the reprinting, in *VKP(b) v Rezolyutsiyakh*, pp. 17-8, of a resolution allegedly adopted on the *Bund*'s suggestion.

93. Zelikson-Bobrovskaya, loc. cit. p. 14.

94. Ibid. p. 17, *Doklady sots. dem. komitetov vtoromu s'ezdu RSDRP*, (Gosizdat, 1930), pp. 91 (Martov's report), 93, and 122-23.

95. Balabanov, op. cit. vol. III, pp. 277 ff.

96. *Voprosy istorii KPSS*, 1957, No. 4, pp. 126 ff.

97. See above, p. 37.

98. English text of both documents in *Selected Works*, vol. II.

99. Cf. my *Central European Democracy*, p. 105.

100. *Sochineniya*, vol. IV, p. 375, *Selected Works*, vol. II, p. 82.

101. Ibid., p. 98. Lenin's italics.

102. Ibid., p. 136.

103. *Sochineniya*, p. 392, *Selected Works*, p. 98.

104. Ibid., p. 141 ff.

105. Ibid., p. 139.

106. By A. Rosenberg in *A History of Bolshevism*, Ist German ed. 1928, Engl. ed. 1944.

107. Cf. note 49 to Lenin's *Sochineniya*, 3rd ed., vol. IV/2.

108. Cf. Lenin's correction to V. Vorovski's article *The Fruits of Demagogy*, reprinted in an annex to the same volume.

109. *Protokoly*, II Congress, pp. 136-37 and 256.

110. Ibid., p. 181.

111. *Sochineniya*, vol. VI, pp. 205 ff.

112. In the following presentation of the events at the II party Congress I use Lenin's statements immediately after the event, in particular, his confidential report to his friends (*Sochineniya*, vol. VII, pp. 5 ff.). It is confirmed by Martov's presentation (see below in the text). Only later has it become customary to treat the dispute about Article One of the Rules as not only the most explicit but also the fundamental of the disagreements during which Bolsheviks and Mensheviks parted ways.

113. L. Martov, *Borba s osadnym polozheniyem v RSDRP*, Geneva 1904, p. VII.

114. Ibid., pp. 67-8.

115. See below, p. 47.
116. *Protokoly,* p. 264.
117. Ibid., pp. 281-82.
118. He used the term in his letter to M. Kalmykova, of September 7, 1903, *Sochineniya,* vol. XXXIV, p. 134.
119. Before the conflict on that Article, Martov and Trotsky had agreed on the election of a small Board of three (*Protokoly* II Congress, pp. 374-75): apparently, the sharpness of that dispute convinced them they had to rely on such emotional appeal as the original Emancipation of Labour group commanded.
120. *Sochineniya,* vol. VII, p. 343. The argument is made in self-defence against a reproach, apparently originating from consistent Bolsheviks within Russia, that Lenin had surrendered to Plekhanov by resigning from the Editorial Board. Apart from the singular authority enjoyed by Plekhanov within the Second International, the dependence of important sources of money on collaboration with the minority may have influenced Lenin's decision; cf. Popov, op. cit. vol. I, p. 114 and Lenin's correspondence with A. M. Kalmykova.
121. Cf. the materials published in *Istoricheski arkhiv,* 1956, No. 1. In the internal correspondence of Lenin's opponents (which by a technical error fell into his hands and was published in his Declaration and Documents on the Spilt—*Sochineniya,* vol. VII, p. 100) it was taken for granted that all the committees with the exception of those of Kharkov, the Crimea, the Southern Mining and the Don Region, sided with Lenin (this picture is confirmed by his own correspondence of the period). Kramolnykov, writing in *Proletarskaya revolyutsiya* (1930, No. 5, p. 42) on conditions in early 1905 concedes Menshevik hegemony also in some of the Caucasian organisations, the Volga Region and Siberia, the Bolsheviks being based upon Northern Russia and the Urals.
122. Cf. his letter to Vlebov (Noskov), *Sochineniya,* vol. VII, p. 438.
123. *Sochineniya,* vol. VII, p. 383.

CHAPTER II

REVOLUTION AND COUNTER-REVOLUTION

(a) THE BOLSHEVIKS IN THE 1905 REVOLUTION

THOSE PARTY organisations in which no overwhelming majority sided with either faction were weakened by the split. The Menshevik Dan, writing forty years after the event,[1] came to the conclusion that a clear-cut break down to the local branches was the only way to fight Tsarism instead of each part being paralysed by continuous disputes with its hostile brother. In 1923 a former Menshevik who because of the Mensheviks' separatist attitude had come to the conclusion that she had to work in a Bolshevik organisation stated that, in late 1904, she could not do so as the Bolshevik organisation of St. Petersburg refused to accept anyone sent to it by the (Appeasing) Central Committee and would accept party workers only from Lenin's centre in Geneva.[2] Even apart from such consequences of the split, the small size of the Social Democrat organisations and the limitation of their appeal to an educated elite of the workers prevented them from playing a predominant role once the masses were mobilised.

In early December 1904 the Bolshevik and Menshevik organisations in St. Petersburg had about three hundred members each ; another hundred Social Democrats supported the (Appeasing) Central Committee. The Bolsheviks had six District organisations, each comprising up to a dozen 'circles'. In two districts three or four sub-districts were formed just before the January events (these were led by committees consisting of the organiser and eight to twelve workers from the circles). The Putilov works, the centre of the revolutionary workers' movement, had seven Bolshevik circles with a total of about fifty party members, some with a revolutionary record dating back to the days of the Union of the Struggle for the Emancipation of the Working

Class. The Petersburg Committee of the Bolshevik Social Democrats consisted of a secretary (at the time of the January events,
G. I. Gussev, who in 1902 had been the *Iskra* agent for Rostov-
on-Don), the heads of the departments for Agitation, Propaganda,
Organisation and Technique (i.e. primarily the underground
printing presses), the editor of the party paper and the District
organisers[3] (most of the latter were undergraduates while the
leading posts were occupied by 'professional revolutionaries').
In the Menshevik camp, even in industrial districts of Petersburg
the district committees consisted of four to seven young intellectuals and about an equal number of workers.[4]

In these circumstances, the workers' mass-movement first
developed in a framework set up by the Government to shield
them from revolutionary propaganda. In Petersburg, the police-
controlled workers' organisation was led by the priest Gapon who
appears to have played a double game. To the workers helping
in the establishment of the organisation he explained his preceding negotiations with the secret police as tactical manoeuvres.[5]
There were, however, a few Bolsheviks amongst the thirty-seven
delegates who had to present to the Putilov management the
workers' demands during the strike of January 3rd/16th (the
strike had been preceded by a meeting of the District organisation of Gapon's Association in which Bolshevik workers spoke
amongst others : the demands were economic but included the
demand for the Eight Hour Day and immunity for elected shop
stewards). After the rejection of the demands, the workers of
other factories were called out by delegations from the Putilov
workers and by the branches of the Gapon organisation. On
the evening of the 5th, 26,000 workers (in six factories) were
already on strike, on the 10th (the day after the massacre),
150,000.[6] Apart from such influence as individual Bolshevik
workers enjoyed in their factories,[7] neither of the Social Democrat factions (which collaborated in those days) could seriously
influence the course of events. At some places they were even
driven away by the workers. The Bolshevik leaflet which, on
the eve of Bloody Sunday, warned the workers of Gapon's and
the Tsar's intentions, was repudiated by most of the workers.[8]
Yet the prolonged socialist propaganda had created conditions in

which radical demands—ranging from the Eight Hour Day to freedom of combination, of the press and of meetings, and the convention of a Constituent Assembly—had to be included in the mass-petition. A stronger influence of the Social Democrat propaganda was felt in the wave of political strikes which swept the country after the massacre. Altogether 440,000 workers went on strike during that month of January.

Now latent disagreements within Social Democracy, and even within its Menshevik wing, came to the fore. The need for an armed insurrection was recognised even by opposition groups outside Social Democracy but there was disagreement about the part to be played by the socialist party in the preparations. Five days after Bloody Sunday[9] Martov denied that it was the party's task to solve the practical and organisational tasks of arming the workers. It could merely enlighten them on the need to arm themselves. The revolutionary situation could not actually be prepared by an underground organisation. It could only develop the political consciousness of the masses.[10] Lenin reproached Martov for overlooking the difference between the situation existing in Russia since January 9th/22nd 1905 and that in every other country where a socialist party was active. (It is remarkable that, in a polemic with the Mensheviks, Lenin could treat the need for an eventual armed insurrection in countries such as Britain and Germany as common ground.) In Russia, the socialists' task was to *organise the revolution*.[11] Lenin was not such an Utopian that he believed in an armed insurrection prepared by the Central Committee of an underground organisation. During that period he quoted again and again from *What Is to be Done?* that the party's ideological homogeneity would enable all its organisations to react similarly in a national crisis. To him, as distinct from Martov and Rosa Luxemburg,[12] centralised preparation was possible. Within the individual factory, locality or district, he regarded initiative in such preparation as a main task of the party organisation. And Lenin was right in stating that Martov's reluctance to tackle the practical problems of armed insurrection was due, not merely to the difficulty of the task but even more to the Mensheviks' refusal to face the consequences of a victorious insurrection organised by Social Democracy.

On the eve of Bloody Sunday Martynov, a former leader of the Economists who had become a leading contributor to the Menshevik *Iskra,* opened his pamphlet *Two Dictatorships* with the statement that, if Lenin's dream of a general insurrection organised by Social Democracy could be realised, 'immediately after the revolution this party, and no one else, would be called by the popular will to form the Provisional Government'. This, however, contradicted the theory that the revolution expected in Russia was bound to be followed by the triumph of the *bourgeoisie.* If Social Democracy took the responsibility for a government which necessarily would have to enact *bourgeois* measures, it would only compromise its future. Two months after Bloody Sunday, the same argument was used in a polemic by Martov, writing in No. 93 of *Iskra,* against Lenin's suggestion that the Socialists should eventually participate in a provisional revolutionary government of Russia. Martov implied that the Russian socialists should aim at a conclusion of the revolutionary crisis by the establishment of a *bourgeois*-liberal government, reserving for themselves the position of a loyal opposition till the far-off time when, under the impact of socialist transformations in the West, socialism in Russia, too, would become possible.

An opposition to this view was started by Parvus and Trotsky. The former was a literary supporter of the extreme left-wing of German Social Democracy, the latter one of the most pugnacious of the Mensheviks during and after the Second Congress who in autumn 1904 fell out with them because of their rapprochment with the liberals. During the 1905 revolution, however, the Trotsky trend became influential amongst the Mensheviks, and Trotsky became the faction's representative in the Petersburg Soviet and editor of its newspaper. Parvus and Trotsky agreed that there were two alternatives—a revolution directed at the establishment of a socialist regime, or the acceptance of *bourgeois* leadership by the working-class. As distinct from Martynov and Martov, however, they accepted the first alternative as the only means of waging a consistent struggle against Tsarism and of making such an impact upon the West-European Labour Movement that its support would be forthcoming. Without that support, they regarded the Russian revolution as doomed. Like Martov, they believed that a socialist government was bound to be faced by the opposition of all the non-proletarian classes. The Bolsheviks, on the other hand, regarded the satisfaction of the peasants' demands as a main task of the revolutionary dictatorship. A dictatorship, of some duration and of a character that would leave some traces in history, was envisaged. However, even a Social Democrat majority in the provisional revolutionary government was a pure Utopia. The government envisaged by Lenin was described as the 'revolutionary-democratic dictatorship of the working-class and the peasantry'.[13]

This concept of Lenin eventually became important, not so much in Russia (where its temporary realisation had to be construed, *post eventum,* in a rather artificial way) as in the recent revolutions in East Asia and the first steps of the East European People's Democracies. In the Russian socialist tradition, Lenin's concept followed from the theory that the Russian working-class could achieve even political emancipation only by its own efforts.[14] The necessity of west European working-class support for the socialist stage of the Russian revolution was taken for granted.[15] Anyone who was not, like Parvus and Trotsky, prepared to concede this, *had* to look for some kind of transition programme going beyond mere liberal democracy but stopping short of 'introducing socialism'. The historical importance of Lenin's scheme lay in its emphasis on the need for an alliance with the *peasantry,* which was to bear fruit in 1917. In 1905 he envisaged the need for an eventual turn towards an alliance with the rural semi-proletariat, in order to crush the resistance of the bourgeoisie to a socialist revolution which would end the instability of the peasantry.[16] The international conditions for the transition from the first to the second stage were never clearly formulated. In 1905, when German Social Democracy was regarded as the model for Russian socialism (and, indeed, it reached the first wave of the Russian revolution by a turn to the left), there was little speculation of an isolated socialist Russia. For Lenin, as for Plekhanov in 1885,[17] it would have appeared ridiculous for a socialist government *not* to make use of such power as it could achieve. He took it for granted that limitations created by the international environment would affect the extent to which the programme could be realised.

Though not without some watering down,[18] Lenin's concepts were adopted by the Third Party Congress. This Congress, though originally convened against the refusal of the 'Appeasing' Central Committee,[19] could assemble with its consent, as in the meantime, majority relations within that committee had been changed by arrests. Under the impact of the revolution, the possibility of reunion with the Mensheviks was already envisaged. In decisions not intended for publication it was ruled that the outcome of such negotiations had to be sanctioned by a special Party Congress ; the Central Committee was warned against rash dissolution (i.e. de-recognition) of Menshevik committees which refused to submit to Congress decisions (Lenin, however, succeeded in removing a sentence which would have prohibited even propaganda against the Mensheviks' views).[20] The Rules were amended in such a way as to make submission acceptable to a minority which insisted on freedom to propagate its views. Not only did Article Seven grant every party organisation the right to produce such literature as it deemed fit, the Central Committee was even obliged to help in the distribution of such literature whenever it was demanded by at least five local committees.[21] Article Nine protected the local committees against dissolution by the Central Committee (which had been denounced by the Mensheviks as a 'state of siege within the party') unless a two-thirds majority of the workers in the organisation concerned demanded it. Lenin described the ruling as protection against the intellectuals' quarrels.[22] He was likely to have had Menshevik intellectuals in mind. But it was impossible to get the workers' support for dissolution of a party committee if the measure was suspected of splitting the party. These amendments were adopted without major disputes in the Bolshevik ranks but Lenin was unhappy about the merger of the (organisational) CC and the Editorial Board (his personal stronghold) in a broader Central Committee. His demand for unanimity within the CC when gaps caused by arrests had to be filled by co-option provoked an opposition by 'Appeasing' members of the out-

5

going CC (whose record had inspired Lenin's precaution) as well as by the 'Committee-men', i.e. the Russian organisers whose abhorrence of complicated procedure in emergencies was combined with distrust of the exiles' theoretical disputes. They had supported Lenin against the Mensheviks' failure to submit to the decisions of the Second Congress, yet were not quite sure whether, with less interest in theoretical distinctions, the split which greatly harmed the party might not have been avoided. In this issue Lenin just escaped a defeat. Bogdanov and he, however, were outvoted when they suggested the introduction of a larger number of workers into the committees which were nearly exclusively composed of intellectuals who had become professional revolutionaries.[23]

As soon as the workers' delusions about the Little Father Tsar had been destroyed by the salvoes fired before the Winter Palace, the Gapon stage of the revolution, in which every demagogue might use the accumulated discontent, was over. At least the industrial workers now accepted leadership of such Social Democrat organisations as were influential. Naturally, modern Soviet historians are more enthusiastic about those movements which arose in places where their faction dominated, (starting with the prolonged strike of the Ivano-Voznesensk textile workers in May-August and culminating in the Moscow uprising in December) than about those where Mensheviks, even of the left wing Trotsky pattern predominated (including the famous Soviet of St. Petersburg and the Siberian insurrections which came closest to a real assumption of power). In Petersburg the Mensheviks started on October 10th/23rd propaganda for the formation of a 'revolutionary (local) self-government', to include all classes which opposed the Tsarist regime. A special Workers' Committee of this was to act as the nucleus of the future united workers' party (this very concept illustrates even the left-wing Mensheviks' refusal to regard the socialist party as something distinct from the broad masses of the workers). Such ambitions may have made the Bolsheviks if not to oppose the Soviets then at least to demand their unconditional support of the existing party.[24] Lenin, however, saw the Soviet as the platform for the common action of all the socialist groups and as the nucleus of the national Provisional Government.[25] After his return to Russia he won his comrades over to his view-point. The Soviet leaders themselves, as they explained at their trial, saw it as an instrument to secure working-class unity and not as a substitute for the parties (three representatives of each of the Bolsheviks, Mensheviks and Social Revolutionaries were admitted to the meetings so that they might be able to carry out the Soviet's decisions). In this they stood near to the Bolshevik standpoint. But their concept of the parties as organs executing the decisions of the workers' parliament (however natural in conditions where organised socialists were the only people likely to carry out actions such as the occupation of newspaper offices) contrasted with the conditions of October 1917, when the Bolshevik party initiated the policy decisions which were carried out by Soviet bodies (the Military Revolutionary Committee of the Petrograd Soviet, and the Soviets of the armies). The Soviet of 1905 was mainly a body expressing the workers' urge for immediate economic gains.[26] It decreed on its own authority the introduction of the Eight Hour Day. The measure, though envisaged by the Third (Bolshevik) Party Congress, was opposed, in the critical November days, by the Bolsheviks as well as the Mensheviks : by the former on the ground that it could not be successful except on a national scale, by the latter because it would alienate capitalist opinion before Tsarism was defeated.[27] Indeed, it gave occasion for the lockout which prepared the defeat of the Petersburg Soviet.

In places where the Bolsheviks were in control of the labour movement, their actions were naturally conditioned by the stage of the movement reached. The Soviet of Men of Confidence of Ivano-Voznesensk, though described with some hindsight by Bolshevik historians since Nevski as having been the first Soviet,[28] was in substance an enlarged strike committee. During the strike it was responsible for provision of the strikers and organised a workers' militia for their protection against the police and strike breakers. It issued permits for essential work, prohibited price increases and ordered the closing down of the public houses (the carrying out of these orders, however, was expected to be done by the normal state machine). But the

Bolsheviks, who were its actual leaders, had to issue their leaflets through the underground press and the Soviet announced its
own dissolution when it had finally decided to break off the
strike. During the December insurrection, on the other hand,
actual power in places such as Sochi and Novorossiisk passed
into the hands of Soviets which preserved public order by their
druzhiniki (fighters' squads, as a rule organised by the socialist
parties), taxed the wealthy and even established People's Courts
(in Sochi according to an elaborate election system) for the
settlement of civil law suits and ordinary conflicts. According
to Tsarist reporters, a similar system introduced in Krasnoyarsk
greatly contributed to the popularity of the new regime[29] (which
was influenced by the Menshevik concept of 'local communes').

In Moscow, the insurgents never assumed power except in
a few districts but the insurrection represented the nearest
approach to 'organising the revolution' made during the whole
crisis of 1905-06. The Bolsheviks of Moscow and of the Federative Committee (formed to re-unite the Bolsheviks and Mensheviks) prepared for an armed insurrection in the spring, when
peasant support was expected. For this very reason they were
not enthusiastic about a premature start.[30] But their hands were
forced by two developments not of their making. On December
2nd/15th half the Moscow garrison was affected by a mutiny.
This was suppressed within a day, but a representative of the CC,
arriving from Petersburg, advised the Moscow Bolshevik leaders
that in view of the capital's failure to react properly to the arrest
of its Soviet leaders, Moscow should take the lead. Their initial
hesitations were only overcome when the CC representative and
the railwaymen's delegates promised that the Government would
be prevented from sending fresh troops into Moscow.[31] Three
days were lost in hesitation before the Soviet took the unanimous decision to start the general strike, three more till the
insurrection, publicly announced from the very start, became
widespread. No general staff was in existence, directives issued
dealt only with the way in which the individual squads should
operate. There was plently of popular sympathy but the fighting
squads numbered a mere 850 men—250 in squads organised by
the Bolsheviks, 200 Mensheviks, 150 Social Revolutionaries. A

few employers even had organised squads from amongst their workers.[32] As the fighting was defensive from the very start whole districts which had no enemy before them were excluded from action. It became hopeless when, because of the failure to include the line to Petersburg in the railway strike, the Government could introduce reliable troops. With the sole exception of Chita[33] the workers' groups nowhere exceeded in strength a few hundred men, nearly all of them members of the revolutionary parties. Such relations of strength excluded any attempt to extend local power to other places by means other than propaganda.

The attitude of the armed forces offered the key to the situation. Any assumption that the majority were pro-Tsarist is refuted by the series of isolated (and hence abortive) outbreaks and by the much larger number of less spectacular movement, which were overlooked in the histories of the movement but partly unearthed on the occasion of the 50th anniversary of the revolution.[34] During the Siberian insurrections Kuropatkin regarded his army—the reliability of which was itself in doubt—as cut off from Russia.[35] The fate of the Moscow insurrection was decided when the Tsarist government succeeded in inducing one reliable regiment into the town. It is difficult to tell what would have happened if some organisation had succeeded in landing at St. Petersburg some of the Baltic sailors, whose sympathies were all the time with the revolutionaries, and who made heavy sacrifices in abortive mutinies. The crucial point, however, was the absence of any revolutionary organisation with capacities other than for propaganda. In such circumstances (which had not fundamentally changed in February 1917) any successful revolutionary movement had to depend on large-scale insurrections in the army. In 1905-06, as distinct from 1917, there were few large-scale army disorders. Numerous as the mutinies were, they were hardly organised above the battalion or ship level, and nearly always started from local grievances. The first and most famous of these mutinies well illustrates their common weakness.

For a considerable time, revolutionary propaganda on the ships of the Black Sea Fleet had been organised with fair response by a special committee of members of diverse Social Democrat groups. Yet far ahead of the organisers' time-table, due to the officers' provocative behaviour a mutiny took place on the battle-cruiser Potemkin—the unit which had been regarded by the revolutionaries as the least prepared one. The insurgent ship moved to the port of Odessa where the workers were on strike and even some street fighting was going on but the landing suggested by the Odessa Bolsheviks was refused because the sailors' committee was afraid that the reliable revolutionary elements on board would weaken, with possibly disastrous effects upon the outcome of the collision between the Potemkin and the main fleet. When the rest of the fleet did meet the Potemkin, its revolutionary sympathies were just sufficient to enable the ship's escape to Rumania.[36] Even in October-November, i.e. at a time when the country had passed through a successful general strike, the sailors' mutinies in Kronstadt and Sevastopol resulted from local grievances. The Social Democrat organisations (from either faction) had to join in movements regarded by them as premature lest they betray the insurgent sailors. But the civilian sympathisers of the naval movement took no armed action. In Sevastopol the infantry remained loyal to the Government; lack of initiative on the part of the insurgent sailors did the rest.[37] We have already seen how the soldiers' mutiny in Moscow (which, too, did not concern politics but conditions of service) encouraged the civilian insurrection which, however, developed too slowly to profit from the soldiers' sympathies. It remains questionable whether an earlier preoccupation of the Bolsheviks with the practical, as distinct from the propagandist, problems of insurrection,[38] or a delay in the trial of strength till spring (when the peasants might be involved in the movement), would have changed the course of events (only in the sense of accomplishing a *bourgeois*-democratic revolution, however). By concluding a peace with Japan, Tsarism could escape from the most threatening element of the situation. We shall see that even the February revolution of 1917 was not 'organised'. Its more successful outcome was due to more favourable circumstances amongst which, certainly, the lessons gained from the 'general rehearsal' played their part.

(b) REUNION AND DEFEAT

The rise of the revolutionary wave put practical action against the common enemy above all theoretical disputes. The reunion of the two Social Democrat factions, however, proved as unstable as its background. The very start of the revolution had encouraged the Third Congress (which was Bolshevik in character) to think of the possible conditions of reunion.[39] In August 1905, when the party organisations already attracted broad sections of workers, negotiations between the two central bodies started. Lenin envisaged the possibility that a mass-influx of formerly less active workers into the party might put the Bolsheviks in a minority within a reunited party : hence he was favourable to the protection of minority rights. As early as in his letter to Krassin, written on September 14, 1905, he thought of having to publish the Bolshevik organ under the authority of the Petersburg or some other local committees, the party organ being controlled by the Mensheviks. He was not afraid of the introduction of a new section of the working-class into the party, yet he insisted on the preservation of the Bolsheviks' identity as a clearly defined group within the reunited party. Those committees which had not yet declared their position should do so before the unification congress so that the reunited party's attitude might be decided in *honest dispute*. Issues of prestige and of the distribution of voting strength at the moment of unification appeared to him as secondary.[40] Lenin's dislike of 'plebiscites' which would grant predominance to the least articulate part of the party found its parallel in the Menshevik camp. There Axelrod and Martov feared that a bloc of Trotsky with the Appeasing section of the Bolsheviks might deprive orthodox Menshevism of its representation in favour of an amorphous 'centre'.[41]

Whatever the ultimate desire of the leaders on either side, the decision was not theirs : the workers pressed towards unification. As long as the 'Trotskyist' tendencies were prominent in the Menshevik camp, there was no case for continuing division between factions which agreed in the demand for an insurrection against Tsarism led by the working-class and disagreed only

regarding the prospects of the revolutionary government emerging
from such an insurrection.   (Conditions became different when
the subsequent defeats of the revolution caused the majority of
the Mensheviks frankly to collaborate with the liberal bourgeoisie
which, on its part, sought accommodation with a slightly reformed
Tsarist regime.)   Immediately after the October strikes the local
organisations of the factions, beginning with Petersburg and
Moscow, established 'Federative Committees' to co-ordinate their
activities.   At Odessa the local Bolshevik Committee, though
inclined to wait for the CC decision, had to work out terms of
local reunion lest it be carried out unconventionally by a majority
of the members of both factions (even an agent of the CC, just
arrived from Petersburg, advised against waiting for the decision
of the two centres).[42]   In these circumstances, questions of prestige and voting strength likely to complicate such moves were
solved in a short series of moves and counter-moves.   The Mensheviks accepted Article One of the Rules (the meaning of which
had changed since party membership had become accessible to
the average worker with readiness to risk the sack) and the replacement of the two existing factional periodicals by one central
organ serving the whole party.   They achieved, however, the
immediate formation of a provisional Central Committee on the
basis of parity and the direct election (on the basis of proportional
representation) of the delegates of the Unity Congress. The points
insisted upon by them suggest that the Mensheviks still expected
to be in a minority position. On February 7th/20th 1906, the
first issue of the new Central Organ was published.   It contained
the political issues on which the two factions contested the elections of the delegates to the Unity Congress[43] which, on April
10th/23rd, opened at Stockholm.

Not before the February revolution of 1917 did Russian
Social Democracy become a legal party, but with the rise of the
revolutionary movement its suppression was sufficiently weakened
to make membership accessible to the average worker with some
readiness to make sacrifices.   In the late autumn of 1905 the
(Bolshevik) Petersburg Committee had already a staff of sixty
agitators, apart from those in the Districts and Sub-Districts.
As early as October 30th one District started the transfer of its

lower organisations to a factory basis. At the meeting of the District Committee which took that decision eight workers as against seven intellectuals were present. One year later, the (united) party organisations of the Donets basin, the Urals, Petersburg and the Ukraine (the latter even without the major towns) had more than 5,000 members each, the Moscow Region (which included the city as well as the central industrial region) 19,000, the Mensheviks' Caucasian stronghold nearly 13,000; apart from 33,000 members of the Bund, 12,000 Latvian and 28,000 Polish Social Democrats (the two last-mentioned potential supporters of Bolshevism) there were 76,000 Russian Social Democrats, amongst them 33,000 Bolsheviks and 43,000 Mensheviks[44] (the competing factions could be relied upon to check excessive estimates in each other's reports). The slight Bolshevik majority amongst those who were prepared to participate in underground activities under pre-1905 conditions turned into a slight Menshevik majority when party membership became attractive for people with more interest in trade unionist and similar activities than in Marxist principles (*a fortiori,* the Mensheviks gained preponderance in the Petersburg Soviet which also embraced the non-party workers). Conditions changed again when open working-class activities were suppressed and most party members regarded their membership as preparation for a future insurrection, which was emphasised by the Bolsheviks. At the Fifth Congress, in May 1907, 46,000 Bolsheviks and 38,000 Mensheviks were represented (the shift was further emphasised by increasing support for the Bolsheviks from the national groups). Amongst the old Social Democrats regional divisions played some part : Moscow, its industrial region and the Urals were predominantly Bolshevik ; the Ukraine, the Caucasus and the western Jewish Settlement predominantly Menshevik ; Petersburg was divided.

In order to secure the subordination of a group outvoted in some decision, the organisation had to be strictly democratic. In Petersburg in 1907, for example, there was a permanent conference of delegates (elected for every 50 or 100 members) which also elected the Committee. The District and City organisations operated in the same way, their autonomy being restricted only by the higher committee's right to send its representatives, with a consultative voice, to the meetings of the lower organisations. In substance, the reunited party was a federation of factions. The Unity Congress demanded that the separate meetings of the two factions should end but only formal tribute was paid to such appeals. When the Congress refused to elect any Bolshevik to the Editorial Board, Lenin accepted it with good grace. As planned before, he published the Bolsheviks' leading periodical—under changing names, as the police closed down one paper after the other—on behalf of the Petersburg Committee followed by a long list of Party Committees controlled by the Bolsheviks. On the other side Dan, speaking for the Editorial Board at the Fifth Congress, stated that its publications had been issued on behalf, not of the party as a whole but of the Menshevik faction, so as to avoid false pretences. The Revision Commission found it quite natural to confirm that a large donation put at the disposal of the Bolshevik faction had been spent according to the donors' wishes.[45] As distinct from the Unity Congress where the Mensheviks had badly misused their majority, elections were now proportional on strictly factional lists. The Mensheviks opposed any choice of the majority even amongst the candidates who were last in the ballot with an equal number of votes. Already at the Unity Congress, all agreements proceeded by negotiation between the leaders of the two opposite camps (only the resolution on armed insurrection was decided by internal dissent in the Menshevik camp).

In his Communication to the Party, published after the conclusion of the Unity Congress, Lenin emphasised unity of action and the subordination of the minority to majority decisions. He enumerated, however, three main points of disagreement, the discussion of which should continue so that the erroneous decisions might be corrected at the next Party Congress. These points were the agrarian problem, the attitude of the parliamentary party in the first Duma, and the decision on armed insurrection. The latter point, in the form in which it had arisen at the Congress, could be described by the Mensheviks as a mere verbal dispute. As regards the two first-mentioned ones, Lenin could not even speak for his own faction. In the agrarian question he voted with the majority of the Bolsheviks who preferred redistribution of the land to nationalisation, so as not to split the Bolshevik front against the Mensheviks' municipalisation proposal. In the issue of Duma tactics, he had allowed himself to be driven by the majority of his faction to the boycott of the first Duma elections ; the same had happened to the more moderate of the Menshevik leaders.[46] When the agrarian problem became topical in October 1917, land nationalisation was proclaimed by the Second Soviet Congress. Stalin, however, who in 1906 as one of the provincial delegates had brought pressure to bear upon Lenin, showed hindsight forty years later. In the introduction to vol. I of his *Collected Works,* he explained the dispute by his inability and that of his colleagues to understand Lenin's alleged insistence upon a direct growth of the bourgeois-democratic into a socialist revolution. In 1917, land nationalisation was enacted because the peasants, and the Social Revolutionary party which was supported by them, demanded it. They demanded it, not because they favoured re-organisation of agriculture on the basis of socialist enterprise but because they understood that establishment of private ownership in peasants' land would soon lead to the small-holders' being involved in debts and losing their land (for the very same reason Lenin [1906] had supported the nationalisation plan : he would have been most unlikely to give way even to a majority of his faction if the basic prospects of the revolution has been involved). Nor did the cleavage in the boycott issue proceed on factional lines. When, in the absence of socialist candidates, the working-class voters disowned the boycott slogan by voting for the Liberals (Kadets), Lenin and a minority of the Bolsheviks supported the Mensheviks in the withdrawal of that slogan for the still outstanding elections. His further conflicts with the Mensheviks concerned the question whether the Social Democrats should collaborate with the Trudoviks and similar Narodnik groups (so as to prepare for the Workers' and Peasants' Government aimed at by him) or with the Liberals, as suggested by the Mensheviks.

The organisation problem, however, again became topical when the progress of reaction turned into a Utopia the prospect of an open party embracing the majority of the industrial workers,

a prospect shared by Lenin.[47] The Bolsheviks wanted an underground party, as large as it could be in the circumstances, but if
necessary, restricted to a nucleus of conscious revolutionaries
prepared for all sacrifices. The Mensheviks, on the other hand,
wanted a party of co-operators and trade unionists active within
the limits now allowed by the Tsarist regime for open workers'
organisation. The first formulation of that alternative was
Axelrod's suggestion of a broad workers' Congress.[48] He
defended it at the Fifty Party Congress on the ground that the
party was a revolutionary organisation not of the workers but
of the lower-middle-class intelligentsia, operating upon the
working-class and using it for its purpose. Working-class members, though now in the majority, could not hold their own
against the intellectuals' longer political experience.[49] The obvious
answer to this was that the workers, most of whom had joined
the party in 1905, should be helped to acquire the experience
necessary for the occupation of leading positions in the party
(there was a definite bias in favour of promoting them). The
majority of the members of the Bolshevik parliamentary party
in the Third Duma already came from the bench; and during the
war men such as Shlyapnikov, Kalinin and Andreyev moved into
the key positions of the underground organisation. When drafting
the resolution of the Fifth Party Congress, Lenin[50] still made a
distinction between Axelrod's propaganda for a non-party
Workers' Congress and those Mensheviks who intended to dissolve the party in such an amorphous organisation (subsequently
described as the Liquidators). In revolutionary times organisations of the Soviet type would unite the working-class and strengthen the party's influence upon it. The resolution adopted by the
Congress[51] emphasised the need for trade unions, co-operatives,
etc. in ordinary times and, for Soviets, in revolutionary times. The
suggestion of the Workers' Congress was rejected as it might
replace the party by non-party organisations of a permanent
character, exposing the workers to the influence of bourgeois
democracy. This argument was supported by Mensheviks like
Plekhanov who, while defending the Menshevik position on the
issue of collaboration with the liberal bourgeoisie,[52] as opposed
to the Liquidators wished to preserve the party's underground

organisation (hence their later description as 'Party-Mensheviks').

For the moment, however, Lenin had to face the organisation problem mainly as a conflict in the Bolsheviks' own ranks. The Bolshevik delegates to the Party Congress elected a permanent factional centre to co-ordinate activities and to supervise the Bolsheviks working in diverse party bodies, in particular in the Central Committee where 'Appeasing' Bolsheviks were likely to predominate. It had, of course, no status in the official setting of the united party but it could meet and publish its decisions, as an enlarged meeting of the Editorial Board of *Proletarii,* the faction's periodical. Though constituted as a check on the Mensheviks it gained importance as the scene of Lenin's struggle against the extremists in his own ranks. Success in this struggle implied further centralisation within the Bolshevik camp.

At the Conference of Russian Social Democrats in August 1907 decisions against a boycott of elections could be carried only by a combination of the Mensheviks and the anti-boycottist minority of the Bolsheviks. Resolutions that the parliamentary party should clearly oppose the Kadets, could be carried only because the boycottist part of the Bolsheviks supported Lenin's motions 'as the lesser evil'. As long as there were any chances of a revolution he doubted whether a conflict on an issue which might then become obsolete was really worthwhile.[53] But while the temporary defeat of the revolution became obvious with the failure even of economic strikes in the weeks following the dissolution of the Second Duma, the 'boycottist' group of the Bolsheviks successively developed formulas intended to restrain the party from activities which might impair its revolutionary purity. These tactical issues were eventually associated with philosophical ones.[54] Lenin believed that Bogdanov's advocacy of adventurist policies was unconnected with his efforts to replace the strictly realistic attitude associated with materialism by the introduction of the 'empirio-criticism' concepts of Mach and Avenarius into the Marxist fold and with the wave of romanticism which after the defeat of the revolution swerved the ranks of the Russian intelligentsia. To these disputes we owe Lenin's *Materialism and Empirio-Criticism,* up to the present day the most serious effort to preserve Engels' materialist approach inde-

pendently of its association with the nineteenth century state of
science and, indeed, to protect the materialist world-outlook
against the assertion, currently repeated after every major progress in science, that it has thereby become obsolete. For the
internal life of the Bolshevik party the incident became important
because, in the decisions of the Bolshevik centre which in
June 1909 expelled the extremists,[55] advocacy of idealist philosophies was paired with 'boycottism' as grounds for expulsion.
Thus, the claim for ideological homogeneity was extended beyond
the basic approach to the social sciences (where it has always
been a truism for orthodox Marxists). Only in appearance was
it mitigated by the declaration that expulsion from the faction,
i.e. from a community of people who within the party fought for
identical views, did not affect the dissenters' status as members of
the party, which might contain different shades of opinion, nor
their right to form their own faction to defend their common
views within the party (which they eventually did). In the
minds of its more ardent supporters, the Bolshevik faction had
a much higher claim to their loyalty than the uneasy coalition
with the Mensheviks and the national groups which was described
as the Social Democrat Party. Lenin himself made his case by
referring to the co-existence of Marxists and Revisionists within
German Social Democracy which was regarded by every left-
winger as a necessary evil.

 Moreover, the resolutions of the Bolshevik conference
described the leftist error as the views of elements which had
entered the party during the revolution, attracted not so much by
the socialist as by the democratic aspects of its programme, and
Lunacharski's 'God-constructing' philosophy[56] as a direct reflection of the struggle of lower-middle-class tendencies against
Marxism. It was implied that for neither trend was there a place
in the party as there should be. The oppositionists (*Vperedists,*
according to the title of the periodical—*Forward*—which supported
their faction) denounced Lenin's collaboration with loyal Mensheviks such as Plekhanov as a betrayal of Bolshevism, in terms
which would well fit later leftist reproaches against Stalin's alleged
Centrism. At least *in nucleo* the concept of the 'monolithic'
party, held together by common views not only on political

principles but also on important issues of tactics, was contained
in the decisions of the Bolshevik conference of 1909. It would
be a mistake, however, to think that this concept was shared
even by the more advanced organisers of the Bolshevik faction.

For two years Lenin had directed the *Proletarii,* as far as the
boycott issue was concerned, in opposition to the majority of the
Bolshevik faction (including organisations as important as those
of Petersburg and Moscow) on behalf of which it was published.
The difficulties encountered in that uphill struggle may have
induced Lenin's application of extremist measures. But these very
disciplinary measures were deplored even by Bolsheviks such as
Stalin[57] and his Baku organisation who had supported Lenin in
the *political* aspects of the dispute. A similar attitude was taken
by the Petersburg organisation when it dropped its original
support of the 'boycottist' line. When Lenin's *Proletarii*
(October 3rd/16th) reprinted the Baku resolution, it added an
editorial note saying that the split had originated only from
Bogdanov's failure to submit to majority decisions. Yet in an
argument with the Petersburg Bolsheviks published in the same
issue Lenin[58] explained that opposition to important decisions
had made the split necessary. Formal submission of outvoted
leaders to majority decision would not prevent them from spread-
ing confusion in the ranks. The implication was that the unity
of action long since postulated by Bolshevism presupposed
common views on major issues of political theory. The subsequent watering down of this argument and the fact that Stalin
had participated in enforcing it, may explain the comparatively
modest tribute paid as late as 1938 in the *Short History of the
CPSU(b)* to the first appearance of seeds which were to germinate
in a later period. To the student, however, it provides an additional argument against artificial distinctions between the Leninist
and the Stalinist period in the development of the Bolshevik
concept of party organisation.

By the time of the expulsion of the Vperedists, the uneasy
coalition of the Social Democrat party was already approaching
its end. Within the Mensheviks' camp the Liquidators' case was
strengthened by the consideration that the party's central bodies
were hopelessly Bolshevik, and bound to remain so in conditions

where people were more interested in legal workers' organisations than in underground activities. The Liquidators working in Russia proudly accepted this description and did not refrain from describing the party as a corpse. A group of Menshevik leaders abroad, headed by Martov and Dan who published in Paris the *Golos sotsialdemokrata* (Voice of a Social Democrat), shared the Liquidators' assessment of the party organisation as practically non-existent and spoke of the Bolsheviks (who had been supported by a majority of the Fifth Party Congress) in terms of 'a foreign circle of corrupt Blanquists' who had no right to speak on behalf of the party. Still, they warned the Liquidators against a formal break with the party which might become useful in the event of another change in the political attitude of the national sections[59] (which, as we know, kept the balance between the two competing Russian factions). In January 1910, an extraordinary Plenary Session of the Central Committee made an effort at reconciliation. The factions should be dissolved, representatives of the minorities (including the Liquidators) be co-opted into the central bodies, *Vpered* as well as Trotsky's *Pravda* be recognised as party organs on condition that they included (Bolshevik) representatives of the Central Committee in their Editorial Boards. Lenin's fears of a 'dissolution of the Bolshevik faction into a party'[60] however, proved unjustified. The only effect of the arrangement was a clear shift of the responsibility for the unavoidable split to the Mensheviks, who, as distinct from the Bolsheviks, refused to carry out their part of the agreement. The three Russian Liquidators refused to join the Central Committee because they found such an institution unnecessary (during the chase for suitable substitutes the two Appeasing Bolsheviks who had to construct the part of the CC working inside Russia, were arrested so that no Russian representation was available). *Golos sotsialdemokrata* continued publication, and Trotsky drove the CC representative (it was Kamenev, his brother-in-law, who stood near to the appeasing section of the Bolsheviks) out of his Board because he disagreed with Trotsky's condonation of the violation of the Unity agreement by the Mensheviks. To Lenin, it now appeared that his own group, attacked within the Bolshevik camp by the *Vpered* faction and Plekhanov's group, attacked within the Menshevik fold by the Liquidators, together formed Social Democracy.[61] He thought so because of the disproportion in strength which excluded any function of Plekhanov's group other than as a bridge for a few Menshevik organisations in Russia to join a party reconstructed under Bolshevik leadership. But it also reflected the continuity of the Russian revolutionary tradition within which disagreements about one's attitude to the liberal bourgeoisie were admissible while anyone who suggested dissolution of the organisation of the revolutionaries was a traitor. In those days of reaction, even Lenin did not envisage an immediate transition of the coming revolution into a socialist transformation of society, but he wished the party to stand for a clear-cut democratic organisation of capitalist society, as had been enforced in France by the defeated revolutions of 1830, 1848 and 1871 (as distinct from the Prussian way which was conditioned by the Liberals' compromise in 1863-65 with a slightly reformed feudal autocracy).[62] With such a prospect, the preservation of the party organisation was infinitely more important than any tactical issue.

By mid-1910 the failure of the conciliation attempt made by the Unity Meeting was evident. By the end of the year, the Bolsheviks demanded the return of the moneys deposited with the German Arbitrators for the benefit of a reunited party because of the other faction's failure to keep the agreement. At about the same time better news came from Russia : workers' demonstrations and strikes had started in protest against atrocities committed in the Tsarist prisons and on the occasion of Leo Tolstoi's funeral. In spring 1911 a private meeting of the Bolshevik members of the CC living abroad—(i.e. of the majority of the *buro* abroad) decided to save funds and documents for the disposition of the reconstructed party. At the CC meeting in June it was decided to set up a Preparatory Committee for the convocation of a Party Conference. The Menshevik representative (who belonged to the Martov-Dan group) and the *Bundist* left the meeting as soon as the intentions of the majority became clear. The Preparatory Committee had two branches, one working abroad and one visiting the Russian committees. The

6

latter met the usual difficulties of disorganisation and police persecution. Rykov was arrested and only Ordzhonikidze succeeded in convening an organised conference. The branch working abroad, however, dominated by the Appeasers as it was, soon became involved in a revolt of the exiled Social Democrats against the split of such unity with the Mensheviks as still survived.[63] Lenin replied by a denunciation of the new faction of Appeasers.[64] As has happened often in the history of political splits, the first result of attempts at reconciliation of fighting factions was their multiplication. But Ordzhonikidze had meanwhile arranged for a meeting of representatives of five party committees from the Southern parts of Russia and the Petersburg organisation was reconstructed in those days.

Lenin now had Russian backing, however weak, for his Conference. It met in Prague, January 1912 : Petersburg, Moscow, the Central Industrial Region, Saratov, Tiflis, Baku, Nikolayev, Kazan, Kiev, Ekaterinoslav, Dvinsk and Vilna were represented.[65] The Conference decided to proclaim itself an all-Russian Conference and to elect a new Central Committee (one of its members belonged to Plekhanov's group). By a special resolution, the Liquidators were described as standing outside the party. Immediately after the return of part of the new Central Committee to Russia some more Russian party workers, amongst them Stalin and Sverdlov, were co-opted. The counter-conference convened in August 1912 by the official Mensheviks and Trotsky failed to establish a bloc of all the non-Bolsheviks. Plekhanov and the Poles refused to participate and the delegates of the *Vpered* group left the conference after the first meeting. With the notable exception of the Georgian Mensheviks, the August Conference remained a meeting of exiles more or less representative of the diverse shades of Menshevism. The split of Russian Social Democracy had become final.

(c) THE BOLSHEVIK UNDERGROUND PARTY

Lenin had chosen the right moment for the re-organisation of the party. The delegates returning from the Prague Conference found a new revolutionary wave in ascendance. It started with the massacre of striking workers on the Lena ; during 1912 the number of strikers reached 1,238,000 (more than in any year since 1905); two-thirds of them participated in political strikes. The movement continued till the very eve of the war, when a strike of the Putilov workers in Petersburg in support of the striking oil workers of Baku grew into a political strike of 150,000 Petersburg workers, with mass demonstrations and barricades. Then the outbreak of the War brought an interruption of the movement of about a year's duration.

In the two years from the Lena strikes to the outbreak of the War (i.e. 1912-1914) the party organisation was restored on foundations different from those prevailing during the mushroom-like growth in 1905-06, which had collapsed with the disappearance of revolutionary enthusiasm amongst the workers and of the unity of the party factions. The statement that, at the Prague Conference, the Bolshevik party was started by a number of people who could be settled on a sofa is slightly exaggerated. It would have had to be a rather larger sofa, and in the given conditions of the Russian underground it meant something to bring together a dozen or so truly representative delegates to a conference abroad. But on the other hand a conference based upon twenty organisations working in Russia—not to speak of the Mensheviks' counterstroke—represented, in the numerical sense, no progress beyond what had been achievable ten years before, in the days of *Iskra*. Eventually the Bolshevik CC established connections with more than sixty groups working in Russia. Not all of these were Bolshevik party organisations. Some were Bolshevik groups within working Social Democrat organisations which included supporters of either faction. But even groups that upheld contact with non-party organisations, and were capable of collecting information and of distributing Bolshevik literature would play their part when, after the February revolution of 1917, the restoration of an open party organisation became possible.

The existing organisations were numerically weak and only a few of them had preserved continuity through the darkest period of reaction. In 1911 the organisation of Baku had about 300 members. The weakening becomes apparent when we remember that 436 party members had voted for Bolshevik delegates in the elections of the Fifth Congress.[66] Nor was the Bolshevik organisation of St. Petersburg, when re-established by Ordzhonikidze, stronger. One year later, when the movement was clearly in the ascendant, Moscow had less than 400 party members in twenty-five groups, the most important of them in the major factories, a few more attached to trade unions.[67] In 1911, the organisation of Ekaterinoslav had 120 members (amongst them only one intellectual), that of Tiflis (Bolsheviks and party Mensheviks together) 70, those of Rostov-on-Don and Nikilayev about 50 party members each. In the Urals, groups of 40-50 party members in cities such as Ekaterinburg, Ufa and Perm were regarded as 'fairly large'. Two years later the party organisations of the six major factories in Ekaterinburg had increased to more than two hundred members. The same number was organised in the Motovolikh works near Perm while the Perm city organisation remained on its former level.[68] It is unlikely that even as much as a tenth of the 46,000 Social Democrats who had supported the Bolsheviks in the elections to the 1907 party Congress continued party work in 1912-14. Yet if the party's numerical strength was hardly superior to that at the eve of the 1905 revolution, its outlook and composition had been greatly changed by the new generation of workers who had joined it in the course of the revolution. The Petersburg Committee, for example, was composed exclusively of workers (however, it elected an Executive Committee consisting of three workers and two intellectuals).[69]

The internal structure of the organisations varied according to local needs. The typical party committee would be composed of elected representatives of the districts or factory groups plus a few co-opted members (as a rule, professional revolutionaries), and perhaps some representatives of the legal workers' associations dominated by the Bolsheviks. In a place such as Petersburg the full committee met every two to three weeks and there might be occasional broader delegates' conferences. In the Motovilikh works, conferences of the 26 shop representatives as well as full party meetings (more than a hundred party members attending) were organised.[70] Local conditions varied not only as regards the methods required to protect the organisations from the secret police but also according to the extent to which the split between Bolsheviks and Mensheviks had occurred. At Samara, for example, there were factory nuclei consisting of both Bolsheviks and Mensheviks and a legal workers' club (established by the Mensheviks but used by all the socialists) where one could meet ; there was also a legal newspaper, the struggle for the control of which caused the convention of delegates' conferences (illegal, of course), attended by supporters of both the competing factions. The Bolsheviks refrained for long from the establishment of a local Party Committee lest it gave the secret police an opportunity to introduce its agents. Only on the eve of the War was a party conference convened by both Bolsheviks and party Mensheviks to elect a committee (meanwhile the Malinovski case had demonstrated that police agents might be introduced even into the Central Committee but that party work could continue in spite of this risk).[71]

Lenin's break with the boycottists had removed those type of old Bolshevik organisations which would have resisted the use of the now available legal opportunities for socialist propaganda. Workers' clubs, cooperatives and associations of all kinds existed in many places. Some had been established by the Mensheviks—so far as these were 'Liquidators' with the intention of offering the workers an alternative to political organisation—some by the Bolsheviks with the intention of creating a broader framework within which the underground organisation could become effective.[72] Even more important were the platforms available to the socialists in the shape of an open press—though severely censored—and of such elected representation of the workers as was available in post 1907 Russia.

In 1912 the Mensheviks started a Petersburg newspaper Lyuch and the Bolsheviks Pravda. Soon the latter had 40,000 readers against a mere 16,500 readers of its competitor. Stalin who edited the first issue of Pravda (of April 22, 1912), in its editorial defined its political basis in very broad terms : collaboration of all Social Democrat workers without distinction was desirable as real party life was inconceivable without disagreements. Those tenets which the diverse Social Democrat trends had in common were far more important than the differences which separated them.[73] However diplomatic the approach, the competition between the two Petersburg papers was a trial of strength between the two socialist trends and a model to which the formulation of the policies of provincial newspapers was oriented.[74] The Mensheviks grudgingly admitted that the Bolsheviks might prevail amongst the supporters of working-class papers in a proportion of 3 : 2 but added that the very possibility of such comparisons showed that the repression of the labour movement was not worse than, say, in Hungary. Moreover, there was no longer any reason for denouncing as Liquidators those who wished to part with the underground organisation[75] (the idea that some underground organisation might be needed even in countries such as Hungary was absent from Martov's mind).

A vivid picture of the activities of the Bolshevik parliamentarians has been preserved in Badayev's Memoirs. The impossibility of improving the workers' conditions by participating in the Tsarist Duma (with its restrictions on workers representation and rights), created closer contacts between the elected and their constituents' non-parliamentary activities than might be found amongst other socialist parties. In the elections for the nine seats reserved for workers six Bolsheviks and three Mensheviks had been returned ; four more Mensheviks were elected in general urban constituencies. Hence the Mensheviks had a narrow majority within the Social Democrat parliamentary party but the total number of industrial workers employed in the Gubernia represented by Bolsheviks was over a million as against a mere 214,000 in the Gubernia represented by Mensheviks.[76] Although some of the Bolsheviks were elected by narrow majorities,[77] their preponderance amongst the industrial proletariat (as distinct from left-wing opinion taken as a whole) was obvious. When the Mensheviks used their narrow majority in the parliamentary party to control all the party's appearances in the Duma and its commissions, the Bolsheviks reacted with the demand for parity in representation. This demand was rejected although even some of the Menshevik deputies found it justified.[78]

The Bolsheviks now formed an independent parliamentary group and appealed for mass support. The appeal was successful though the Bolsheviks' insistence offended so basic an instinct as the preservation of working-class unity.[79]

The Bolsheviks' preponderance amongst the industrial proletariat was also demonstrated in the election of workers' representatives to the Social Insurance Committees. This was one of the few legal opportunities open to elected workers' representatives for participation in the administration of social services, and practically the only one where the elections were straightforward. In the outcome, the Bolsheviks won 84 per cent of the seats in the capital, and 82 per cent in Russia as a whole. As this was an activity in the very field in which the Mensheviks had expected further progress, the result weighed perhaps more heavily than the Bolsheviks' control of most of the trade unions in Petersburg and Moscow. The Bolsheviks' greater readiness to face the persecutions still involved in trade union activities granted them an organisation influence superior to that of post-1917, when trade union activities were no longer suppressed. From the order paper of the VI Party Congress the convention of which, for mid-August 1914, was envisaged by a CC meeting in April,[80] it is evident that a prolonged use of the meagre legal opportunities given by Tsarism was envisaged. In that document, the revolutionary potentialities of Russia are found only in the nationalities question and in the party's attitude to the 'Narodniki' (i.e. the Social Revolutionaries). They would be important if in the course of the industrial workers' movements the need for allies in the village would arise. Consciousness of the increasing importance of underground work was reflected in the establishment of a special department of the CC which, under strict security arrangements, would help the work in the legal organisations, prepare the party Congress, guide the Petersburg Committee and restore it after arrests (as we shall see, this activity was in great demand during the war years).[81]

(d) BOLSHEVISM IN THE WAR CRISIS

Because of the Russian socialists' revolutionary tradition, the majority of them refused to accept the government's war propa-

ganda (amongst major belligerents, only the Italian labour movement proved similarly immune). The fact that Russian Social
Democracy was split, enabled the left-wing clearly to elaborate its
position without being handicapped by thoughts of organisational
unity. It is, however, incorrect to describe an internationalist
position as the privilege of the Bolsheviks or (more important,
as the internationalist-minded Mensheviks eventually proved a
small minority) to identify the position of the Bolshevik party
with that taken up by Lenin and his narrow circle of exiles.

After some hesitations on the Menshevik Chkheidze's part,
both the Social Democrat Duma factions agreed on a joint statement on internationalist lines.[82] Further aspirations of the Bolshevik deputies are indicated in their eventual indictment, not only
for having rejected Vandervelde's appeal to support the Allied
war-effort but also for having appealed to the soldiers to use
arms in the cause of socialism.[83] Badayev's self-critical statement that the joint declaration of the Social-Democracy deputies
'did not contain a clear and precise characterisation of the war
or of the position of the working-class and did not give a well-
defined revolutionary lead'[84] appears as hind-sight applied after
Lenin had elaborated theories with the understanding of which
the Bolshevik deputies can hardly be credited. Their political
adviser, Kamenev, understood them and on the occasion of the
parliamentary party's trial in February 1915, dissociated himself
from Lenin's line. Lenin,[85] on the other hand, dissociated himself in public from such behaviour and directing for obvious
reasons, the criticism of mistakes committed in his opinion by *all*
the defendants at Kamenev (who was not a deputy elected by
the workers). But this did not prevent him from speaking, in
March 1917, of Kamenev as a person who should understand
that he bore responsibilities of world historical importance.[86]
Nor did such criticism of Kamenev's behaviour, as Muranov and
Stalin were later alleged to have expressed in joint exile,[87] prevent
them from accepting Kamenev as their editorial colleague as a
matter of course.[88] This shows that Kamenev's mistake was
regarded merely as a minor tactical error. Lenin's capacity to
make those distinctions which we are soon to discuss, enabled him
in the historical crisis of March 1917 to see further than his

comrades in Russia, and eventually transferred the Russian Schism of 1903 to the international stage. Such hind-sight, however, should not cause us to indentify his attitude with that of the Bolsheviks who unnecessarily continued to defend, with the tenacity and readiness for self-sacrifice characteristic of their struggle, such tenets as were already accepted by left-wing socialists in Russia and, as the resolutions of the International Socialist Congress of 1907 and 1912 had shown, at least in theory even abroad.

Much of the argument developed by Lenin during the War was relevant only in the given ideological setting. While accepting the theory of modern monopoly capitalism developed by Hobson and Hilferding he opposed the right-wing Social Democrats' references to Engels' attitude to wars in the pre-monopoly stage of capitalism.[89] His concept of a narrow workers' aristocracy, corrupted by imperialism, explained the behaviour of the western Social Democrat parties without admitting that the working-class of the advanced countries, in its large majority, was itself affected by imperialism.[90] Thus Lenin and his party did not realise that Russia would have to face the difficulties of socialist reconstruction unaided except by other nations of the East. Even on the eve of his return to Russia Lenin held the traditional belief that Russia, by accomplishing her bourgeois-democratic revolution,[91] would precipitate the socialist revolution in the West. But as early as 1915 he concluded from the unequal development of the political and economic conditions in the diverse capitalist countries that the traditional concept of a simultaneous socialist revolution was unrealistic. The triumph of socialism would start from a single capitalist country.[92] When the Russian revolution proved to be isolated, this statement was naturally quoted as the first proclamation of the possibility of 'socialism in one country'.

Apart from an interpretation of the international framework, however, the war demanded clarification of the idea of revolutionary dictatorship envisaged by the Bolsheviks since 1905. The war delayed for two more years the overthrow of Tsarism, which was visibly on the cards in summer, 1914, but eventually turned it into a comparatively easy process. The peasants, for the conquest of whose sympathies a prolonged struggle had been envisaged by Lenin, were now in uniform and in a mood in which they would easily join working-class insurgents. The bourgeoisie, against whose alliance with the Tsarist regime the 'democratic dictatorship of the workers and the peasants' had been envisaged, came into conflict with the regime because of the latter's attempts to find a way out of the war by a separate peace. What Lenin in 1905 had anticipated as a prolonged struggle during which the class-fronts would become clear and the bourgeoisie be forced to drop Tsarism, was in March 1917 reduced to a short attempt of the Liberals to preserve constitutional monarchy. In the autumn of 1915, when the defeats of the Russian armies had made revolution in Russia a vital issue, Lenin analysed the different meanings of the 'democratic dictatorship of the workers and peasants'. Now, as distinct from 1905, the connection of the bourgeois-democratic revolution in Russia with the socialist revolution in the West had become visible. In these conditions, the decisive division within the Russian progressive movement was no longer that between those who aimed at a bourgeois-democratic revolution and the big bourgeoisie which wished to avoid it by a compromise with Tsarism. It was between the petty bourgeois in town and countryside who regarded the Russian revolution as a means to defeat Germany without defeating capitalism, and the socialist proletariat which desired it in the interest of the proletarian revolution in the West.[93] Still, this was an issue for the future. In a discussion of a report on the activities of the Petrograd Committee,[94] which was inclined to skip the bourgeois-democratic stage of the revolution, Lenin emphasized that the Russian proletariat had first to complete the bourgeois-democratic revolution in Russia in order to kindle the socialist revolution in Europe. Although because of the war, the second task had now become extremely close to the first, it was still a separate and second task. The solution of the first demanded collaboration with the petty-bourgeois peasantry of Russia.[95]

Like many socialists Lenin regarded Russia as the country likely to *start* the next revolutionary wave. On the other hand, as we have just seen, without sharing Utopian dreams about a simultaneous revolution in *all* the major European countries, he stated in conventional terms that the Russian proletariat could not *complete* socialist reconstruction by its own efforts. This did not prevent him from appealing to the Great Russians' legitimate pride in their revolutionary national traditions which would be continued by the coming revolution.[96] This attitude sharply contrasted with Trotsky's statement that the war, 'breaking up the nation-state, was also destroying the national basis for revolution' and Trotsky's warning against 'that national revolutionary Messianic mood which prompts one to see one's own nation as destined to lead mankind to socialism'.[97] Lenin believed that the proletariat which first had conquered power in some country, 'having expropriated the capitalists and organised at home the socialist production, would confront the capitalist rest of the world'.[92] These words, coming from a Marxist, need not be interpreted as suggestions of an aggressive foreign policy. Foreign intervention would force war (or a series of wars) on the first socialist country, and these would have to be fought with political means. Appeal to the oppressed classes in other countries, and if necessary even armed support of their insurrections, would form one of these political means, help one's own national pride and the revolutionary plans of others. There was no contradiction between the two unless one believed (as Trotsky did) in the necessarily European character of the socialist revolution to come. To Lenin a scheme for tackling socialist reconstruction in isolated Russia was available once the political situation could enforce it. To envisage it definitely as long as there were any chances of sparing socialist Russia the difficulties of isolation would have contradicted Lenin's general approach to revolutionary politics. His death just after the defeat of the German communists in 1923 made Russia's isolation an accomplished fact. His last articles, however, give a clear indication of the way which the world revolution, in which he believed to the last, would have to go when revolutionary attempts were defeated in the capitalist countries of the west.[98]

Arguments amongst the Bolsheviks about specific problems of revolutionary policy were very much within the family. Lenin's main tenets, however, were sufficiently clear and repeated often enough for even an occasional copy of *Sotsial-demokrat* to serve as a guide, should it reach some Russian committee or Siberian place of exile. At least as far as Petrograd was concerned (and there existed always some tenuous links between the organisations of the capital and of the Provinces) it was quite feasible for the Stockholm Bureau of the exiled Central Committee to supply literature and even to send individual agents. In autumn 1915, a new Russian *Buro* of the CC was formed in Petrograd, to replace the old one which had been arrested in connection with the prosecution of the Bolshevik Duma deputies. It consisted of Eremeyev (like Molotov a former member of the Pravda staff), one of the Bolshevik members of the Social Insurance Council, and one worker who had played a leading part in the Ivano-Voznesensk Strike Committee of 1905. As they could not cope with the work, A. Shlyapnikov was sent by Lenin as representative of the organisation abroad to Petrograd. In August 1916 he reformed the Russian *Buro,* co-opting Zalutski and Molotov (who meanwhile had escaped from the Siberian exile where he had landed in consequence of a failed attempt, as an emissary of the Petrograd Committee, to restore the Moscow organisation). From then on the Russian *Buro* could continue to work till the fall of Tsarism enabled the establishment of a legal party organisation. In late 1916 the *Buro* was connected with Moscow, Nizhny-Novgorod, Kiev, Tula, Voronezh and some organisations in the Donets basin, the Urals and Siberia. Its main activities were associated with the two capitals and the Ivano-Voznesensk industrial district.[99] However, it would be incorrect to think that the underground Bolshevik party could carry out an agreed political line say in terms of the French CP during World War II. On the other hand, comparisons with the conditions of the German or even Japanese parties during that War would be mistaken for it was certainly stronger.

As natural, the local organisations directly connected with the workers functioned with much greater regularity than the centre. According to Mints,[100] the Petrograd City Committee was destroyed by the Police thirty times during the war, that of Moscow ten times (the Moscow breakdowns occurred because a police spy had infiltrated into the committee arranging re-elections : in consequence, the newly elected committees were arrested on the occasion of their first meetings, the last one on December 1, 1916). Some of the 'destructions' recorded from Petrograd may have amounted to nothing worse than the arrest of two or three party officials, the consequences of which were exaggerated in the reports of ambitious police officials while the rest of the committee continued till a real breakdown occurred. Yet it is obvious that the average member of a city committee (who at least after the loss of the first rank was likely to be a worker with average political experience) simply lacked the time necessary for him to grow up to the responsibilities of his office. The lower ranks of the organisation, however, showed a fair stability. In February 1916 when there was no working city committee whatever,[101] Moscow had five District organisations with 31 groups and 550 organised Bolsheviks ; Petrograd by the end of that year had nine District organisations (apart from the separate language groups) with some 1500-2000 party members. Large party groups such as those in the Putilov works and the Rozenkrants and Lessner factories counted 70-100 party members, average ones, 15-30.[102] For the party as a whole, a strength of 23,600 members existing on the eve of the February revolution was assessed retrospectively in 1922. Even if deductions are made for those living in foreign or Siberian exile, this figure is quite disproportionate to what we know about the actual working strength of the two largest organisations.[103]

Yet even in a realistic assessment, the party's numerical strength appears remarkable enough in relation both to the means of repression available to a Government in war-time[104] and to the number of the old-standing industrial workers who remained in the cities during the war, the gaps being filled by peasants, small traders, etc. who entered the war industries as a means of avoiding the call-up.[105] The Bolsheviks could influence the course of events only through the 'hard core' of the working-class. The changes in social structure due to the war explain both the slowness with which they could make their impact upon the revolutionary developments (including the Soviet elections which followed the fall of Tsarism) and the rapidity with which they conquered such large sections of the population of the capitals as soon as the mood of the peasantry changed.

In the summer of 1915—at the very time when the Tsarist armies had suffered decisive defeats—a new wave of strikes started in Kostroma and Ivano-Voznesensk. There were many killed and wounded. In protest, in September alone about 150,000 workers struck work in Petrograd, Moscow, Nizhny-Novgorod and other centres. Shcherbatov stated in the Council of Ministers on August 24, that the situation in Ivano-Voznesensk had been so serious that for one critical moment it had been uncertain what the garrison would do. Shavkovski added that the workers were much aroused and that any kind of spark might kindle a fire. At the meeting of September 15th, Shcherbatov doubted whether more than a thousand soldiers in the capital were reliable in an emergency, while the 30,000 convalescent soldiers might easily join an insurrection.[106] Yet there was still some equilibrium between the supporters and opponents of the war effort within the labour movement of the capital. In September the workers were called upon to elect their representatives to the War Industrial Committees, the formation of which implied recognition of the status of labour as a partner in negotiations on economic problems.[107] Consciousness of these implications[108] may have strengthened the position of the Mensheviks who advocated participation while the Bolsheviks, in order to demonstrate the workers' opposition to the war effort, campaigned for the election of electors (the elections were indirect) who would refuse to elect Workers' Representatives to the Committee. In the first meeting of the electors the Bolsheviks, with the help of sympathising non-party delegates, achieved a majority in favour of non-participation but after a prolonged propaganda campaign against the Bolsheviks, this decision was reversed in a second meeting held two months later. The War Industrial Committees thus established clashed with the employers as soon as they established sub-committees for labour questions even when their interference was restricted to such modest issues as provision of medical aid in the factories. The employers felt that in the very activities of these committees potential recognition of trade unions was implicit.[109] The Bolsheviks' abstention from the committees, natural though it was as an anti-war demonstration, contributed to the Mensheviks' predominance in the Soviets formed after the February Revolution, under the strong influence of the workers' section of the War Industrial Committee. On the other hand, the employers' refusal to collaborate with the Committees, as well as the Liberals' refusal to admit representatives of the Menshevik and Social Revolutionary parliamentary parties to the Conference of the City Unions,[110] may explain the apparent contradiction, noted by Trotsky, between the Mensheviks' readiness to support the liberal bourgeoisie and the initial Menshevik leadership in the Soviets which could not develop except as an alternative to bourgeois rule.

Perhaps because of the consolidation of the military situation the next revolutionary wave developed only gradually. October 17, 1916, saw the start of a political strike of 85,000 Petrograd workers which continued for four days ; some soldiers of the 181st Infantry Regiment joined in the demonstration. In protest against their arrest and against the court-martialling of the members of the committee of the Bolshevik naval organisation, the Bolsheviks called a second political strike from October 26 to 29 which proved even stronger : 95,000 workers in 98 enterprises participated.[111] All in all, that year saw 1.3 million workers strike (during the first seven months of 1916), most of them for political aims. The traditional political strike on Bloody Sunday, 1917 proved stronger than its predecessors : in Petrograd alone some 150,000 workers participated. The slogans issued by the Bolsheviks and the Menshevik Internationalists were directed against the War, for a Constituent Assembly and a Democratic Republic. In early February the Russian *Buro* of the Bolshevik CC discussed with other democratic groups joint action for the overthrow of the Tsarist government. But the Liberals' hopes were put on the planned 'palace revolution'. The Menshevik parliamentary party under Chkheidze (as distinct from the Mensheviks in the War Industrial Committee under Skobolev) organised demonstrations in support of the Duma on February 14, when its meetings were reopened. Their hopes, too, were put in the 'palace revolution', which might be disturbed by independent working-class action. Hence February 13 and 14 saw competing demonstrations. Those organised by the

Bolsheviks in Petrograd to commemorate the anniversary of the arrest of the Bolshevik Duma deputies were moderately successful, the pre-Duma demonstrations of the Mensheviks—and also the Bolshevik demonstrations in Moscow—complete failures. The wave of strikes, most of them economic in character, continued without interruption until the lock-out of the Putilov workers on February 22, which set major events into motion. Already on February 14, the strikes carried slogans such as 'Down with the War' and 'Long Live the Second Revolution'. Some Bolsheviks still doubted whether the coming upheaval would not be premature in view of the party's insufficient preparation. Others, however, suggested that the party's fighting squads (*druzhiniki*) should be made ready for action.[112]

On February 23rd, International Women's Day, there were demonstrations against the bread shortage. The workers of the Vyborg District moved into other districts to call the workers out to strike ; a total of nearly 90,000 went out. On the following day 200,000 Petrograd workers struck in 131 factories, on the 25th the strike was fairly general. The Bolshevik organisation was apparently unable to keep step with the events : the draft pamphlet considered by the Petrograd Committee on the 25th (on the eve of its arrest) envisaged a mere three days' strike of protest. Some of the District and factory organisations, however, started arming their members. On the morning of February 26 the *Buro* of the Bolshevik CC invited the Vyborg District Committee to assume leadership in place of the arrested City Committee. It also decided to lift the suggested time-limit, to extend the strike to Moscow and bring into the movement soldiers, who would supply arms. Still, organised withdrawal after a temporary setback was regarded as the most likely outcome.[113] Such a prospect explains the strict refusal of Shlyapnikov and his fellow-members of the *Buro* to allow the participation of armed workers' *druzhiniki* in the demonstrations.[114] Measures which would turn the general strike into a struggle for power, such as the building of barricades and the cutting off of essential supplies, were announced by the Petrograd organisation as late as on February 27th, i.e. at a time when the troops were already changing their allegiance. On the preceding evening, when the first overt mutiny of troops sent against the workers had occurred, the Vyborg Committee, having met representatives of the *Buro* and the remnant of the Petersburg Committee, had decided to transform the general strike into an armed insurrection. However, there was still no plan for armed action. During the decisive events of February 27, the Bolsheviks could do no more than encourage the workers' and soldiers' spontaneous action.[115] Yet on the evening of the 26th, the delegates of the Volhynian regiment had decided not to shoot at the people. On the following morning, the soldiers of the training battalion of that regiment killed their commander, brought two other regiments out of the barracks and moved to the Vyborg District to join the workers. Passing from barrack to barrack, together with the workers, they moved to the centre of the town. On February 27, at 4 P.M., Tsarism had lost effective power in the capital. During the following days, power was transferred without major incidents in the armies and in the Provinces.

If anything is evident from this record, it is that the Bolsheviks had prepared the revolution but not organised it. They had been by far the strongest and most zealous of all the underground groups working within the country,[116] and they had been the only one which clearly and consistently opposed the war. It was due to their propaganda within the army as much as to such disagreements within the High Command as had originated from the preparations for the 'place revolution', that no one had challenged the victory won by the revolution in the capital at a time when the rest of the country had hardly dared to strike. They had been right as against the Mensheviks in stating that, if there was any chance of dividing the Liberals from Tsarism, it rested precisely upon the workers' independent action which would face the Liberals with a *fait accompli*. Finally, they were the only ones who had proclaimed a clear and consistent platform (the manifesto of February 27th/28th[117] was as far advanced as anything which Lenin had suggested for Russia upto those days). If Rosa Luxemburg's definition of the tasks of the revolutionary vanguard is accepted, the Bolsheviks did everything that could reasonably be expected from them in February 1917. The Bolsheviks, aiming at 'organising the

7

revolution', had opposed that definition. Still it may be said that an underground party could hardly do more. An elemental upheaval, strong enough for Shlyapnikov's failure to arm the *druzhini* not to matter, was necessary to confront Bolshevism with problems the solution of which required actual organisation of a revolution. The tasks, in approaching which the Bolshevik concepts of organisation had been formulated, however, had been obviated by the 'spontaneity' of the February revolution. Some re-orientation was now needed.

NOTES AND REFERENCES

1. Op. cit. p. 280.
2. A. L. Sokolovskaya in *Krasnaya letopis,* No. 7 (1923), pp. 24-5.
3. L. S. Kuznetsova in *Voprosy istorii,* 1955, No. 1.
4. Cf. Somov's article 'On the Social Democrat Movement in Petersburg 1905', *Byloye,* 1907.
5. Cf. Yaroslavski (op. cit. 1926) vol. I, pp. 394 and 398.
6. Cf. Kuznetsova, loc. cit., and the Ministerial Reports published in *Vestnik akademii nauk SSSR,* 1955, No. 1.
7. Amongst the Mensheviks, even the advice of young intellectuals that the Social Democrat workers join Gopon's organisation in order to be influential amongst the masses, was rejected by the workers (Somov, as quoted in note 4).
8. Pankratova, op. cit. p. 60 ; Doroshenko, writing in *Krasnaya letopis* 1925, No. 3 ; V. Nevski, ibid. 1922, No. 1 (pp. 14-15 in the reprint in *Khrestomatiya,* vol. III).
9. The date of January 9th according to the Old, January 22nd according to the Gregorian Style. From here on, we are dealing with dates well-noticed in the contemporary western press : therefore we give the dates in both calendars up to the revolution of October 25th/ November 7th, 1917, after which the Old Style (Julian) calendar was abolished and the Western (Gregorian) introduced.
10. Editorial of *Iskra,* No. 85, main parts reprinted by Dan, op. cit. pp. 339 ff.
11. *Sochineniya,* vol. VIII, pp. 144 ff.
12. In his articles of that, and the immediately preceding period, Lenin made fun of such expressions of hers as 'organisation as a process', 'arming the workers as a process', etc. In her *Massenstreik, Partei und Gewerkschaften,* which was published in 1906 as a polemic against the German Right-wing Social Democrats, Rosa Luxemburg described even the start of political strikes as 'a task of the revolu-

tionary period itself', as distinct from the party which, by proper propaganda, should ensure that the most advanced suggestions were always available to inspire mass-spontaneity (*Ges. Werke*, vol. IV, pp. 445-46). It should be kept in mind that Rosa Luxemburg's opposition to 'organising the revolution' was associated with a Menshevik approach to the Russian organisation problem but in no way with the Right-wing Menshevik interpretation of the tasks of the Russian revolution (on that issue, she sided with Parvus and Trotsky).

13. *Sochineniya*, vol. VIII, pp. 260 ff., ; *Sel. Works*, vol. III, pp. 33 ff.
14. See above, pp. 30-31. 15. See above, pp. 24-25.
16. 'Two Tactics of Social Democracy in the Democratic Revolution', *Sochineniya*, vol. IX, p. 81 ; *Sel. Works*, vol. III, pp. 110-11.
17. See above, p. 26.
18. Cf. Dan, op. cit. pp. 371 ff. 19. See above, pp. 48-49.
20. *VKP(b) v Rezolyutsiyakh*, vol. I, p. 54, and Kramolnykov's article in *Proletarskaya revolyutsiya*, No. 5, p. 45.
21. We may remember (see above, p. 39) that in 1902 members of the Rostov-on-Don party organisation were not allowed to circulate party literature other than that approved by their Committee. At that time, however, the ban was directed against the Economists, who were regarded as unorthodox by all the Social Democrats : the ruling of 1905 protected Bolsheviks and Mensheviks against the danger of being deprived of their freedom of expression if the alternative faction happened to control the Central Committee (even by a narrow majority, as occurred in 1906 as well as in 1907).
22. *Sochineniya*, vol. VIII, p. 383.
23. Lyadov in *Proletarskaya revolyutsiya*, 1922, No. 3 (pp. 496 ff. in the reprint in *Khrestomatiya*, vol. III). With hindsight, Yaroslavski (op. cit. 1926, vol. III, pp. 441-42) dates Lenin's disagreements with Bogdanov back to that early period.
24. Cf. B. Radin-Kuznyants' article in *Novaya zhizn*, 1905, No. 1, reprinted in *Istoriya RKP(b) v Dokumentakh*, vol. I, pp. 333 ff.
25. His article 'Our Tasks and the Soviet of Workers' Deputies' (*Sochineniya*, vol. X, pp. 3 ff.) was not published at the time by the Bolshevik organ *Novaya zhizn*, but certainly circulated amongst committee members.
26. Dan, op. cit. p. 382, regards the demand for amnesty for the naval mutineers at Kronstadt (whose lives, indeed, were saved) as a mere cover for that economic urge. See also Gorin, op. cit. p. 205.
27. Pankratova, op. cit. p. 154, Cherevanin, *Proletariat v revolyutsii* (Moscow, 1907), p. 68.
28. F. Samoilov, who makes this case in *Proletarskaya revolyutsiya*, 1930, No. 12, admits, however, that initially a large section of the strikers opposed any raising of political issues at the meetings. For a criticism of the approach described, see Gorin, op. cit. pp. 11 ff.

29. Cf. Sokolski's article in *Voprosy istorii*, 1955, No. 12, and the materials from Sochi, published in *Istoricheski arkhiv*, 1955, No. 6.

30. Lenin (*Sochineniya*, vol. XXXIV, p. 312) shared this opinion.

31. Gorin, op. cit. pp. 272 and 377 ff. ; Yakovlev in *Voprosy istorii*, 1955, No. 12.

32. Griva, speaking at the 1906 Conference of the Social Democrat Military Organisations (*Protokoly*, p. 57). Ostapchenko (ibid. p. 59) stated that the rank and file's enthusiasm was conducive to the overcoming of the leaders' hesitations.

33. Where 2000 workers joined the squads (but more than 25,000 rifles had been captured by the revolutionaries), cf. Vetoshinin, op. cit. pp. 247-48, and *Istoricheski arkhiv*, 1955, No. 6, pp. 76 and 90-1.

34. For example, the very detailed data given in *Bakinski rabochi*, October 11, 1955, show that nearly every garrison in the Caucasus was involved.

35. Cf. the materials reprinted in *Krasny arkhiv*, vol. XI-XII, 1925, pp. 320 ff.

36. Cf. the contemporary documents published in *Istoricheski arkhiv*, 1955, No. 3 ; Kovalenko's report in *Byloye*, February 1907 ; also Nevski in *Khrestomatiya*, vol. III, pp. 230-1 and Yaroslavski, op. cit. (1926), vol. II, pp. 465 ff.

37. Cf. Gorin, op. cit. pp. 197 ff. and 222 ff.

38. The documents dealing with these problems, published in *Partiya v revolyutsii 1905 goda* (Partizdat, 1934) start about mid-September, i.e. three months after the Potemkin mutiny.

39. See above, pp. 65-66.

40. Letters to the CC of August 24 and October 3, 1905, *Sochineniya*, vol. XXXIV, pp. 274, 279 and 298.

41. *Axelrod-Martov Correspondence*, pp. III (note 7) and 120.

42. Pyatnitski, op. cit. pp. 90-1.

43. This description was officially accepted by the Congress in order to avoid disputes about the legitimacy, or otherwise, of the Third (Bolshevik) Congress. The next (Stockholm) Congress had a Bolshevik majority which, however, for the sake of reconciliation, did not insist upon its numeration as the Fifth, however much Lenin disliked this concession (*Protokoly*, 1933 ed. p. 601). There were no more Congresses other than of the Bolshevik party which, of course, kept to its accepted numeration from the Sixth (1917) Congress onwards.

44. Cf. Yaroslavski, op. cit. (1926), vol. II, pp. 531 ff. and 658, Lenin's *Sochineniya*, vol. XI, pp. 235-7.

45. *Protokoly*, pp. 115 and 608.

46. Stalin, *Sochineniya*, vol. IV, pp. 396-7 ; Dan, op. cit. pp. 411-2 ; *Axelrod-Martov Correspondence*, p. 148 (and note to it) and No. 54.

47. *Sochineniya*, vol. XI, pp. 322-3.
48. Cf. Dan, op. cit. p. 407. In its original form, Axelrod's suggestion had been aimed at a pressure group acting upon the Duma, i.e. something leading to 'dual power' rather than competing with the party.
49. *Protokoly*, p. 511.
50. *Sochineniya*, vol. XII, pp. 120-1.
51. *VKP(b) v Rezolyutsiyakh*, p. 107.
52. *Protokoly*, V Congress, p. 428.
53. Cf. note 13 to Lenin's article 'Against the Boycott' in the 3rd ed. of his *Sochineniya*, vol. XII.
54. In his letter to Gorki on February 25th, 1908 (i.e. written three months before he regarded the split in the Bolshevik faction as inevitable) Lenin still maintained that the philosophical disagreements did *not* coincide with the political ones. The extreme Empirio-criticist Bazarov had sided with Lenin on the boycott issue (in the following disputes Bazarov left the Bolshevik camp without joining any other faction).
55. *VKP(b) v rezolyutsiyakh*, pp. 153-5.
56. Its impact is clearly felt in Gorki's *Mother*, which has always been regarded as the outstanding reflection of the Bolshevik party in Russian classical literature. Gorki sided with the opposition in 1909, and went in 1917 to the length of sharply opposing the Bolsheviks' conquest of power.
57. *Sochineniya*, vol. II, pp. 149 ff. and 160 ff.
58. *Sochineniya*, vol. XVI, pp. 49 ff.
59. Dan, op. cit. pp. 439-40.
60. *Sochineniya*, vol. XV, p. 399, and also vol. XXXIV, p. 363.
61. The 'Unity Crisis in our Party', *Sochineniya*, vol. XVI, pp. 187 and 228, *Sel. Works*, vol. IV, pp. 37 and 63-64. See also Stalin's *Sochineniya*, vol. II, p. 219.
62. *Sochineniya*, vol. XXXIX, pp. 358-59 and 385.
63. Cf. O. Varentsova's survey of the party crisis in 1910-12, published in *Khrestomatiya*, vol. VI, pp. 80 ff.
64. *Sochineniya*, vol. XVII, pp. 226 ff., *Sel. Works*, vol. IV, pp. 92 ff.
65. The delegates of Rostov, Samara, Nizhny-Novgorod, Sormovo and Lugansk were absent for various reasons; in the Resolutions of the Conference the existence of organisations in Ufa and Tyumen also was mentioned.
66. Stalin, *Sochineniya*, vol. II, pp. 147 and 182, *Protokoly*, V Congress, p. 461, Moskalev, op. cit. p. 39.
67. F. L. Alexandrov, writing in *Voprosy istorii*, 1954, No. 9.
68. Moskalev, op. cit. p. 39, *Khrestomatiya*, vol. VI (reprinted from *Sotsial-demokrat*, Nos. 25 and 26), pp. 152 and 171; Shmorgun writing in *Voprosy istorii*, 1954, No. 10, CC Correspondence pp. 12-15.
69. Ibid. p. 17.

70. Ibid. pp. 7, 17 and 36. *VKP(b)* v *rezolyutsiyakh,* p. 201, Badayev, op. cit. pp. 61-62.

71. Pyatnitski, op. cit. pp. 193 ff ; CC Correspondence, pp. 36-37.

72. Ibid. p. 7, and Moskalev, op. cit. p. 39.

73. Quoted in *Voprosy istorii,* 1956, No. 11, p. 4. The fact that the article was omitted from Stalin's *Sochineniya* supports the reporter's opinion that, written in the midst of the struggle against the Liquidators as it was, it showed a tendency towards 'unity at every price'. Young Stalin was in no way the Leninist diehard that he appeared in his later career. Up to his arrest Stalin served as the main representative of the CC on the editorial board ; sharp criticisms of *Pravda's* policies arose only after the arrest of Ordzhonikidze, Sverdlov and Stalin in connection with the publication of an article of Bogdanov's. Cf. Loginov's article in *Voprosy istorii KPSS,* 1957, No. 1, pp. 119 ff.

74. Cf. Lenin's *Sochineniya,* vol. XX, pp. 362 and 513 ff., and Pyatnitski's memoirs.

75. Axelrod-Martov Correspondence, pp. 290-91.

76. Lenin's *Sochineniya,* vol. XX, pp. 358 and 475.

77. Cf. Badayev, op. cit. pp. 21 ff. and 29-30.

78. Ibid. pp. 131-32.

79. Ibid. pp. 113-14 and 122 ff.

80. CC Correspondence, published in *Istoricheski arkhiv,* 1957, No. 1, p. 30, and 1958, No. 6 ; see also *Voprosy istorii KPSS,* 1957, No. 7, p. 112.

81. The CC decision has been reproduced, from Lenin's manuscript, by M. V. Stechova, ibid. No. 3, p. 175.

82. Text in *Khrestomatiya,* vol. VIII, p. 178.

83. Ibid. p. 183.

84. Op. cit. p. 200.

85. *Sochineniya,* vol. XXI, pp. 149-50.

86. Ibid. 3rd ed. vol. XX, p. 55. In the 4th ed. vol. XXXV, p. 253, the passage is omitted, for reasons which were obvious in the Stalin period.

87. Moskalev, op. cit. p. 182.

88. This will be discussed later on.

89. Engel's pro-German attitude of 1891, reference to which during World War I would obviously have been open to misunderstandings, was explicitly disowned as late as July 1934, in a letter written by Stalin to the members of the Politburo, which was published in *Bolshevik,* 1941, No. 24, i.e. on the eve of the German attack on Russia. Cf. *Soviet Studies,* vol. II, p. 152.

90. I have discussed this issue at length in my *Central European Democracy,* pp. 80 ff.

91. *Sochineniya,* vol. XXIII, p. 362.

92. 'On the Slogan of the United States of Europe', ibid.

93. *Sochineniya*, vol. XXI, pp. 345 ff. ; Sel. Works, vol. V, pp. 149 ff.
94. The party organisation did not accept the renaming of St. Petersburg as Petrograd at the beginning of the war as it had been caused by chauvinist (anti-German) motives.
95. *Sochineniya*, vol. XXI, p. 367, *Sel. Works,* vol. V, pp. 155-56.
96. *Sochineniya*, vol. XXI, p. 86.
97. *Nashe slovo*, February 24, 1915 and April 12, 1916, summarised by Deutscher, op. cit. (1954), pp. 236-38.
98. This will be discussed later on.
99. I. P. Leiberov, in *Istoriya USSR*, 1957, No. 1, p. 49. The main sources for the following presentation are Moskalev and Mints. op. cit., both based on the police archives (Moskalev, of course, has the biases current during the Stalin period).
100. Op. cit. p. 17. Mints states that his figures, which, as he himself states, are two to three times higher than the current estimates, are based on perusal of the police archives. See also K. Ostrovityanov in *Voprosy istorii KPSS*, 1957, No. 3, p. 188.
101. According to Moskalev, a Moscow branch of the Russian *buro* of the CC was established in its place in May.
102. Leiberov, op. cit. p. 48 ; Moskalev, op. cit. p. 207 (quoting police documents published in *Istoricheski zhurnal*, 1940, No. 3, pp. 35-36). D. I. Erde in *Izvestiya agademii nauk*, History and Philosophy Section, vol. VIII (1951), No. 6. There is no full agreement between the sources even about such elementary data as the number of Districts existing at a certain time in Moscow or Petersburg (possibly questions of definition are involved) ; the Moscow figure is in any case smaller than that given by Pyatnitski (op. cit. p. 103) for Moscow in 1906, which itself reflects the defeat of the preceding insurrection (two major working-class districts were served by one District Party Committee).
103. The figure quoted in the text was derived, by the organisers of the party census of 1922, from the fact that, in that census, 10,483 members claimed party membership dating from before the February Revolution. An (unspecified) allowance was made for the increased mortality of party members during the civil war. Mints (op. cit. p. 21) is dissatisfied even with the calculated figure. This counter-argument, however, is in reference to the very quick rise in party membership after the February Revolution. Those immediately admitted must also have been in touch with the party from before. This is true but does not imply that those admitted were already *Party members* at some earlier date (and even if this were true, it would not prove that their membership in an underground party was uninterrupted).
104. According to Leiberov (l.c. p. 48) in consequence of the October

strikes of 1916, 1750 active Petrograd workers were drafted to the front army.

105. Leiberov (l.c. p. 44-45) estimates the 'hard core' of the Petersburg working-class (to speak more precisely, amongst males exempted because of their jobs for military service) as 60-70,000. Not more than a thousand party members can have worked in the war industries of the capital.

106. Golder, op. cit. pp. 142 and 184.

107. I have discussed analogous phenomena in my *Central European Democracy*, pp. 127 and 152.

108. Golder, op. cit. pp. 126 ff.

109. Balabanov, op. cit. vol. II, pp. 380 ff.

110. Shcherbatov's report to the Tsar of September 29, 1915, reported by Golder, op. cit. p. 153.

111. Leiberov, l.c. p. 47.

112. Shlyapnikov, op. cit. pp. 43 ff. and 56 ff. ; K. E. Barshtein and L. M. Shagalinova, writing on the basis of police documents in *Voprosy istorii*, 1957, No. 1. Shlyapnikov emphasised the lack of party guidance (for this reason his book was criticised immediately after publication) ; Barshtein and Shagalinova (who still avoid quoting Shlyapnikov) show the opposite bias and may be supposed to give the best evidence in favour of active party guidance available in the archives. Leiberov, as quoted in note 99, at least quotes Shlyapnikov and argues against his standpoint.

113. Barshtein-Shagalinova, l.c. p. 135, Shlyapnikov, op cit. pp. 72-73.

114. Moskales's assertion (op. cit. p. 233) that Shlyapnikov's attitude on the arms question was overcome within the *Buro* of the CC (for this Molotov is credited) is contradicted by Shlyapnikov's statement (op. cit. p. 105) that the representative of the Vyborg District repeated the demand for arms as late as on the 27th, 11 a.m., and that Shlyapnikov still remained firm. This he would not have done, and certainly not noted with pride after the event, if he had been out-voted in the *Buro*. The issue on the 27th was settled within a few hours as the Vyborg workers meanwhile got arms from the soldiers. This was the kind of development which had been envisaged on the evening of the 26th.

115. Leibenov, l.c. p. 62.

116. This is confirmed by the Police reports quoted by Trotsky, op. cit. Vol. I, p. 57 ; the Leninists were said to have behind them 'an overwhelming majority of the underground Social Democrat organisations'.

117. Printed as Annex to Lenin's *Sochineniya*, 3rd ed. Vol. XX/2. Because of the delay in publication, the date of the Manifesto has been an issue of argument amongst Soviet historians. Cf. Leiberov, l.c. p. 64, note 148.

CHAPTER III

THE BOLSHEVIKS BECOME THE STATE PARTY

(a) POLITICAL RE-ORIENTATION

IN THE evening hours of February 27th, two alternative centres of power were formed in Petrograd. During the talks about a 'palace revolution' a 'Government of National Confidence' had been envisaged. Now a Duma Committee, in due course to be transformed into the Provisional Government, was established, headed by the more liberal landlords and bourgeoisie. On the other side, the Menshevik members of the War Industrial Committee, together with some Co-operators and Menshevik Duma deputies, convened a Provisional Executive Committee of the Soviet of Workers' Deputies. With some effort, Shlyapnikov[1] induced the initiators to wait until at least 20-30 workers' representatives were elected but the delay failed to strengthen the Bolsheviks' position.

The failure of the strongest underground party to secure adequate representation in the Soviet has caused much heart-searching. Shlyapnikov found an explanation in the Bolsheviks' pre-occupation with street-fighting and re-establishing the workers' organisations rather than with electioneering.[2] Later, part of the responsibility was put on the change in the social and political structure of the Petrograd industrial workers because of the war.[3] At the meeting of the Petrograd Committee of March 18/31, 1917, the minority position of the Bolsheviks was explained by 'the spontaneous course of the revolution' (and by mistakes, committed in particular by the *Buro* of the CC which had failed to secure party leadership).[4] This implied reluctant recognition of the fact that this revolution, like every true one, had drawn into political life new strata of workers who had never been touched by the underground propaganda but had heard something of the Menshevik's legal activities (similar conditions developed during the next year in Germany when leaders of the anti-war struggle failed even to be elected to the first Soviet Congress). The right-wing of the Petrograd Soviet was further strengthened by the initially overwhelming representation of soldiers[5] amongst whom the defencist Mensheviks might be popular. Intellectuals with moderately left-wing views serving as non-commissioned officers had good chances of being elected as soldiers' delegates. The defencist Mensheviks were conscious of the long-term implications of involving the army in political strife. At first, they worked with the knowledge that in a joint Soviet the workers' delegates might be submerged amongst the soldiers (eventually they put all their energy into propaganda amongst the soldiers and, for the time being, achieved considerable success).[6]

Already in the evening hours of February 27th, the initiators of the Provisional Executive Committee demanded that the Provisional Committee of Duma Deputies assume power. Even the left-wing Menshevik Sukhanov[7] expressed deep satisfaction that, by this decision of the liberal bourgeoisie, the ship of revolution had at last put up sail. At that moment, Mensheviks still entertained the delusion that, according to their old platform of 1905, they had enforced a break of the bourgeoisie with the supporters of the *ancien régime*. (A more realistic view of the alternatives was expressed a few days later by Sir G. Buchanan[8] when he was asked by Milyukov whether he would prefer him to resign since Milyukov had been compromised by his unsuccessful attempts to keep Grand Duke Michael : Buchanan without hesitation expressed his preference for Milyukov's keeping to his post.) The Soviet majority's policy was disputed only by small minorities. The right-wing (defencist) Mensheviks' demand for a coalition government in order to strengthen the war effort was rejected by the initiative group of the Executive Committee (i.e. the bulk of the Mensheviks) as the bourgeoisie should be left with the sole responsibility for government in a bourgeois revolution.[9] On the other side, a Bolshevik motion to have the Provisional Government elected by the Soviet so that it would more consistently carry out bourgeois-democratic reforms (before Lenin's return, no one questioned the bourgeois-democratic character of the revolution) was supported only by 19 of the 40 Soviet members who had been elected as Bolsheviks.

The Bolsheviks' real problem derived from the easy victory of the February revolution. They had lost their original platform, yet were prevented from formulating a new one by established Marxist orthodoxy.[10] True, the issue of land reform was still open. Because of the Mensheviks' refusal to break with Kerensky (who, on his part, refused to break with the Kadets and their appendage of reactionary generals) even the convention of the Constitutional Assembly was a part of the Bolshevik platform up to, and including, the October revolution.[11] Yet in view of the Mensheviks' prolonged refusal to join a coalition government, the differences between the two Social Democrat parties were not large enough to justify in the eyes of the masses—and even of some of the Bolshevik leaders—a continuation of the split. Due to the Stalin cult and the reactions against it, the course of the disputes among the Bolsheviks before Lenin's return to Russia has been frequently misrepresented. The basic facts, however, are sufficiently clear[12] to allow for a survey.

After the February Revolution, the Vyborg Committee and Molotov, speaking on behalf of the *Buro* of the CC at the meeting of the Petrograd Committee of March 5th/18th, demanded the replacement of the existing Provisional Government by a new one based upon the Soviets which would have to realise the minimum programme of Social Democracy, confiscate the big estates and convene the Constituent Assembly. The Committee, however, decided not to oppose the Provisional Government as long as its actions were in the interests of the people but to oppose any attempt to restore monarchial institutions. These motions illustrate the lack of clarity on either side. Molotov called for a 'Provisional Revolutionary Government' based on a Soviet which, at that time, had not the slightest intention of doing so, while the majority of the Petersburg Committee reserved its threat for a most unlikely eventuality. The real issue, of course, was that of the war, and the attitude to the Army. On March 7th/20th the Committee adopted a resolution which appealed to the Soviet and to the socialist parties of the other belligerent countries for a democratic peace (a motion of Podvoiski's, who demanded a *direct* approach of the Bolsheviks to the army in order to revolutionise it, and wished the Soviet to bypass the socialist parties of the other belligerent countries since they were compromised by their war policies, was rejected). On March 14th/27th the Soviet Executive Committee adopted, indeed, an appeal to the peoples of the world against their governments to take the question of war and peace into their own hands. Immediately before, within the Bolshevik camp, the shift towards the Soviet majority had been accentuated because of the return of Muranov, Stalin and Kamenev from their Siberian exile. Notwithstanding the protests of the *Buro* of the CC, Muranov claimed for himself as representative of the old parliamentary party control of *Pravda*. On March 15th/28th, Kamenev's article 'Without Secret Diplomacy' lent unqualified support to the Soviet's appeal of the preceding day. Stalin, too, supported the appeal. He criticised, however, its conception of the struggle for a democratic peace as a process within the Allied camp. Russia, acting as an independent agent, should invite *all* governments to open peace negotiations on the basis of the right of *all* nations to self-determination. Like Kamenev and the Bolsheviks, Stalin regarded the Provisional Government as the agent of revolutionary Russia and it should be forced by the Soviet to take the necessary initiative. It should, however, be checked by a workers' militia lest it serve as a legal shield for the organisation of a counter-revolution.[13] Stalin's attitude is also reflected in the resolution of the Russian *Buro* of the CC submitted to the Conference of Party Workers which, in connection with the all-Russian Soviet Conference, met on March 27 (old style). Yet while he wished to avoid a premature trial of strength the majority of the *Buro* wished the Soviets to develop into an alternative government.

The attitude to the war also coloured the Bolsheviks' approach to the issue of re-uniting the Social Democrats. Molotov demanded the formulation of a positive platform, acceptance of which would be the condition for re-union. Stalin found the anti-war platform of Kienthal and Zimmerwald sufficient as a basis for re-union (a right-wing under Voitinski, who regarded the Provisional Government as the agency of the national defence of revolutionary Russia, soon solved the problem by leaving the Bolshevik party). At that stage of the discussion, only Lenin's first *Letter from Afar* was available (it had been published in *Pravda,* March 21, i.e. five days before the *Buro* of the CC elaborated the draft motions for the Conference). In pronounced opposition to the Trotskyist formula 'replace Tsarism by a workers' government' Lenin rejected the idea of jumping over the peasant-dominated, non-socialist stage of the democratic revolution. He refused, however, to keep the further development of the revolution within that stage; it was questionable whether a specific 'revolutionary-democratic dictatorship of the working-class and the peasantry' was still feasible.[14] A relentless struggle against the Provisional Government and its supporters within the labour movement should be waged as a bourgeois government was incapable of ending the imperialist war. Lenin did not yet suggest a positive alternative to the existing combination of Soviet and Provisional Government. Hence it is hardly astonishing that he failed at first in convincing his fellow-Bolsheviks of anything other than the inherent connection between capitalism and war, which they had long taken for granted.

Before his return to Russia, however, Lenin had elaborated his concept of the new regime, following the example of the Paris Commune. It would be based upon revolutionary self-government of the insurgent masses headed by the Soviets (under Bolshevik leadership). It would dissolve all the pacts, propose to all belligerents an immediate armistice, proclaim the conditions of a democratic peace and annul the debts entered into by Russian capitalists. If no peace on this basis was accepted, it would wage a revolutionary war, supported by the toilers of the world. In his famous *April Theses,* first read to the Bolsheviks attending the Party Conference,[15] Lenin envisaged transitional economic measures such as nationalisation of the land, creation of special Soviets of the poor peasants and labourers and model farms operated by them, amalgamation of the banks under the Soviet control and Soviet supervision of industry. Such reforms would not yet imply 'introduction of socialism' but a net of emergency measures similar to those applied during the war in a number of bourgeois states. Socialism would eventually follow when the

large majority of the people had understood its necessity.[16]   It
was impied that the transition, though its final success depended
on international developments, was primarily a Russian matter.

Lenin's unorthodox theses caused perplexity, less amongst
the Bolshevik rank and file who wished to carry the revolution
forward than amongst the leaders who were sensitive to the
finesses of theoretical distinctions. As it was later not regarded
as creditable to have opposed Lenin, only part of the
record of the discussions has been preserved, and even this has
been unearthed in our days under much official resistance. In
any case it is clear that party committees such as those of
Petersburg, Kiev and Saratov originally had majorities opposed
to Lenin.[17] In view of Lenin's radical break with existing party
tradition it is hardly surprising that Stalin, as he himself stated
before his becoming the subject of a 'cult', was convinced only
after weeks. Kemenev who resisted up to the April Conference
was not an isolated sinner.

At that time, Lenin regarded his transition programme as no
more than an indication of the revolutionary path.[18] He still
envisaged the consolidation (for a considerable period) of a
bourgeois regime based upon the upper strata of the peasantry.[19]
It was, however, important to protect the working-class from the
danger of becoming an appendage of those groups, at home and
abroad, who had opposed Tsarism because of the inefficiency of
its war effort.[20] Hence pupils of Lenin such as Zinoviev who
believed in the dependence of Russia on the world revolution
might support his principal platform in April, yet oppose in October the action through which it was put into practice in isolated
Russia.[21] Lenin tried to impress upon the international labour
movement the reorientation of the Russian party by suggesting,
e.g. that the old party description as 'Communist' be resumed
and that the left-wing of the Zimmerwald group form a new
International. These suggestions were practically irrelevant to
a trial of strength in the Russia of 1917. The very break with
the past indicated by them provoked the opposition of a large
majority of Lenin's supporters. As the issue of the party's name
was associated with the Bolsheviks' long and successful struggle
for representing the Social Democratic party, Lenin gave way on

this issue as well as on some minor questions. But he insisted on polling a lonely vote of protest against the majority decision to remain in the Zimmerwald International. This, he believed, delayed the formation of the Third International and burdened the Bolsheviks with a dead weight.[22]

Lenin's stand on this international question was associated with the question how far, within Russia, re-unification should go. That *some* re-unification was necessary was obvious in this revolution as it had been in that of 1905, and for the same reason. There appeared to be little sense in maintaining divisions which had grown from disagreements about the functions of the underground party in Tsarist Russia. A new cleavage had arisen in consequence of the war. The Russian Bolsheviks were not the only socialists who regarded 'social patriotism' as a betrayal of socialism, but they remained the only ones who drew organisational consequences from this. Unanimously, though with ten abstentions (probably by delegates who shared Lenin's cautious approach to the more moderate supporters of Zimmerwald), the April Conference adopted a resolution in favour of unity with all those who 'standing in fact on the platform of internationalism would break with the lower-middle-class policy of betraying socialism'. Stalin's definition of the common minimum requirement was thus combined with the approach of the Prague Conference which had left it to the Mensheviks to decide whether they preferred unity with their Liquidator wing (now it was the question of the defencists) or unity with the Bolsheviks. As the very essence of Menshevism was a refusal to break with the right-wing of the labour movement there was little chance of the Internationalist Mensheviks joining.

Even before Lenin's return to Russia it had been noted by a majority of the Petersburg Committee that a suitable partner for re-union was available in the shape of the *Mezhrayontsy,* a minor group which accepted the anti-war platform and excluded the defencists from its advocacy of re-union with the Mensheviks.[23] These 'inter-regionalists', i.e. Social Democrats who for some reason stood outside the two major factions, formed a small group which during the last period of the war had carried out some underground propaganda. Eventually it served as a temporary political home for many returning exiles who were not prepared simply to join either of the main factions (which, by now, had become well-established parties). Some of them, such as Trotsky, might be described as left-wing outsiders of Menshevism who had so far been divided from Bolshevism on the organisation problem but approached them when the War made a split in the socialist ranks unavoidable. Others, such as Lunacharski, were former *Vperedists* who (as distinct from their comrades who rallied round Gorky's *Novaya zhizn*) wished to end the split with the main body of Bolshevism. There were also Social Democrats who had long stood between the factions such as Ryazanov. The tendency of the contemporaries to think in terms of factions, and of later historians (Stalinist as well as Trotskyist) to think in terms of outstanding individuals (Trotsky being the foremost), has obscured the fact that the *Mezhrayontsy*, a group of officers without soldiers, served as a clearing house for socialist intellectuals who had lost their bearings.[24]   When, eventually, the end of the revolutionary upheaval again turned political problems into practical issues of organisation and made the Party the central institution of Soviet society, nearly all the *Mezhrayontsy* became involved in the new conflict, ranging from Lunacharski's slowly receding into the background to Trotsky's tragedy.

Even now the *Mezhrayontsy*'s re-union with the Bolsheviks was delayed by their demand for the convention of a Unity Congress which would create a new party on the Zimmerwald basis, including the Centrists.[25]   But when, after the July crisis, the Bolsheviks became the subject of persecution and calumny by the right-wing Mensheviks, the *Mezhrayontsy* joined them while the Menshevik Internationalists would go no further than to dissociate themselves (from the behaviour of their fellow-Mensheviks) by a fraternal message to the VI Congress. More important, however, than the admission of minor groups of intellectuals was the fact, only recently established,[26] that nearly a fifth of the party organisations existing in 1917 were 'united', i.e. contained Mensheviks as well as Bolsheviks. In many cases the consistent Mensheviks were not numerous—only a few left the united organisations when later in the year the final split came. While the 'Party Menshevik', as a political figure, disappeared from the scene, the united organisations formed the bridge across which many thousands of workers with a Menshevik past, or at least earlier Menshevik sympathies, joined the Bolshevik party.

(b)   THE BOLSHEVIK MASS-PARTY

The period between the February and October revolutions of 1917 was the only time during which the Bolshevik party enjoyed what in western countries are regarded as the normal conditions of party life : facilities for propaganda of its views but not a monopoly of power. (Even the two months from the July events to the Kornilov revolt in September, during which the Bolsheviks' opportunities were restricted and some of their leaders had to go into hiding, compared favourably with the most liberal conditions enjoyed under Tsarism, say in early 1906.)   Only during that period did the cadre party of devoted revolutionaries (more workers than intellectuals amongst them since 1905) become a force capable of ruling and reconstructing a large country.

Within the six weeks from the February Revolution to the April Conference, party membership increased from a few thousand to 79,200, largely by the re-activisation of former party members and by the enrolment of former sympathisers.[27]   Already it was felt desirable in Petrograd to create guarantees against the influx of unreliable elements, similar to those taken later when the party was in power.[28]   Between the April Conference and the VI (July) Congress the number of party organisations on the city, district and subdistrict level increased from 390 (78 of which were represented at the April Conference) to 530; between July and October by another hundred.[29]   By July the number of party members, according to the more conservative of Sverdlov's two estimates, had increased to 200,000.[30]   At the CC meeting of October 13/29 he even gave a figure of 400,000 : this figure presumably expressed his desire to strengthen the hands of the supporters of insurrection.   If there was any truth in it, the party's membership at the time of the VII Congress[31] would have indicated, not just the deflation natural when the demobilised soldiers returned to their villages (most of them as mere sympathi-

8

sers) but a political breakdown for which there is no other evidence. But certainly some increase took place between July and November even in the old organisations.[32] At the Moscow Regional Conference in December 1917[33] it was stated that the party organisation of Ivano-Voznesensk had 5871 members; not all of these can have been industrial workers (the total number of such workers was 50,000 as against 70,000 before the war). In large engineering centres such as Petrograd the percentage of party members amongst the industrial workers may even have been larger than in a centre of textile industries (though with an old-standing Bolshevik tradition) such as Ivano-Voznesensk. At the VI Party Congress already all the more important organisations from Russia proper, Finland and the Ukraine were represented. Still, the average district town had no party organisation unless it happened to be the seat of a major factory. The new organisations formed between July and November, even if small, and the much larger army organisations[34] made substantial contributions to the party's total strength.

We have no direct data about the social status of those who joined the party in 1917 but conclusions may be drawn from the statistics of those who were registered during the party census of 1927. Of those entrants of 1917 who ten years later were still in the party, 68.9 per cent had orginally been industrial workers. (This percentage is nearly the same as that amongst those who had joined the Bolshevik party in the underground.) With 25.5 per cent, now salaried employees and intellectuals formed a slightly smaller part than they did amongst the Old Bolsheviks (where they constituted 29.7 per cent of the group, perhaps more intellectuals among them than salaried employees). For the first time in the party's history, in 1917, recruitment of a considerable number of peasants (6.6 per cent of the new entrants) became possible.[35] Although being organisationally by far the strongest of the revolutionary parties, the Bolsheviks met serious competition. For instance the Social Revolutionaries' strength at the time of the VI Congress was assessed, for Moscow Province, as a third of that of the Bolsheviks; in Perm they nearly equalled the Bolsheviks' strength. Within the working-class itself the Mensheviks were the Bolsheviks' immediate competitors. Their strength in Petrograd Province was estimated by Volodarski as 8000 against the Bolsheviks' 36,000 ; in Perm there were a mere 300 Mensheviks.[36] The radical workers, it seems, were more easily organised than the looser type of socialist sympathisers. This fact, too, was an important element in the coming events.

The VI Congress provided for local, District and Provincial organisations. Definite rules were established for the admission of members (on the recommendation of two Party members, and with the agreement of the group meeting), on membership fees etc. The old-established Bolshevik rules for members' activity, centralisation, and subordination of the minority to majority decisions, were preserved, so also were the guarantees for the autonomy of the local organisations, including the right to have publications of their own (ample use of which was made in the following year by the Left Communists) and the right of a minority (now a third) to enforce the convocation of an extraordinary Party Congress. This last rule has remained on the Party's statute book up to the present day, perhaps with an intention of preserving the continuity of party legality in the case of the centre's becoming the victim of some *coup*.

(c) THE WAY TO POWER

Six months after the clarification of their political orientation at the April Conference the Bolsheviks assumed power. This half-year was characterised, not only by the organisational growth but also by a change in the party's relations with the masses. Without the backing of a spontaneous mass upheaval Bolshevism could not dare to oppose all those famous leaders who enjoyed the prestige of having been the open opponents of Tsarism. These forces, however, had to be disciplined so that they might provide the basis of a successful insurrection and the establishment of a new political system. Through bitter experience the Bolshevik party developed its capacity of leading the masses, not merely as before, by issuing slogans which indicated the general direction of the movement, but also by political tactics, restraining mass-action when it appeared to be hopeless and initiating action which would further the desired aim even by indirect means.

On the very eve of the April Conference the Petrograd organisation of the Bolsheviks had sympathised with the demands of radical workers for the immediate overthrow of the Provisional Government, and had to be curbed by the Central Committee. (This incident made Lenin's argument against Kamenev at the Conference more moderate than it would have been in conformity with the interpretation by either side of the importance of the issues discussed.) In a country such as Russia there was an obvious danger that the revolutionary capital, whose workers had overthrown Tsarism single-handed, might become isolated from the Provinces. The anti-Bolshevik attitude of the first Soviet Conference (two-thirds of the representatives, mostly soldiers, were from the Provinces) sharply differed from the friendly relations between the Bolsheviks and most of the Mensheviks existing in the first Petrograd Executive Committee. When the May crisis which followed Milyukov's declarations on foreign policy, had resulted in the formation of a coalition government, the Bolsheviks' opposition at the I Soviet Congress (June 8/21) was supported only by the small groups of the *Mezhrayontsy* and Internationalist Mensheviks. Shortly before, the leader of the Soviet majority parties, the Social Revolutionary Chernov, had appealed to the first all-Russian Peasants' Congress to guard the big estates against local peasant initiative until the Constituent Assembly had disposed of the land.[37] The Bolsheviks on the other hand encouraged such initiative. In due course the peasants, and the peasant-dominated army, would come into line with the revolutionary workers. In a mood which appeared to many as over optimistic, Lenin, at the First Soviet Congress, interrupted Tserreteli's statement that coalition government was unavoidable in view of the unwillingness of any party to assume power by the statement that there was such a party, Lenin's own. For the time being, however, the Petrograd workers had to be restrained from premature action.

During the session of the I Soviet Congress a demonstration of the Petrograd workers was called for June 10/23 to demand that it should assume full power. When the majority of the

Soviet denounced such 'conspiracy' and prohibited all demonstrations during the Congress session, the Bolshevik CC called them off, to the great displeasure of the Petrograd organisation. Some of the workers were said to be so disillusioned that they even left the party.[38] The Petrograd workers got some satisfaction one week later, when the Soviet majority called a mass-demonstration. It was dominated by Bolshevik slogans. But on that very day the offensive on the Galician front, which had been demanded by the Allies and was regarded by the masses as evidence of the new government's unwillingness for 'democratic peace', was started. As soon as its failure was evident, on July 2/15, the bourgeois ministers resigned from the coalition government under the pretext of disagreements on the Ukrainian question. This left the Menshevik and Social Revolutionary members of the Provisional Government alone to cope with a situation which had become tense because the employers had closed down many factories ; in Petrograd alone, 125 with 39,000 workers in June, 206 with 48,000 workers in July.

On July 3/16 the soldiers of the First Machine Guns Regiment, threatened with 're-organisation', against the advice of the Bolsheviks but under the influence of anarchist groups decided to move into the streets and to call the factories and other regiments to join them. As late as one hour before the demonstration the Petrograd City Conference of the Bolsheviks advised against it so as to deprive the Soviet leaders of any pretext for enlisting public opinion against an alleged Bolshevik *coup d'etat*. The Bolsheviks' success in preventing an outbreak on June 10/23 evoked undue optimism that they could repeat the performance.[39] While the columns of the demonstrators were already marching towards the city-centre, in the Putilov works Ordzhonikidze and others went on defending the party decision, without success. Shortly before midnight, when the demonstration was already in full swing, the Bolshevik CC decided to head the armed demonstration on the following day so as to secure its orderly course and to prevent provocations. Since the party had lost the initiative, Trotsky's suggestion for an unarmed demonstration was bound to be rejected. It could not have been realised.[40] The demonstration of July 4th, under the slogan that the Soviet leaders should assume power, was impressive yet served the unwilling invitees only as a pretext for outlawing the Bolsheviks. In the evening, when the Bolsheviks had already declared the demonstration concluded, troops were called to suppress it. Bolshevik newspapers were destroyed so that the appeal calling off the demonstration could not be published.[41] The anti-Bolsheviks had been waiting for a pretext, and forged 'documents' to demonstrate that Lenin was a German agent were ready for publication that very night. The professional anti-Communists of our day have built up this device of a Government lacking support into an 'explanation' of the October revolution. Stalin, being the only Bolshevik representative on the Soviet Central Executive Committee who had not gone into hiding, had great difficulty in arranging the surrender of the troops participating in the demonstration in order to avoid the massacre which the Government had planned.

In the progress of the Russian revolution the July crisis was a minor setback. Already at the VI Congress party workers from the Provinces who were just gaining control of their local Soviets found the Petrograd comrades unduly pre-occupied with their local defeat. Hence they objected to Lenin's drawing far-reaching conclusions from that incident.[42] In Lenin's mind, however, the events of July 1917 clarified the basic concepts of the party's task. Before, that task had been seen as that of over-throwing a reactionary regime and replacing it by a combination of all democratic parties ('democratic dictatorship of the working-class and the peasantry' or, since March, rule of the Soviets) in which the Bolsheviks would collaborate. From now on, however, the party's function was conceived as that of the sole controller of the new regime. The former slogan 'all power to the Soviets' had been inspired by the existence of 'dual power', the armed forces being controlled by the Soviets. The transition of the revolution from its first, bourgeois-democratic, to its second, socialist stage would come about by a mere shift of influence within the Soviet. The workers' wish for comprehensive measures was bound to follow from the Provisional Government's inevitable attempt to end the 'dual power' in its favour.[43] Yet during the July crisis, the Soviet leaders had helped the bourgeois Government to repress the Bolsheviks. There was no longer any sense in the Bolsheviks' demanding the transfer of power to them. Lenin, however, kept to his argument that Soviets represented the highest form of government yet known. In the coming revolution, new Soviets would appear 'but not the present Soviets, not organs of compromise with the bourgeoisie, but organs of revolutionary struggle against it'[44]—in short, Soviets led by the Bolsheviks. Stalin, reporting at the VI Party Congress, had to face opposition against the dropping of the slogan 'all power to the Soviets'. Apart from Provincial party workers who were already on the way towards control of their local Soviets this opposition included former Mensheviks who did not wish to break with their old comrades[45] and right-wing Bolsheviks who eventually would oppose the conquest of power.[46] Presumably in agreement with most of his colleagues in the CC, Stalin mitigated the sharpness of Lenin's approach. He explained that the end of the attempt at collaboration with the Soviet leaders implied no rejection of the Soviets as the most suitable form of organising the masses. The party, however, should speak not in institutional terms but in terms of political reality.[47] A few weeks later, during the Kornilov crisis, Lenin himself turned back for a moment to the political concept of the transfer of power to the (Menshevik-dominated) Soviet but a difference in approach was noticeable even during the October crisis.[48] On a later occasion, Stalin[49] used the incident to demonstrate that occasionally the party had been right even against Lenin.

Another incident at the VI Congress showed the way in which the latent contradiction between the April Theses' concentration on Russia's institutional crisis and the traditional views about the international conditions for a socialist revolution in Russia was eventually resolved. In his report to the Congress, Bukharin had moved a resolution which defined the conventional distinction between the two stages of the Russian revolution. During the first the Russian working-class, supported by the peasantry, would defend the latter's interests; during the second the Russian working-class, with international woking-class support, would achieve socialism. Bukharin was not optimistic about the prospects of the Russian revolution. With the end of the division of power between the Soviet and the Provisional Government, these prospects were no longer better than in the other imperialist countries. But if the Russian revolution should triumph before that in the West, its prospects, Bukharin said, rested upon a revolutionary war against the western capitalists so as to incite the socialist world revolution which alone would free the Russian revolution from its isolation.[50] Stalin replied with the restraint required from a fellow-reporter. He claimed for the Russian revolution an active and constructive part even apart from its international impact, and reproached Bukharin for his failure to define the specific socialist task of the revolution within Russia.[51] He rejected both excessive concessions to the *kulak* in the first stage and a purely working-class policy in the second stage of the Russian revolution. When, however, Preobrazhenski moved an amendment to Stalin's motion on Bukharin's lines, (declaring that the Russian revolution could pursue socialist aims only in the event of a proletarian revolution in the West), Stalin came forward with a declaration which, against all the traditional caution of Marxist orthodoxy, amounted to 'Socialism in one country' if the Russian revolution should remain isolated :

> You cannot rule out the possibility that precisely Russia will be the country that paves the way to socialism. Up to now there has not been such freedom in times of war in any other country, nor have attempts to establish workers' control of production been made outside Russia. Apart from this, the basis of the revolution is broader in Russia than in western Europe where the working-class has to face the bourgeoisie in isolation, while in our country it is supported by the poorest strata of the peasantry. Finally, the German state machine works with incomparably higher efficiency than that....of our bourgeoisie, which is itself a tributary (*dannitsa*) of European capitalism. We ought to discard the obsolete idea that only Europe can show us the way. There exists a dogmatic Marxism and a creative one. I stand for the latter.[52]

Stalin took it for granted that the Russian revolution would pave the way for an era of working-class revolutions in the West.[53] Omission of this point would not only have expressed a pessimism unwarranted at a time when, under the impact of the war and of the Russian February revolution, the German workers and sailors had just started to move. But it would also have played into the hands of those who refrained from using the revolutionary opportunities existing in Russia[54] for the benefit of Western revolutions. But what in 1917 were mere differences in emphasis existing amongst Bolsheviks turned into cleavages within the international setting.

The Bolsheviks' July defeat strengthened the hand of reaction. In countering these developments, the Bolsheviks became the only force capable of defending the revolution. Though they had suffered temporary losses both in prestige[55] and in opportunities for open propaganda, their hold on the industrial proletariat was hardly weakened by the July crisis. The right-wing socialists, on the other side, were compromised by their connections with Kerenski who, on his part, was compromised by his dealings with Kornilov and the latter's supporters, the Kadets. Immediately after Kornilov's abortive coup the Bolsheviks won majorities in the Soviets of the two capitals. The right-wing socialists were soon reduced to an insignificant minority within the industrial proletariat. When Kerenski, against the wishes of the majority of the Democratic Conference convened by him, formed a coalition government with the Kadets, this cabinet was bound to appear to the Petrograd workers a direct betrayal of the promise to fight the supporters of Kornilov. As the left-wing Menshevik Sukhanov[56] put it, it was a clique of usurpers, insurrection against whom was legitimate.

The history of the struggle which Lenin waged in order to convince his own party of the necessity of insurrection has frequently been told. For the purposes of the present study, we need only to correct two widespread misconceptions. Firstly, due to Trotsky's efforts to belittle the part played in October 1917 by the Old Bolsheviks, and to draw generalisations from the behaviour of a few, the impression has been created that Lenin had to force insurrection on an unwilling party. It is certainly true that Lenin had difficulties with a section of the Central Committee which, at first, was large[57] and which even at the joint meeting of the CC with the leaders of the Petrograd organisation, on October 16th/29th, was not confined to Zinoviev and Kamenev.[58] The election of the first Politburo, at the CC meeting of October 10th/23rd, may have been intended as a precaution against questioning the validity of important decisions taken in the absence of CC members who had to work in the Provinces.[59]   But during the whole conflict Lenin acted on the assumption that he was supported by the major party organisations, and threatened his opponents in the Central Committee with an appeal to the rank and file.[60]   He was, indeed, supported not only by the Petrograd Committee, which as late as October 24th/November 6th found it necessary to elect a special committee for the organisation of the insurrection,[61] but also by the Moscow Provincial Committee which on September 27 disapproved the CC's decision to participate in the Democratic Conference.[62] Lenin's threat to bring the issue before an extraordinary Party Congress could be effective only because those concerned were convinced that a majority would back him.

The second issue which requires clarification has been produced by the Lenin cult.   In Lenin's life-time, both Trotsky and Stalin[63] claimed that they—and the majority of the CC which backed them—had been right when they insisted on the party's conquering power on behalf of the Soviet Congress rather than on its own account, as otherwise the elected delegates of the soldiers and workers would have been alienated.   From Lenin's correspondence and from the evidence recently collected[64] it is evident that up to the very moment of victory he was afraid of delays, not only on the part of the opponents of insurrection within the CC but also on the part of the CC majority.   The latter he expected to pay undue heed to the possible vacillations of the II Soviet Congress. Lenin, not without reason, was afraid of vacillations even of some Bolsheviks; hence, he and a majority of the members of the Military Revolutionary Committee of the Petrograd Soviet wished immediate assumption of power by the latter on the eve of the Congress—although that Congress might be expected to have a Bolshevik majority.   In a historical analysis, these disputes may be associated with the earlier ones on the question whether, after the (Menshevik-dominated) Soviets' failure to play the part of a Government alternative to the Provisional one, the Bolshevik party was to aim at overthrowing it and establishing its dictatorship (later to be based upon re-elected Soviet) or whether it was to strive to obtain a majority in the Soviets so that the decisive struggle could be carried out by Bolshevik-dominated Soviets against a Provisional Government dominated by the bourgeoisie.[65]   The October revolution had been carried out in the second way and its leaders—perhaps including Lenin—found it correct *post eventum*. Neither the official party historians nor those participants in the events who published their recollections during the first fifteen years after the revolution found basic principles involved in those disputes. Some recent Soviet publications[65] try, perhaps being confused by Zinoviev's and Kamenev's suggestions, to show a delay in the actual decision on insurrection up to the consultation with the Bolshevik delegates to the Soviet Congress and the CC's decision immediately to start a 'purely defensive concentration of forces', as explained by Trotsky and Stalin at an internal meeting. Having in mind the revolutions which have failed because some leader, under some apparently sound pretext, was afraid of crossing the Rubicon, Lenin was right in suspecting the second approach to be a cover for the first. In fact, so also did the Petrograd Committee. It is possible that he suspected even those who sincerely aimed at carrying out the coup on behalf of the Soviet Congress, and establishing a coalition government of all the Soviet parties, and that his struggle on the timing of the insurrection was already the first stage of the disputes which followed.[66]   Being here concerned not with the biography of leaders but with the party's internal development, we are on firm ground when stating that the Bolsheviks regarded the October revolution as one brought about by their party and that the latter had fulfilled its function.

Indeed, the gravest crisis of the October revolution followed its triumph in Petrograd.   That triumph had been easy because Kerenski had obviously betrayed the democratic programme accepted by all the Soviet parties, including even the convocation of the Constituent Assembly, and because many feared another Kornilov coup (this time under the sole responsibility of Kerenski).   Even such reliable supporters of the Bolshevik cause as the Central Committee of the Baltic sailors enumerated, in their appeal of October 29th, the immediate convocation of the Constituent Assembly as one of the achievements of the victorious revolution (apart from the land law, the offer of an armistice, the abolition of capital punishment in the army, and the establishment of workers' control of production).[67]   When virtually all the non-Bolshevik parties protested against the Bolsheviks' conquest of power many Bolshevik leaders, to whom these parties and organisations had been serious realities during the struggle against Tsarism, refused to analyse whether they were still backed by real social forces. In fact, the opponents to insurrection in the Bolshevik camp were more numerous during the crisis which followed than the preceding one.

While Kerenski's counter-attack on Petrograd was on the way, on a suggestion originating from the international Mensheviks, the Central Executive Committee of the Railwaymen's Union (*Vikzhel*) tried to force the Bolsheviks to the negotiation table under the threat of a railwaymen's strike (it had been chosen because only pro-Bolsheviks sat on its Central Committee). Some workers' delegations from individual factories urged the disputing socialist parties to come to a compromise[68] (according to Chernov,[69] *Vikzhel* offered its support to a Government formed at Army Headquarters, i.e. to a military counter-stroke against the Bolsheviks). Kamenev and Ryazanov, who participated on behalf of the Bolsheviks in the negotiations with *Vikzhel* late in the night of November 13 (new style),[70] pending the sanction of the Central Executive Committee of the Soviets, agreed to the formation of a new government from which Lenin and Trotsky were to be excluded on one side, Kerenski and Avksentiev on the other. In the supervising body, neither the Bolsheviks and their supporters, nor the advocates of political and military offensive against the Soviets were to have a majority. But on that very night Kerenski's troops were defeated near Petrograd. The Bolshevik Central Committee, which up to then had allowed the Appeasers to proceed as they might delay the action of potential opponents, demanded clarification of the situation.[71] Lenin, Stalin and Trotsky had been absent at the CC meeting of November 11 which had decided in favour of negotiations, perhaps because they had more important things to do, but perhaps also because they found it opportune to let the Appeasers have their run.

On November 14, the Central Executive Committee elected

by the Second Soviet Congress declared that all socialist parties should agree to the political platform adopted by the Congress. The Central Executive Committee, to which the new government would be responsible, was to be enlarged by representatives of the trade unions (including *Vikzhel*) and the Peasants' Soviets, after new elections to these bodies.[72] At the evening meeting of that day, however, this decision was disowned by the Left Social Revolutionaries as making civil war inevitable. The suggestion was immediately taken up by some of the Bolshevik members of the CEC, including Kamenev, its Chairman. When rebuked by their CC, they responded with open revolt and induced the majority of the Bolshevik members of the CEC to amend the decision adopted on the 14th so as to meet the demands of the Left Social Revolutionaries. Now Lenin persuaded nine members of the CC and one candidate member to sign an ultimatum to the minority (Zinoviev, Kamenev, Milyutin, Nogin and Rykov).[73] Unless they submitted unconditionally to party decisions an extraordinary Party Congress would be convened to decide on their expulsion from the party. If, against expectation, the Congress should support them, they would have to form a coalition government with their socialist partners but Lenin and his friends would fight that government as an embodiment of vacillation and anarchy (i.e. would refuse submission to the Congress decisions). The Moscow City Committee, which had just signed a two-day armistice with Kerenski's supporters, sent a delegate to Petrograd to support the minority of the CC. On the other hand, the Petrograd Committee, on a note from Lenin, sent a delegate to support him.[74] On November 17th the ultimatum was read to the minority. As the latter was neither prepared to retract its views nor capable of accepting the threatened trial of strength, its members resigned their posts in the Central Committee and in the Sovnarkom (i.e. complied with the demand made upon them by the CC decision of November 15)[75] under protest. The coalition government aimed at by them, they said, would have secured the convention of the Constituent Assembly and would have acted on the peace programme of the II Soviet Congress. They also expressed their solidarity with the Left Social Revolutionary members of the Military Revolutionary Committee who had just resigned in protest against the suppression of the newspapers of the *bourgeois* right-wing. The Central Committee answered with a public denunciation of the oppositionists as deserters from their posts and—with reference to their behaviour on the eve of the insurrection—as 'strike-breakers'.[76] On this act of condemnation, Zinoviev demanded, and was granted, re-admission to the Central Committee. The others waited for three more weeks, with an evident intention to see how events would turn out. At the CC meeting of December 12 their demand for re-admission was submitted but rejected by the majority on the ground that they still maintained their political viewpoint and, indeed, misinterpreted the coalition government formed meanwhile with the Left Social Revolutionaries.[77] As late as December 24 the CC found it necessary to dissolve the parliamentary committee elected by the Bolshevik members of the Constituent Assembly on the ground that it showed 'a bourgeois-democratic outlook on the Constituent Assembly without consideration for the real conditions of class struggle and civil war'. All the well-known oppositionists with the sole exception of Zinoviev (who, as we know, had submitted to the party majority) and a few members of the party majority (including Stalin) had sat on the dissolved committee.

In fact, the crisis had already been decided on November 28 when, under the impact of the military decisions near Petersburg and in Moscow, the Second Congress of the Soviets of Peasant Deputies rejected the Right Social Revolutionaries' suggestion to move the Congress to Mogilev, i.e. to Army Headquarters, and granted full votes to the District delegates (amongst whom, as distinct from the Gubernium delegates, the Left Social Revolutionaries formed a majority). The right-wingers seceded from the Congress and the left-wingers decided in favour of fusion, on terms of equality, of the Peasant Soviets' Executive Committee with that of the Workers' and Soldiers' Soviets. The formation of a coalition government of Bolsheviks and Left Social Revolutionaries was implied. The fusion of the Soviets on the Gubernium level was a prolonged process. In Petrograd Province, where the Right Social Revolutionaries at first retained the lead, it was achieved as late as February. In March, when it was fairly complete, Bolshevik-dominated district Soviets were already more numerous than Soviets led by Left Social Revolutionaries.[78] Although, at first, the Soviet government's power hardly extended beyond the industrial towns and the army, the peasants' sympathy with its peace policy was quite enough to keep the Bolsheviks in control and to condemn the Left Social Revolutionaries' later armed protest against the Brest Litovsk treaty to failure. The supposed alternative to Bolshevik dictatorship, backed by a long tradition of the democratic movement though it was, was exposed as unrealistic when the dissolution of the Constituent Assembly failed to evoke any serious protest and when, eventually, its majority parties, assembled under the protection of a foreign intervention army, were superseded by Kolchak, who easily disposed of them.

(d) THE TURN TO RECONSTRUCTION

The responsibilities of state power implied a more realistic approach to foreign policy than was necessary for an opposition party, as well as a more realistic approach of the workers to the needs of production. On the very first day of the Soviet regime, Lenin rejected suggestions to give the Soviet proposals for a democratic peace an ultimate character. The imperialist governments should not be given a pretext to reject the Soviet proposals because a point might appear unacceptable.[79] As for internal tasks, once a socialist government was in power, it was necessary 'to fight against the old habit to approach the amount of work to be done and the means of production from the standpoint of an unfree man who wished to get rid at least of some avoidable task and to snatch away at least something from the bourgeoisie'.[80]

Applied to the peace issue, the realistic approach necessitated propaganda for such conditions of peace as the Soviet Republic regarded as just and desirable, followed by negotiations. At the same time there had to be resistance against unacceptable demands. Already in late December Lenin submitted to a soldiers' conference (which was convened to discuss the demobilisation of the army) a confidential questionnaire concerning the possibilities of resistance or at least of an ordered retreat into the interior of

Russia in case of the Germans' insistence on annexationist demands. It also sought the best way of conducting the peace negotiations leading to the creation of psychological conditions for resistance. (For publication, he sent the conference a message emphasising the need for creating a socialist army and addressed[81] the first detachments of volunteers sent for that purpose to the front). Once he knew what conditions in the army were like, he waged a consistent struggle, inside and outside the Central Committee, for the acceptance of the inevitable. For this purpose he made full use of the propaganda opportunities available in Brest Litovsk. However, he never went as far as letting the Germans have an excuse for breaking the armistice, which is what actually happened as a result of Trotsky's proclamation of "neither war nor peace."

I may suppose my readers to be familiar with these disputes, which eventually ended with the signing of the treaty of Brest Litovsk.[82] In the framework of the present study we are interested only in the impact which they made on the party. Events at the top are fairly clear. Up to and including the decisive meeting of February 23, Lenin had no majority within the Central Committee (the signing of the treaty was made possible only by the abstentions of Trotsky and his friends which were motivated by the mere impossibility of waging a revolutionary war against Lenin's opposition). In consequence, Lenin and his supporters could only offer advice (and, eventually, threats with actions unconstitutional from the standpoint of party legality). Trotsky's declaration of "neither war nor peace", however costly to the young Soviet Republic, involved no breach of party discipline.[83] The Left Communists' reactions, in particular their combinations with the Left Social Revolutionaries against a section, and eventually a majority, of their own party, were clearly unconstitutional.[84] Yet Lenin could not treat them with a severity comparable to that applied against the right-wing Bolsheviks during the November crisis. Apart from any sympathy for their sentiments, it was obvious that, during the Brest Litovsk crisis even more than in November, decisions had been based not upon the Rules but upon universal conviction that he was historically right and that events would convince his opponents. When, at the decisive CC meeting, the Left Communists resigned from the CC in spite of their being granted full freedom of propaganda within the party, Stalin put the question whether such resignations from the CC might not be regarded as resignations from the party also, but Lenin denied this.[85]

Much more complicated, and difficult to analyse at least till local archives are opened, are developments in the lower party organisations, even their numerical strength. It is fairly clear that the conquest of power was immediately followed, not by any considerable influx of new members but by a loss in membership. Lenin spoke occasionally of 'October Communists'[86] but the connection in which the remark was made leaves little doubt that he had former members of other socialist parties in mind. They were to be prevented from having a voice in the drafting of the new party programme. An influx of turncoats from the ranks of civil servants and technical specialists was prevented by the boycott of the new regime proclaimed by these groups, and observed partly for months. Even when it had ended, those who had taken part in it would have to wait for years before they could gain the party's confidence. On the other side, party membership was bound to be reduced by the dissolution of the army and by the flight of starving workers from the capitals to their villages, where land distribution was in full swing. Most of those returning were likely to remain sympathisers and a few of them even helped to start new party organisations in the villages. However, from the standpoint of membership records the balance was bound to be negative, in particular if we remember that even the more moderate of Sverdlov's enthusiastic estimate of 1917[87] cannot be explained except on the assumption of a great share of the army organisations in total membership. As, in those days, a majority of the party members was still in the old and large organisations which were represented at the VII Party Congress, its sudden convocation can hardly explain the small figures of party members represented.[88] (Bubnov, writing in 1931,[89] gives the figure of 115,000, which would be no more than forty per cent of even a modest estimate of party strength at the time of the October Revolution).

At the opening of the VII Congress Sverdlov announced on

9

behalf of the Central Committee that the Congress would be
regarded as competent if attended by more than half the number
of delegates present at the preceding (VI) Congress. A competent Congress was obviously needed in order to prevent later
questioning of the legality of the Brest Litovsk treaty by the
oppositionists. Sverdlov opposed too close a scrutiny of membership figures such as 36,000 in the Petrograd, or 20,000 in the
Moscow organisation, lest the validity of Congress decisions be
questioned.[90]   It was stated that Kronstadt, which claimed
3500 members, was not likely to have even 500 left of the
3000 members existing on the eve of October. Kronstadt had
always been the centre of Left Social Revolutionary, if not anarchist, tendencies. Disappointment with the course of the revolution may have been particularly strong there even amongst those
who had joined the Bolshevik party on the eve of the October
revolution. Because of the high percentage of sailors amongst
its members the Kronstadt organisation was particularly affected
by demobilisation. Of the active Bolsheviks amongst them many
were transferred to posts of responsibility all over the country.
But the loss of up to half of the party membership existing in both
the capitals on the eve of October can hardly be explained in
similar ways, nor even by the disorderly management of membership records before October, overestimates of actual membership
resulting from continuing registration of people who had joined
only for a few weeks. Some real loss in membership is likely.
Presumably it was due to new entrants with little previous revolutionary experience who were shocked by the deterioration of conditions of living after the conquest of power. It is impossible for
us to assess the weight of each of these factors in determining the
loss in registered membership between the eve of October and the
VII Party Congress. Even at the time the Central Committee could
hardly assess the state of things with the embryonic machine
it possessed.

A recent publication[91] illustrates the work of the Secretariat
of the CC immediately after its transfer to Moscow, and up to
the eve of the VIII Party Congress. Three women officials
worked there, under general guidance by Sverdlov (who did this
work as a sideline of his main work as Secretary of the Soviet

Central Executive Committee). Stasova, the Secretary of the CC, remained in Leningrad and paid only occasional visits to Moscow. The work consisted in the reception of the numerous visitors from the provinces, correspondence with local organisations, registration of party workers who (mainly in consequence of the German advance and the progress of counter-revolution) came to Moscow and formed a reserve for Sverdlov's disposition, and the posting of literature. Only from June 1918 did reports from the localities begin to arrive with some regularity and instruction letters issued by the CC. From the time of the Czechoslovak mutiny onwards special surveys of the situation in party organisations near the front line were made and posted to Lenin, Sverdlov and Dzerzhinski, as the CC members most immediately concerned.

The signing of the peace treaty enabled a turn to economic reconstruction. The Bolsheviks had conquered power with the programme elaborated in Lenin's *Can the Bolsheviks Retain State Power?* The banks, being in the key-position of a modern monopoly-capitalist economy, had to be nationalised. In the individual enterprises workers' control was to be established in order to prevent closedowns and misappropriation of funds in the owners' interest. After the conquest of power, control of the factories was transferred to various combinations of the former management with representatives of the staff, and sometimes already of the local trade unions, according to circumstances. Similar combinations continued to administer individual factories even after nationalisation.[92] Full control by the workers, and eventually nationalisation, were enforced in many individual cases if the old management failed to co-operate or if it diverted funds for payment to the owners. Yet the workers' interest, not only in continuous production but also in improvement of their conditions outside the factory formed a main incentive to nationalisation.[93]

Lenin undoubtedly regarded workers' control as a transitional step to nationalisation, though he disliked the pace forced upon the Bolsheviks, partly by external circumstances[94] and partly by the workers' elemental urge. He sought to introduce orderly approach to economic organisation. This idea was elaborated in his pamphlet *The Next Tasks of Soviet Power*. With a frankness foreign to the treatment of similar issues during the Stalin period, Lenin conceded that the attraction of competent *bourgeois* specialists by higher remuneration involved a sacrifice of socialist principles. It was, however, necessary.[95] Socialist principles were in no way violated by a replacement of the current management of factories by collegia (to which the trade unions clung). The class character of an administrative arrangement depended, not on its institutional form but on the distribution of power in the state on behalf of which it operated. The description of managerial power in terms such as 'dictatorial' may be due to the fact that the immediate dispute had originated from a decree on the restoration of discipline on the railways. But the basic concepts of the pamphlet have been repeated by Lenin again and again.

Lenin wanted the workers to develop a system of accounting and control to check, not only the bourgeois specialists and the careerists who would find their way into the party but also each other so as to secure regularity of work and to increase productivity. Use should be made of piece-work and of organisational methods such as the Taylor system. The organisation of socialist competition was all-important. The press should devote itself to the popularisation of exemplary behaviour even at the price of neglecting some material on current politics.[96] The elemental democratic urge of the masses had to be combined with iron discipline and unconditional subordination to the manager's orders during working hours ; the court was also to enforce a proper working discipline.[97]

Already in their Theses submitted to the VII Party Congress[98] the Left Communists had outlined the danger of a degeneration of the Soviet regime (a warning characteristic of most of the later oppositions). Such degeneration, from a workers' party into a 'general people's party' dominated by the soldiers' interest in peace at any price, was bound to follow from the very acceptance of the Brest Litovsk treaty. In the Theses published by them in their periodical *Kommunist*, April 20, 1918[99], the theme was further elaborated. The party was now supposed to be degenerating into a lower-middle-class party, operating an economy based upon state capitalism but bound to become dependent upon foreign bankers and upon the Russian capitalists serving as managers. The Left Communists had in mind quite definite negotiations about the establishment of mixed trusts, which since November 1917 were carried out between the VSNKh and the managers of the Sormovo-Kolomna combine. These negotiations ended in April 1918 under evident pressure from the workers' delegates (the Sormovo combine was nationalised as late as June 18th).[100] The Left Communists objected to Lenin's demand for better working discipline which, they alleged, was a threat to the initiative and freedom of the working classes. Much more was at stake than the practicability of a particular organisational arrangement. Lenin accepted the challenge and denounced the leftists' advocacy of Russia's anarchic state, which followed from the predominance of the lower-middle-classes. In such a country even state capitalism, if associated with the Soviet regime, which secured its eventual transformation into socialism, would mean a great step forward.[101] Under the impact of the war the two elements of the new social order—state regulation of the economy and Soviet power—had been separately developed in Germany and Russia. The Russian workers, having established the second, had to learn the first from the Germans and from Russian organisers of industrial combines.[102]

NOTES AND REFERENCES

1. Op. cit. pp. 117-18.
2. Ibid. pp. 166-67. Similarly Zalezhaki, as quoted by Leiberov, l.c. p. 71. A. Kondratev writing in *Krasmaya letopis* (No. 7, 1923, p. 69) reports that even in the New Iessner Works, which had been a Bolshevik stronghold before and during the War, at first Mensheviks were elected. When, however, on March 1 he and other Bolshevik leaders released from prison addressed the workers, the Mensheviks were recalled and the Bolshevik list (which included some non-Bolsheviks) elected.
3. A. Fedorov and G. Faustov in *Kommunist*, 1957, No. 3.
4. *Pervy legalny Peterburgski komitet bolshevikov v* 1917 g., Gosizdat, p. 51.
5. Cf. Trotsky, op. cit. p. 201. A few days later, however, the represen-

tation of workers and soldiers was equalised, with one delegate for 2000 electors.

6. Shlyapnikov, op cit. pp. 158-59.

7. Quoted by Trotsky, op. cit. p. 179.

8. *My Mission to Russia,* Vol. II, pp. 90-91.

9. There was collaboration between moderate Mensheviks and Bolsheviks on minor issues such as Shlyapnikov's demand to exclude Khrustalyov who had been the first Chairman of the Petersburg Soviet in 1905 but had since collaborated with the Tsarist government. (Cf. Shlyapnikov, op. cit. pp. 179 ff.). Incidents, such as this, illustrate the great difference in attitude between the Mensheviks and the German Majority Social democrats who were soon confronted with similar issues, but answered them in a way which preserved the generals' power.

10. See above, pp. 97-8.

11. See above, pp. 124-7.

12. Trotsky's important contribution to the argument was his publication, in *The Stalin School of Falsification,* of the proceedings of the Conference of Bolshevik representatives in March 1917. All references to that conference were dropped in Soviet publications until 1956 when F. I. Drabkina, on the basis of her personal memories as well as of archive documents, gave a fairly balanced account (*Voprosy istorii,* 1956, No. 9). A presentation of the whole course of events, with a sharp anti-Stalin bias, was given by E. N. Burdzhalov in his article, ibid. No. 4, and his reply to Bugayev's party-official criticism (*Partiinaya zhizn,* 1956, No. 14), ibid. No. 8.

13. Stalin's *Sochineniya,* Vol. III, pp. 7 ff.

14. *Sochineniya,* vol. XXIV, pp. 28 ff. In an argument against Kamenev, the unprovoked use of the old Trotskyist formula of 1905 may have been intended to anticipate a possible reproach of Kamenev that Lenin now was turning to the position taken by Trotsky in 1905 (as Trotsky, and all the Trotskyists since have suggested).

15. *Sochineniya,* vol. XXXVI, pp. 395 ff. The omission of the item in the 4th ed. was evidently caused by reluctance to mention the very fact of the March Conference.

16. Ibid. vol. XXIV, pp. 34 and 52-53 (*Sel. Works,* vol. VI, pp. 43 and and 61-62).

17. Burdzhalov, l.c. pp. 51-52.

18. His draft for a Speech or Article in Defence of the April Theses, *Sochineniya,* vol. XXIX, pp. 13-14, though not published or directly used, may indicate the way in which he conducted his campaign.

19. Ibid. pp. 27-28 ; *Sel. Works,* vol. 6, pp. 35-36.

20. This argument, evident already in the first *Letter from Afar,* may partly have been influenced by the presentation of events in the western newspapers from which Lenin drew his information while in Switzerland.

21. See below, pp. 120-1.
22. Proceedings of the April Conference ; see also V. Evgrafov's article 'From the April Theses to the April Conference', *Kommunist*, 1957, No. 7 and Lenin's pamphlet on the Conference, *Sochineniya*, vol. XXIV, pp. 66-67.
23. *Pervy legalny Petersburgski komitet*......, as quoted in note 4, pp. 63 ff. (meeting of March 21/April 3).
24. An illuminating record of the way the group of intellectuals around Trotsky—not identical with, but prominent amongst the *Mezhrayontsy*—was formed during successive efforts in revolutionary journalism abroad, is given by Deutscher (op. cit. 1954). Even some of those *Mezhrayontsy* who eventually were considered as party candidates for the Constituent Assembly stood far to the right of Trotsky. In October Lenin (*Sochineniya*, 3rd ed. vol. XXI, p. 289 ; *Coll. Works*, p. 64 [omitted in the 4th ed.]) praised Trotsky for his behaviour which compared favourably with that of his colleagues. See also Trotsky, op. cit. 1937, p. 108.
25. Cf. Lenin's *Sachineniya*, vol. XXIV, pp. 394-95 ; Carr, op. cit. p. 89, Deutscher, op. cit. (1954), pp. 158 ff. Even Trotsky qualified his agreement with the Bolsheviks by the condition that they had 'de-bolshevised' themselves. This last statement was not published by Lenin in his *Pravda* article but kept in his private notes which he had shown to the members of the Central Committee. The fact seems to prove that after the April Conference he, too, regarded a token of Bolshevik readiness to admit other Social Democrats as more important than the risks involved in union with partners who started with such provocative delimitations.
26. Mints, op. cit. p. 22. A large amount of material has been collected by V. V. Anikeyev (in *Voprosy istorii KPSS*, 1958, Nos. 2 and 3), which opposes the emphasis on the occurrence of united organisations which became current during the historians' reaction against the Stalinist embellishment of party history. It shows that 150 of 720 surveyed organisations were united but these included a mere 14,000 of the 80,000 members represented at the April Conference, and 27,000 of the 240,000 members represented at the VI Congress. The evidence given by Anikeyev shows the tendency of the Bolsheviks to break with the *defencist* Mensheviks. By implication, this allowed for continuing unity with the internationalist Mensheviks. As the latter formed only a small minority in the Menshevik camp, 58 united organisations became purely Bolshevik before, and 90 more shortly after, the VI Congress. But in the major towns of Central Asia, for example, the formation of separate Bolshevik organisations started only in September and was concluded as late as in early 1918 (*Istoriya SSSR* 1959, No. 5, p. 18).
27. According to the data given by K. T. Semenov in *Voprosy istorii KPSS* 1957, No. 2, p. 148, the Urals organisation by the beginning

of March had nine party organisations with a total of 500 members, but by mid-April had grown to thirty organisations with 16,000 members.

28. Cf. the draft Rules elaborated for the April City Conference by a sub-committee of the Petrogard Committee (Protokoly VII-April-Conference, 1934 ed., pp. 21 ff.). The suggested requirement of two recommendations by existing members for every new admission was accepted by the City Conference, but not that for confirmation of every admission by the District Committee, nor that for the basing of the party organisation on factory nuclei.

29. Anikeyev, l.c., p. 132.

30. Sverdlov managed to give two estimates in the course of one speech (*Protokoly*, VI Congress, pp. 36-37). The higher one—240,00—appears to have been based upon a very copious estimate of the army organisations and upon granting the newly admitted *Mezhrayontsy* at least as many members as they claimed. But according to the reports made by the delegations, the city organisations of Petrogard and Moscow, had, indeed, more than doubled their membership since April.

31. See below, p. 129.

32. *Protokoly* VI Congress, and Mints, op. cit. p. 29.

33. Its proceedings were published in *Proletarskaya revolyutsiya*, 1930, No. 10.

34. At a Conference shortly before the July crisis, sixty army organisations (43 from the front, 17 from the rear) with a total of 26,000 members had been represented : it is questionable whether this represented a major progress against mid-April when, according to Semenov (l.c. p. 151), the Petrograd army organisation alone had 6000 members. The July crisis brought a setback and at the VI Congress only two Army organisations were represented. From then on to October, however, the losses were more than made good.

35. *Izvestiya Tsk RKP(b)*, 1928, No. 1.

36. *Voprosy istorii KPSS*, 1957, No. 2, p. 113.

37. Text of Golder, op. cit. p. 375.

38. *Pervy legalny komitet.......*, as quoted in note 4, pp. 153 ff. and 164.

39. Ibid. p. 172.

40. Cf. I. V. Petrov's article in *Voprosy istorii*, 1957, No. 4, and the sources quoted there.

41. See also the documents published in *Voprosy istorii KPSS*, 1957, No. 2.

42. For example, Dzhaparidze (Baku), *Protokoly*, pp. 120-21, and Yaroslavski, ibid. pp. 135-36.

43. *Sochineniya*, vol. XXIV, pp. 40-41 ; *Sel. Works*, vol. VI, p. 49.

44. Ibid., vol. XXV, p. 170 ; *Coll. Works*, vol. XXI/1, p. 49.

45. Larin (*Protokoly*, p. 69) declared that left-wing Menshevik Inter-

nationalists joined the Bolsheviks in demanding transfer of power to the Soviets ; Yurenev, speaking for the *Mezhrayontsy* (ibid. pp. 113-14), found that Stalin's motion combined undue pessimism as regards the prospects of conquering the Soviets with undue optimism as regards the Bolsheviks' chances of conquering power in opposition to the Soviets : this might result in an isolation of the working-class from the peasantry. Stalin's motion, which had been drafted jointly with Lenin, was thus reproached for what would later have seen described as a typical Trotskyist error !

46. Nogin, ibid. pp. 123-24. At an enlarged CC meeting, held on July 13-17, Lenin's standpoint was not accepted by a majority of those present. Cf. A. M. Sorokin's article in *Voprosy istorii KPSS*, 1959, No. 4.

47. Ibid. pp. 117 ff. ; Stalin's *Sochineniya*, vol. III, pp. 179 ff.

48. See below, p. 122.

49. *Sochineniya*, vol. VI, pp. 340-41.

50. *Protokoly*, VI Congress, pp. 100 ff.

51. Ibid. pp. 138-39 and III, Stalin's *Sochineniya*, vol. III, pp. 182-83.

52. *Protokoly* Sixth Congress, pp. 233-34, Stalin's *Sochineniya*, vol. III, pp. 186-87.   Deutscher's (op. cit. p. 154) comparison of Stalin's statement with the contemporary attitudes of Trotsky and Lenin misses the decisive point that what they had in common were necessary implications of the policies of *every* supporter of a Bolshevik insurrection in 1917: it was precisely the differences in emphasis that mattered.   The hints regarding 'dogmatic' and 'creative' Marxism, directed by one of the main reporters against the other (Lenin eventually repeated this point about Bukharin in his 'Will'), cannot have been lost on an audience familiar with all the intricacies of intra-party disputes.

53. *Protokoly*, pp. 138-39 ; Stalin's *Sochineniya*, vol. III, pp. 182-83.

54. At the decisive CC meeting of October 20, Stalin argued in favour of insurrection with emphasis on its international implications (ibid. p. 381).

55. The armed forces naturally felt the impact of the events most strongly. Control of the Central Committee of the Baltic Fleet, for example, was lost by the Bolsheviks in July but regained after Kornilov's coup. Cf. the Protocols of its meetings, published in *Istoricheski arkhiv*, 1957, No. 4.

56. Op. cit. vol. VII, p. 11.

57. On September 21/October 4 the CC advised against entering the pre-Parliament with so narrow a majority.   The decision was transferred to the Bolshevik delegates to the Democratic Conference who decided with 77 votes against 50 in favour of participation as suggested by Kamenev, Nogin and Rykov ; Trotsky and Stalin had opposed it. The reader who obtains most of his information about these disputes from the reflections of the later feud between Trotsky and Stalin

in western publications, may be surprised to find the two in one camp at this and other occasions. This is, however, not astonishing : unless they had in the majority of cases supported the line which eventually proved correct, neither a newcomer whose previous record was highly compromising in Bolshevik eyes, nor a practical organiser who was unable to challenge the more brilliant speakers and publicists, could have arrived at a position where the struggle for Lenin's succession was bound to be fought out between the two of them. Stalin and Trotsky stood jointly against Lenin in a number of cases. The one instance where they differed, Trotsky—but not the CC majority—supporting Lenin, concerned the latter's suggestion to expel Zinoviev and Kemenev from the party because of their indiscretions in Gorki's *Novaya zhizm* (October 18/31). Stalin's approach on this issue conforms to what is known of his earlier attitude to the application of sharp organisational measures. It was subsequently confirmed by everyone concerned (including Lenin himself), by forming political alliances with Zinoviev and Kamenev whenever this was demanded by the expedience of disputes within the party. (When, eventually, these alliances had broken up, impressive 'revelations' about the October events were bound to follow.)

58. There were three abstentions but an alternative motion of Zinoviev, which sought delay of the intended action, got six votes, and three more abstained on it.

59. This interpretation is supported by the composition of the Politburo, which included all the well-known leaders present in Petrograd (including Kamenev and Zinoviev who had voted against insurrection) and Pubnov, the head of the party's military organisation. It is supported by the very fact that no more was heard of that first Politburo (even in later years, when the Politburo was an actual working body, CC members present in Moscow were expected to attend. The existence of disputes about the quorum is confirmed by Lenin, *Sochineniya,* vol. XXVI, p. 193 (*Coll. Works,* vol. XXI/2, p. 134). Only ten of the twenty-one CC members had voted in favour of insurrection but most of the nine who were absent could be supposed to support it.

60. Cf. ibid. pp. 34 ff., and 251 ff. respectively. Trotsky's suggestion that Stalin's move to circulate Lenin's letter, after its rejection by the CC, amongst the party organisations was directed against Lenin's policies (Stalin, p. 222) appears as a mere product of factional propaganda.

61. Minutes, as quoted in note 4 above, pp. 326 and 329.

62. *Proletarskaya revolyutsiya,* 1926, No. 10, pp. 178 ff. There was a difference between the attitude of the Moscow Provincial and City Committees. At least after the October insurrection, the latter supported reconciliation with Mensheviks etc.

63. In Stalin's *Sochineniya* (vol. IV, pp. 317-18) it is claimed that Lenin later approved of the procedure applied by the majority of the CC.

64. Cf. E. N. Gorodetski's book *Rotheleniye Sovetskovo gossudavtoa* : 1911-8 Moscow, Nauka, 1965, pp. 96 ff., and his article in *Voprosy istorii* 1957, No. 16 ; and M. E. Naidelov's survey of the presentation of the October events in Soviet historiography (ibid).

65. See above, pp. 117-9.

66. See below, p. 131.

67. *Istoricheski arkhiv* 1957, No. 5, p. 94.

68. Cf. Bunyan and Fisher, op. cit. pp. 167-68 and 193 and R. Abramovich's article in *Sozalistichesky esrnik*, May 1966.

69. Ibid. p. 209.

70. A. Anski's report, ibid. p. 169. From here on all the dates are given only in the new style.

71. Ibid. pp. 192-94. *Protokoly* Ts. K., pp. 144 ff.

72. Text in Appendix 2 to Lenin's *Sochineniya*, 3rd ed., vol. XXII.

73. Perhaps because no absolute majority of the CC members was present in Petrograd to support the move, and perhaps because of the formally incorrect character of the threat, Lenin let his supporters sign the ultimatum individually.

74. *Pervy legalny komitet*, as quoted in note 4, p. 340.

75. The three points of the CC decision to which reference here is made were first published in 1932, in the Appendix volume XXX to the 3rd edition of Lenin's *Sochineniya*.

76. Lenin's *Sochineniya*, vol. XXVI, pp. 268 ff. ; *Sel. Works*, vol. VI, pp. 412 ff.

77. Cf. Lenin's *Sochineniya*, vol. XXXVI, p. 416.

78. Cf. Kh. A. Eritsyan's article in *Istoriya SSSR*, 1957, No. 3.

79. *Sochineniya*, vol. XXVI, pp. 222-23.

80. Ibid. pp. 370 ff.

81. Ibid. pp. 381 and 388.

82. Cf. Carr, op. cit. vol. III, chap. 21 ; Deutscher, op. cit. (1954), chap. XI ; Wheeler-Bennett, *Brest-Litovsk, the Forgotten Peace*, London 1939 ; Schapiro, op. cit. chap. VI.

83. For the facts see Protokoly VII Congress, p. 116 ; Lenin's *Sochineniya*, vol. XXVI, p. 471 and vol. XXVII, p. 90.

84. Bukharin's presentation of the facts in his trial (*Court Proceedings* 1938, pp. 447-48) coincides with his article published in *Pravda*, January 3, 1924, and with what was known in party circles (even as far away as Vienna) shortly after the events. The existence of a plan to arrest Lenin is also confirmed by J. Steinberg, *Souvenirs d'un Commissaire du Peuple*, Paris 1930, p. 234. Vyshinski's propaganda, and the pressure brought to bear upon some of the witnesses, introduced into this historical record the legend that the oppositionists' plan included any physical harm to be inflicted upon Lenin, Sverdlov and Stalin (on the contrary, the oppositionists would have

been glad to return them to leading positions after a short arrest, during which war would be declared on Germany) and the assertion that the intrigue was continued even after the Moscow party organisation's decision on May 15th against the left-wing.

85. *Sochineniya*, vol. XXXVI, p. 440.
86. Ibid. p. 434.
87. See above, p. 113.
88. Such an explanation is suggested in the *Short History of the CPSU(b)*, p. 212, and also in the *Istoriya kommunisticheskoi partii Sovetskovo Soyuza*, p. 261, where an actual number of 300,000 party members is claimed for the time of the Congress.
89. Quoted by Carr, op. cit. p. 305.
90. Protokoly VII Congress, pp. 4, 120 and 122.
91. By B. Z. Stankina, in *Istoricheski arkhiv*, 1958, No. 3.
92. Cf. Drobizhev's article in *Istoriya SSSR*, 1957, No. 3.
93. Cf. the dispute, at the I Congress of Soviets of National Economy, between Lozovski and Smirnov, quoted by Bunyan, op. cit. pp. 447-48.
94. On June 28, 1918, general nationalisation of large-scale industries was enacted in order to prevent their seizure by the Germans; provision was made for the retention of former owners as managers. Cf. Liberman, op. cit. pp. 50 ff., Debb, op. cit. p. 95.
95. *Sochineniya*, vol. XXVII, p. 222 (*Sel. Works*, vol. VII, p. 322).
96. Ibid., pp. 177 and 230. These suggestions already indicate the characteristic features of the present Soviet press.
97. Ibid., pp. 240-41 (343-44 and 234-46). Lenin includes decision on the conditions of labour, as distinct from its actual performance, amongst the subjects to be left to 'meeting democracy' outside working hours. The right to elect the managers, whose orders must be obeyed, was mentioned in Lenin's draft of *The Next Tasks of Soviet Power* (*Schineniya*, vol. XXVII, p. 186) but not in the pamphlet as published.
98. Reprinted also as Appendix 11 to vol. XXII of Lenin's *Sochineniya*, 3rd ed.
99. Reprinted ibid., as Appendix 12. *Kommunist* became an organ of the Left Communists during the comparatively short period (between February 11 and the VIII Party Congress) when they were in control of the Petrograd organisation (as they were already a month earlier in Moscow), e.g. B. F. Bagayev's article in *Nauchniye Ookladi vyshdai shkoli, istorideskige nauki*, 1961, No. 1.
100. Cf. the note published by P. V. Bolobuyev and V. Z. Drobizhev in *Voprosy istorii*, 1957, No. 9. The Sormovo negotiations had been attacked in *Kommunist*, No. 1 (which also published the Left Communists' Theses), p. 19.
101. Lenin's *Sochineniya*, vol. XXVII, pp. 261, 267 ff. and 302 ff. (the last-quoted passage contains Lenin's analysis of the five different social formations co-existing in Russia).
102. Ibid. pp. 137 ff. and 262 ff.

CHAPTER IV

THE PARTY, THE STATE AND THE MASSES

(a) PARTY POLICIES IN THE CIVIL WAR

LENIN'S concepts of the use of state power for building a socialist economy had to wait for full expression. In some essentials they had to be discarded as soon as they were adopted because of resistance within the party.

The left-wing Social Revolutionaries could not carry their opposition to the Brest Litovsk treaty to extremes as their supporters, the peasants, demanded an early peace most earnestly. But as soon as the peace was concluded and the land redistributed, an open antagonism appeared between the peasants who were not prepared to part with their grain reserves (at least not as long as the town had few industrial commodities to offer in exchange) and the government which could not allow the towns to be starved, even though this meant a reduction of the peasants' standard of life.[1] A number of decrees issued since May 9th[2] provided for requisition by armed workers' detachments. The procurement price for grain not voluntarily delivered by a well-to-do peasant was to be shared between the denouncer and the village community. The situation became desperate during the last days of May when the Czechoslovak legions mutinied along the Trans-Siberian Railway. By their occupation of Samara on June 8th, the industrial centres were cut off from the grain supplies of the East (the South was already lost to the Germans and to White troops operating under their protection). On June 11th the establishment of Committees of the Village Poor was decreed. In co-operation with the workers' detachments these committees were to confiscate all grain surpluses to safeguard supplies for the towns. They distributed, for the benefit of the poor, all kinds of commodities and agricultural implements held by the *kulaks*. The agrarian revolution which had started in October was now completed. The *kulaks'* private lands, which had remained unaffected hitherto, were now included in the egalitarian re-distribution of the land.

Lenin[3] described the operation of the committees as hard and cruel but necessary in view of the starvation of the towns. In fact it amounted to an armed struggle of the industrial workers against those peasants who had some grain, with such support as could be found in the village. It was not much : Stalin who had just been sent to Tsaritsyn said that the former soldier, the 'righteous peasant', had turned from support of the Soviet regime to opposition. 'He hates with all his soul the grain monopoly, controlled prices, requisitions and our struggle against black-marketeering'.[4] Occasionally 'the kulaks'—i.e. those opposed to grain deliveries to the towns—controlled even the Committees of the Poor. The (real) kulaks might successfully incite the (real) poor against the Government by using their influence in such a way that the taxes were levied not according to the wealth but to the number of members of a family so as to hit hardest the poor peasants with their large families.[5] After a few months the Committees of the Poor, having enforced re-elections of the village Soviets, were dissolved.

The food crisis, aggravated by the Czechoslovak attack, caused the gravest crisis in the whole history of Soviet Russia (Denikin's advance in 1919, and Hitler's in 1941 not excluded). Its first victim was such freedom as was still allowed to parties opposing the Soviet regime. On June 14th the right-wing Social Revolutionaries and Mensheviks were expelled from the Soviets as being in sympathy with the counter-revolutionaries. Yet the left-wing Social Revolutionaries, though no longer represented in the Government, held strong positions in the Soviets and in the Army. In view of the peasants' dissatisfaction they had obvious cause for an attack against the regime. In the (erroneous) assumption that the Brest-Litovsk treaty was unpopular, and in order to involve the Soviets in a new war with the Germans, an attack was opened, on July 6th, with the assassination of the German ambassador. It was accompanied by insurrections at Yaroslavl and Rybinsk organised by right-wing Social Revolutionaries. Four days later the commander of the Eastern front, Muraviev, a left-wing Social Revolutionary, attempted to open the front to the Czechoslovaks. By July 8th the feeble insurrection in Moscow was suppressed and the left-wing Social Revolutionaries outlawed. For the time being no legal party other than the Bolsheviks was left on Soviet territory. But although Muraviev was liquidated in a matter of hours and the Yaroslavl insurrection within a fortnight, the situation continued to deteriorate. On August 6th Kazan was taken by the Czechoslovaks, while Trotsky was just assembling the forces for counter-attack. The culmination of the crisis was reached when, on August 30th, Lenin was seriously wounded by a right-wing Social Revolutionary terrorist. The same organisation assassinated, on the same day, Uritski, one of the outstanding communists in Petrograd.[6]

The very gravity of the crisis carried its remedy. The shots fired against the recognised leader of the Russian working-class by people who still described themselves as socialists, destroyed any residue of the illusion that the questions under dispute were merely theoretical. The former hesitations[7] gave way to the proclamation of the red terror. The workers, having got an *ad oculos* demonstration that the revolution was in mortal danger, joined the colours. Within a fortnight Trotsky had retaken Kazan and Zimbirsk while Stalin had broken the threatening encirclement of Tsaritsyn. Thereby the Volga was returned to Soviet Russia. Another six weeks later, the western front was liquidated by the German revolution. From now on, the Ukraine and the Northern Caucasus were battlefields of the civil war but no longer cut off from Russia by a superior foreign army.

Eventually, the Western Allies replaced the Germans as the protectors of counter-revolution. Under their auspices the White generals gathered a strength surpassing anything experienced during the critical year 1918. But so also did the Bolsheviks. The war against Germany having come to an end, there was no possibility of using western conscript armies for intervention in Russia (the one attempt made by the French ended in mutiny). The effect of whatever material support the Whites got from their western friends depended upon the reliability of a conscript Russian peasant army. Comparatively short experiences with White rule were sufficient to destroy whatever delusions about the only possible alternative to Bolshevism were current amongst

the peasants. Even hard requisitions appeared as the lesser evil
in comparison with a return of the landlords. The very fact of
foreign intervention discredited the cause in favour of which it was
exercised. A number of serious military crisis followed one another during the year 1919, but retrospectively it is clear that no
individual incident could have brought about the fall of the Soviet
regime. In 1920 it fought a national war with Poland, easily
successful so far as the defence of the national territory was
concerned and failing only in Lenin's more ambitious aspirations.
In the autumn of that year Wrangel's army was destroyed by a
comparatively minor effort. The following year brought the
re-union of Transcaucasia and of the Far East, though (for
another year) the latter was admitted only in a compromise form
dictated by foreign policies.

For the time being, the civil war defeated Lenin's plan to
build the new society with such personal and organisational
resources as were found available in the estate of the old one.
'War communism' was taking its course, first of all in the field of
distribution. Out of the necessity produced by the monetary
inflation a virtue was made of letting the workers be remunerated
in kind.[8] Even Lenin silently replaced his old-standing interest
in the banks as an organisational form of the new society elaborated by the old one by emphasising the cooperatives as 'the
only machinery created by imperialist society which we must use'.
He insisted on their full use. Notwithstanding their Menshevik
or Social Revolutionary background there was no reason why
the co-operatives should not work as well for the Bolsheviks as
they did before for the capitalists. And, as distinct from the
communists, they knew how to organise commodity exchange.[9]

At the height of the summer crisis Lenin did not think that the
necessary economic concessions to the non-working class implied
a need to admit non-Bolshevik parties.[10] But to him the one-
party system was never a matter of principle. The German
revolution made a great impression upon intellectuals who up to
then had regarded the Bolshevik revolution as a hopeless adventure, while the continuation of Allied intervention in Russia after
the end of the German war and the progressive replacement, in
the White regions, of bourgeois-democratic supporters of the

Constituent Assembly by military governments of the Kolchak or Yudenich type demonstrated the real purposes of that intervention. With non-Bolshevik intellectuals in mind, Lenin, in *Pravda,* November 21st, 1918, suggested the re-admission of non-Bolshevik parties, provided they were prepared to collaborate in the defence of the fatherland.[11]   On the eve of the Moscow Party Conference the Mensheviks, answering Lenin's observations, announced support of the Soviet government against the Whites. After a sharp discussion in the Moscow Committee of the CP, at the end of which the opponents of the admission of non-Bolshevik parties rallied a mere five votes, legal status was returned to the Mensheviks and Social Revolutionaries on November 30th. There is no reason to suppose that Lenin had reservations about the basic merits of the one-party system. He simply desired to rally all those who were ready to defend the Soviet regime. A glance at the political background of the majority of the officials working in the Soviet economic, legal and administrative—not to speak of the educational and academic—institutions shows how justified this consideration was in view of the political structure of the pre-revolutionary progressive intelligentsia. One year later the VII Soviet Congress was addressed by delegates of the Mensheviks, of the *Bund* and of the pro-Soviet minority groups of the Social Revolutionaries. The Mensheviks and Bundists protested against the rare convention of plenary meetings of the Soviets (an argument also used by oppositional Communists but easily refutable in view of the civil war) and against the activities of Cheka. Martov demanded civil liberties, an end of repression and (a pious hope at that stage of the civil war) closer relations with the outside world. Lenin's reply was no more conciliatory than had been Martov's speech but drew a definite distinction between convinced opponents of Bolshevism, such as Martov, on the one hand, and the pro-Soviet section of the Mensheviks on the other.[12]

The very conditions of civil war prevented the non-communist intellectuals from becoming that link in an orderly transition from capitalism to socialism as was intended by Lenin. There was, however, one field of state activities in which the non-communist (in most cases, even non-sympathising) specialist played a

10

prominent part : this was the Army itself. The need for a large and well-organised army was obvious. No one except left-wing communist fanatics could seriously advocate a predominance of guerrilla warfare (which continued to play its part wherever workers and peasants rose in the rear of the White armies). With a few exceptions, nearly all of whom had to be immediately promoted to the top-ranks, the existing military specialists regarded Bolshevism as the lesser evil in comparison with a White dictatorship dependent on western support. As even from the loyal specialist no understanding of the policies of the Soviet government could be expected, he had to be accompanied, supported and supervised by the Commissar, a party representative who in the best case aimed at gradually acquiring military knowledge. It was taken for granted that his success in this effort, i.e. the formation of a body of people capable of military as well as of political leadership, would render the institution of special political commissaries superfluous.[13]

Some tension was inherent in this arrangement. Within the army itself this tension found expression in a series of frictions between those army commands which were in the hand of communists—with an orthodox military training hardly above the rank of sergeant—and Trotsky's High Command, whose General Staff was naturally dominated by the specialist element. The Tsaritsyn dispute, which created tension between Trotsky and Stalin, was the most famous but by no means the only one of these conflicts. Since it has been realised that much of Stalin's and Trotsky's assertions about the horrible crimes committed by the other in the years 1917–1919 belongs to the realm of factional mythology and that both of them have proved to be capable military organisers who committed occasional strategic mistakes, there has been some tendency to describe the origins of their conflicts to trivial incidents as happens in every organisation and at the most to their personal characteristics.[14] Yet the more one thinks about what might have happened if, say because of a greater foresight on Lenin's part as to the personal characteristics of the two most outstanding organisers, incidents such as the Tsaritsyn arguments had been avoided, the more one is forced to conclude that the men and the parts eventually played by them were more shaped by jobs which had to be carried out than by their personal characteristics.

The army had necessarily to be divided between specialist and political management. Conflict between Trotsky and Stalin, however, was inevitable. There was a series of disputes between the former who, although a newcomer to the party, had to preside over the re-organisation of the army and its command, and the latter who, being one of the most experienced and trusted representatives of the party machine, was periodically sent to danger spots to supplement shortcomings of the High Command and to investigate the causes of military failures. In some respects, Trotsky represented the familiar case of the opposition leader who, having become minister, still depends on his permanent staff. The fact that he could hardly dispose of permanent staff above the rank of Colonel and that those who worked with him had in their subjective consciousness broken with their past, might weaken criticism of his collaborators. The army of a new Russia was to be built on terms familiar to them. The ranks had to be filled by general mobilisation of all citizens, and strict subordination of the lower ranks of the hierarchy to the higher was the most elementary condition of success. To Stalin, in this respect quite typical of the Bolsheviks, the war was a mere continuation of the class struggle. Defeat was bound to follow from indiscriminate mobilisation of the peasantry and from the inclusion of persons exploiting the labour of others in the reinforcements sent to the front. There they could cause whole formations to go over to the Whites.[15] Since the Politburo had sent him to the front with extra-ordinary power, Stalin felt that his task was of paramount importance. Trotsky's interference—whether caused by a different conception of priorities or, even worse, by the assumption that in times of war the head of the Army was allowed to overrule the party organisation[16]—was a threat to success. When Stalin's military commanders, reliable revolutionaries, would clothe their natural conviction that their front was the most important one and deserved the largest supply of ammunitions, with considerations about the political unreliability of the old officers and the need for local initiative, Stalin would side with them. Trotsky's own behaviour is characterised by the very different degrees of chari-

tableness which he could show, many years later, on the one hand
to Voroshilov's and his fellows' indisputably honest desire to serve
the party best, and on the other hand to the 'moments of inspiration' of his Chief of Staff, Vatsetis, when the latter would issue
orders 'as if the Soviet of Commissaries and the Central Executive
Committee did not exist. . . .perhaps before going to sleep, the
chap had been reading Napoleon's biography and confided his
ambitious dreams to two or three young officers'.[17]   For the party,
it was most natural to distrust Trotsky, not because some Vatsetis
might carry out a coup d'état—this was impossible—but because
he relied on people who owed little loyalty to the party and would,
presumably, back their commander-in-chief in a conflict with the
party majority.

All this belonged to a future still in the clouds, yet within the
scope of minds trained to think in terms of the French revolutionary experience.   To the present belonged a series of conflicts
in which the organisation and the use of the army would be
hammered out.[18]   Many communists still thought in terms of
guerrilla warfare and felt that all the revolutionary enthusiasm
could thus be mobilised, while to the left-wing communist it
was a matter of principle.   Even to those who did not think in
such terms the alternative was compromised by repeated cases of
betrayal by military specialists.   These instances were not so
numerous if the large number of such specialists, their close
connection with friends and relatives fighting on the other side,
and the very varied means by which they had been recruited for
the Soviet government, were kept in mind.   Yet they were
numerous enough to provide material for a score of impressive
speeches at a party conference.   Those who had just suffered
some local defeat because of treason and whose comrades had
been delivered into the hands of the Whites, would not consider
that, on the whole, the republic fared better with specialists than
it would do with a purely communist officers corps which would
have to learn the art of warfare by trial and error.   Those party
leaders who emphasised the political against the specialist interest
would defend the present arrangement against the opposition but
be in sympathy with some of the arguments brought forward by
the latter.[19]

The basic conflict was exaggerated by oratoric excesses on both sides and by the manner in which Trotsky made the case for military discipline—including threats to have disobedient communists executed. The opposition, however, agreed that the times of guerrilla warfare and voluntary recruitment had passed, took the need for non-communist military specialists for granted and polemised mainly against too strict military discipline—especially in the rear where the need for quick decision and unconditional subordination appeared less urgent.[20] The compromise resolution adopted after very sharp disputes[21] recognised the need for strengthening party work in the army, for a re-organisation of the General Staff and for stronger supervision of the reliability of the military specialists. It also acknowledged the valuable service rendered by their huge majority. The demand for a change of the party line on this question was explicitly rejected, and so were the mutual recriminations concerning Bonapartist tendencies.[22] The two aspects of the party line in military matters were re-emphasised a few months later in the CC's appeal to party members when Denikin was *ante portas*. Frictions between those members who, from the existing party decisions, wanted to proceed through a 'prolonged school' in military art with the specialists as teachers, and those who wished for 'ruthless suppression of treason' wherever it might threaten, were said to be inevitable. These could, however, be settled within the party organisation without affecting the party's general policy.[23]

In the spring of 1918 ten to fifteen per cent of the soldiers (at that time volunteers) were party members. The Czechoslovak attack, and the following threat from the East, were followed by a general mobilisation as well as by a special mobilisation of party members. As the first was more effective than the second, at the beginning of 1919, of half a million Red soldiers[24] 35,000 were party members. Because of the mass-recruitment of soldiers for the party which followed Denikin's threat, the number of communists serving in the army increassed from 29,540 (to whom 32,140 organised sympathisers had to be added) on October 1, 1919, to 104,238 by the end of the year. By the spring of 1920 the army party organisations had 146,000 members. This would amount to about a third of the total party membership (the same proportion is recorded from the Petrograd and Moscow party organisations).

Originally, party groups operated on the regimental scale. At the Eastern front, where most of the party's forces were concentrated, their average strength amounted to 25–30 members plus 40–45 organised sympathisers. In view of the army's special tasks and discipline, by a CC decision of October 1918 party groups were deprived of the right to supervise operations. In the operational army (as distinct from the rear organisations which remained part of their District organisations, with the usual rights) the functions of party bodies above the group level were exercised by Political Departments nominated from above. At the culmination of the Polish war, 2962 primary party organisations (now down to the company level) with 120,185 members and probationers were active in the operating army. The rear formations were served by another 3975 organisations, with 157,858 members and probationers.[25]

The military party organisations should not be regarded only as the political and moral backbone of the mass army. They made quite considerable contribution to the army's fighting strength. The large numbers of men mobilised should not obscure the fact that relatively few fighters were actually engaged on the battle fronts, and that *elite* formations played an important part on either side of the civil war. On the side of the Whites, the number of available Tsarist officers far exceeded the actual need for commanding officers; hence special 'officers' battalions, and even regiments were formed, all the soldiers of which had held commissions in the old army. They could naturally be expected to fight with greater devotion than the mobilised peasants. On the Red side, the shortage of officers led to the formation of numerous training centres. According to Gusev, less than two-fifths of the entrants were workers by social origin (but only one-fifth had higher than elementary education). In 1918, only 13 per cent of those entering the training centres had belonged to any political organisation but when graduating practically all had joined the C.P. The communists recruited during the civil war, with more regard for military merits than for social and political background, provided a new stratum of party

members, in addition to the old Bolsheviks of pre-1917 standing
and the workers and soldiers who had joined during revolutionary
upheaval. Used to command and to obey as they were, they would
provide, for many years to come, many of the middle and higher
officials—with the exception of the top ranks which were reserved
for Old Bolsheviks by the established demands on party record
(stazh). At this time whole divisions could be formed in critical
moments from amongst the pupils of the officers' training centres
and their achievements were in no way inferior to those of the
best officers' divisions existing in Denikin's and Wrangel's armies.
Apart from such special formations, it was usual during a crisis
to concentrate the party members at the decisive points of the
regiment's or division's front.

The impact made by some tens of thousand enthusiastic
fighters upon the outcome of the civil war can be realised by the
fact that at the turning point of his fate Denikin had 98,000 men
(another 43,000 lay in hospital) against 140-160,000 Red
soldiers,[26] and that Yudenich started his offensive in October 1919
with 18,500 men and that a former member of his government
regards it as quite natural that that army was routed when Trotsky
could concentrate 22,500 men against it.[27] By the infusion even
of moderate numbers of people who knew what they were fighting
for, the peasant soldiers' tendency to desert after defeat could be
prevented. On its panicky retreat in December 1918, the Third
Red Army lost half of its 35,000 men but Stalin believed he had
prevented the worst when he moved 2200 men as reinforcements,
properly vetted as to political reliability, to the decisive points.[28]
In such a war the 20,000 communists sent against Denikin after
the party recruitment of the autumn of 1919, and the 5,000 sent
directly by the Petrograd organisation to the front against
Yudenich,[29] made a substantial contribution to the defeat of the
forces which Russia's traditional ruling classes could mobilise.
It is true that mobilisation of party members for service at the
front might weaken local party organisations to such an extent
that 'detachments for special tasks' had to be formed to prevent,
or if necessary to suppress, counter-revolutionary uprisings in the
rear.[30]

On the industrial front, everything depended on the prolonged efforts of perhaps a million workers—a third of the number at the October revolution—who, in spite of starvation, had stayed at their jobs in the key industries. Party members formed only a small minority amongst those workers;[31] the major contribution which they could make to the production effort was by their example and by force of persuasion. These factors were important in the army too, but there, example concerned elementary manly virtues and persuasion aimed mainly at peasant soldiers very far from the Marxist outlook, in order to show them the general advantages of the new regime. In the factory, however, the communist had to defend measures of the government which *prima facie* contradicted traditional interests of labour. He could not show the benefits of the democratic revolution (which had been completed in October 1917) but had to emphasise the needs of the socialist transformation to come. The communist in the army was the backbone of the new state. The communists in the factory, once sufficiently numerous, would become the dynamic factor of its further development.

The importance of the example set by the communists in the production drive was emphasised in the resolution on organisational problems adopted by the Ninth Party Congress, which met on the eve of the Polish attack in spring 1920 when there was hope for peaceful reconstruction. It was necessary to explain to all party members that even the most unskilled and inconspicuous workers was responsible for party work of the highest importance and that they had no privileges whatsoever, only the obligation to be models in their production activities as well as in their everyday lives. They should be sent to the most important places, as a rule, according to their profession or specialisation. The need for politically reliable administrators was met by the ruling that every lower party organisation, on its own responsibility, should send to the higher one at least every second month a list, comprising 5–10 per cent of its members with an indication of the kind of job for promotion to which they were suitable.[32] At first, this rule was not complied with in actual practice. The Personnel Departments of the higher party organisations (*Uchrazpred*) whose functions had been emphasised already in the decisions of the VIII Party Congress[33] were concerned mainly with the mobili-

sation of party members for certain urgent campaigns. Krestinski reported to the X Congress that during the report year the
Department had carried out six 'mobilisations' for military and
another six for civilian campaigns, apart from smaller ones intended to find party members with the necessary background for the
reconstruction of the state machine in the liberated national
districts. A total of 46,154 party members (i.e. nearly a tenth
of the party's actual strength) had been redistributed from one
province to another, apart from movements within the provinces
ordered by their party committee for the purpose of agricultural
campaigns. From the start, however, the party's power to shift
its members from one place to another (apart from mobilisation
for the army) was in practice more modest than in theory. Even
in an emergency, such as the breakdown of railway transport in
spring 1920 which resulted in starvation of the towns, the Party
Congress had to be appealed to because a mere thousand Communists, instead of the 5000 demanded, had been mobilised by the
local organisations for work on the railways.[34]

Only a small minority of the party members were transferred
to permanent jobs outside their Gubernium—3226 during the
period from April 1919 to February 1920. When normal conditions returned and civil assignments had to be expanded, the
absolute figures of transfers increased, yet not in proportion to the
increase in total membership. During the second half of 1927
two thousand four hundred were transferred by the ordinary
procedure (i.e. apart from special recruitment for new tasks).
Half of those transferred in 1927 had secondary or higher education, 9.2 per cent were Old Bolsheviks,[35] both percentages being
very much higher than in the party at large. Since the Lenin
recruitment of 1924,[36] the average party member turned out to
be an ordinary man or woman following his ordinary occupation,
with the difference that he was expected to show greater civic
discipline, to make some extra effort in his job and to perform
some unpaid civic activities which satisfied ambition but greatly
reduced leisure. In the life of such an average party member
assignment to a post other than one within his normal career
would constitute quite an extra-ordinary event (except, of course,
in times of war). Literature on Soviet institutions, however, was

produced not by the average man or woman with some civic interest but by the more vocal type of persons, usually with a grievance. Complaints that *Uchrazpred* (which later was renamed the Cadres Department) rewards with promotion and punishes by removal to faraway places (possibly under the heading of promotion) according to a party member's subservience or otherwise to the party machine, are as old as the institution itself.

(b) NEW DEVELOPMENTS IN PARTY ORGANISATION

The setback in party membership which followed the demobilisation of the old army[37] was followed by a gradual increase. In speeches at the VIII Congress, in March 1919, a figure of 350,000 party members was claimed. The figure is most unlikely as Petrograd, for example, claimed no more than 12,000 members, and Moscow 15,834 (plus 4818 candidates).[38] Even the figure of 280,000 given by a comparatively early critical source[39] may have included a large number of merely nominal members. At least in Moscow, re-registrations of party-members, with the intention of eliminating the nominal members, were an annual event since 1918. In the country as a whole, such a re-registration was announced immediately after the VIII Congress, with an intention to shift out people not properly attached to the party. Since a new mobilisation of party members for the front was carried out at the same time, most of the unsuitable elements who had attached themselves to the party in power were said to have vanished under the double threat. In the instructions for re-registration party members were required to deliver their old tickets, to pay the fees due (apparently they were expected to be in arrears), to fill the questionnaires required and to present recommendations from two party members of not less than six months' standing and known to the local committee as reliable communists. Party organisations not complying with these requirements were to be dissolved. This happened, indeed, to 2500 of the 8000 primary party organisations existing in March 1919. Nearly half of the dissolved party organisations operated in villages ; in one district party membership was reduced from 2500

to 150. But even a city organisation such as that of Astrakhan
might be reduced from 3500 to 1300 members.[40] A large proportion of the loss, in particular in the towns,[38] was due to the
elimination of merely nominal members; another part to the 64,000
members reported at the VIII Congress as belonging to the Polish
and Baltic party organisations. Many of them were ordinary
political refugees who eventually settled in Russia without retaining their party membership. Yet the high proportion of completely dissolved party groups, in particular in the villages, suggests
that developments of a more fundamental nature than a mere
straightening of the party's records were involved. The instructions for the re-registration anticipated nearly all the terminology
applied during later purges (chistki): the term was already used
for progress reports. The very small number of expulsions from
the party published under this heading shows that expulsions of
people as morally unworthy of party membership were exceptions.
By far most of those who failed to get the new party-tickets were
expelled for non-attendance at party meetings or for a failure to
observe party discipline (e.g. for evading a mobilisation order).
A large proportion of the village groups dissolved may have
originated from mere renaming of groups non-Bolshevik in character (e.g. local groups of the Left Social Revolutionaries).

Already in 1919 the principles which eventually inspired the
great *chistka* of 1922 made their appearance in efforts to apply
stricter standards to ordinary workers, intellectuals and to persons
who, before joining the Bolsheviks, had been members of another
party.[41] Yet the idea of systematically restricting party membership was prevented from realisation by the Denikin threat. With
direct reference to the purge just completed it was explained that
recruitment for the party, with preference for workers and
peasants, should now be resumed. An article of Lenin's suggested a strict approach to the members by assigning them to work
involving high responsibility, of course within the limits of their
capacities.[42] The recruitment campaign was carried out at a time
when, as Lenin said, in the event of Denikin's victory the party
ticket was a sure way to the gallows. However, it resulted in
allegedly 200,000 new admissions. The available data suggest
that half of these were non-workers serving in the army who

would describe themselves as 'soldiers'.[25]   Amongst the party recruits of 1919 who remained party members by the end of 1927, workers (by social origin) formed just a narrow majority (14.9 per cent were peasants, 34.7 per cent salaried employees and intellectuals).[43]   As the recruitment figures published included at least every admission during the second half of 1919, the figures of 431,000 for January 1st, 1920, and of 585,000 for January 1st, 1921, given even by the most cautious of sources, are likely to be exaggerated. The much higher figures mentioned at the Party Congresses may be explained by the majority's reluctance to open itself to the reproach of restricting minority representation by the application of very strict standards of verification.

By the end of 1919, the party may have been slightly stronger than on the eve of October. The new recruits made up for those who had dispersed to their villages and for the losses at the front and in the territories occupied by the Whites. This overall picture covers much varied local developments. We have the precise figures[44] for Saratov, an oldstanding centre of the revolutionary movement, not unduly inflated by the war (and hence unlikely to have been greatly deflated by the post-war-dispersal) and never subject to the White terror, yet sufficiently near to the fronts to have sent a major part of the party members to the fighting armies. Of the 1001 members re-registered in Saratov · city, 6.3 per cent had joined the party before 1905, 11 per cent between 1905 and February 1917, 24.8 per cent between the two revolutions of 1917, and 55 per cent after the October revolution (these figures, it should be emphasised, concern the eve of the mass-recruitment against Denikin). Although the age-group 20-30 surely made the largest contribution to the fighting army, it comprised also nearly half of those who remained at Saratov (38.4 per cent were in the 31-45 group). As to their social origin, 20.4 per cent of the male members had been unskilled workers, 53.6 per cent skilled workers, 27.1 per cent intellectuals (a mere 9 per cent of the members—a majority of them intellectuals—were women). At the time of the re-registration, however, 68.1 per cent of all the party members were employed in state and trade organisations ; nearly 20 per cent of the total (who evidently included the higher administrative personnel, full-time

members of trade union factory committees, etc.) described themselves as being on full-time party work. 6.4 per cent of the re-
registered members had higher, 20.8 per cent secondary education; another 9.3 per cent had attended special trade schools, yet
there were even 2.6 per cent illiterates (of course attending
literacy classes). If Saratov occupied an intermediate position
between the capitals which retained a larger proportion of their
old membership and those cities which had been temporarily
occupied by the Whites, we may conclude that, on the eve of the
new recruitment drive (which doubled party membership) there
was a near-equilibrium between those who had joined the party
before, and those who had joined it after the conquest of power.
We cannot say how many of the intellectuals had a revolutionary
tradition (most of the women intellectuals apparently had) and
which was the share of the post-1917 recruits amongst those
employed in 1919 in the civil service.

Even in Moscow Province, it was established as late as
September 1918 that the District party committees, which were
small in those days, should be composed of full-time workers.[45]
According to data (covering only part of Russia) on the composition of party committees which were submitted to the Party
Conference in December 1919:[46] on the district (*uyezd*) level
the predominant age group was that between 25 and 30 (with
36.6 per cent of all the committee members), followed closely by
those of 30-35 and those of 20-25, these groups forming together
more than 80 per cent of the committee members. Less than
10 per cent were in the group 35-40, i.e. were likely to have
played any part in the 1905 revolution. Nine per cent of the
committee members were on full-time party work, nearly all the
rest in leading Soviet positions as full-time workers. A personal
union between the party and Soviet bodies appears to have been
in existence. According to their original occupation, 45 per cent
of the District Committee members had been workers, 26 per cent
salaried employees, slightly over 10 per cent members of the
village intelligentsia, and nearly 10 per cent peasants. On the
Gubernium (Provincial) level, the 25-30 age group was nearly
as well represented as on the District level but there were a mere
10.7 per cent in the 20-25; 28.6 per cent in the 30-35 group, and

18 per cent in the 35-40 group. According to their earlier occupation, 40 per cent of the committee members were workers, 38 per cent intellectuals (including students), a mere 4 per cent peasants. 33.8 per cent had joined the party before February 1917 (less than half of these before 1907), 41 per cent between February and October: a quarter of the committee members had joined the party when in power (no data about their earlier membership in other socialist parties are given). As the number of former 'professional revolutionaries' was small, the typical member of a Gubernium Committee appears to have been a worker or intellectual who joined the Bolshevik party between 1912 and October 1917. The leading positions were occupied by persons with a long revolutionary experience, including the revolution of 1905-07. It was natural for a member of a Gubernium Committee—i.e. of the second-highest link in the party hierarchy—to serve party or state in a full-time capacity. Otherwise the small committees established in those days could not have managed their business.

Already in late 1918 it was found necessary to make clear on every party ticket when the owner had joined the party[47] lest rogues should attempt to get important posts on false pretences. Such precautions were directed only against individuals. As we have seen, there were many newcomers whose devotion to the party's cause was unquestionable though their admission did not increase the proportion of members of working-class origin. The VIII Congress demanded careful scrutiny in the admission of persons who were neither workers nor peasants.[48] In the Rules adopted in December 1919,[49] the minimum duration of probationer status was given as two months for the privileged groups, six months for the rest. Lenin declared that, the party being now victorious, there was no need for more members. Applicants of non-proletarian origin should not be admitted unless their reliability could be carefully tested.[50] Lenin knew very well that unless he formulated the terms with extreme sharpness, the average intellectual without a definitely anti-Bolshevik record would presumably find two party members, possibly even old Bolsheviks, who would recommend him as worthy of admission. Naturally, people whose career might be greatly promoted by membership in the

state party would be more eager to gain admission than the
average worker.

Exaggerated estimates of the influx of careerist elements into
the party had since become current, partly because of repeated
warnings against such a possibility, partly because of the assertion of opposition groups that they represented the true
working-class interest and that, by definition, their defeat was
due to the infiltration of non-working-class elements. Further
exaggeration was made by the denunciation of the motives of
those intellectuals who collaborated with the regime by others
who persisted in boycotting it.[51] Some deterrents for careerists
or people who acted from still darker motives, were given by the
double prospect of the hangman in the event of a White victory
(the outcome of the civil war regarded as most likely in lower-
middle-class and intellectual circles) and of the Cheka's execution squad which threatened the party member involved in any
bribery or speculation.[52] Certainly, there were people who
entered the party in order to enrich themselves, directly at the
public expense or indirectly by the protection which they could
give to professional profiteers for an appropriate consideration.
And there were more who, when suddenly faced with the responsibilities of office, could hardly resist its temptations in a time of
extreme scarcity. The small number of reliable party members
with administrative qualifications secured quick promotion to the
careerist. Even a few thousand of this kind, connected by private
channels with some ten thousands of profiteers and simple thieves
could do immense harm, even more to the prestige of the new
regime than to its material resources. So it was most natural to
mobilise public opinion against them and to treat them, when
caught, by the only means which could work as a deterrent in
times when the very survival of the regime was at a stake. To
some extent the intensity of the official denunciation of the
dangers threatening from the careerist and the person aiming at
becoming a *nouveau riche* was conditioned by the consciousness
that precisely this type of person had brought down the Jacobin
dictatorship in Thermidor, 1794. In any case, such publicity
might exercise some healthy effects on the chances of promotion,
within the party hierarchy, of people of non-working-class origin

who had joined the party after October 1917 and whose personality was not above suspicion.

The success of these policies was evident 20 years later when
in the trials of the oppositionists—the less outstanding of whom
had joined the party just during the civil war—in only very few
cases (most of them from Central Asia) was non-political misbeha-
viour in the defendants' early careers introduced into the
'amalgam'. The NKVD used whatever information it had on
such occasions, and the defendant with such a record usually
behaved in the preliminary investigation in such a way that he
formed quite a suitable candidate—from the prosecution's point
of view—for public trial. The remarkable fact about the information about corruption within the CP collected from all sides,
including the party itself in the diverse stages of its development,
is just its paucity if measured by Russia's size and traditions of
administration. Yet, while the official warnings might increase
vigilance against the less desirable type of non-working-class
recruit, they could not prevent the state party from reflecting the
social structure of the state, with some bias in favour of the
workers and the left-wing of the intelligentsia. Of course, the
exclusion of the capitalist and feudal elements still persisted.
There is no reason to question the statement of the Workers'
Opposition, in its appeal to Comintern in 1921, that the party
had just about 40 per cent members of working-class status.
For many years this percentage remained constant.

Although individual factory organisations were already in
existence, the Rules of 1917 still regarded the local committee
as the basic unit (as had been the norm in the underground).
According to the Rules of 1919, however, the local organisations
presented combinations of nuclei (groups) formed in the individual enterprises, offices, military formations, etc. At least so far
as Moscow is concerned, the transition to the new organisational
basis appears to have taken place during the second half of 1918.[45]
The links of hierarchical subordination downwards and of democratic control upwards, connected these primary organisations
through the local, district and Gubernium committees with the
party's central institutions. The party's representatives in non-
party institutions such as the Soviets or trade unions were bound

to obey the instructions of the corresponding Party Committee but had the right to demand a reconsideration of instructions with which they disagreed. The second decision, however, was definitive (Art. 62). This was a mere regulation of relationships which were as old as the institutions of Bolshevik M.P.s and Bolshevik ministers.[53]

Party and State functions could hardly be separated. At the very start, the Bolshevik members of the steering committee of the coalition government (Lenin, Stalin and Trotsky) also formed an unofficial policy-making body within the Central Committee. All-Russian Soviet Congresses offered convenient opportunities to convene Party Conferences without keeping the leading Communists longer than was necessary away from their local jobs. The VIII Party Conference, which met in December 1919, adopted the Party Rules, the outlines of which had been decided in May as well as the directives given to the communist faction to the VII Soviet Congress. In the formulation of these directives the CC was outvoted by the opposition, yet Lenin advised his fellowers not to bring their case again before the full Soviet Congress. Indeed, they withdrew their motion.[54]

In the period of the civil war, the Central Committee was the actual policy-making body. Fifteen members and eight substitutes ('candidates') were elected at the VII Congress, nineteen plus twelve at the IX Party Congress. The strength of the policy-making body was thus about the same as it was in later days under a different description (the Politburo, and from 1952 till 1966 the Presidium of the CC). Also the broader forum (Party Congress or Party Conference) before 1920 was no more numerous than the present Plenary Meetings of the CC, which however meet more frequently.

The composition of the Central Committee was conditioned by its function as a supreme political council. Outstanding leaders had a moral claim to be elected and excellent service by a person who fulfilled the qualities of a party leader would be rewarded by election to the CC. But in cases of political disagreements the Congress would ensure that such a group be safely put into a minority by suitable demotions. In cases of very severe attacks against the party line even a well-known leader such as Kamenev

11

might be removed from the Central Committee for years, without any detriment, however, to his occupation of most responsible posts in the Government. On the other hand, an opposition leader such as Bukharin, whose removal from the Central Committee was undesirable because he was an excellent party propagandist, might by an honourable mission abroad be kept safely away. His zealous fellow-factionists on the other hand would get suitable assignments where high administrative or military responsibilities would detract their attention from the game of theses, counter-theses and factionalism of all kinds. Resignation from the Central Committee because of political disagreements was regarded as something near to a split.[55] The Party Congress itself would see that its political attitudes were properly reflected in the new CC and would, in most cases, re-elect the outstanding leaders even if it had to teach them some hard lessons. Not being re-elected to the CC implied no political stigma, as there were plenty of instances of return.[56] In later periods continuous failure to be re-elected presumably signified the unsuitability of a leader of the underground or an emigre literator to play a leading part in the new conditions. Apart from diplomatic assignments new party functions especially in the Central Control Commission were available so that long-standing service would be recognised without any special demand for administrative capacities or adaptability to changing political conditions. At a lower level, Lenin demanded that a Provincial Committee, such as that of Moscow, should include every healthy tendency existing within the party, whether it had already formed itself into a definite trend or was in the process of formation. The whole group, however, should be capable of working together in good comradeship on the basis of the decisions of the conference.[57]

A body supposed to include important leaders from all over the country could not conduct the party's everyday business. At the VI Congress, when the Rules of 1917 were adopted and the memories of the underground were still fresh, meetings taking place every second month appeared as the maximum which could be prescribed to the Central Committee. For its current work it might elect from its midst a 'narrower CC'.[58] Under this heading the Politburo made its first appearance in the days of October.[59] The concept that it was essentially a list of CC members who *had* to be present when important decisions were taken survived even when the institution was stabilised. The VIII Congress in March 1919 ruled that all CC members not belonging to the Politburo, when present in Moscow, were entitled to attend its meetings with a consultative voice[60] (this provision was not retained in the final text of the Rules adopted in December of the same year, but the practice continued for much longer).[61] With the party in power and its leaders busy in the two capitals, or at the headquarters of fronts which were not more than 600 miles away from Moscow, it appeared possible in 1919 to have plenary meetings of the CC twice a month on days fixed in advance and to institutionalise those already existing informal bodies which, in the government of a huge country, made policy decisions everyday. Since the end of the coalition government and its steering committee, the composition of these bodies had depended upon who happened to be on the spot. On various occasions even diverse informal bodies made their appearance.[62]

Trotsky's and Stalin's military activities appear to have given rise to Ossinski's complaint at the VIII Congress that Lenin and Sverdlov did most of the work together without consulting other CC members. Even more significant than this complaint of an oppositionist are the arguments in defence of the CC by Sosnovski and Avanesov. Were party members coming to Moscow on State business not benefitted by having a talk with a first class leader such as Sverdlov and did the leading party organisers not take part in the specialist congresses of communists working in the diverse fields of administration? In accordance with his general outlook, Ossinski would have liked an inner cabinet to control party policies.[63] The Congress, however, established definite *party* bodies of five members each to conduct the CC's current political and organisational business respectively. Lenin, Stalin, Trotsky, Kamenev and Krestinski (with Bukharin, Zinoviev and Kalinin as candidates) sat on the first Politburo. Stalin and Krestinski (the latter soon became Party Secretary) headed the Orgburo, too. The evident purpose of this arrangement was to make them responsible for carrying out the agreed policy by suitable assignments and redistribution of the available party workers. By 1920 the machine of central party leadership was working in a fairly regular way. According to Krestinski's report to the X Congress,[64] during the preceding eleven months the full CC had met, on the average, thrice every month. In addition, the Politburo held six and the Orgburo nine to ten meetings per month. A total of 5500 issues appeared on the order papers of those 189 meetings. Only a few of them may have been really discussed and most must have been passed in a very formal way, *nemine contradicente*, by what by now had become the established machinery for supervising legislation and adminstration as well as the assignments of party members to senior posts.

The actual work of party administration was now concentrated in the hands of the Secretariat. By May 1919 its staff had increased from the five people available a year before to fifteen but since the VIII Congress had appointed Krestinski, a member of both the Politburo and Orgburo, as Party Secretary, the staff increased to eighty persons by December 1919. In the spring of 1920, two more members of the CC (who also sat on the Orgburo), Preobrazhenski and Serebryakov, were appointed secretaries of the CC. On the eve of the X Party Congress the staff had increased to 602 members (most of them were, of course, office workers).

With the expansion of the central party machine, it became increasingly specialised. From 1918 Stankina had no more to report than a table put up by Alexandra Kollontay, who specialised on propaganda amongst women, and the preparations for the foundation congress of *Komsomol,* the communist youth organisation. But when the Secretariat was re-organised under Krestinski, departments for information, for organisation and instruction of lower organisations, for inspection, party schools, distribution of party workers (*uchrazpred*), finances, and for secret work (*spetsotdel*) were established. In July followed a department for organising the work in the villages, in September a proper department for work amongst women. Strangely enough, a department so conspicuous during the following period as that for Agitation and Propaganda was established as late as mid-1920.[65] The progress made by the establishment of a central office with direct and regular connections to the localities may be measured by the fact that as late as May 1919 it had been found necessary to publish in the CC's *Izvestiya* very detailed instructions to Gubernia and District Committees on the organisation of military formations by the political departments, on the release from normal party propaganda and administrative work of party workers better used at the front, and on the rights and duties of the CC representatives sent to the Provinces to direct the mobilisation. (On arrival at his destination, the representative had to convene a meeting of party workers to arrange necessary measures, but he was also responsible for appointing agents in the districts who would act on his behalf.) Such a tendency of the CC to act directly, using the *Gubernium* Committees as mere auxiliaries, was hardly avoidable since its Inspection Department had just fifteen permanent workers other than the three members of its *collegium*. The only activity of the Instruction-Organisation Department was the drafting of the new Rules.

A student who has the opportunity to compare present methods of lobbying amongst the more influential party organisations with the earlier ones would probably discover strong analogies. The present practice of having the main party organisations represented in the Supreme party body,[66] which in any case is a post-Stalin development, was only foreshadowed by having part of the Central Committee operating in Petrograd. But consultation of the leaders of the major party organisations, at least in cases of disagreements within the CC, was institutionalised. If a disagreement proved so serious that it threatened party unity,[67] or in the event of a strong opposition amongst the rank and file (as on the military question) the decision would lie with a Party Congress. In the first case, the Congress decision would be final. In the second a compromise would be sought with every important trend in party opinion, and re-adjustment of the relationships among the leaders would take place. It was taken for granted that members of the Central Committee, unless they had approached the Congress with a demand to settle their internal disagreements, would act as a corporate body and defend each other against outside attacks. Differences of opinion would be thrashed out behind the closed doors of the committee which drafted the compromise resolution. Trotsky's later attempts to make political capital out of the fact that Lenin and Stalin behaved according to the convention[21] illustrates the outsider's failure to understand its importance. It was also Trotsky who, according to his own record,[68] on the issue of signing the Riga Peace Treaty with Poland resorted to an outvoted CC member's *ultima ratio* at a moment when the majority was already reconsidering its position. The incident may have added to the bitterness with which Lenin treated the disagreements on the trade union question which were more suitable for public discussion.

If not the rank and file then the middle ranks of the party hierarchy, who claimed to speak on its behalf, had ample opportunities to discuss the party line. Alternative policies could be, and were, advocated at the annual Party Congresses. Party Conferences whose rights differed from those of the Congresses only in that they could not re-elect the Central Committee, met in the intervals. (This practice was formalised in point 26 of the Rules of 1922—point 26 of the Rules of 1919 had even demanded quarterly convention of the Party Conferences, which proved to be impracticable.) None of the frequent discussions, even where the status of individual party leaders was involved, could affect the fact that Russia was governed by the Central Committee. But the appearance, as a fairly regular phenomenon, of organised opposition against individual aspects of centralism served as a counterweight to the natural implications of the war emergency.

(c) ADMINISTRATORS AND TRADE UNIONIST *VS.* THE CENTRAL COMMITTEE

Retrospectively, the fair freedom of expression allowed even during the crises of the civil war to dissenters has been explained, firstly by the common danger which secured co-operation amongst the supporters of the revolution and secondly by the absence of a new bourgeoisie which might use them to achieve political power. From the sociological standpoint, however, it is clear that the Bolshevik party itself contained many non-Bolshevik, in particular syndicalist, elements whose co-operation had to be purchased by their having a say in the party's affairs. Their legitimate criticism of grievances was even regarded as a valuable check on the current misuse of bureaucratic power. There was no lack of groups interested in making the most of these complaints : the old-Russian evil of local monopolists in power (in Peter I's days they had been called *Velmozhi*) provoked permanent friction. To this was now added the trade union leaders' belief that 'their' industries should be controlled by themselves. An organised opposition which would cherish continuity with its predecessors belonged to the realm of a Party Congress or Conference. Two years were still to pass before, in changed circumstances, Lenin found organised opposition incompatible with the party's survival.[69]

The recognised and loyal oppositions of the civil war period fed on feelings very similar to those upon which those denounced during the NEP period operated. In theory, at least, Soviet Russia was a 'proletarian' State. But, to the average worker the non-proletarian army officer or manager is much more visible an object of class opposition than the vested interests in a capitalist State. The 'bourgeois' specialists working for the Soviet government and the very policy of employing them, became the current object of attack. There were all kinds of specialist-intellectuals devoted to the revolution but incapable of bearing the party's internal discipline. For instance, there were officers and engineers who simply loved their country and their job, ordinary family fathers who took their salaries from whoever happened to rule (without identifying themselves with the rulers of the day to such an extent that they would endanger themselves in case of a counter-revolution). Then there were people who were incapable of understanding that their tasks had changed with the regime, and also some real traitors and saboteurs. Accordingly, there was a complicated mixture of correct and incorrect statements in the platform of every opposition. The party leaders correspondingly differed in their treatment of such an amalgam. Some leaders listened to the opposition's criticism, as indeed some of the instances they quoted were scandalous. Others dismissed such criticism with the observation that these were inevitable, though deplorable by-products of a healthy development. These bodies would then be designated as involuntary tools of bourgeois influences which would disintegrate the

proletarian dictatorship. Lenin was strong enough to keep
a balance and yet be firm against the oppositions. As he
died in time to become an authority to which the opponents of
his successor appealed,[70] he was even allowed to enter the records
as a person who had *not* 'betrayed the revolution'. Yet all the
basic criticisms of the opposition, and also the party's reply to
them, had already grown in his time. In principle, these issues
formed a mere continuation of the cleavage with the left-wing
Communists of 1918.

During the year 1919 when the White threat was at its
highest, opposition to the basic principles of the new State was
a mere overtone in disputes about the practical arrangements.
This holds true of the 'military opposition' at the VIII Party
Congress as well as of the dispute on administrative questions
which started at that Congress and concluded in the same year
at the VII Soviet Congress and the VIII Party Conference, which
was held concurrently with it. The use of agricultural specialists—in some cases even former estate owners—in the administration of the State-farms offered the opposition an obvious point
of attack. Sapronov went so far as to denounce management of
economic or administrative institutions by individuals as contradicting the proletarian character of the State which demanded the
inclusion of as many proletarians as possible in directing bodies.
Ossinski even feared bureaucratic infection of trade unionists by
their collaboration with bourgeois specialists in the administrative
centres (*glavki*). At the same time he warned against the
dangers involved in the transfer of factory management to
workers who quite recently had been peasants (perhaps even
kulaks) and might plunder State property.[71] No such arguments
could affect the impact of the needs of war upon the organisation
of the economy, but lasting results came out of the disagreements
between the administrative centres and the Executive Committees
of the Provincial Soviets (*Gubispolkomi*), which backed the
opposition. (The third party to the dispute, the village Soviets,
remained in the background although they had as many grievances
against the *Gubispolkomi* as the latter had against the national
centres. Kalinin maintained that transfer of power to the *Gubispolkomi* would even strengthen Soviet bureaucracy.)[72] During

the discussion on whether special city Soviets should be established in towns where the higher (District or *Gubernium*) Soviet
Executive Committees were located a delegate remarked that,
if this decision was left to the *Gubispolkomi,* there would be no
city-Soviet whatsoever.[73] At the preceding (VIII) Party Congress
a delegate had explained these conflicts by a predominance of the
peasant interest in the *Gubispolkomi* while the workers dominated
in the city-Soviets.[74] The first half of this statement is questionable but it was surely true that the industrial cities were the only
places where the workers could make their impact upon Soviet
government.

The opposition's stand in the discussion at the VII Soviet
Congress was strong. Vladimirski, speaking for the majority of
the CC, did not defend the *glavki* against the advocates of decentralisation. Even Lenin avoided fighting out the issue as a matter
of principle.[75] The opposition achieved a compromise which, as
a principle, has survived up to our days. According to this
principle of 'double subordination', Soviet Departments are
subordinate both to their own Soviet and to the corresponding
Departments of higher Soviets up to the Ministry. If they receive
from the latter an order which appears infeasible they may
protest through the Presidium of their own Soviet to the higher
links of the Soviet hierarchy, without stopping the execution of
the order.[76] (It is true, in the working of such compromises all
depends upon the spirit in which they are applied.)

The opposition, however, failed when it attacked the principle
of party leadership from the standpoint of the Soviet organs. At
the VIII Party Congress Ossinski suggested a fusion of the *sovnarkom* (i.e. the Government) with the Presidium of VTsIK (i.e.
the Supreme Soviet body). He argued that the duplication of
their functions was unnecessary, yet attacked, in substance, the
CC's habit of correcting Government decisions through the cons-
titutionally higher body. He suggested that twelve leading
members of the CC should be delegated to the new ruling State
organ in order to exercise, in their capacity as cabinet ministers,
the functions of the Politburo. The rest of the CC might be left
to manage the party machine (as an Orgburo). Zinoviev
answered, quite correctly, that the adoption of Ossinski's plan

would abolish the leading function of the CC in relation to the Government.[77] The adopted Congress Resolution envisaged further development of the functions of the Presidium of VTsIK.[78] At the IX Party Congress, Trotsky replied to the opposition's complaints that the Congress was free to elect whatever CC it found fit but that no CC could lead the party without controlling all the existing State organisations, including VTsIK.[79]

The advocates of separation of the State organisation from the party, or at least from its CC, described themselves as Democratic Centralists—implying that the first half of this official description of the party's structure was not taken seriously enough by the party leaders. It is not necessary here to discuss the question whether the *Gubispolkomi,* headed by a weak government deprived of direct association with the party organisation, would have made for more democracy. Clearly they would not have been able to cope with Russia's tasks in peace and war. Within the party, the Democratic Centralism group enjoyed little support outside the organisations of the Ukraine. A much more serious opposition to the party leadership occurred, on the eve of the IX Party Congress. It actually amounted to a revolt of the communist trade union leaders against the CC.

In view of the catastrophic transport situation the CC had established a Transport Commission with dictatorial powers[80] under Trotsky. To strengthen its position, the party organisations working on the railway lines were taken out of their normal connection with the District organisations and concentrated under a special Transport Department of the CC, analogous to the Military Department under which the Political Commissaries and the party organisations in the army worked. Trotsky spoke of the change in terms of an emergency measure which might become superfluous within a few months,[81] but it was feared that it might be repeated in one key industry after the other. Stalin, indeed, had established a Political Department for the Donets Coal Industry in view of its breakdown.[82] A lot of talk about the militarisation of labour was abroad in connection with the formation of labour armies (in itself hardly a controversial measure).[83]

The trade unionists' reactions varied to the supposed threat. An extremist wing, led by Shlyapnikov, demanded that the

necessary centralisation of economic life should be effected by
concentration of management in the hands of the unions. The
communist groups in the trade union centres claimed control of
its groups working in the local trade unions and of the party's
factory nuclei, i.e. of the party's whole industrial organisation
(according to existing Party Rules, every party group was subordinated to the party organisation of its area, and all party groups
in national institutions directly to the Central Committee).[84]
With an evident intention of facing the IX Party Congress with
a consolidated trade union position, the Trade Union Congress
was convened for a date immediately preceding the opening of the
former. The party's CC had to intervene in order to have it
delayed until after the Party Congress.[85] The longstanding protests against the appointment of specialists as managers with
decisive power were revived. A majority of the communist trade
unionists demanded collegiate administration of industry, from top
to bottom.[86] The Moscow Provincial Committee explained that
socialism implied overcoming the division of labour and that only
the collegiate system enabled the workers to alternate in the
exercise of managerial functions. As against these outbreaks of
Utopianism, Lenin, supported by a large majority of the IX
Congress, upheld his position of 1918.[87] He reiterated that the
class character of a society depended not upon the method of
management but upon the ownership of the means of production.
The task of introducing not only a small *elite* but broader strata
of workers and peasants into the administration was closely
connected with that of learning from the available, non-proletarian
specialists. It was a great pity that so few of them were available.
Lenin hit the opposition's weakest point when he denied that
management by collegia of a few trade union appointees implied
an increase in the say which the average worker had in the
factory.[88] New forms of social organisation, including the socialist democracy demanded by the opposition, could not be realised
before large scale industry was developed. This implied the need
to catch up with the organisational achievements of more advanced
nations.[89] Having gone so far in the statement of unpopular
truths, Lenin made short shrift with the opposition's complaints
about the interrelations between Orgburo and Politburo, the

alleged banishment of its supporters to assignments far away, etc., etc. The party could not carry out its policies unless it appointed capable people to key posts.[90]

The theses on trade union organisation which, on Trotsky's report, were adopted by the IX Party Congress described the Soviet regime as 'the broadest organisation, concentrating all the social power of the working class'. With the development of the communist consciousness and creative activities of the masses, the trade unions must gradually become auxiliary organs of the Soviet State, not the other way round. Trade unions participated in the organisation of production in all stages, from the Factory Committee of the Supreme Council of National Economy, but were not entitled to interfere with the management. Their participation in the latter consisted in the suggestion, but not election, of suitable candidates for managerial jobs, especially from amongst the workers.[91] Management by individuals was the desirable aim. As long as the necessary number of managers who combined the political and technical qualifications required was not available, diverse combinations of skilled engineers with working-class activists, or even small collegia were to be admitted. In every case, decisions arrived at by a collegium should be carried out under the command of an individual manager.[92]

(d) THE BREAKDOWN OF WAR COMMUNISM AND THE TRANSITION TO THE NEW ECONOMIC POLICY

The impact made by the civil war upon communist thought is seen by the conclusions drawn from their military occupations by the two outstanding leaders between whom, eventually, Lenin's succession was to be contested. Trotsky felt that military discipline and assignment of priorities, which had brought victory in war, would also solve the problems of reconstruction, at least in its first difficult stages. The use for urgent industrial tasks of armies which still had to be kept in readiness during the interval between Denikin's defeat and the Polish invasion was hardly controversial. However, there arose problems, which to some extent anticipated those of China's 'Great Leap' of 1959, when Trotsky regarded the use of Labour Armies for timber collection not as an issue of mere technical expediency but as a means 'to show the *muzhik* how to work'.[93]   Soon Stalin was forced to say, however, that the Labour Army would be of little help in coal production unless the professional miners' working discipline was improved.[94]   Already on the eve of the IX Party Congress, Smirnov, one of the leaders of the Democratic Centralism group, explained in Pravda[95] that militarisation, though helpful in disciplining the peasant soldier even for civic tasks, could not solve the problem of skilled industrial work.   Trotsky was prepared to introduce some material incentives by granting bonuses to units doing exemplary work but argued against Smirnov's thesis that free wage labour was necessarily superior in its productivity to a labour force working under strict discipline.   He saw similarities between the problem of desertion from the army and the workers' escape from the starving towns.[96]   On the Central Committee's insistence, Trotsky included in his thesis on Urgent Economic Tasks a paragraph which emphasised 'the unity of the economic plan' and enumerated the priorities.[97]   At the Congress it was noticed that similar plans might be applied in any country whose economies were disrupted by the war.

Stalin's theoretical conclusions from his civil war experience were first summarised, in the summer of 1921, in the draft for a pamphlet which was never written[98]—perhaps because these conclusions appeared to his colleagues in the Politburo more outspoken in the revision of traditional Marxist concepts than might be good for the Comintern, perhaps simply because he took too many leaves from Smirnov's book.   (The draft, however, formed the basis of *Leninism,* written three years later.)   Although the term is not used, politics is interpreted as an art, comparable to military art. Marxist theory analyses the objective aspects of the development of society.   It has to be supplemented by an analysis of the subjective contribution to that development made by the conscious and planned behaviour of the organised proletarian vanguard, i.e. by strategy which deals with the long-term, and by tactics which deal with the short-term, aspects of the art of politics.   These concepts are illustrated by examples from Bolshevik tactics which are treated as examples of typical behaviour, just as in a military textbook.   However, as distinct from military art which deals with forces already organised and subject to military discipline, the art of politics deals with an organised minority which has to motivate much broader masses of people to take decisions in line with its general aims. In the process of following such courses of behaviour the masses become convinced of the correctness of those aims. There is no suggestion that the aims themselves may develop during the process. The October revolution is treated in its international connections but, as already in 1917,[99] the proletarian revolution in Russia is regarded as stronger than that in the West because of its close association with the peasants' struggle for emancipation from the feudal yoke.[100]

Stalin's draft, which dealt with long-term concepts of communist strategy, slumbered for years in his desk. Trotsky, however, happened to be in the centre of the next conflict which occurred between his Transport Department and the Union of the Workers of the Waterways in the autumn of 1920. At that time, Lenin's group began to doubt whether the crisis of industry could be overcome by Trotsky's programme of militarisation. The dimensions and consequences of the debate showed that much more than emergency solutions in a critical field of economics and a personality specially proud of military discipline were involved.

The dispute exploded in early November 1920, at the time of the V Trade Union Conference. The Party's CC demanded 'a most energetic and systematic struggle against the degeneration of centralism and military methods of work into bureaucratism, high-handedness, red tape and fussy guardianship over the trade unions'. The Political Administration of Transport should be abolished since the special conditions which had required the application of such extraordinary methods had ceased to exist. Trotsky reacted with the demand for a 'shaking-up' of the trade union leadership. The communist delegates to the Trade Union Congress endorsed the CC's resolution and made a further contribution of their own in the shape of Rudzutak's Theses on the Tasks of the Trade Unions in Production.[101] The preoccupation of trade unions with the organisation of production and the duplication of managerial functions between themselves and the State's economic organs were described as temporary necessities, conditioned by the weakness of economic administration. In future the trade unions, while still participating in the drawing up of plans and the organisation of competent management, should devote their main attention to the strengthening of labour discipline, to production propaganda and to increasing the workers' interest in the full utilisation of labour power and of technical resources. Wage rates and bonuses should be closely connected with the fulfilment of the production plan. In susbtance, Rudzutak's Theses already defined that attitude to the trade union problem at which the party has again arrived in our days, after the intermezzo of NEP and the distortions of the Stalin period as a victim of which Rudzutak fell, like so many of his antagonists.

Lenin hesitated to open a dispute against Trotsky because he regarded a split in the party leadership as harmful. Eventually, however, he came to the conclusion that Trotsky's dictatorial approach to the trade unionists threatened a split between the party and its working-class support. Open argument was the lesser evil.[102] Hence, he and his closest collaborators sided with Rudzutak, supporting the latter's suggestion of bonuses for plan-fulfilment. Lenin stated later that the actual subject of the trade union discussion had been a problem eventually solved by the NEP although the participants in the discussion had not been conscious of it. Indeed, bonuses could not encourage good work unless there was something on the market to buy. Stalin explained the struggle mainly by Trotsky's failure to realise the difference between enforced discipline as necessary in the army and voluntary discipline as characteristic of the working-class. Trotsky had provoked such criticism by describing the very statement of the difference as a Menshevik deviation.[103] Not only at the time of the events but when writing his memoirs, Trotsky believed that he had represented the economic interest in high production as against Lenin's and his friends' preoccupation with strengthening the mass-basis of the regime.[104] He did not consider the possibility that his opponents might have regarded the military-administrative method as inferior even from the economic point of view.

At the CC meeting of November 9, Bukharin established a 'buffer' group—combining a majority of the CC—to blunt Lenin's attacks against Trotsky. There was much confusion on the basic issue whether, and for what reasons, a specific representation of the workers' interests against the workers' State was necessary (an *a priori* refusal to recognise this question as legitimate was the basis of Trotsky's approach). At first Lenin answered the question by stating that the Soviet State was not just a workers' State but a State of the workers and peasants. It followed that the workers' sectional interest might need special representation against that State. After having realised the implications of this statement (which, indeed, might lead to the position taken up by the Opposition in the middle twenties), Lenin corrected himself and explained the need for a specific representation of the workers' interest by the fact that the Soviet State was a workers' State established in a country with a peasant majority, and handicapped by bureaucratic distortions.[105]   In this form, the statement has entered Soviet ideology although Soviet leaders were not always fond of quoting it.

Meanwhile, what had started as a dispute amongst leading communists and trade unionists about the appropriate relationship between State and trade unions, had turned into the nearest approach to a revolt of the rank and file against the party leaders. At the Moscow Regional Party Conference of November 20, 1920, factionalism had come to such lengths that the two factions met in different halls and proportional representation in the Party Committees was demanded. Lenin, addressing the Conference, still maintained that the Opposition contained many healthy elements and criticised many actual shortcomings. But he insisted that the specific Opposition line had to be brought to an end.[106] He regarded Trotsky's refusal to collaborate in a settlement of the dispute by negotiation within the Commission established by the CC and his insistence on open discussion and decision by the next Party Congress, as a disruption of the party's working unity. Bukharin added to the confusion by suggesting that the trade unions' nominations for economic appointments should have binding force. Lenin denounced this as a transfer of economic control to the trade unions, 90 per cent of whose members were non-communists.[107] Although Bukharin's syndicalist excursion remained an episode, syndicalism proper found its opportunity to erupt.

At the meeting of the Central Committee on December 7, Trotsky voted for a resolution of the 'buffer group' so as to form a majority against Lenin's suggestion to dissolve the Transport Commission immediately. The point was reached where a settlement of the differences within the walls of the CC had become impossible, and a public discussion was opened. Soon it assumed such dimensions that Lenin spoke of a party crisis and of a threatening split between the proletarian party and the masses of the proletariat.[108] The Petrograd organisation declared its solidarity with Lenin and Zinoviev, but soon the Moscow organisation, that old leftist stronghold, reacted. To the theses of Trotsky and Bukharin further platforms of diverse opposition groups were added. The Democratic Centralism group, led by Sapronov, went to the length of describing the difference between Zinoviev (i.e. Lenin) and Trotsky as being merely that between 'two trends within the same group of ex-militarisers of the economy' and of demanding for the trade unions the right to nominate the VSNKh. 'The Workers' Opposition', under Shlyapnikov, demanded transfer of the control of economic life to a 'Producers' Congress' based upon the trade unions. From this platform it was not a very long way to the demand for 'Soviets without communists' which since long had been the banner of all those who wished to preserve some achievements of the October revolution but to dispense with the party's rule[109] and which, within a few weeks, was to inspire the Kronstadt mutiny. Lenin reproached the factions within the party for their competition in offering the maximum of concessions to non-party people.[110] Precisely in order to avoid it, he had refrained so long from opening the discussion. Yet since the summer of 1920 the peasants of the Tambov-Gubanium, one with a fairly high component of *kulaks,* were in a state of insurrection under quite formal Social Revolutionary leadership and under slogans such as 'for free trade', 'for free Soviets'. In February 1921 the movement, which has been greatly overlooked in favour of the more spectacular events of Kronstalt, reached its culmination with 30,000 participants; after the introduction of the New Economic Policy it became weaker but was defeated, since mid-May, only by major military operations.

While the political framework of war-communism was

12

exploding, its economic basis had to be dropped. Lenin, who was not happy about the introduction of the Tax in Kind, explained it, three months later,[111] by the bad harvest of 1920 which had prevented the fulfilment of the plan of grain collections, and hence also of the industrial production plan. A mere four million tons of grain, instead of the seven million envisaged by the plan, had been collected. It was still more than at the corresponding time of 1920 but, as the war was over, the extreme exertions demanded from the people in 1919-20 could not be repeated. Two and a half million tons were already distributed by February 1, 1921. Then, as coal supplies from the Donets basin had come to a standstill, even coal for Petrograd had to be bought abroad so far as this was possible in the circumstances.[112]   On February 8 Lenin drafted a Politburo resolution on replacement of the grain levies from the peasants by a tax in kind, with freedom for the peasants to sell the surplus in the local markets.[113]   The issue was decided in the Politburo on February 19, and in the Plenary Meeting of the CC on February 24-25.[114]   Already on February 12 the grain requisitioned in the Tambov-Gubanium had been stopped. On the order paper of the CC meeting appeared also 'the situation in Moscow' ; in Petrograd a serious strike-movement was in full swing. The strikers' demands included that for the right to trade freely with the villages. The Kronstadt mutiny, which in historical mythology is described as the cause of the transition to NEP, was no more than one in a chain of similar events. In particular, its impact helped to make the argument on the introduction of the Tax in Kind at the X Party Congress a near formality.

On February 28 the crew of the battleship *Petropavlovsk* adopted a decision which, on the following day, was submitted to the vote of a mass-meeting. The party organisation in Kronstadt, dominated as it was by a 'fleet opposition' analogous to the 'workers' opposition' influential in Moscow, Petrograd and other places, offered no resistance.[115]   The preceding campaign of the Petrograd party organisation against the Political Administration of the Baltic Fleet, i.e. against Trotsky's machine, may have contributed to the development of the radical opposition movement.[116]   This would seem analogous to the Hungarian revolt of

October 1956, which was promoted by the criticism of the Stalin regime by the XX Party Congress. However, the analogy should not be driven too far since Kronstadt, 1921, kept on a platform at least theoretically compatible with the preservation of a Soviet regime, though not of party rule, while the Hungarian revolt of 1956, within a similar period of success, had already gone to the length of establishing a coalition government with bourgeois parties, violent destruction of communist party organisations and appeal for Western help. The Kronstadt sailors' demands included abolition of the preference rations enjoyed by party officials and specialists, which was already envisaged by the IX Party Conference in September 1920,[117] and freedom of economic activity of the peasantry. It was possible to negotiate on *these* points, but the party could not accept demands such as that for full freedom for non-communist parties and abolition of its privileged position in politics. At a meeting on March 2, the delegates of the town and naval establishments installed a Temporary Revolutionary Committee, pending the re-election of a Soviet no longer dominated by the communists. In these conditions, an effort of Kalinin's to bring about a peaceful settlement was bound to fail. Corresponding to the peasant basis of the movement, anarchist and Left Social Revolutionary influences were prominent. Large-scale publicity from foreign anti-Bolshevik sources soon came forward and there was no lack of counter-revolutionary minded naval specialists, to help in the defence of the stronghold. The party had to bring the adventure to an end before the ice broke and a counter-revolutionary stronghold at the very doors of Petrograd could be established with foreign support. In order to make clear that the party was united in its resolution not to allow its internal disagreements to help the forces of counter-revolution, the delegates of the X Party Congress, many oppositionists amongst them, headed the columns which under heavy losses advanced over the ice of the Finnish gulf against the mutineers.

Six months after the introduction of the Tax in Kind, when addressing the Moscow Regional Party Conference, Lenin remembered the days of Brest Litovsk. In the present economic war, as in the former military one, the dangers involved in any retreat

had to be faced: the alternative was capitulation.[118]   In appearance, the demands of the Kronstadt sailors and workers had only
meant a minor shift in the policies of the Soviet regime—introduction of free trade.   In fact, however, the non-party elements who
raised such demands served as a bridge over which the White
counter-revolutionaries made their appearance.[119]   The implication was that the party must firmly hold on to its monopoly of
power.   Any sharing of it, even with groups which had supported
it during the civil war, might provide the thin end of the wedge
by which the achievements of the October revolution would be
lost.

The first application of such an analysis concerned the
Mensheviks and Social Revolutionaries who as late as 1920 had
enjoyed considerable freedom.[120]   Now they were described as
helping mutineers and White Guards.   Their appropriate place
was in prison or in exile: the government would not prevent them
from leaving the country.   But it would label them as 'non-party'.
And if the usual conferences with the non-party people should
serve the ends of anti-Bolshevik elements, these consultations
must be replaced by other methods of testing the mood of the
masses.[121]

The real danger, however, lay within the party's own ranks
where all political life was now concentrated.   A split amongst
the Jacobins—the Thermidorians using even leftist slogans—had
brought about their downfall.   Lenin warned the 'workers' opposition' of the demagogy implied in its very description.   In the
economic field, he said, the situation demanded concessions
to the peasant; in the political field, prevention of any further
organised opposition within the party's ranks.[122]   The X Congress
defined its attitude to the Opposition in two motions, 'On Party
Unity' and 'On the Anarcho-Syndicalist Deviation', adopted after
private meetings in which representatives of all the trends participated.[123]   The first of these motions explained the need for party
unity and truly comradely relationships between party members
in view of the increased vacillations of the lower-middle-class
population and of the use made by the Petrograd Mensheviks, on
the eve of the Kronstadt insurrection, of the disagreements with
the party.   Even before that, discussion on trade unions within

the party factions had arisen, i.e. groups operating on a special platform and developing some elements of internal group discipline. These factions had to be dissolved under penalty of immediate expulsion from the party. All party organisations must take strictest precautions, lest the necessary criticism of the party be carried out from any specific group platform. In order to create a suitable forum for such criticism the publication of a regular Discussion Paper and of special symposia was envisaged. Critics, however, should take account of the party's difficult position in its hostile environment and help in the correction of its mistakes by participation in its *practical* work. The last (seventh) point, which by Congress decision was not to be published,[124] authorised a joint meeting of the members and candidates of the CC and of the Central Committee who had infringed the party's discipline or encouraged any factional activities. The ruling was not strictly applied at a time when nothing more serious than the Workers' Opposition threatened the party's unity. But precisely because reference to any specific faction had been removed in the preparatory committee, up to the present day point 7 has remained a Damocles' sword over the head of any leader whose activities might be described as 'initiating or encouraging the formation of a faction'.

NOTES AND REFERENCES

1. An illustration of the sacrifices demanded from either side (one year later) was given at the II VSNKh Congress by Bryukhanov (Proceedings, p. 120). Even if the peasants' consumption could be kept within 12 pood (192 kg) per head instead of the usual 16-18, and the consuming centres could be kept at the semi-starvation ration of $7^1/_2$ pood per annum, a deficit of 53 million poods had to be replaced by potatoes.
2. Reprinted as Appendices to Lenin's *Sochineniya*, 3rd ed., Vol. XXXIII.
3. *Sochineniya*, vol. XXVII, pp. 479-80.
4. Stalin's *Sochineniya*, vol. IV, pp. 122-23. See also Bunyan and Fisher, op. cit. pp. 474-75.
5. Ibid. pp. 214-15. For an illustration of the difficulties met by the agitators sent from the towns, cf. A. P. Demidova's diaries, published in *Istoricheski arkhiv*, 1956, No. 4.
6. According to the statements of the right-wing Social Revolutionaries

in their trial of 1922, the decision to apply terrorism against the Bolsheviks was taken by one wing of the Social Revolutionaries in February 1918, i.e. after the dissolution of the Constituent Assembly. On June 20th, 1918, Volodarski was killed by a member of a group organised by the party's Military Committee. As the group, however, was disowned by the Social Revolutionaries' Central Committee, it refused to carry out further attempts without formal guarantees against further disavowals. These were given, and kept, since the Social Revolutionary Central Committee, now safe in Samara, had no particular reasons for diplomacy. The attempt against Lenin was a well-organised operation, carried out with an effort comparable with that made in earlier days against Tsars. Later, the Social Revolutionary leaders, working with the support of western Social Democrats as they did since 1920, had an interest in dissociating themselves from that phase in their struggle against the Bolsheviks. Schapiro (op. cit. p. 154), while conceding that they may have known that plots of assassination were afoot, asks what they could have done about it short of informing the Cheka. The simple answer is that a party official declaration against interpretations of the party's opposition to Bolshevism in the sense of permitting terrorist activities, would not only have warned Cheka but also discouraged the terrorists who were clearly disinclined to murder except on their party's behalf. Hence Cheka would have had no opportunity to operate.

7. Cf. Lenin's sharp protests (*Sochineniya,* vol. XXXV, p. 275) against Zinoviev's and his colleagues' refusal to head the demands of the Petrograd workers for mass reprisals against the assassination of Volodarski (see the preceding note).

8. Proceedings, II VSNKh Congress, p. 74.

9. *Sochineniya,* vol. XXVIII, pp. 198 and 365-66.

10. Letter to the Workers of Elets (who had admitted a left-wing Social Revolutionary group after its dissociation from the anti-Bolshevik activities of the Social Revolutionary CC), ibid. pp. 32 ff.

11. A valuable acknowledgement by Peter Sorokin, ibid. pp. 165 ff.

12. Proceedings, pp. 56 ff. and 75 ff. *Sochineniya,* vol. XXX, pp. 210 ff. For the further fate of the non-Bolshevik parties see Carr, op. cit. pp. 172 ff., and Schapiro, op. cit.

13. Gusev, op. cit. *passim.* 20,838 party members were directed to political work in the army (commissars and propagandists) between December 1, 1918 and August 1, 1920 (i.e. the culmination of the Polish war) ; 3452 during the preceding period (between July 21 and November 18, 1918) and 3611 during the concluding period of the Polish and the Wrangel war, i.e. up to the end of 1920. (Cf. N. I. Shatanin in *Voprosy istorii KPSS,* 1958, No. 1, p. 21).

14. Cf. Deutscher, op. cit. pp. 200 ff. Liberman, who, at the time, could collect what observations the party leaders would make to a trusted non-party specialist (but, of course, no inside information), states (p. 127) that the conflict was regarded broadly as one between Trotsky and the party and that most of the party leaders sided with Stalin, not because of sympathy for him but because of distrust of Trotsky. When they had to appease the latter by recalling Stalin, their distrust of Trotsky only grew. From the note published (*Trotsky papers*: 1911-22, vol. I, Mouton, The Hague, 1964) in a particular document 315, it appears that Trotsky's protest against the replacement of Vacetis as Commander-in-Chief by Kamenev, the victor on the Eastern front appears to have played an even larger part in his tensions with the Party than the Tsaritsyn incident. In that case, not Stalin but Lenin was involved.

15. *Sochineniya,* vol. IV, pp. 206-07.

16. Ibid., pp. 120-21. The mentioning, in a contemporary document, of the French Military Mission amongst the people to whom Trotsky gave mandates may be an indication of political disagreements of a more serious nature : but little use can be made of such materials before all the archives are available.

17. *My Life,* pp. 340 and 375 ff. See note 14 above ; and, for example, document 168, p. 331 of *Trotsky Papers,* 1911-22.

18. The report made by Stalin and Dzerzhinski on the reasons of the Perm catastrophe (reprinted in Stalin's *Sochineniya,* vol. IV) is the most substantial contemporary evidence of a confidential and non-propagandist character. In a study of the civil war, its arguments would have to be compared with those made, at the same time, in the party press by the supporters of the 'military opposition' (enumerated in note 30 to Lenin's *Sochineniya,* 3rd ed., vol. XXIV).

19. Some reminiscence of this attitude is preserved in Stalin's statement, in the *History of the CPSU(b)* (p. 235) that the 'military opposition' also attracted support from Party workers 'who had never participated in any opposition'. This is explained by the changed meaning of the term 'opposition' : what in 1919 was regarded as simply denoting a group of comrades who voiced disagreement on some point of policy was taken, in 1938, as denoting a group opposed to the 'general line'.

20. Smirnov, *Otchet,* pp. 125 ff. See also Carr, op. cit. (1959) pp. 375 ff.

21. In the military section of the Congress the opposition rallied a majority in favour of its demand to grant the Political Commission the right of interference with the course of military operations. The supporters of the party majority, headed by Sokolnikov and Stalin, walked out in protest against the way in which the debates were conducted (Trotsky had gone to the front where he was urgently needed). Even in the secret session of the full Congress the opposition was supported by more than a third of the delegates ; this was

no more than the strength of other oppositions but surely sufficient
ground for the majority's seeking an agreed solution. (Of the proceedings of the secret session, only parts of the statements of Lenin—
in Yaroslavski's *Party History*—and of Stalin—*Sochineniya*, vol. IV,
pp. 249-50—have since been released.) See also S. F. Nerida, *O nekotorykh voprosakh istorii grazhdanskoi voini v SSSR*, Moscow, Voiniz-
dat, 1958, pp. 167 ff. Stalin, who at the Congress had been one of the
fervent representatives of the party majority, a few months later under
the impact of his Petrograd experiences wished the question of the
military specialists to be reconsidered by a plenary meeting of the
CC. This suggestion, however, was rejected on the ground that the
issue had been decided by the Party Congress (ibid. pp. 183 and 186).
Trotsky's presentation of the conflict (reproduced, on the basis of his
personal archives which now are available in original, in Deutscher,
op. cit. 1954, pp. 426 ff.) reflects his bitterness about the party
majority's applying, in a case where his personal prestige was involved,
its usual method of defending basic principles while meeting the
opposition's criticism of actual shortcomings in administration.

22. *VKP(b) v Rezolyutsiyakh*, pp. 309-311.

23. Ibid., p. 721.

24. Cf. Vatsetis' report to the Sovnarkom, *Istoricheski arkhiv*, 1958, No. 1,
pp. 47 and 53. By May 1, 1919, the army's fighting strength had
fallen to 357,200, to which another 105,000 had to be added for
security formations (ibid., No. 2, pp. 45-46).

25. Cf. the CC report to the IX Party Congress (also in *Izvestiya Tsk
RKP(b)*, March 24, 1920; Yu. Petrov in *Partiinaya zhizn*, 1957,
No. 10; N. I. Shatanin, as quoted in note 13 above, with quotations from archive materials). The estimate of 200,000 new party
recruits during the anti-Denikin campaign appears to be exaggerated.
The fairly vague data given (from 21 gubernias) in the CC report
suggest on closer analysis that about half of those recruited were
already serving in the army (these may include the 32,000 organised
'sympathisers' existing on the eve of the drive and many peasants
and blackcoated workers serving in the army, who would normally
prefer description as 'soldiers' to that of their normal civilian status
while workers would be proud to register as such).

26. Cf. his *Memoirs*, Vol. I, pp. 230, 261 and also 345 (on the Volunteers'
Army's campaign in spring 1918).

27. V. Gorn, *Grazhdanskaya voina v severo-zapade Rossii*, Berlin 1923,
pp. 283-84.

28. *Sochineniya*, vol. IV, pp. 199 and 222-23.

29. Krestinski's report to the IX Congress, *Otchet*, p. 39.

30. *Izvestiya TsK RKP(b)*, No. 1 (May 28, 1919).

31. According to Shlyapnikov's statement at the X Party Congress
(*Otchet*, p. 30) two per cent of the metal workers in Petrograd, and

four per cent of the 22,000 workers employed in 41 engineering factories surveyed in Moscow, were party members ; it may be supposed that many of these held administrative posts or were full-time trade union officials.

32. *VKP(b) v Rezolyutsiyakh*, pp. 350-51 ; *Otchet*, IX Congress, p. 323.
33. *VKP(b) v Rezolyutsiyakh*, p. 313.
34. Ibid., p. 355. *Otchet*, IX Congress, pp. 76 and 331.
35. *Izvestiya Tsk RKP(b)*, No. 15 (March 24, 1920) and 1928, No. 3.
36. See ch. v, sec. (b).
37. See above, p. 149.
38. *Otchet*, p. 185. *Moskovskaya organizatsiya RKP(b) v tsifrakh*, Vol. I, Moscow 1925, quoted in K. I. Bukov and G. A. Nagapetyan's article in *Voprosy istorii KPSS*, 1959, No. 6. Since the figure is characterised as valid before the party recruitment, when Denikin was *ante portas*, it may be supposed to include the results of the 're-registration' already carried out in the summer of 1919. But if some clearly propagandist interpolations, such as a round figure of 16,000 new admissions during the mass-recruitment of 1919, and a total of 52,264 party members and probationers before the re-registration of 1920, are excluded, the source just quoted shows a fairly stable development of the Moscow party membership (including probationers) : 14,697 in 1918, 20,652 in 1919 before the mass-recruitment, 27,816 after the re-registration of 1920 (if the lower, and better specified, of two estimates differing by about 10,000[!] is taken). That last re-registration is said to have led to the elimination of 15,000 members, but a mere 620 of these were actually expelled from the party, an unspecified number going to the polish front. I suspect that, in fact, some 8-10 thousand members allegedly recruited during, and immediately after, the anti-Denikin campaign were excluded and that the re-registrations, in general, dealt more with paper accumulated in the offices (perhaps from people who under some persuasion had signed a membership form without taking it in any way seriously) than with actual party members. Moscow differs from other places only in that we have some opportunity to check its figures. The Commission of the VIII Congress felt it necessary to express its doubts about figures such as 16,000 in Kursk Province, 12,000 in Smolensk, 13,700 in Tambov (*Otchet*, p. 237).
39. F. E. Smitten, *Sostav VKP(b)*, Moscow-Leningrad, 1929, p. 6, quoted in Lenin's *Sochineniya*, 3rd ed., vol. XXIV.
40. *Izvestiya Tsk RKP(b)* Nos. 1, 2 and 6, 1919 ; see also the archive sources quoted by Z. S. Moronchenkova in *Voprosy istorii KPSS*, 1957, No. 4, pp. 65-66.
41. *Vyatka* report in *Izvestiya TsK RKP(b)*, No. 3, 1919.
42. Ibid. No. 6 (September 30, 1919).

43. Ibid. 1928, No. 1, and March 24, 1919 (reprinted as an Appendix to the Proceedings of the IX Party Congress, pp. 547 ff.).

44. *Izvestiya TsK*, 1919, No. 3.

45. Bukov and Nagapetyan as quoted in note 38.

46. *Izvestiya TsK*, 1919, No. 3. The sample given for the Gubernia is very small—51 members of fourteen committees. As in every partial investigation, the sample is more likely to over-represent the strength of those groups whose membership on committees was regarded as particularly desirable.

47. Lenin's *Sochineniya*, vol. XXVIII, p. 330.

48. *VKP(b) v Rezolyutsiyakh*, p. 311.

49. Ibid. pp. 327 ff., articles 6 and 7.

50. *Sochineniya*, vol. XXX, p. 165.

51. The characteristic illustration of the attitude of these circles is the discussion by A. A. Goldenvaizer (*Arkhiv russkoi revolyutsii*, Berlin, vol. VI, p. 244) on whether the barristers of Kiev, after the reconquest of the town by the Red Army in February 1919, acted wisely when resuming their work under the conditions offered by the Soviet Government (which had been greatly modified to save them from moral conflicts). True, Goldenvaizer says, they acted according to the advice of their colleagues of the Northern capitals ; but the latter had resumed work only after having gone on record with one year of sabotage activities, while the Kiev lawyers were to continue working under the Red regime as they had done under the White one. Even the mere exercise of one's profession under the new regime is thus disapproved of ; it is not difficult to imagine what people like Goldenvaizer thought of colleagues who joined the party.

52. Carr's (op. cit. p. 212) assumption of a difference between the Cheka and the GPU in that 'the former directed its activities exclusively against enemies outside the party, the GPU acted impartially against all enemies of the regime, among whom dissident party members were now (1922) commonly the most important' is mistaken in regard to the period for which it is made. A large proportion of the corruption cases dealt with by the Cheka concerned party members (who, of course, were, immediately on conviction, expelled from the party) while, on the other hand, as late as 1926 the use of the GPU in intra-Party disputes was resented as contradictory to elementary party ethics (cf. Carr's, op. cit., 1959, p. 221).

53. See above, ch. 3, sec. (b).

54. Cf. notes 171 and 196 to Lenin's *Sochineniya*, 3rd ed., vol. XXIV.

55. See above, pp. 128-9.

56. An analysis of the elections to the Central Committees by the Party Congresses of 1918, 1919 and 1920 shows that of the 15 members of the First Committee, seven (apart from Sverdlov, who would undoubtedly have been re-elected had he not died) were re-elected everytime

(Bukharin, Dzerzhinski, Zinoviev, Krestinski, Lenin, Stalin and Trotsky). In the three elections to a total of 53 seats on the CC (at the IX and X Congress, committees of 19 members each were elected) 32 names appear. Two of them are promotions from the candidate stage, four returns of persons who had been members or candidates of the CC of 1917. Of the eight candidates elected in 1919, two were demotions from full membership, and one reelected as a candidate in the following year. Apart from this member, the list of 1920 (12 candidates) contains three demotions and returns of former CC members each. Three of the candidates of 1920 became full members in 1921, while four (amongst them two former CC members) retained their status.

57. *Sochineniya*, vol. XXXI, pp. 400-401; the argument was made against a minority which demanded proportional representation for all factions within the party which had put up lists of candidates. Against that demand the document is fairly mild in terms of what became recognised standards during the twenties. It was not included in the 3rd, and was first published in the 4th, edition of Lenin's *Sochineniya*. It appears to be identical with one of the two speeches which are described in note 225 to vol. XXV of the 3rd ed. as lost.

58. Point 13 of the Rules, *VKP(b) v Rezolyutsiyakh,* p. 267.

59. See above, pp. 121-3.

60. *VKP(b) v Rezolyutsiyakh,* p. 312.

61. Cf. Lenin's *Sochineniya,* vol. XXXVI, p. 547.

62. Cf. Lenin's *Sochineniya,* vol. XXXV, p. 308.

63. *Otchet,* pp. 141, 148, 152, 270.

64. *Otchet,* pp. 9-10.

65. See note 91, below p. 189; N. Kitayev's article in *Partiinaya zhizn,* 1957, No. 7, and the sources quoted there. Local Agitprop Departments were operating already at an earlier stage (*Izvestiya TsK RKP(b)*, No. 1 has a report from Voronezh, mostly concerned with classes— which were poorly attended—and slightly better attended meetings on topical problems of financial, economic or agrarian policy). At the centre, training of party and Soviet workers was managed by the School Department, which established a special school with 500 students in two faculties for party and Soviet work respectively (ibid. No. 2). The intended three months' curriculum could not be concluded, because after Denikin's successes the pupils—all active party workers—had to be sent to the Provinces to carry out the mobilisation. But the school was later re-organised as the Sverdlov University (ibid., No. 8).

66. The present Politburo has to be compared with the old CC. The counterpart of the present full CC are the old Party Conferences.

67. Apart from the Brest Litovsk crisis, the trade union discussion of 1920 provided an instance in which premature convention of the Party Congress was at least envisaged. In July 1919, Trotsky's opposition on the Vatsetis-Kamenev issue (see note 14 above) grew so wild that, to prevent his resignation (at the height of the Civil War), his colleagues offered him the convocation of an extra-ordinary party Congress if he so wished.

68. *My Life*, pp. 391-92. In the preceding discussions, both Trotsky and Stalin had opposed Lenin's suggestion of pursuing the defeated Poles up to Warsaw. But while Trotsky always emphasised that he had been right against Lenin on this point, Stalin at the time confined his public utterances to some interviews and recalled their memory only at the 15th anniversary of the events (true, in the *Communist International*, where, in 1935, it would not fail to reach the appropriate audience). Cf. his *Sochineniya*, vol. IV, pp. 333 and 339-40, published in 1947.

69. See ch. 5.

70. At least as a rule: Ciliga (op. cit. pp. 274 ff.) describes the shock which was caused to him, a Trotskyist, when his comrades in the concentration camps—oppositionists of the early periods—proved to him that not Stalin but Lenin himself was responsible for those developments to which he objected.

71. Proceedings of VII Soviet Congress (Organisational Section), pp. 199, 201, 217 ff., 223.

72. Ibid., pp. 220 ff.

73. Sokolski (Proceedings, p. 239).

74. Minkov (*Otchet*, p. 181).

75. *Sochineniya*, vol. XXX, pp. 223-24.

76. Point 7 of the Congress Decision (*VKP(b) v rezolyutsiyakh*, p. 334) speaks of infeasibility 'for any reason', i.e. apparently also of disagreements about the expediency of the order. If the order were 'infeasible' in the verbal sense no prescriptions about its provisional execution would have been needed. For a short time, by decision of the VIII Soviet Congress in 1920, Gubernium Executive Committees (but not the lower ones) were even allowed to stop the execution of orders received from some People's Commissariats, pending decision about their protest (which would, of course, lie with the Sovnarkom or the CC). Excessive use of this right was, however, discouraged. (Carr, op. cit vol. I, pp. 217-18.)

77. *Otchet*, VIII Congress, pp. 164-65, 178, 250, 270-71, 281.

78. *VKP(b) v rezolyutsiyakh*, p. 314.

79. *Otchet*, IX Congress, p. 82 (see also Krestinski's speech, ibid. p. 46).

80. These included even the application of capital punishment (which, at that time, was restricted to the immediate rear of the fighting

armies) for crimes committed against railway transport. *Otchet,* IX Congress, p. 327.

81. Ibid., p. 120 ff.

82. Ossinski, ibid. p. 132.

83. See ch. 6, sec. (a).

84. Point III/3 of the Resolution of the IX Party Congress on Trade Union problems.

85. *Otchet,* IX Congress, p. 89.

86. Point 7 of Tomski's Theses (reprinted ibid. as an Appendix, from *Ekonomicheskaya zhizn,* March 10, 1920), and also as an Appendix to Lenin's *Sochineniya,* 3rd ed., vol. XXXV.

87. He emphasised the continuity : *Sochineniya,* vol. XXX, pp. 442-43 and 469-70.

88. Ibid. pp. 379-80, 400 ff., and Lenin's speech in the communist group of the trade union centres, March 15, 1920.

89. Lenin's *Sochineniya,* vol. XXX, p. 474.

90. Ibid. pp. 413-14 and 435 ff.

91. *VKP(b) v rezolyutsiyakh,* pp. 346-47.

92. Ibid. p. 341.   93. Liberman, op. cit. pp. 131-32.

94. *Sochineniya,* vol. IV, pp. 292-93 and 300-301.

95. March 27, 1920.

96. Proceedings, IX Congress, pp. 99 ff.

97. Ibid., as Appendices 9 and 10, Trotsky's first draft. Lenin's observations and the text of the Theses as finally submitted to the Congress.

98. *Sochineniya,* vol. V, pp. 62 ff. Stalin's reluctance in using that draft has contributed to the myth of his alleged failure to develop original theoretical ideas.

99. See above, pp. 119-20.

100. Ibid. pp. 86-87. The statement forms the conclusion of the draft.

101. Reprinted in Lenin's *Sochineniya,* vol. XXXI, pp. 18-22 ; *Sel. Works,* vol. IX, pp. 23-26.

102. *Sochineniya,* vol. XXXII, pp. 34-35. Lenin's reference to his disputes with Trotsky during the Brest-Litovsk crisis illustrates the sharpness of the argument.

103. Stalin's *Sochineniya,* vol. V, pp. 5 ff.

104. Cf. Lenin's *Sochineniya,* vol. XXXII, p. 62 (p. 54 in *Sel. Works,* l.c.) and Trotsky's *My Life,* p. 397. Lenin himself emphasised in the quoted passage the priority of the political approach ; in any case he wrote in 1921 and not, as did Trotsky, in 1929.

105. *Sochineniya,* vol. XXXII, pp. 6 and 26-27 (pp. 9 and 33 in *Sel. Works,* vol. IX).

106. Ibid. vol. XXXI, pp. 395-96.

107. Ibid. vol. XXXII, pp. 29 ff. (*Sel Works,* vol. IX, pp. 35 ff.).

108. Ibid. pp. 23 and 54.

109. Already in spring 1919 (in a report from Nizhny Novgorod, published in *Izvestiya CC RKP(b)*, No. 1), the slogan is mentioned as current amongst the peasants.

110. *Sochineniya*, vol. XXXII, p. 31.

111. *Sochineniya*, vol. XXXII, p. 383.

112. Ibid. pp. 149 and 159.　　　113. Ibid. p. 111.

114. Chronicle, vol. XXXII of Lenin's *Sochineniya*, pp. 522-23.

115. A summary of the main facts, written with sympathy for the mutineers but in clear realisation of the implications of a victory on their part, was published by R. V. Daniels in *The American Slavic and East European Review*, December 1951. The main Soviet source is A. S. Pukhov, *Kronstatski myatezh v 1921 g*, Leningrad, 1931.

116. As suggested by Schapiro, op. cit. p. 299.

117. *VKP(b) v rezolyutsiyakh*, pp. 361-62 (points 17 and 18).

118. *Sochineniya*, vol. XXXIII, p. 75.

119. Ibid., vol. XXXII, p. 160 (*Selected Works*, vol. IX, p. 98).

120. *The Report of the British Labour Delegation to Russia*, 1920, gives an illustration of the conditions prevailing at that time precisely in the type of complaints made by the legal representatives of the Mensheviks, including the Moscow Printers' Union, and the type of 'illegal' activities (including an appearance of V. Chernov, the former Chairman of the Constituent Assembly and leader of the right-wing Social Revolutionaries, which would clearly have been impossible had not even his underground status been fairly formal) which went on in those days.

121. Lenin, *Sochineniya*, vol. XXXII, pp. 340-41, (pp. 189-9 in *Sel. Works*, vol. IX), cf. also Carr, op cit. pp. 176-77.

122. *Sochineniya*, vol. XXXII, pp. 166 and 170-73.

123. Ibid. p. 225. A comparison between Lenin's draft (Ibid. pp. 217-20) and the finally adopted text of the Resolution on Party Unity (*VKP(b) v rezolyutsiyakh*, pp. 373-75) shows changes which resulted from these discussions. The specific references to the 'Workers' Opposition' (whose behaviour at the Moscow Party Conference in November 1920, and in Kharkov was originally quoted) and in slightly milder form, to the 'Democratic Centralism' group, were eliminated. The statement that the White Guards disguised themselves 'as communists or even as the most left-wing communists' was reformulated so as to say 'as communists or even "to the left" of them'—hitting at anarchism rather than at the extremist groups with the party.

124. The decision to publish it was taken by the XIII Party Conference, on Stalin's suggestion, at the culminating point of the dispute with Trotsky.

CHAPTER V

THE VANGUARD OF THE WORKING CLASS BECOMES THE ORGANISER OF INDUSTRIALISATION

(a) THE PARTY ORGANISATION IN THE SETTING OF THE NEP

WHEN THE New Economic Policy was introduced, industrial production had fallen to a minimum : in 1921 coal production amounted to 30.8 per cent., steel production 4.3 per cent., of the 1913 level.[1] The decision of February 1921 meant that the solution to the difficulty was sought neither, as Trotsky had suggested during the trade union discussion, in the mere strengthening of labour discipline in industry, nor in workers' self-government. It was sought in the restoration of a market in which the peasants would sell food; such private industry as was admitted might compete with the nationalised one in the supply of consumers' goods. Such goods could then be bought from wages as well as from the proceeds of peasants' sales on the market. Yet the very creation of a free market, however limited, involved dangers for the regime. According to Lenin, every sale of grain on the market, every instance of black-marketing and profiteering, implied some restoration of capitalist relationships.[2] Half a year before the introduction of the NEP he noted that the lower-middle-class elements were more numerous and stronger than the socialist economy.[3]

In order to hold its own under the new conditions, and in due course to return to the offensive, the party had to do two things. It had to preserve, and even strengthen, its unity, and it had to protect itself against contamination by the capitalist environment produced by NEP. Failure to do this would result both in labour support for the opposition groups and in the opening of channels through which the bourgeoisie could bend the state machine to its will. The first need was catered for, apart from the disciplinary sanctions envisaged in the resolution on Party Unity, by the condemnation of the two opposition platforms by the XI Congress.

Trotsky's standpoint was rejected by the admission, in point 5 of the resolution on Trade Unions, that the quick transformation of the unions into State organs was a grave political error. The Workers' Opposition's demand for the organisation of the national economy by a Producers' Congress was rejected, in sharper terms, in the resolution on the 'Syndicalist and Anarchist Deviation in Our Party'. Propaganda for these views was described as incompatible with party membership.[4]   An outlook still very different from later concepts of ideological homogeneity was expressed by the rider that the prohibition of propaganda addressed to a broader forum did not imply prohibition of these views in specialist publications, symposia, etc.   When, after the rejection of their views, Shlyapnikov and his friends refused to accept the seats in the CC offered to them, the Congress, in a special motion,[5] asked them to submit to party discipline and refused to accept any resignation. The procedure not only differed from that applied three years before to Bukharin who, in an analogous situation, was invited to consult his political friends[6], but it also differed from that of later days when ideological deviation meant exclusion from party office.

In shaping the institutional safeguard of party morals, Lenin avowedly took a leaf out of the opposition's book.[7]   To meet the opposition's complaints, the IX Party Conference, in September 1920, had established a Control Commission which should examine complaints about misuse of power by party bodies, including the CC.   If no agreement could be reached, it should report to the Party Congress.   The institution had as its models the Conflict Commissions established in the Central European Social Democrat parties in order to prevent suppression of oppositions by unconstitutional means as well as to safeguard party ethics.   The exercise at least of the first function presupposed independence from the CC.   The inclusion of two CC members in the first provisional Central Control Commission was explicitly described as a temporary measure.[8]   Additional CC members were elected by the party conferences of four most important industrial Gubernia.   The X Party Congress elected a permanent CCC ; similar institutions were to be established in the Gubernia. In the definition of its tasks, functions such as the struggle against

bureaucratism, careerism and misuse of official position of party
members were supplemented by such as the struggle against violation of comradely relationship within the party, against the sprea-
ding of unfounded rumours and other assertions detrimental to
the party's unity and authority, i.e. against possible excesses of
intra-party struggle.   Ten years' party membership was demanded
from candidates for the Central, five for those for the Regional,
and membership since the February Revolution of 1917 from
candidates for the Gubernial Control Commissions.   In order to
preserve their independence, they could not be members of party
committees nor hold administrative posts of responsibility.   All
the members of the Central, and some members of the lower
Control Commissions had to be full-time workers.   The Control
Commissions were elected by the Congress of the corresponding
party organisation and reported to it.   Their members were
entitled to participate in all meetings not only of their party
committee but also of all the party and Soviet institutions within
their region of competence.   Their decisions had to be carried
out by the corresponding party committee.   In case of disagreement, the party congress had to decide.[9]   For some years, the
Central Control Commission served as an agency of reconciliation
but the Gubernium Control Commissions soon acquired a reputa-
tion of supporting the party committees by prosecution of dissenting party members.   A motion to abolish them was defeated by
the XI Party Congress only with a narrow majority.[10]

At the X Congress seven members of the CC were elected.
Two years later the XII Congress[11] broadened the institution so
as to include fifty members, 'predominantly from amongst the
workers and peasants, with a good party record and suitable for
the exercise of supervisory functions in party and State'.   The
change was made in connection with Lenin's suggestion, in his
article 'Better Fewer but Better', to re-organise the People's
Commissariat for Workers' and Peasants' Inspection (Rabkrin)
which had originated as an institutionalisation of mass-participation
in supervisory functions.   It was a supervisory body consisting of
a moderate number of political workers, selected by the party.[12]
The combination of CCC and Workers' and Peasants' Inspection
(Rabkrin) in one supervisory body might avoid the reproach that

13

State officials who were party members were put above effective supervision. On the other hand, it protected the communist in charge of some State organisation who had disagreements with the CC majority against unjustified attacks on his administrative activities. Demands on party record similar to those made by the X Congress on CCC members would obviously have excluded the participation of workers in the new supervisory body, but a Presidium of nine members 'of a type suitable for CC membership' was to be elected. It should include the leading members—including the People's Commissary—of the PC of *Rabkrin*. At least half of the CC members (whose number was increased at the XIII Party Congress to 151) should work within the Commissariat, according to directives established by its Collegium in agreement with the supreme party bodies.

At the time of the XII Congress the CCC was still regarded as safeguarding party ethics rather than political homogeneity. Shkiryatov reported on the arrangements made between the CCC, the Courts, the GPU, and also the Political Department of the War Office which had to decide upon the opening of prosecutions against members of the armed forces. He emphasised the need to help the comrade who had inadvertently come into trouble and to avoid unfounded arrests which, even if followed by an acquittal, would result in a diminishing of the authority of the communist involved. On the other hand, it was necessary to stop the habit of high-standing communists to interfere with the course of justice against State officials with whom they had worked and of whose good character they were convinced. In some cases such interventions were symptoms of the communists' infection by the spirit of the business environment in which they had to work. The CCC had put some of its party investigators into the GPU's offices[13], (presumably to have criminal offenders expelled from the party before they came under public trial). Such arrangements did not yet involve the GPU in matters outside its competence as conceived in those days. However, some influence of the police approach to investigation might have affected the general work of CCC investigators returning to their ordinary work, i.e. the prosecution of disciplinary offences which might include the expression of political dissent.

Prosecution of obvious cases of corruption, however, did not solve the problem of protecting general party standards under the conditions of NEP. This was the formulation, in personal terms, of preventing a restoration of capitalism. More numerous than provable offences was the use of a party member's power within his legal field of discretion in a way fitting the interests of the new capitalist or of the *kulak,* if the communist was accessible to the influence of wealth, or if his class-interests were opposed to those of the Soviet regime. From a multitude of decisions of this kind a degeneration of the regime into a shield protecting the growth of the new *bourgeoisie* could follow. The safest precaution against such dangers was the investigation of every party member's fitness to be a member. In point 5 of the Resolution on Party Unity—i.e. at the point where the justified elements in the opposition's demands were recognised—the X Congress mentioned the need to discover and to expel alien elements who had attached themselves to the party. The organisational resolution stated that no quantitative broadening but qualitative improvement of the party's ranks was necessary. The recruitment of workers should be accompanied by 'purging the party from non-communist elements by a precise account of every individual party member according to his work in office and also according to his fitness as a member of the Russian Communist Party'.[14]

This decision was carried out by the 'revision of the personal composition of the party', carried out during the second half of 1921.[15] Special commissions composed of old Bolsheviks appeared on all party organisations. Regional Commissions and a Central Commission served as supervisory organs with which complaints could be lodged. This check proved to be important as most of the local purge commissions used the opportunity to settle accounts in local frictions and personal matters.[16] Every party member had to give a self-critical account of his background and activities, followed by a public discussion in which everyone present, including non-party members, was expected to state all favourable and unfavourable facts about the activities of this particular communist. Quite apart from expulsions or reductions of full members to probationer's status, the campaign popularised the standards of the Old Guard of Bolshevism. The reports of its members about their experiences in prison and in Siberia, as well as the experiences which older and younger communists could report from the battlefields of the civil war, set a standard, compliance with which was expected from everyone who wished to become a member of the state party, or to make good short-comings which had resulted in his getting a reprimand. Expulsion from the party was envisaged for those members who had lost contact with the masses by bureaucratisation and by pursuing their private interests, not to speak of those whose egotism, if not corruption, compromised the party in the eyes of the masses. Expulsion for political reasons was envisaged only for those Mensheviks who had not been truly converted to Bolshevism. At the X Congress satisfaction had still been expressed about the decision of some minor Ukrainian revolutionary groups and of the *Bund* to join the CP. As for the Mensheviks, Smilga had noticed that their healthier elements, disgusted by their leaders' joining the counter-revolutionary camp as they were, wished to join the CP in whole groups.[17] In his article which opened the purge, however, Lenin suggested that 99 of 100 former Mensheviks who had joined the party later than early 1918, should be purged.[18] It is hardly surprising that local organisations, taking Lenin's advice literally, committed 'excess purges'.[19] Even after correction of these mistakes, a total of 5000 former members of other parties (amongst them 2000 Mensheviks) were expelled in the purge. Expulsion of oppositional communists—except for direct breach of discipline, in which case no purge but mere application of the Rules was needed—was excluded by the Purge Commissions' terms of reference. In order to give the opposition some guarantees, its supporters were included in the commissions (e.g. Shlyapnikov in the Central one). The commissions were under definite instructions to be stricter with intellectuals and officials than workers. If there was any truth in the description of a 'Workers' Opposition', its working-class members (though not the intellectuals in sympathy with them) should have profited from this ruling.

By the time of the XII Congress, in April 1923, total party membership amounted to a mere 386,000, as against 659,000 which, according to Shkiryatov's report at the XI Congress, had

been registered on the eve of the purge. At the time of Shkiryatov's report, 136,000 members (i.e. 20.7 per cent of the total
membership) had been expelled (another 12,000 were subsequently expelled in Turkestan); 18,000 (i.e. 2.6 per cent) left
voluntarily.[20] Although the pre-purge figures were presumably
exaggerated, it is obvious that there must have been a considerable number of resignations after the conclusion of the purge.
Many workers—old Bolsheviks amongst them—left the party,
disappointed with the realities of NEP.[21] (The purge itself
would have increased the percentage of workers amongst party
members. In the main industrial centres, including the two
capitals, about 18 per cent of the members were expelled—in
Ivano-Voznesensk Province even a mere 12 per cent, as against
thirty and more per cent in the agricultural regions. Of those
expelled 27,800 were workers, half of them still working in the
factories; 61,000 peasants, two-thirds of them still engaged in
agriculture; 43,000 intellectuals and salaried employees by social
origin; the army and the national minorities in the border regions
were treated in a charitable way.) A mere 624 of those expelled
were Old Bolsheviks, 4360 had joined the party between the
February and the October revolutions of 1917, two-thirds of the
expulsions concerned members of no more than two years'
standing. The purge changed the party's social structure in the
direction wanted by Lenin but its very procedure must have
disgusted many people who were useful party members or, in due
course might have become such, if less drastic methods had been
applied.

The XI Party Conference in December 1921 noticed that
a line must be drawn across all the mutual recriminations which
had been raised during the purge. In future every party member
should be judged solely by his devotion to the proletarian cause
as shown in his activities.[22] Very soon the struggle against a
tendency of the less stable members to desert the party, or at
least to threaten with leaving it, was described as a topical task.[23]
But Lenin, who had taken the initiative in the purge, regarded
the reduced number of party members as still too high in view of
their insufficient preparedness for their tasks. Everyone who
honestly faced realities must recognise that the party's proletarian

policy was based, not upon its social composition (as was asserted by the Workers' Opposition) but upon the undivided authority of a very thin stratum, the old party guard. Even a small conflict in its midst would, if not destroy, still weaken its authority to such an extent that it would lose control of events. Hence Lenin drew the conclusion that joining the party should be made more difficult for all candidates, especially those who did not belong to the working-class.[24] The XI Congress, though it did not go as far as Lenin would have desired, prolonged the length of the probationer's status for all groups and demanded increased references—for workers and peasants from three party members with no less than three years' standing, for salaried employees, intellectuals, etc. and for all persons who formerly had belonged to another party, from five party members with no less than five years' standing : their admission had further to be confirmed by the Gubernium Committee. Special rules as to the responsibility of the sponsors for the fitness of the recommended were to be elaborated.[25]

Strict as these rulings may appear, in reality, no insurmountable obstacles prevented non-proletarian elements, or even former Mensheviks, from joining the party. Without the additional organisational barriers, the average intellectual with a slightly left-wing pre-revolutionary record and ample opportunity to make the acquaintance of some leading communists would have enjoyed a privileged position. Lenin's other suggestion that a simplified procedure for getting rid of unsuitable elements should be established[24] was by-passed by the Congress, with the experience of one purge in mind. He achieved no more than the statement that, in view of the tendency of careerists especially from the urban lower-middle-classes to join the State party, further purges might in future become necessary and that the Control Commissions should intensify their struggle against the penetration of bourgeois habits into the party and the tendency of some pseudo-communists to use NEP for their personal enrichment.[26] Lenin sought guarantees against the infection of the State machine by its NEP environment through its fusion with the party, the purity of which was to be maintained by Old Bolshevik standards. The suggestion made sense as regards the supervisory bodies and the Foreign

Office (to both of which Lenin referred), and also as regards the GPU (where it was taken as a matter of course). In general, however, party opinion was opposed to fusion of party and State.[27] In the conditions of NEP, party members working at different posts had to defend legitimate aspects of the national interest. The XI Party Congress demanded specialisation of the party institutions at least from the Gubernium level upwards according to the different branches of administration which had to be supervised. Direct interference with management was prohibited because it reduced the responsibility of the executives and threatened the party with bureaucratisation and involvement with details. These warnings have not ceased to be relevant up to the present day.

The growth of an independent party machine built under war communism into an all-embracing body arose, however, from the party's relations with the working-class. On the basis of reports made by representatives of diverse trade unions (Shlyapnikov being one of them) in the meeting of December 28, 1921, the CC meeting of January 12, 1922, adopted a resolution on the tasks of the trade unions, drafted by Rudzutak, Andreyev and Lenin.[28] In the private enterprises admitted by NEP class conflicts between capital and labour were unavoidable. Even in the State enterprises, now put under a regime of economic accountancy, management had to defend aspects of the public interest which were to some extent opposed to those interests of the workers which the trade unions had to defend. The inevitable collision of interests might assume a more serious character if management approached its tasks from a bureaucratic standpoint. Trade unions, the resolution said, should defend the public interests as well as those of the workers; they should again be based on voluntary memberships. Their tasks included the negotiation of collective agreements as well as the raising of labour discipline and the education of the workers. In particular they should also struggle against egalitarian or formal-democratic ideologies as propounded by Menshevik and anarchist groups. Trade unions should participate in the higher administrative and planning bodies of Soviet economy and aim at developing from amongst the workers suitable administrators but must not directly interfere with factory management. Under a Soviet regime, strikes could be caused only by extremely bureaucratic distortions of Soviet management and capitalist remainders on the one side, and by the cultural backwardness of the working masses on the other. Strikes in State enterprises should be settled as quickly as possible by way of negotiation, if necessary with superior State organs. Trade unions should insist on the removal of justified grievances and on satisfaction of those interests of their members that were compatible with the interest of the workers' State.

Such policies could not be pursued unless it was strictly supported by the communists working in the trade unions. But difficulties arose precisely in this field. During the first year of NEP, real wages fell even below the level current at the time of its introduction.[29] Discontent found expression in the Workers' Opposition whose supporters held important positions in the trade unions (in particular in those of the metal workers and miners). Occasions for expression of discontent with the conditions of the workers in the nationalised enterprises were offered by the admission of private enterprises (which, however, by the end of 1922, occupied no more than 70,000 workers against three million in the nationalised industries) and of concessions to foreign capitalists (which, however, never became a factor of importance). Specialists of bourgeois origin—whose employment and privileges had provided a long-standing grievance of the opposition groups[30] —became a favourite subject of demagogy, sometimes with tragic consequences.[31]

In August 1921 Lenin attempted to get Shlyapnikov expelled from the party, because in a speech before the party nucleus of the Moscow Electric Station, he had attacked the Government decrees on leasing enterprises to private persons[32] (i.e. carried disagreements within the CC into the party at large). Lenin failed to rally the two-thirds majority of the members of the CC and the CCC required by point 7 of the Resolution on Party Unity[33], but the CC decided unanimously to remove Shlyapnikov from the Central Purge Commission. Even this was declined by a two-thirds majority of the CCC—presumably on the grounds that Shlyapnikov had been included in the Purge Commission precisely in order to give the lesser oppositionists a guarantee of fair play ; the CC then withdrew its proposal.[34] Amongst the Gubernial Party Committees only those of Samara and Omsk had majorities of supporters of the Workers' Opposition, and were dissolved by the CC.[35] Amongst the communist trade union officials, however, the opposition was much stronger. At the IV Congress of the Metal Workers' Union a list of members of its Central Committee, composed, against the instructions given by the CC of the party, exclusively of supporters of the Workers' Opposition received 120 votes against a mere 37 polled for the party official list; the CC, however, intervened to put the minority list into office.[36] Not only supporters of the Workers' Opposition but also supporters of Trotsky in the discussion before the X Congress were removed from key positions in the trade unions and given other assignments. Kossior, one of the victims, pointed out that the administrative method of settling disagreements in the trade union field would easily drive workers out of the party, or into the ranks of the most radical opposition groups which were just being formed.[37]

The standpoint of the extremist opposition was formulated by Myasnikov. If the CC pursued a policy opposed to the interests of the working class and used its organisational powers to prevent criticism of that policy, it followed that the working class must end the totalitarian control of political life. Already in May 1921 Myasnikov, in a letter to the CC, suggested that political stagnation and lack of political criticism could be removed only by restoration of the freedom of the press to all political trends, from the anarchists to the monarchists. In July, returning to his home in the Urals, he started a successful agitation on these lines. Lenin[38] attempted to convince Myasnikov that this slogan would only promote the political restoration of the bourgeoisie which still enjoyed sufficient economic strength to turn freedom of the press to its benefit. When Myasnikov continued his campaign he was expelled from the party and employed in Soviet trade missions abroad, which he used to establish connections with leftist groups in the western communist parties.[39] The 'Workers' Group' organised by him in early 1923 jointly with some members of the Workers' Opposition expelled from

the party continued the syndicalist line of the old Workers'
Opposition, culminating in the demand for the transfer of political
and economic administration to 'producers' Soviets' and trade
unions, and in the denunciation of NEP as the 'New Exploitation
of the Proletariat'.   More moderate, at least in that it aimed at
reforming the party from within, was the Workers' Truth group,
formed after the X Congress by followers of Bogdanov. It
published an underground paper and attacked NEP in the sharpest terms, yet without a syndicalist programme. The importance
of either group lay less in its direct influence (though individuals
associated with them played their part in the strikes of the late
summer of 1923) than in their proclaiming ideas even at the XII
Party Congrss, which disciplined oppositionists could not ventilate
in public.[40]

The XI Congress settled accounts with the Workers'
Opposition as a more or less organised body (it continued and
played its part within later oppositions).[41]   Apparently no worse
offence could be found than the joint appeal of twenty-two
members of the Opposition to the Comintern. This appeal could
not be criticised as such. The party itself regarded the Comintern
as the supreme tribunal which might judge on disputes between
Soviet trade unions and the State organs.[42] But the harshness of
the reproaches (including A. Kollontay's envisaging the possibility
of a split) and the formal violation of the Rules involved in
Myasnikov (who was already expelled at the time) being one of
the twenty-two, offered an opportunity for disciplinary measures.
A special committee of the XI Congress confirmed the conclusions
at which an investigation committee of the Politburo, consisting
of Dzerzhinski, Zinoviev and Stalin, had arrived but refused the
expulsion of Kollontay, Shlyapnikov and Medvedev which had
been recommended by the three—presumably with Lenin's approval.   The highest disciplinary penalty was reserved for two minor
figures who, if the assertions about their political past were true,
could have been expelled by any ordinary purge commission.
(However, as expulsions of active oppositionists were approved
by the Party Congress, local 'purges' were encouraged.)[43]   At the
XII Party Congress it was reported that the CCC had to consider
1413 appeals of party members expelled by the Gubernial Control

Commissions. As a mere fraction of those expelled appealed, it may be assumed that the large majority of those expelled for non-political reasons acquiesced, and that a high proportion of those who appealed had been expelled for *political* reasons.

Repression of oppositions which might reflect the workers' spontaneous urge was one part of the party's struggle for the preservation of power under the difficult conditions of NEP. It was supplemented by the party's effort to maintain an outlook of its own, different from that of the State machine which was exposed to the pressures of NEP. Confidential information letters of the CC were issued to local party organisations so that international problems could be discussed with the necessary frankness.[44] From the modest beginnings noticeable in the period of the civil war,[45] party schools were developed so that the early period of NEP, indeed, may be regarded as the time of the growth of modern party educational activities. On the recommendations of a conference of the organisers of party and Soviet schools held in December 1921, the XI Party Congress decided during 1922-23 to organise three types of schools : (i) elementary, with a three-months curriculum, one for two or three districts; (ii) higher with a one-year curriculum, to be established in all the *Gubernia* and autonomous regions; and (III) Communist Universities with a three-year curriculum. The schools were not exclusively intended for party members : only fifty per cent of the places in the elementary, seventy-five per cent of those in the higher Soviet and Party schools were reserved for members of the party and *Komsomol*. By January 1923, 158 elementary and 53 higher Soviet and Party schools, with 10,300 and 10,400 pupils respectively, were operating ; the eight operating Communist Universities had 5,558 students.[46] The comparatively small attendance at elementary Soviet and Party schools suggests only moderate popularity of a course necessarily restricted to Marxist theory and hardly conveying knowledge useful in practical appointments. The traditional 'circles' and classes, attendance at which did not interrupt the pupils' normal work, were preferred for such purposes. The XIII Party Congress decided to turn the Soviet and party schools into Party Schools aiming at the preparation of party organisers and propagandists for the villages as well as for the towns. Their purposes thus being more clearly defined, the school made some progress. In the school-year 1925—6179 elementary and 67 higher Soviet and Party schools with a total of 26,800 pupils, and another 120 evening schools with 9000 pupils were in operation. 8400 students attended the Communist Universities.[47] Elementary political education had been transferred to classes ('politics schools'), particularly designed for the education of the 'Lenin recruits'.[48] In 1925-26, 6178 such 'schools' were said to be attended by 185,000 people. There is no reason to assume that the statistics of Adult Education in the USSR were not subject to exaggeration as they are in other lands. The Soviet and Party schools, like their modern successors, mainly prepared professional party workers and administrators, but a very high proportion of the workers recruited for the party got *some* kind of general political education.

The XI Congress confirmed rules regarding the party machine which had been elaborated by a conference of the Regional and Gubernial party Secretaries. There was to be a full-time secretary of the party *nucleus* in enterprises with more than 1,000 workers, or more than twenty-five party members (the rule shows that *nuclei* of that size were still regarded as large and important). Each Gubernium and District Committee should appoint about three full-time instructors to support the organisational work.[49] Salaries were regulated, four months later, by the resolution 'On the Material Condition of Party Officials', adopted by the XII Party Conference.[50] There should be 15,000 of them : 325 at the centre (fifty CC members, 100 salaried staff, the rest in regional agencies of the CC), twenty (three of them for the *Komsomol*) in each of the hundred *gubernia* and regions, eight (one of them for the *Komsomol*) in each of the thousand districts (*uyezdy*), two thousand secretaries of primary party organisations (*nuclei*) in the major enterprises and institutions and three thousand for those of the existing fourteen thousand rural districts (*volosti*) where there was already an established party office. These figures were soon exceeded : in 1923 there were 26,000; in 1924, after a general campaign to reduce office staffs, 23,000 salaried employees in party offices (not all of them party members). Certainly this was a small fraction of 1.6 million

salaried officials working at that time in Soviet political institutions, without those paid from local budgets.[51] But already the
suggestion was made that these 23,000 people were actually
controlling the whole political machine.   In fact, Stalin found it
necessary to refute the idea.[52]

In the decisions of the XI Party Congress[53] as well as of the
XII Party Conference[50]—the latter met when Stalin was already
in charge of the Secretariat—the conditions of full-time party
workers were treated along with those of party members in general.
These were extremely difficult during the first year of NEP.
Provision had to be made for securing them at least a subsistence
minimum and prevent extreme differences in the material conditions of party members.[53]   The resolution adopted by the XII
Conference emphasised that the party could not shoulder the
responsibility for the material conditions of its members.   They
should not indeed be very different from those of other workers
and peasants who, when unemployed, depend on insufficient social
services. In fact, half of all the members' contributions and all the
deductions from excessive incomes of party members were earmarked for a special fund for mutual assistance of party members
in emergencies (the modest benefits offered by that fund could
hardly counteract the tendency of party members still at the bench
to move into the civil service where there was less risk of unemployment). The resolution 'On the Material Conidtions of Party
Officials' elaborated the principle of a maximum income for party
members, wherever employed.   This figure was to be established
by the Council for Labour and Defence.   So far as my knowledge
goes, this was a fairly hypothetical figure, relevant perhaps for a Communist *prima ballerina*—if such a creature
existed—or, perhaps, for an engineer who had made an invention
(though, being a Communist, he would presumably be rewarded
by promotion and not by a money prize).[54]   The figure usually
referred to as the *partmaximum* was the maximum earning
provided for in the ordinary salary scale, i.e. the 17th wages
group plus 50 per cent addition in consideration of responsible
work which could not be managed within a regular Eight-Hour
Day (of course, the addition became in itself a symbol of status as
a worker occupying a post of responsibility).   In 1925-27 this

ordinary maximum income amounted to 225 rubles monthly, witn a purchasing power which I would compare, if at all,[55] with that of the corresponding amount in gold—480 Mark—in the Germany of those days, where it was characteristic of the junior manager, the middle ranks of the civil service or the university lecturer (German MPs got half as much remuneration). In the USSR at that time, the *partmaximum* was earned, in the Government or in the office of the CC, by a head of a Department, in the Universities by the holder of a Chair, in the local party service by the Gubernium Secretary (the salary of the 12th wages group was earned in the lowest grade of the administrative civil service, in the party, by the secretary of a small factory, or rural district party organisation). Twenty-five per cent of and literary and other incomes exceeding the *partmaximum* had to be delivered to the fund for mutual assistance of party members. In academic and similar institutions such extra incomes were fairly widespread; the highest state officials had less opportunities for extra earnings but enjoyed many privileges in kind.

The above data illustrate the social status aimed at by the leading stratum of the Soviet republic. It was in no way ascetic, and far above that of the broad masses of the workers (not to speak of the peasants) notwithstanding the occasional occurrence of skilled workers, precursors of the later Stakhanovites, who earned very well and were not reminded of the *partmaximum* so as not to discourage their efforts. But while differentiations within the stratum were moderate, and transfer to a faraway place need not mean loss of such modest comfort as one was used to, a clear barrier divided this stratum from the standards of the new bourgeoisie and those specialists, artists, etc. who shared its way of life. This barrier was necessary, not because of mere abstract standards of social justice but in order to prevent corruption. The party machine formed not a very numerous party of the leading stratum of Soviet Russia, out was very important in that it was capable of giving assignments to a much larger number of communists who occupied leading positions in most fields of life (perhaps with the exception of the arts and the sciences, where communists of high professional standing were so rare that they would be forgiven unorthodox views).

In order to answer the long-standing opposition argument that *Uchrazpred,* by its dispositive powers, kept the mass of the party members in material dependence[56], Stalin emphasised that the number of assignments in a year such as 1922 had been much smaller than in the times of the civil war with its mobilisations of all kinds.[57] He omitted, however, the point that once the war was over, people thought in terms of normal careers. Eight thousand assignments for permanent work (amongst these 5,167 concerning persons holding positions of responsibility) might not be proportionally more than what had been usual in 1919-20[58], but it affected quite a considerable portion of those communist officials in positions of responsibility who changed jobs during a year. Moreover, for everyone who was actually promoted or demoted by party decision there may have been a few whose behaviour was influenced by the hope, or fear, of similar experience. Certainly the Central Committee's dispositive power influenced the personal fates only of a small minority of party members. A real rebellion of the rank and file could easily have swept them away, as no one would have dared to violate the Rules in those days. In the absence of such a rebellion, however, with the average communist being inclined to follow the lead of those in positions of authority, the power of the CC and of its Secretary General was quite strong over dissenters in the Central Committee.

It was another question as to how far the party machine could dominate the machine of the State. The percentage of party members in the higher Soviet organs amounted to 80-90 per cent; it depended on the party's policy of how high to make it—at least outside those branches of public life where a certain proportion of qualified specialists was needed in the visible positions. A narrow half of those working in leading economic posts were communists. With some efforts the percentage amongst the managers of the largest enterprises was increased from 31 per cent in 1923 to 61 per cent in 1924. The percentage was much smaller—four to seven per cent—in the organisations of commerce and credit. The quality of many of these party members was illustrated by the fact that the numerous communists working in a leading organisation of Foreign Trade had in 1923-24 to be purged cent per cent ! Amongst the leading officials of the

State Bank a mere twelve per cent were communists. But there were seventeen per cent communists amongst those employees of the grain purchasing agency who came in direct contact with the peasants and whose policies might be more important (and less easily accessible to control from the centre). Amongst the army officers, there were 13 per cent communists in 1923 and 18 in 1924, but the total number of communists in the Army fell from 61,000 to 52,000 (in spite of the reduction of the Army's numerical strength, which implied some reduction of the percentage of party members in the ranks). Less than one per cent of them had joined the party before 1917, slightly more than three per cent between the revolutions of February and October 1917, just a third during the civil war, 23 per cent in 1920 and 20 per cent in 1921-23.[59] The scarcity of Old Bolsheviks in all walks of life is illustrated by the result of the great efforts made between 1922 and 1923 (according to a decision of the XI Party Conference which was caused by the struggle against the Workers' Opposition) to increase their percentage amongst trade union leaders. The percentage of members who had joined the party before October 1917 amongst the Chairmen of the Gubernium trade union centres (i.e. the highest-standing officials below the national leaders) was raised from 27 to 57.[60]

Stalin, who since Sverdlov's death had been the party's leading organisation specialist, presided over these developments since the X Party Congress had replaced Krestinski, Preobrazhenski and Serebryakov—supporters of Trotsky and of the 'buffer' group, respectively, during the trade union discussion—by Molotov, Stalin's associate since the old *Pravda* of 1912, and Yaroslavski, who soon became Stalin's main supporter in the CCC. The policies of the Secretariat can hardly have been affected when the man who had directed its activities as head of the Orgburo now became Secretary General, with Molotov and Kuibyshev as assistants. But certainly the importance of organisation was emphasised now that one of the party leaders made it the main field of his activities. Apart from Trotsky's motivated assertion[61], there is no ground for the assumption that Lenin at that time—as distinct from his afterthoughts eight months later—was opposed to the appointment. The only criticism to which it was exposed at the XI Party

Congress—in very polite terms, the meaning of which was accessible only to the initiated—was directed against both Lenin and Stalin.[62]   Stalin, however, would not have moved to the job had he not regarded the party machine as the nucleus of the whole party organisation, superior in importance to the political-propagandist aspects of party work in which much popularity could be gained, as well as even to the highest offices of the State. His success shows that his interpretation of the dynamics of the Soviet system was correct.   That it was due not only to the particular conditions of NEP was demonstrated, in later days, by the success of Khrushchev against Malenkov who, when faced with the decision which of the two highest offices to keep, chose the Premiership.[63]

(b) THE OLD BOLSHEVIKS ASSERT THEIR LEADERSHIP : TROTSKY'S DEFEAT AND THE LENIN-RECRUITMENT

One year after the introduction of NEP it was clear that the communists had succeeded in maintaining the essential position of power.   At the meeting of the communist group of the Metal Workers' Congress on March 6, 1922[64], Lenin proclaimed that the retreat had come to an end : no further major concessions would be made to capitalism.   Shortly before, he had emphasised the need to restrict the rights of private enterprise in the new civil code : 'We do not recognise anything "private"; for us *everything* in the field of economics belongs to *public* and not to private law.'[65]   Evidently Lenin understood by 'retreat' concessions to the capitalists, not to the peasants.   In the very speech in which he announced to the XI Party Congress the 'end of the retreat', he also emphasised the need for further steps to alleviate the peasants' lot and threatened the Workers' Opposition with expulsion from the party because its propaganda might prevent the workers from making Socialist State enterprise a success, or bring the alliance with the peasants to an end.   Lenin believed that the State industry could not only be restored after the devastations of the war and hold its own in competition with private enterprise, but also eventually move the peasant economy forward on socialist lines if proper relationships (*smychka*) with the peasants were

14

established.[66] In his last articles, written during his illness, Lenin elaborated on the theme : with political power in the hands of the Soviets, agricultural co-operation might provide a transition to socialist forms of production accessible to the peasants' understanding.[67] Improvement of administration and management, for which purpose Lenin suggested the reorganisation of the Workers' and Peasants' Inspection[68], might raise the level of savings; every kopeck saved should be devoted to the development of large-scale industry and to electrification.[69] After the first difficult steps an incomparably quicker development could be achieved. In the field of international relations the avoidance of new foreign intervention[70] was the main aim. Soviet socialism, built by the efforts of Soviet workers and peasants, would be able to assume the leadership of the underdeveloped nations. 'Ultimately', Lenin wrote, 'the outcome of the struggle is determined by the fact that Russia, India, China etc. together constitute the overwhelming majority of mankind.'[69]

The size of the instrument of such an historical transformation grossly contrasted with its purpose. Lenin himself, being afraid of the influx of heterogeneous elements under NEP, had made his contribution towards narrowing down the party's size.[71] Zinoviev, speaking at the XI Congress,[72] found that the party could well fulfil its tasks with the half million members which (because of an underestimate of the extent of the 'purge') it was believed to have at the time. 100,000 were needed for the army, 25-50,000 for the higher links of the State apparatus, 100,000 for local government, and the rest in the factories. In prerevolutionary days, he said, there had been thirty to forty Bolsheviks in the Petrograd Putilov works (a giant with tens of thousands of workers) but those were real leaders. Now there were sixty communists in the works—but what benefit could come of such an increase, or even a further one, unless the quality of the communists greatly improved? Evidently he acquiesced in a state of affairs in which the average worker would hardly meet a communist except in the capacity of a trade union official or manager.

Two more years were to pass before the solution of the problem was found in a broadening of the party at the expense of the traditional standards of the Old Guard. In 1922 no one, except the Workers' Opposition which desired an identification of the party with the Workers' sectional demands and opposed the compromises of NEP, would have suggested such a solution. The idea of narrowing down the party arose in order to save it from the careerist who in the conditions of NEP might easily have introduced a bourgeois scale of values. Many workers, dissatisfied with their standard of life and busy recovering their private affairs from the devastations of the preceding period, even left the party. But part of the difficulty was due to an inarticulate feeling that no really broad appeal was possible without some symbol of unity. The Old Guard was united by hardly anything except the recognition that State power had to be preserved by complicated manoeuvres in a difficult time. The following crises, painful though they were, saved the party from death by stagnation.

At the centre of power, Stalin made his first appearance in the foreground with the suggestion at the XII Congress that the CC be broadened by the inclusion of new members who were not affected by the personal tensions and conflicts which had naturally developed during six years within a narrow body of people working together. In due course the new members must replace the Old Guard which was gradually being worn out.[73] *Prima facie,* this statement was no more flattering to the Old Bolsheviks than to Trotsky. In view of the tactical position, however, it was watered down by Stalin's defence, in so many words, of a 'nucleus'—consisting of Kamenev, Zinoviev and himself—which had formed itself within the Central Committee in the course of years of common work.[74] Its stability should not be overrated. In informal discussions conducted in September 1923, Zinoviev suggested its replacement by a triumvirate consisting of Stalin, Trotsky and a third person—himself, Kamenev or Bukharin. Later he described this effort at what today would be described as 'collective leadership' as an attempted 'politicisation of the Secretariat'[75] (the assumption being that, under Stalin, it was mainly a technical body). For us it is noteworthy that already in those days the Secretariat was regarded as the appropriate locus for effective party leadership even by persons critical of Stalin.

Leading nuclei, based on a tradition of common work, were formed in the Gubernium Committees as well. In spite of the disputes and tensions which accompanied their formation, Stalin found them quite healthy and legitimate manifestations. Indeed, they were preliminary conditions of effective collective work, provided that the frictions were prevented from becoming personal.[76] Grouping of people at the centre and at the periphery, according to common understanding of the practical tasks, implied mutual support. The idea that this might contradict the statements of the X Party Congress about the inadmissibility of intra-party groupings was completely alien to Stalin. If anyone had questioned him on that point he would have answered, as he did two years later, that 'the Party cannot be a faction', identifying the majority group with 'the Party'. But, surely, someone had to rule the country. Should it be done by the State machine of a country with a peasant majority, most of the education and much of the ostensible wealth being concentrated in the hands of the old and new bourgeoisie regenerated by NEP ? This would naturally assume that the Bolshevik Party and the leader of its army had done a good job in saving the country's independence and prospects of development. Or should it be done by the Old Bolsheviks exchanging during long nights interesting memories and pointed formulations on controversial points of doctrine ? Apart from the questionable merits of such forms of leadership at the centre, elaborate qualifications demanded of every candidate for any office might easily result in a situation where office holders could no longer be elected but had to be nominated. Moreover, there was no guarantee that the narrow group of party members which represented Bolshevism in some factory, would be able even to answer the questions of their non-party fellows.[77]

Lenin had not seen this problem : hence his 'will'[78] failed to influence the party's fate, in spite of his insight that the personal qualities of Stalin and Trotsky might result in a dangerous split within the leadership. That he did not wish to be succeeded by Trotsky is evident from his remarks about the latter's 'non-Bolshevism'. That he now was afraid of Stalin's using his enormous power in order to throw Trotsky aside was made explicit.[79] Obviously he did not wish to be succeeded by any single individual. (His own personal leadership might appear to him as due to the peculiarities of the revolutionary situation, not easily repeatable as the party, once in power, could no longer be regarded as the outcome of efforts led by any individual.) Stalin owed much of his eventual triumph to the fact that individual leadership appeared as the alternative to the rule of the party machine and that Trotsky, because of his popularity as the successful war leader, was the obvious candidate for individual leadership based upon non-Party forces. Since we have not seen a Trotsky-dictatorship we cannot say whether its methods would have been any less brutal than those eventually applied by Stalin. Lenin apparently wished to concentrate leadership in the hands of a body so authoritative that the holders of the highest offices in party and State would have to accept within it positions of equality. Emphasis on everyone's shortcomings might appear as a useful device of bringing home to the party leaders the need for collaboration. In fact, Lenin's criticism initially worked as a brake upon the person eventually chosen and allowed the party, thirty years later, to dissociate itself from Stalin's shortcomings without impairing its founder's, and its own, authority.

Presumably in order to establish for any future Politburo majority inclined to drastic solutions handicaps similar to those which he himself had experienced from the party organisers,[80] Lenin suggested an increase in the membership of the Central Committee to fifty or even a hundred. (The opposite method was applied after Stalin's death in order to put a brake on any individual's aspirations to individual leadership.)[81] The XIII Congress in May 1924, to the leading delegates of which Lenin's 'will' was communicated, elected a CC of 53 members.[82] The figure of 71 plus fifty candidates (increased to 67 in 1930) was reached as late as 1927. From such an array of party organisers Stalin might experience an occasional setback when he wished to expel the opposition leaders, as in July 1927. But if conflicts were driven to extremes they would be even more bitter than those among a narrow circle of Old Bolsheviks, linked to each other by many memories of the underground struggle, would have been.

The situation within the party leadership, tense for years and bound to become tenser as the course of Lenin's illness made the succession problem topical, came to a head during the 'scissors' crisis, so called with reference to the graphs which marked the development of industrial and agricultural prices respectively. Immediately after the introduction of NEP, the extremely low level of agricultural and industrial production allowed for such exchanges as were possible, roughly on the pre-War price level. But since, as in other lands gravely hit by the war, agriculture recovered much quicker than industry at first, price relations changed with the result that the peasants could not afford to buy industrial goods and had less incentive to increase their sales of foods. Unemployment in industry followed. It was aggravated by the strictly deflationist policy of the State Bank, which was just engaged in replacing the devaluated paper money by a new currency (*chervontsy*) stable in terms of gold.

The very fact of economic depression caused disputes. Amongst the economists, Kondratev, defending the agricultural interest, was opposed by Strumilin and other advocates of the industrial interest. Then there was Preobrazhenski who regarded the 'scissors' as an instrument of the necessary 'primitive accumulation', at the peasants' expense, of the investment funds necessary for industrialisation.[83] It would be erroneous to associate any of the senior party leaders with extreme suggestions. The resolution of the XII Party Congress, supported by Trotsky as a result of a compromise within the leadership, emphasised the importance of planning. It said that it was impossible to replace the working of the market by administrative regulation, the necessary foundation of which 'had not yet been created by economic experience'.[84]

Undoubtedly the existing production capacities of industry were badly used, and moreover, burdened with excessive overall costs. On the eve of the XII Congress (in April 1923) the CC considered suggestions going as far as the closing down of the Putilov and the Bryansk Railway works because they showed a deficit. Such radical suggestions were withdrawn in the preliminary talks of the Congress, but even the resolution eventually adopted stated that all secondary considerations which might contradict a radical concentration of production must give way to 'the basic economic task', i.e. securing the necessary circulating means for State industry, reduction of cost prices, expansion of the market, achievement of profits. A permanent and general improvement of the workers' conditions was possible only on the basis of industrial expansion which was impossible unless industry made profits. Keeping inefficient factories working, or keeping staffs larger than those justified by the actual productivity of some enterprise, was the most expensive and irrational form of social security.[84]

The results of the economy drive were considerable. 21 per cent were saved in overhead costs of coal production as well as in labour costs in the Donets basin, 24 per cent in the overhead costs[85] of iron production, 18 per cent in those of cotton spinning. In November 1923 all prices of industrial goods were cut by 23.7 per cent (those of textiles even by 33 per cent), and in spring 1924 the stabilisation of the currency was accomplished. The peasants obtained industrial commodities at more satisfactory rates; even if they could not get enough of them they got money which it was worthwhile to hoard and which, according to a decision of the XII Party Congress, would be accepted in payment of taxes. The index number of agricultural prices rose from its lowest level (56 per cent in 1913) to 74 per cent at the end of 1923, while the industrial index had fallen from 172 to 147 per cent. This made the disproportion less than 2:1 : it fell further to less than 1.5 to 1 by October 1924. Two-thirds of the price reduction in industry were covered by economy of costs; the rest was borne by a reduction of industrial profits (which meant the investment rate). The 'scissors', though continuing on a much reduced level, ceased to be a first-rank political problem.

While being successful for a while in restoring equilibrium prices in the market, the economy drive and the strict anti-inflationist policies pursued by the Government were bound to cause dissatisfaction among the workers. Delays in paying wages figured prominently amongst the reasons for the wave of strikes which, in August 1923, started from the engineering works at Sormovo. The party organisations of the enterprises involved were either by-passed by the workers, and hence were surprised by events, or they were controlled by underground groups such as the Workers' Group and Workers' Truth.[86] The party's threatening isolation from the working class was bound to create alarm. It may have led to Zinoviev's above-mentioned efforts at preventing a split amongst the leaders. On September 23-25 a Plenary Meeting of the CC discussed the situation : three special committees were appointed to report on the general economic situation, on wages, and on the internal situation in the party. Trotsky and his friends abstained from work on these committees. Attempts made at the time to weaken Trotsky's control of the supreme military council[87] may have brought about that attitude. Appeals from the extreme leftists, suggesting a *bloc* of all the opponents of the majority group and the elimination of Zinoviev, Kamenev and Stalin from the Central Committee had been made already at the XII Party Congress. There Kossior, one of the moderate oppositionists, demanded the repeal of the resolution of the X Congress on Party Unity : the prohibition of groupings within the party, though justified in the conditions of the Kronstadt crisis, had outlived its usefulness.[88] There is no evidence that Trotsky reacted strongly to any of these moves before the August strike, yet on October 8 he issued a letter to the CC which, at the same time, was circulated by him amongst leading party workers, as an avowed appeal over the heads of the CC to 'every party member whom he found sufficiently mature'. Secret grouping, about which the CC committee on internal party matters had complained, were said to follow from the party's unhealthy state and from the secretarial hierarchy's monopoly to express party opinion and to form party decisions.[89] Responding to Trotsky's letter, forty-six well-known party members, with the background of diverse opposition groups, submitted to the Politburo a document composed of diverse declarations.[90] The basic document, which was accepted by a majority of the 46 only with reservations, forecast impending economic and political breakdown unless the internal party regime was fundamentally changed. The only positive suggestion upon which all the signatories, and soon also the Central Committee, agreed was the convocation of a Party Conference to which some oppositionists should be invited.

Neither the criticisms expressed in the document nor the alarmist statements about threatening dangers were novel. But the gravity of the crisis was made evident by the combination of groups which pursued different aims yet were united by the desire to overthrow the existing leadership. Such a combination had, on the ninth of Thermidor, brought the Jacobin phase of the French revolution to an end. A party such as the Bolsheviks, which regarded competition amongst political parties for the electorate vote as incompatible with the preservation of the revolutionary regime, could hardly tolerate competition of parties (slightly disguised as factions) for control of the diverse parts of the State machinery. Once one of the competing groups claimed that the policies of the leading group threatened the collapse of the revolution, in a communist's eyes any counter-measure would be justified. In fact the consequences of a struggle for power within the ruling party was eventually the destruction of the freedom even of political argument within its ranks. This possibility would be reinforced by the absence of a leader of Lenin's authority who could admit blunders without fearing the loss of his own and the party's leadership.[91]

For a moment, the implications of a struggle against a leader of Trotsky's calibre as well as the German crisis (which in the interpretation current in Moscow just approached a revolutionary climax)[92] favoured moderation. A meeting of the CC and the CCC on October 25 to 27, which was attended by representatives of the ten biggest party organisations and (with a consultative voice) by twelve representatives of 'the forty-six', deplored Trotsky's breach of corporate discipline which had led to the factional grouping of the forty-six, yet asked the Politburo to accelerate the work of the preparatory committees.[93] On November 7, Zinoviev announced, as a token of the era of internal democracy, the opening of the discussion. Within the Politburo a committee consisting of Stalin, Trotsky and Kamenev had to elaborate a resolution on party structure. Its draft was unanimously adopted at a joint meeting of the Politburo and the Presidium of the CCC on December 5 and published immediately. The resolution did not attack the party machine as such—the existence of bureaucratic tendencies within it was recognised by all the majority leaders, including Stalin.[94] 'Workers' democracy' was defined in a positive way, so as to mean
the freedom for all party members openly to discuss the most important issues of party life....and the eligibility of

all party officials. . . .from below to the top.   But it does in no way suppose the freedom of factional groupings which are highly dangerous for a ruling party for they always involve the danger of a split. . . .of the government and of the government machine as a whole. . . .

Only by a continual, lively, intellectual life can the party be preserved such as it was formed before and during the revolution, continuously submitting its past to a critical study, correcting its mistakes, and collectively deciding the most important questions.   Only these methods of work can provide real guarantees against the transformation of ephemeral disagreements into factional groupings with all the consequences indicated above.

In order to prevent such developments, the leading party bodies must listen to the voice of the broad party masses and must avoid an interpretation of every criticism as a manifestation of factionalism which would drive conscientious and disciplined Party members on to the road of secrecy and factionalism.[95]

The compromise had been achieved by the reservation of explicit condemnation of the underground groups which no one could defend and by the replacement of condemnation of groupings as such[96] by reference to the resolution 'On Party Unity'. As usual in such cases, the compromise in form failed to bridge the cleavage in substance.   When explaining the need for democratisation of party institutions, Stalin noticed the limitations placed (under the conditions of NEP) upon free eligibility for candidates for office by the well-considered requirement of a certain party record (*stazh*).   There was also the need, recognised by Trotsky himself, to keep discussion within such limits as were compatible with the party's character as an acting community.[97]   Occasionally the majority would defeat opposition amendments even when it was difficult to explain why they were mistaken.[98]   Trotsky, on the other hand, gave his interpretation of the agreed resolution in a letter to his local branch 'On the New Course', which was distributed to all the organisations by the opposition and sent to *Pravda* for publication.[99]   He described it as a mere first instalment, which could be realised not by the party machine but by 'the party subordinating its apparatus to itself'. The constitutional definitions and limitations of party democracy, however important, were only of secondary importance. 'What needs changing we will change'; first of all it was necessary 'that the party, in the person of all its local branches and associations, should restore to itself its collective initiative. . . .revive and renew the apparatus, making it feel that it is the executive mechanism of the collective whole'. It was a healthy phenomenon that the youth, 'the most reliable barometer of the party', reacted sharply against party bureaucratism (indeed, Trotsky got resolutions supporting his views mostly from the party nuclei of the Moscow high schools and in the army). It was an unhealthy state of affairs if critics were asked to show the length of their party record. History had already known examples of degeneration of an 'Old Guard' of a workers' party, the leaders of the Second International being conspicuous.

The meaning of such statements was obvious, and so was also Stalin's short and nearly casual reaction.[100] The theoretical possibility of a degeneration of the Bolshevik Old Guard should not be excluded, but a far more topical danger was implied in the presence of former Mensheviks in the party. The party should be on its guard when one of them appealed against the Old Bolsheviks to the young generation who had joined it when in power. The position of Trotsky—the most popular of the leaders surviving Lenin, the head of the army and the outsider in Bolshevism—was unique. All forms of discontent, both within the party and counter-revolutionary, tended to group themselves in sympathy around him.[101] Precisely for this reason, party opinion was bound to rally against him once the issues had come into the open. Stalin could wait and leave it to Trotsky either to submit, or to repeat his attacks and thus to create a situation where compromise would be less favourable after every loss of prestige brought on himself by defeats in the party caucus. Trotsky's hesitancy at many points may be explained by his reluctance to accept such non-Communist (and, in the conditions, counter-revolutionary) support as was potentially available.[102] He had no chance whatever, except as another Bonaparte, and the traditions of the Russian revolutionary movement were strong enough to prevent him from following that course. It is also true that Zinoviev, as distinct from Stalin, did everything to make reconciliation more difficult and its conditions unacceptable for Trotsky's self-esteem.[103] Fear, lest a defeated Trotsky, without a personal claim to leadership, but still useful, should become a potential ally of Stalin, may have determined such an attitude of Zinoviev. Trotsky's failure to compromise in time can be explained either by an excess of personal pride which outweighed whatever knowledge of the party setting he must have acquired in twenty years of conflict and collaboration,[104] or by some application of his concepts of Permanent Revolution to intra-party strife (in the sense of a series of attempts to wrest leadership from those hands into which it was bound to fall because of the objective conditions). The latter explanation was, naturally, preferred in his later writings ; it is not incompatible with the first.

Already in that first trial of strength Trotsky's defeat was a foregone conclusion. Of all the major regions, he obtained considerable support only from the old strongholds of 'Democratic Centralism'—Moscow (where 67 of the 346 industrial *nuclei* voted for him) and the Ukraine. Even in the army, where the party's propaganda machine was still in the hands of his supporters, the latter claimed to be backed by only a third of the *nuclei*.[105] Amongst the under-graduates, supporters of the party majority were so rare that those of them who, like Zhdanov and Malenkov, showed organisational abilities thereby also made the first steps in a successful party career, not too easy for an intellectual in those days. Even a minority of ten or twenty per cent of the delegates to a Party Congress supporting an opponent of Trotsky's standing would have been undesirable from the majority's point of view. The delay in the decision of the next Congress (or the convention of an extra-ordinary one) involved insecurity, and also the risk that less responsible minds might get the upper hand in the councils of the opposition. Hence the issue was decided by the XIII Party Conference, meeting a few days before Lenin's death. The resolution on party organisation, as agreed in the Politburo, was adopted unanimously; the condemnation of 'the lower-middle-class deviation in our party', as Trotskyism now was described, against a mere three votes. The Trotskyists were required to dissolve their factional organisation : as a warning to their leader, point 7 of the resolution 'On Party Unity' adopted three years before on Lenin's proposal, was published. Trotsky remained, however, on the Politburo to which he was also re-elected at the two subsequent party congresses.

While the Trotskyists' formal rights as party members remained unimpaired by the sharp condemnation of their views, the handicaps under which they had in future to work were demonstrated by two measures announced by Stalin to the Conference. Firstly, Antonov-Ovseyenko, the head of the Army's Political Demonsration, was to be transferred to another assignment (he soon became a diplomat) because he had influenced the discussion in the Army's party organisation in favour of the Opposition. Secondly, two relatively unknown undergraduates were to be expelled from the party because they had driven the Opposition's criticism to extremes (one of them had described the regime as a dictatorship of the party over the proletariat; the other had demanded that all the political decisions should be taken in the party cells, and the CC be reduced to the status of a mere executive organ).[106] The first measure, in itself no party penalty (though a heavy blow against Trotsky's position in his war office) was remarkable mainly in that its political reasons were honestly proclaimed. The second, like the measures taken at the XI Congress against two minor supporters of the Workers' Opposition, was remarkable mainly in that it was so solemnly announced. The majority followed its victory by a purge of the party nuclei other than those in factories, but strongly denied that the expulsions had been caused by political disagreements. Preobrazhenski found this unfair to those purged who thus got a moral stain on their record, instead of a note of disagreement which eventually could be rectified.[107]

The warning given was emphasised by Stalin's argument against Trotsky's explanation of factionalism as a healthy reaction to bureaucratism in the party. In fact, Stalin said, factions arose from the co-existence of different social groups in a country which contained all kinds of social formation from mediaevalism to growing socialism. Competition of diverse factions within the party, far from being an expression of party democracy, was thus interpreted as a manifestation of the presence within the working-class party of non-working class elements. If there were maximum freedom of internal discussion, there would be even more factionalism (the struggle against minorities, far from being a settlement of disagreements amongst comrades, thus became an act of class-struggle). From a monolithic organisation, with a common will and uniting all shades of opinion in common action, as according to Stalin it had been in Bolshevik thought, the party, if Trotsky's theses were adopted, would be turned into a discussion group or, at best, into a union of groups and factions which entered into only temporary agreements with each other.[108] Stalin formulated the objective conditions in which democracy in his sense was possible and thereby in substance—though still without the unorthodox formula—his concept of 'Socialism in one country'. Industry must rise, its material conditions must at least not deteriorate, the party must include in its ranks the best elements of the working class, and peace must be preserved. The party could not preserve internal democracy when arms had to be taken up to defend the country.[109] The last observation still indicates an interpretation of democracy as opportunity of voicing disagreements. But a few months later, at the XIII Party Congress, Stalin reproached Trotsky for his description of bureaucratisation as the greatest evil. Even a highly democratic party machine, if divorced from the masses, would fail in its purpose. On the other hand, even a party with bureaucratic shortcomings could develop if it was linked with the masses and enjoyed their confidence.[110] The workers' readiness to join the party was the supreme sign of this confidence. Stalin found the answer to the apparent alternative between the stagnation of the Old Guard and transferring its work to a young generation divorced from its tradition in a large-scale expansion of party membership under the guidance of a machine dominated by Old Bolsheviks.

Of all the results of the discussion on democracy within the party the most important was the mass admission of workers from the bench. By special decisions of the Plenary Sessions of the CC of January 31 and March 31 such workers got a monopoly of admission for periods of three months ; conditions of admission were relaxed to allow the admission even of workers who did not have recommendation from long-standing party members. On the other hand, discussion of the applications in meetings of non-Party workers would strengthen the links between the party and the masses. To enhance the new recruits' self-confidence and to put a premium on successful recruitment, probationers were given a full vote in the election of delegates to the XIII Congress (of course, they could not be elected themselves). This ruling was added to the decisions of the CC Plenary Session which met after Lenin's death, together with a warning against repetitions of the aggravation of tensions within the party which had been characteristic of recent discussions. This warning was directed against Zinoviev's friends who, behind the closed doors of the majority's caucus, urged Trotsky's expulsion. But while the minority got some protection against the danger of expulsion, it found its possibilities of criticising the majority reduced by the presence of newcomers unfamiliar with nuances of party doctrine and inclined to vote against anyone who appeared as a disturber of unity and diverted attention from the practical tasks.

Lenin died a few days after the Party Conference had opened the recruitment campaign which was now connected with his name. The overwhelming sense of loss demonstrated by the broadest strata of the people gave his party an additional sanction. Not one hundred thousand, as originally intended, but two hundred thousand workers could be admitted : the party's strength rose from 446,000 members and probationers to 647,000 by July 1, 94 per cent of the new recruits being industrial workers. 60 per cent of the total membership and 76 per cent of the probationers now were workers by social origin. In the factories the percentage of communists among the total labour force rose from 3.9 to 11.4 per cent. The recruitment campaign had been carried out with a mass appeal. At some places whole shops applied for membership; *Izvestiya*[111] reprinted with approval the declaration of Tver workers who deemed that it was criminal to remain outside the RKP when the dead leader had to be replaced by collective thought and efforts; a total of 300,000 applications for membership was submitted.[112] The CC decided that although group applications were acceptable, decisions on admission should be taken on an individual basis : the type of applicant who had simply 'swum with the current' thus got an opportunity for second thought. But it is hardly conceivable that an applicant who really desired admission was rejected unless he was a notorious drunkard or laggard. No demands on earlier political education were made : sixty per cent of the party members existing in June had none whatsoever and Stalin found it advisable to concentrate on qualitative rather than quantitative strengthening of the membership, through more intensive schooling.[113]

The fact that a mere 8.4 per cent of the new members came through the Komsomol[112] shows that the success of the Lenin recruitment was not due to a mere relaxation of restrictions which, before, had prevented the entrance of workers not sufficiently ripe from the Old Bolsheviks' point of view. The typical entrant may have been a worker who had left his village not too long ago. Entrance involved a decision to make industry his life's career to increase his professional qualifications and to acquire political knowledge. The workers recruited in 1924, or at least the more ambitious amongst them, provided the cadres for Stalin's industrialisation, long before they replaced the Old Bolsheviks in the key positions of the party machine.[114] For this reason the repeated demand to create within the party a majority of workers at the bench (as distinct from workers by social origin) was never realised. After the admission of another 163,000 of such workers in 1925, their percentage amongst the total membership (of 1025 million, including probationers) reached a temporary maximum of 40.8 per cent; still there were 46.6 per cent salaried employees, whose number increased by promotions. The aim for a majority, amongst the party members, of workers at the bench was not even realised during the first five-year plan when very serious efforts were made to achieve it.[115] Recruitment for the party amongst the industrial workers prospered best in times of quick industrial expansion which were, however, also the times of increased promotions of party members to junior managerial jobs.

The Lenin recruits not only provided the nucleus of the party's future cadres : their schooling also offered the occasion for the formulation of the Leninist theory which inspired party politics for nearly twenty years. Many contributions were made to the new systematisation, which was required by the needs of the new

recruits as well as by the desire for a strict delimitation from
Trotskyism. The one written by Zinoviev, the most polemical in
character, was dominated by peasant and colonial problems,
elaborating his statement in 'Bolshevism or Trotskyism', his contribution to the discussion on Trotsky's *Lessons of October,* that
Leninism was 'the Marxism of the epoch of imperialist wars and
of the World Revolution which has immediately started in a
predominantly peasant country'[116]. Stalin's *Leninism*—the only
book which gained more than ephemeral importance—elaborated
a scheme drafted by him three years before.[117] The 'subjective
factor' was systematically introduced into the presentation of
Marxist theory : politics had become an art. Although Stalin
explained Leninism in relation to the specific Russian background,
he regarded it as '*the* Marxism of the period of imperialism and
of the proletarian revolutions'.[118] By implication, the specific
conditions of Russia (plus some more 'underdeveloped countries',
the inclusion of which Lenin had envisaged at the end of his life)
represented the problems of actual socialist revolutions. This
was the real content of Stalin's later concept of 'socialism in one
country'. Whatever its shortcomings (Stalin died before socialism
was completed in his country and a second world power establishing socialism was in existence), it was useful in rejecting
pessimism or adventurism caused by the temporary isolation of
the Russian revolution.

Every systematisation carries the danger of dogmatism; this
danger is multiplied if systematisation accompanies the awakening
of masses which had formerly never taken active part
in political life. Far from being a mere guide and an
application of past experiences to changing circumstances,[119] the
systematised theory may become a symbol of the acceptance of
leaders supposed to be repositories of that theory. The mass
recruitment of workers at the base and the broadening of the
CC by electing workers at the top,[120] was intended as a means
of introducing into the party an element not interested in the long-
standing quarrels. Indeed, it saved the party from the stagnation
threatening in 1923 and has enabled it to provide fairly comprehensive leadership ever since. Potentially, the mass party created
by Stalin is a framework of opinion-making in which democracy

15

may develop long before the rest of the country are ready to join in an argument which, by the very nature of things, goes deeper than short-term interests with which party struggle in the western countries is concerned. But even today, in spite of all the enormous educational progress made since the Lenin recruitment, the average member of the ten million party is more remote from the leading cadres than was the average member of the 400,000-strong party of 1923 from the Old Bolsheviks. The responsibilities facing the nucleus have increased. Since the Lenin recruitment, the party's closer connection with the masses became an established fact, but so also did the bureaucratisation which Stalin, in 1924, was prepared to accept as a lesser evil.[110] It is still early to forecast the results of the struggle against it which has been waged with increased intensity since Stalin's death.

The further elaboration of Stalinist theories was conditioned by a split in the party majority of 1923-24. Already when reporting on the results of the XIII Party Congress Stalin went out of his way to polemise against imprecise theoretical statements made by Kamenev and Zinoviev.[121] The tension appears to have been directly connected with problems of agrarian policy. In some Georgian districts, the Menshevik insurrection of August 1924 was supported by the peasants. As in the case of the workers' strikes in August 1923, the party organisations, which were fairly numerous in the region, had failed to notice the fermentation amongst the population. Discontent with grain prices and non-payment of taxes were widespread in regions ranging from Belorussia to Siberia.[122] Mass disturbances reported by the police in the RSFSR increased from 393 cases in the first quarter of 1924 to 1,597 in the second; then followed a decline which at first was slow; only in the third quarter of 1926 a minimum of 22 cases was reached.[123] The party was still poorly represented in the villages : for every 26 of them there was one party nucleus, for every 250 adult villagers one communist; 13,558 rural *nuclei* with 99,700 party members and 53,293 probationers were now in existence[124] (slightly more nuclei than in the towns, yet with less than a third of the urban party membership). The most active of their secretaries were assembled in Moscow to learn that the party's approach to the peasants must be changed.

Real life must be brought into the Soviets so that they might show the feelings of the non-party peasants.[125]

Dissatisfaction with the new concessions made to the peasants may have led to Trotsky's decision to take a step which, though undoubtedly within the limits of party legality,[126] was bound to be regarded as a challenge. The *Lessons of October* dwelt, not unnaturally, on Zinoviev's and Kamenev's record in the crisis of 1917. By way of generalisation, the capacity of 'old guards' to adapt themselves to the quickly changing needs of revolutionary times was questioned. The generalisation was applied to the defeat of the German communists in 1923 which had made the isolation of Soviet Russia absolute. Lenin's action in 1917 appeared as that of a genial individual who—jointly with another genial individual, Trotsky—overruled rather than convinced a resistive caucus.

Trotsky's book was bound to be interpreted by his oppenents not only as a continuation of his attack against the Old Bolsheviks (which it obviously was) but also as a renewed bid for power. In fact, it is difficult to suppose that he pursued any aims other than that of making a demonstrative stand. In the short run, he was bound to be defeated : any exchange of recriminations about the past must bring up his own past conflicts with Lenin. Stalin's position was strengthened as he was the only member of the triumvirate who had a good October record (whatever details Trotsky might bring forward). He also enjoyed the opportunity of being generous both to his less fortunate fellow-triumvirs, whose mistakes he played down (for the time being), and to Trotsky. When Zinoviev and Kamenev wished to expel Trotsky from the party or at least from the Politburo and mobilised the Leningrad organisation for that purpose, Stalin did not join this move to discredit Trotsky (whose past anti-Leninism and whose mistakes in the civil war could now be brought into the open without his opponents bearing the responsibility for having reopened old accounts). He avoided any organisational measure. Trotsky resigned from the War Office (which was unavoidable in the circumstances). Already in the summer of 1924 the party majority had formalised its caucus in the Politburo so as to make the outvoting of Trotsky in that body a foregone conclusion. One year later, when his conflict with Zinoviev and Kamenev had come into the open, Stalin defended his avoidance of organisational measures against Trotsky by the basic undesirability of surgical operations from the party's point of view. A policy of amputations was infectious. Once one had started that way, where would one stop ?[127] Some element of threat against Stalin's temporary allies was unmistakable, but there is no reason to doubt the sincerity of his view both when it was expressed within the Central Committee and two years later, when it was made public. As late as 1929 Trotsky's forcible expulsion from the USSR in order to avoid imprisoning him was strongly resented by party opinion. More brutal methods of surgery became possible only when a new generation assessed the past of party leaders in the light of the mythology in which they had been brought up.

The discussion on *The Lessons of October* offered Stalin the opportunity to make the theory of 'socialism in one country' explicit. As his own intellectual development pointed to that conclusion,[128] his avoidance of the theory in the first edition of *Leninism* must be explained by tactical considerations for established orthodoxy. However the main heresy, the prospect of the Russian revolution's emerging triumphant by internal reconstruction and alliance with the underdeveloped East, had been expressed by Lenin himself in his last articles. As Trotsky's new attack concerned the communists' defeat in that very country upon which Marxists since the days of the Communist Manifesto had put their main hopes,[129] the question of what the victorious Russian revolution should do, pending the triumph of world revolution,[130] became the most devastating argument against the opposition. Stalin inspired the new cadres by showing them that the worker's everyday job was part of a great historical process. The conditions for Soviet Russia's security against external threats and fulfilling her functions as a centre of socialist reconstruction were formulated in very ambitious terms, which however are low compared with what has been achieved since : fifteen to twenty million industrial workers (in comparison with the four million available in those days), electrification of the main industrial regions, cooperative organisation (without further specification) of agriculture, and a well-developed metal industry.[131]

Zinoviev, who knew his quotations by heart[132], kept silent until later in 1925, when disagreements on agrarian policies developed. The policy of 'enlivening the Soviets', i.e. replacing their nomination by small cliques of local communists by real elections (under observance of the laws which disenfranchised *kulaks* and priests), resulted in the ascendancy in many places of those middle peasants who were politically influenced by their more prosperous fellows. In the village Soviets of the Kuban region, the percentage of workers fell from 20 to 7 per cent., that of *Komsomol* members from 7.5 to 1 per cent. Former Red Army men (who during their service had been prepared to play an active part in local government) constituted a mere quarter of the members of the village Soviets, while before they had formed the majority all over the country. The percentage of communists in the village Soviets fell from 12 to 6.5 per cent and even in the District Executive Committees from 61 to 44 per cent.[133] The Plenary Meeting of the CC, which met in April 1925 concurrently with the XIV Party Conference, hence decided to lift restrictions on the applications of wage labour as a regular basis of farming and on the lease of land (in Russia, as a rule, the *kulak* with the necessary capital rented land from the poor peasant who could not cultivate his share in the *mir*, and therefore had to sell his labour) so that the social struggles which followed from the social differentiation in the village might be fought out in the open.[134] It was, however, questionable whether the party organisations existing in the villages were capable of conducting these struggles. Labourers formed a mere 1.3 per cent of their membership. 11.1 per cent of the members of some village nuclei investigated by the CC and CCC had to be expelled,[135] because most of them were exploiters of labour.

(c) THE PARTY BECOMES 'MONOLITHIC'

The 'extension of the NEP to the village', as it was officially called, allowed for different interpretations. According to the official one, the class struggle could be better conducted on an open stage than if application of wages labour and long-term leases of land continued as an underground activity. But during the discussions which preceded the Plenary Meeting of the CC,

Bukharin appealed in an article to the wealthy peasants 'to enrich themselves' and thereby to promote country's economic development. Krupskaya sent *Pravda* an article criticising Bukharin who in turn wrote a reply. Against the votes of Krupskaya, Zinoviev and Kamenev it was decided that neither of the two articles should be published and that Bukharin should withdraw his slogan.[136] He did so in a somewhat diplomatic way, but after a few weeks the slogan was repeated in a slightly modified form by one of his supporters in the Komsomol, Stetski by name. In a letter to the editors of *Komsomolskaya pravda,* which was not fully published at the time,[137] Stalin, Molotov and Andreyev explained that the party was not in favour of private capitalist accumulation but admitted it only in order to promote its own aim of socialist accumulation. But at the XIV Congress, when Zinoviev and Kamenev attacked Bukharin again, Stalin declared their attacks to be unsubstantiated.[138] Bukharin himself, naturally glad of such publicity as he got, explained in a pamphlet[139] that even kulak-dominated cooperatives would be integrated in the country's progress towards socialism as they had to invest their profits in state-owned banks. It was obvious that the socialism to be built in one country could be interpreted in very different ways.

Before these interpretations became a matter of open dispute, the very slogan of 'socialism in one country' was attacked by an opposition gradually rallying against Stalin's machine. At the April 1925 session of the CC Zinoviev stated that Russia's backwardness prevented the building of socialism. As capitalism abroad experienced temporary stabilisation, increased pressure should be applied against capitalist tendencies in the villages. When reporting on the session, Stalin rejected these arguments in sharp terms without mentioning their author.[140] As divisions on majority policy problems were avoided, Stalin, reporting to the XIV Party Congress on the antecedents of the crisis, could refer only to the earlier demands of the Leningrad organisation for expulsion of Trotsky and to its efforts to establish its authority on the national scale.[141] Petrovski found some analogy between the present situation and that of 1923 : there had been personal frictions, afterwards practical disagreements, and lastly attempts to find theoretical foundations for these frictions and disagreements.[142]

Stalin stated fairly frankly that it was an issue of power : the party could no longer bear the institution of 'viceroys', especially since there was no longer a Lenin to keep them under control.[143] As there was now a fairly broad body of agreed tenets—including even some general concept of 'building socialism in one country'[144] —the struggle for power was described, in esoteric terms, as a dispute about which of the two present deviations was the more dangerous one : that of under-estimating the *Kulak* danger (with the implied risk of its getting out of control) or that of overestimating it (with the implied risk of recourse to the methods of war-communism, and destroying the alliance with the peasantry). The October meeting of the CC which prepared the XIV Congress described both dangers as equally great. On the eve of the Congress, however, the Moscow organisation (which was not disinterested in view of the large part played in it by Bukharin's supporters) described the second, leftist deviation as the more dangerous one. Stalin, who four years later would surpass the war-communist infringements in the peasants' way of life, supported the Moscow move. Because of its whole past, he said, the party was more immunised against the first, rightist deviation.[145] The fact that this statement eventually proved correct provides, however, no answer to the question whether the trial of strength with the Zinovievists was, indeed, necessary in order to prevent a premature breakdown of NEP.

So far as Zinoviev's group was characterised by any theoritical attitude prior to the personal and organisational conflicts, it was embodied in the statement in his 'Philosophy of the Epoch' that the driving force of the revolution had been the desire for equality. The inapplicability of the slogan to any possible aspect of Soviet society in the near future was so generally realised that the point was emphasised mainly by Zinoviev's opponents, and played down by himself. In the opposition's theoretical armoury there were, however, two tenets more threatening in case they were turned into slogans of a mass agitation.

The statement that state capitalism played a predominant part in Soviet economics appeared in diverse ways. At first Zalutski, one of the Leningrad propagandists, described the Soviet State industries in this way (with the obvious implication that their

workers needed to defend their interests against the management
in ways similar to capitalist enterprises). This definition had to
be withdrawn by its author. The interpretations given by the
opposition speakers at the Congress emphasised the dependence
of the State industries on a market largely dependent on the NEP
men and the *kulak*. With Kamenev, the slogan of State capitalism
amounted to little more than a refusal to accept Bukharin's description of all existing peasant cooperatives as potentially socialist.
Zinoviev, however, in his co-report pointed out that the state
enterprises, being dependent on the market, paid quite unsatisfactory wages; therefore they should not be described as socialist in
more than in their eventual prospects.[146] A questioning of the socialist tendencies of the party itself was implied in the suggestion that
its social structure should be changed so that 90 per cent of its
members worked at the bench or (in an alternative formulation)
that 90 per cent of the workers should become party members.
To make these suggestions *ad absurdum*[147] was not difficult as
long as Lenin's concept of the party as the organised vanguard of
the working-class was taken for granted. For this reason the opposition's suggestions frequently varied, some of the new ones being
even less fortunate than the old, while others were reduced to
organisational detail. Yet Zinoviev, in his concluding remarks
at the Leningrad Party Conference of December 3 described
the issue as 'involving the character of our party and the further
leadership of our revolution'.[148]

During the preparation for the Congress, the Leningrad and
Moscow organisations worked as crystallisation centres of the
main trends. In the election of the Leningrad delegates supporters of the majority of the CC were excluded and the need for a
'homogeneous' Leningrad delegation emphasised. Moscow reacted with attacks against the diverse statements made in Leningrad.
The latter made a fairly quiet reply. Moscow's rejoinder maintained a standard of orthodoxy even of specifically Bukharinite
tenets, such as the growth into socialism *without the intermediate
link* of peasant cooperation as existing in Soviet Russia, as opposed
to Safarov's description of it as State-regulated capitalism.[149] On
the very eve of the Congress, Stalin and his friends suggested a
compromise which included representation of Leningrad in the

centre of the party machine[150] and reinstatement of those Leningrad party officials who had been dismissed because of their support of the national majority. The resolution of the Moscow Conference should be accepted as the basis of the Congress resolution.[151] Mutual attacks should be avoided but the statements of two leading Leningrad officials (Safarov and Zarkis) about State capitalism and introduction of the bulk of the workers into the party should be disowned. At the Congress, Tomski stated that the negotiations had broken down on that last point only. According to Andreyev, however, the Opposition leaders had also insisted on freedom to defend their views even after the Congress. Zinoviev himself stated that the acceptance of the Moscow resolution in substance, though not in form, would have implied the Opposition's agreement to the description of its views as non-Leninist.[152] In fact, Leningrad's support of the Opposition had been so strongly associated with the most radical statements made in the course of the factional struggle that disowning them would have implied repelling its most faithful supporters. Even supposing that Stalin and his closest friends were prepared for an equal sacrifice—i.e. for the disowning of Bukharin's standpoint, in whatever polite terms—they could hardly do so without appearing ambiguous. Clearly they wished for a trial of strength. The Opposition leaders, on their part, preferred overt proclamation of the cleavage, and the inevitably following overt defeat, to the acceptance of the junior position within the leading group which Stalin was prepared to grant them, and in which they would have had the sympathies of many of his followers who were afraid of the right-wing danger[153] and who also disliked Stalin's tendency to drive every disagreement to extremes.

Since 1921, there had been no co-report on the Report of the Central Committee. The very demand for it, made on behalf of the Leningrad organisation when the existence of disagreements on basic principles was denied, indicated the distance of Lenin's Old Guard from the nucleus of the party's leadership. It alienated a large section of the Congress, including men such as Kalinin, Ordzhonikidze and Mikoyan, who would have liked to go far to heal disagreements. There had been much provocation from the majority's side. The CCC, in Lenin's intentions an organ of reconciliation between conflicting groups,[154] interpreted its task as that of supporting the majority of the CC. Its reporter, Kuibyshev, even deplored its original attempts to avoid a conflict as a mistake and described denunciations of fellow-party members who attacked party unity as a public duty.[155] But the fact that the co-report was made by a member of the Politburo who had previously agreed to Stalin's report made it obvious that critique of the report was unimportant as against the need to break Stalin's control of the Secretariat. This, indeed, was the only definite suggestion made in Zinoviev's co-report. But this very mode of attack was bound to rally the majority round Stalin's person and thus to strengthen his position. Zinoviev interpreted the setback suffered by himself in the struggle for power as impending counterrevolution. A meeting of the Leningrad Provincial Committee refused to submit to Congress decisions. In private discussions with Ruth Fischer (whom a few months before he had ousted from the leadership of the German CP in deference to a Politburo decision) he described Stalin's victory in terms of an approaching Thermidor of the Russian revolution[156] (a terminology hitherto reserved even in the most private utterances of his supporters, such as Zalutski, to the Bukharin group). Such an analysis implied a call, if not for civil war, then at least for a specific opposition party to defend the sectional interests of labour within a framework bound to become capitalist in essence.

Within a few days, however, that potential party lost its asset, the Leningrad organisation. Armed with a special declaration of the Congress which emphasised the need for party unity, a delegation of the Central Committee, headed by Kirov (the frictions of those days contributed to his assassination, nine years later), visited the Leningrad organisation, called for the disowning of the Leningrad delegates and a re-election of the Local Party Committees. Many individuals may have simply turned to the victorious side on which the party official's job depended, but there is no reason to believe the defeated side's assertion that its defeat was the outcome of pure terror. In Leningrad, like elsewhere, the delegates had been elected on the assumption that there would be a unanimous vote in favour of the general policies of the Central Committee (which was still regarded as the outcome

of the struggle between the Old Bolshevik Guard and Trotskyism).
Nor had the homogeneity of the Leningrad delegation been
achieved with less pressure from the party machine than Stalin's
majority in other regions. The Leningrad organisation, the
majority of whom were ordinary workers at the bench, must have
been shocked by the Opposition's tactics at the Congress even more
than were many of the delegates who, being Old Bolsheviks,
knew how to read *cum grano salis* the official mythology about
the infallibility of majority decisions.

Stalin had to offer to the Leningrad and other workers more
than the emotional appeal of party unity. Five years later he
described the XIV Congress as 'the Congress of industrialisation'.[157] The resolution approving the Report of the CC instructed the latter 'to carry on economic construction with a view to
transforming the USSR from a country importing machinery and
equipment into a country producing machinery and equipment so
that the USSR, surrounded as it is by capitalist countries, may
not on any account become an economic appendage of the capitalist world economy but may form an independent economic unit,
developing on socialist lines'.[158] The point of industrialisation
played no central part in the deliberations of the Congress and in
the disputes accompanying it. The party majority concentrated
on the need to strengthen the alliance with the peasantry (the
differentiations within the latter being treated vaguely, so as to
preserve the alliance with the Bukharinites). On the other hand
the opposition devoted itself to the issue of intra-party democracy,
which included the defence of the industrial workers' sectional
interests within, and against, the existing enterprises. The industrialisation point was not even mentioned in the opposition's
demand for improvements in the resolution. (In fact, the opposition's approach to the problem was not homogeneous : at least
Sokolnikov would have been bound in honesty to reject the
majority resolution as being an expression of the 'super-industrial-
isation' tendency.)

Three months later Stalin, when speaking to the Leningrad
organisation, specified the meaning of industrialisation. Not
mere development of the light industries but also the development
of the heavy industries could secure the country's independence.

The USSR, being unwilling to become dependent on foreign investors, could accumulate the means necessary for industrialisation only by economies in her own industry, trade and administration. The point was directed against the opposition which, at the Plenary Meeting of the CC in April 1926, suggested a wage increase (it was rejected then, but in September an increase was actually granted, with special consideration for the worst paid workers and with the declared intention of reducing wage differentials).[159] It also marked, however, a departure from the standpoint of Bukharin who, three months later, reproached the opposition for its statement that the development of industry was lagging behind that of agriculture and, as against the opposition's demands for quicker industrialisation, pointed out that industry could not develop quicker than the peasant market. This statement made no sense unless industrialisation was conceived by Bukharin as development mainly of the light industries and industries producing agricultural implements.[160]

In his Leningrad speech, presumably with an eye to the rapproachment between the Zinovievites and the Trotskyites, Stalin had appealed for support against those who interpreted intra-party democracy as freedom of factional groupings instead of active participation of all party members in the discussion of the practical problems of socialist reconstruction, and against those who might re-open the discussion on issues on which a party Congress had decided and turn the party into a discussion meeting.[161] Rykov would not go quite as far. He recognised that democracy within the party was meaningless unless different shades of opinion were tolerated. Like Stalin, however, Rykov described any organised collaboration between party members whose views differed from the adopted party line as illegitimate factionalism while organised collaboration of the supporters of the majority view against the opposition was legitimate.[160] By implication, factionalism was found in the very effort of a minority to become the alternative majority, no change in the party line being possible except by the majority's own correction of its ways.

The Opposition, on its part, after its defeat in Leningrad, faced the alternative of either limiting its efforts to practical suggestions (if possible with a popular appeal, such as the suggestion of wage increases) within the party's leading bodies, or bringing maximum pressure to bear by the threat of a split. From the second point of view a combination of all the discontented elements was desirable. But this course was unadvisable in a prolonged effort to influence party opinion. A combination of Zinoviev and Kamenev on the one, and Trotsky on the other side, would deprive either partner of his specific moral assets, since Zinoviev and Kamenev were notorious for their opposition to the conquest of power in 1917, and Trotsky for his opposition to the Old Bolshevik tradition. No one in the party could regard the Oppositionists' declarations about the withdrawal of their mutual recriminations as sincere.[162] If they were not, the new *bloc* could have no purposes other than the overthrow of the existing regime within the party.

The new opposition policy found its first expression in a meeting of the Zinovievites held on June 6 with the usual precautions of underground conspiracy in the woods near Moscow. Its aim was to overcome the last hesitations against the *bloc* with Trotsky and to discuss the formation of opposition groups within the army.[163] It was immediately disclosed, yet the organisers—members of Zinoviev's staff at Comintern headquarters—refused to give the CCC any explanation. The first serious reprisals followed : at the Plenary Meeting of the CC on July 14-23, 1926—the one at which Zinoviev and Trotsky formally announced their *bloc* and withdrew their earlier mutual recriminations—Zinoviev was removed from the Politburo, Lashevich from the CC and his military post. As the main culprits, in view of their revolutionary past, had to be treated comparatively mildly, the minor organisers went off with mild reprimands[164], but expulsions from the party occurred already in September.[165]

In the last days of September and the first days of October 1926 the Opposition leaders, after some preparation by underground propaganda, appeared in a number of Moscow factory organisations to enforce a general discussion on the eve of the XV Party Conference. At that time, nobody could believe any longer in Kamenev's assertion that 'once Zinoviev and Trotsky would appear on a common platform, the party would find its

true central committee'.[166]   From what I heard in those days
from some oppositionists as well as from moderate supporters of
the party majority who wished to get rid of the Opposition (whose
strength they overestimated) without having to apply Draconian
measures, it appears that the Opposition aimed at an impressive
success in some industrial centres.   Though falling short of a
majority, this would induce the party majority to recognise the
Opposition as what would be in fact, if not in form, a second legal
party within the Soviet framework.[167]   Although the opposition
leaders had selected the most suitable points of attack, they were
successful only in a single railway depot where party members
belonged to the Democratic Centralism group.[168]   As soon as
major factories were involved, the outcome was sufficiently clear
to cause the opposition leaders to submit, on October 4, a
declaration in which they promised to stop their factional activities.   The party majority, however, insisted on a straightforward
dissolution of the Opposition's caucus and an explicit dissociation
from those of its allies who denounced the allegedly established
kulak rule in Russia and the 'thermidorial' degeneration of the
VKP(b).   To this the Zinoviev group would not agree.   Its
leaders made another effort in their Leningrad stronghold.   The
reception was characteristic of the mood of the 'Lenin-recruits':
as against the advice of the party machine, in each of the major
factories hundreds of party members voted in favour of hearing
them, but once they had made their dogmatic speeches, their
motions did not receive more than twenty or thirty votes of
organised supporters in each meeting.   Hence they had to accept
the majority's demands.   Stalin[169] formulated them in a comparatively moderate way, admitting the Oppositionists' right to defend
their views in constitutional ways and promising the re-admission
of those already expelled if they admitted their mistakes.   The
Opposition was allowed to include in the final text of its declaration of October 16[170] the request for such re-admission.   The
Central Committee stated, in its reply, 'with satisfaction' that by the
Opposition's declaration the elementary conditions of Party unity
had been maintained.   Disciplinary measures were restricted to
the removal of Trotsky and Kamenev from the Politburo, and
Zinoviev from the Comintern (where his position in any case had

become untenable). Even a declaration of Shlyapnikov and Medvedev, who promised to stop factional activities and to submit to party decisions and regretted the tone of their attacks against the majority, was accepted as satisfactory.[171]

Within the Opposition camp, the defeat was bound to cause reconsideration of its position. Some of the leaders, Trotsky in particular, had gone so far that it was difficult for them to regard the new position as anything more than an armistice, bound to lead to a resumption of the struggle. Others were inclined to regard what had happened as a demonstration, to be followed by patient work as a pressure group within a homogeneous party. From what I experienced in those weeks on the spot, I am inclined to conclude that the second tendency would have got the upper hand, at least amongst the Zinovievites, had not Stalin used the XV Party Conference for a renewed attack the sharpness of which, though not contradicting the letter of the compromise of October 16, certainly violated its spirit.[172] Having admitted the Opposition's right to remain in the party without disowning its views, Stalin, in his theses for the Conference, characterised those views as being in essence Social Democratic. When Trotsky complained about the infringement of possible collaboration involved in such a description, Stalin replied that the even sharper description of Trotsky's own views as a 'lower-middle-class deviation' had not implied organisational discrimination against him, nor even prevented his present allies from collaborating with him. It was the party's task to convince the Opposition of the wrongness of its views, but the Opposition had the right to defend these views, as long as they were held by constitutional means, provided only this was done without factionalism, and without exploiting the difficulties of reconstruction in order to form a second party.[173] The speeches made by Opposition leaders during the debate evoked sharper formulations in Stalin's reply.[174] Rykov, in his concluding speech, expressed disappointment with those speeches in view of what could be expected from the preceding negotiations. In the decisions of the Conference, recognition of the right to voice opposition by constitutional means was coupled with a definition of these means which reduced to a minimum an opposition's prospects of becoming an alternative majority. In future, general discussions were to be admissible only in the following cases:[175] (i) if this was demanded by at least some Provincial organisations, (ii) if, within the Central Committee, there existed no sufficiently stable majority on important political questions, (iii) if the CC in spite of the existence of such a majority, felt it desirable to check the correctness of its policy by a party discussion. In none of these cases, however, should a general discussion be opened without a CC decision.[174] Without this last condition (which, indeed, reduced the alternative (i) to nought) the point was included in all the Party Rules since 1934 up to the present day.

With an opposition's *ultima ratio*—the threat of a party split— and any potential preparations for it being efficiently removed from party life, a legal opposition could, in future, be no more than a grouping of like-minded people (very loose, for otherwise it would have invited the penalties against factionalism) who tried to modify the party line in some definite direction. In that case the very formulation of the existing disagreements must be in proportion to the constitutional means available to voice them. It is quite possible that Stalin and Rykov had, indeed, been induced during the preceding negotiations to expect more in the way of reducing disagreements than the most vociferous section of the opposition (including most of the famous names) was ready to grant. If, however, the Opposition's struggle was aimed at the overthrow of the existing party regime, its declaration of October 16 could be only to gain some breathing space.[176] A tendency to keep the 'truce' to the very minimum compatible with the preservation of formal discipline was evident during the XV Conference as well as immediately after when, as I remember, quite suddenly the Opposition leaders decided to address the VII Plenary Meeting of the Executive Committee of the Comintern. The speeches of Trotsky and Zinoviev emphasised the existence of a conflict hardly bridgeable (Kamenev's speech reflected a more conciliatory approach). This kind of behaviour of the opposition (constitutional though it had become) after its defeat, prevented that gradual dying away of the tensions which would have been possible if the opposition had conceived its activities as those of a pressure group working in favour of an increased rate of investment and stronger pressures upon private enterprise and against bureaucratic degeneration of the State machine. As soon as the party majority got more involved in the problems of industrialisation and collectivisation, its temporary alliance with the Bukharinites was bound to break once these problems were faced.[176a] Trotsky notes that at the beginning of 1927 Zinoviev envisaged gradual capitulation, whatever this may mean. The decisions of the Plenary Meeting of the CC in February 1927 on capital investments and price reductions were adopted unanimously.[177]

While sharply rejecting the Opposition's attacks, the majority was conscious of the need to remove their grievances. In a speech on October 2, Molotov recognised the existence of serious shortcomings in the realisation of democracy within the party, of bureaucratism in party practice and of class-alien influences originating from the state machine. In December the CC adopted a decision on the work of party members in Soviet institutions: uneconomic management, embezzlement, red tape and a formal approach to work came under attack.[178] Some party organisations had apparently regarded the struggle against the opposition as implying a reversal of the former preference for recruitment from the industrial workers. During 1926 the percentage of salaried employees amongst party members rose in Astrakhan Province from 12 to 22, in Tambov Province from 25 to 40. A CC decision of December 31, 1926, emphasised the need to restore the balance. On January 10, 1927, a census of the whole party membership was carried out: at that date, there were 774,798 members and 372,276 probationers, a total of 1.15 million. According to social origin, 56 per cent of these were workers, 19 per cent peasants, 22.6 per cent salaried employees, but according to actual occupation there were a mere 30 per cent industrial workers, 10 per cent peasants actually cultivating their land but 38.5 per cent salaried employees. A mere 0.8 per cent of the total membership had higher, and another 7.9 per cent secondary education; there were still 2.4 per cent illiterates. Apart from the narrow stratum of the old revolutionary *intelligentsia*, the party was recruited from the lower classes of pre-revolutionary society but promotion as well as

16

natural ambitions tended to increase the weight of officialdom. Certainly it comprised the larger part of those 45 per cent of the party membership who had any political schooling.

The party had a total of 42,715 primary organisations. Just a fifth of these—8,446—with 485,000 members and probationers (i.e. about 40 per cent of the total) operated in industry. In the villages there were 20,878 groups with 265,000 members, i.e. a fifth of the total. But 3,500 of these were mere probationers' groups formed in the absence of a sufficient number of full party members ; 16,500 party groups were formed on a village basis. Apart from peasants they included local officials and members of the village *intelligentsia*. About five hundred groups each worked in state and in collective farms respectively ; 6,233 primary organisations, with a total of 228,000 members, operated in the diverse state institutions, 6,486 with 95,000 members in the army ; 672 with 67,000 members in the institutions of higher education. The latter's specific weight in university life must have been considerably stronger than that of the industrial cells (which comprised a mere 10.5 per cent of the industrial workers at the bench). In consequence of the measures taken after the census, the percentage of industrial workers amongst new admissions increased from 42 per cent in 1925 to 56 per cent in 1927.[179]

Gradually the 'Lenin-recruits' moved into the front line. If, with the defeat and denunciation of the oppositions, the exciting argument about the general prospects of the Revolution had died down, activities intended to propagate and to carry out the agreed party line had greatly expanded. There was a lot of honorary posts to be filled from the party group upwards. The party *aktiv*, defined as comprising the members of the *buros* of party groups, the shop organisers, propagandists, women's organisers and members of the committees of trade unions and other social organisations, increased in Leningrad from 28 per cent of the total membership in January 1926 to 37 per cent one year later, in Moscow from 10,620 in early 1926 to 38,815 by the end of 1927. Nor were the young party members confined to junior positions : of the secretaries of primary party organisations elected in the autumn of 1927, entrants of the years 1924-26 already formed a narrow absolute majority (in a place such as Leningrad the

elimination of the Opposition was bound to result in an even
greater proportion of young party officials). Higher up, Old
Bolsheviks were still in the key positions at the Provincial level,
and the entrants of 1917 and the civil war period in the positions
next in importance. But the entrants of 1924 and later already
provided more than 27 per cent of the Provincial, more than 40
per cent of the District and City Committees (at the village level
they formed an absolute majority).[180] The share of young party
members in the total strength of party committees was not subs-
tantially higher than it had been in 1919. Its political weight
may have been even smaller since at least the higher committees,
which in 1919 were actually directing bodies, had since turned
into a kind of local party parliament. Yet while people who
joined the party in the great revolutionary upheaval had still been
influenced by Lenin's concept of the organised vanguard, those who
had joined during the three years preceding 1927 were ordinary
people with a slightly over-average degree of civic interest—in
some cases also with over-average ambitions—who led fairly
settled lives in a firmly established state to the further progress
of which they made their contribution. When, eventually, they
moved into the key positions—and Stalin's 'great purge' would
see to their doing it quickly and thoroughly—the struggles in
which the party's outlook had been shaped would appear to them
as a mere disturbance of its orderly development, and the man
who had put an end to those disturbances as their natural leader.

The last stand made by the United Opposition in the summer
and autumn of 1927 was important mainly because it promoted
the association, in the minds of the young generation, of its political opposition and civil disloyalty. The chronic dispute between
Leningrad and Moscow should not be regarded as a mere conflict of personal ambitions. The struggle about Bukharin's
enrichissez-vous had concerned a really important issue of the
development of the revolution. But there was no justification
(other than abstract concepts of a degeneration of the Russian
revolution supposedly unavoidable if it remained isolated) for a
renewal of all-out attacks against Stalin on the ground of tactical
mistakes—real or imaginary ones—committed by him when
instructing the Chinese communists and the Soviet trade unionists

in favour of collaboration with the Kuomintang and with the leaders of the TUC. When the Chinese events were followed by the Arcos raid, the British Government's breaking off of diplomatic relations and the assassination of the Soviet ambassador to Warsaw, a demonstration of national and communist unity was clearly required. But Trotsky drew the opposite conclusion. In an article sent to *Pravda* he promised that, if and when the western interventionists should approach Moscow, the Opposition would save Soviet Russia by over-throwing Stalin just as Clemenceau had saved France, when, the Germans being fifty miles from Paris, he demanded the replacement of the existing government because of its vacillations and inefficiency.[181] The party majority's reluctance finally to break with a part of the Old Guard was demonstrated, in August, at the Joint Plenary Session of the CC and CCC. The Opposition was faced, by way of an ultimatum, with the question of whether it would renounce the 'Clemenceau thesis', abandon its description of the regime as potentially Thermidorian, and sever its organisational links with anti-Comintern groups abroad such as that of Ruth Fischer-Maslow. Its fairly vague answers were seen as indicating a temporary truce from which more peaceful relations might emerge.[182] The Opposition, however, now elaborated its platform[183] and propagated it by means of its own clandestine organisation and printing press. According to good 1905 tradition, the hall of a High School was occupied to hold a public meeting. Even the formation of a new International jointly with its sympathisers abroad was prepared.[184]

On October 16 the CCC demanded from the Opposition leaders that they should refrain from underground meetings and make their case in the regular discussion to be opened one month before the Congress.[185] It was obvious that their opinions would be condemned at the Congress but they would have retained some status in the party after a demonstration of party discipline. Yet Zinoviev and Trotsky refused to comply with the demand : on October 23 they were expelled from the Central Committee. An attempt of the Opposition to organise on November 7 separate street demonstrations parallel with the official ones was followed by Zinoviev's and Trotsky's expulsion from the party. Stalin now confronted every oppositionist who wished to remain in, or return to, the party with the demand of renouncing those points of the Opposition platform which contradicted the party's principles,[186] as formulated by the XIV Congress. On this ultimatum the Opposition split on the eve of the XV Congress, yet the Zinovievites hesitated to break openly with the Trotskyites which Stalin had made a condition of reconciliation.[187] During the preceding campaign, some of them may have been driven by their allies' pressure further than they would themselves have liked to go, but they had taken the responsibility for thousands sacrificing their careers, and some their freedom, in the defence of the views to which they subscribed.[188] The leaders' submission would have been the simplest way to ease the followers' fate but it would also have prevented any future support from those who felt themselves betrayed. So the Zinovievites continued, though with some differences of opinion, to defend their position during the first part of the Congress and thereby forfeited the support which the communists' abhorrence of expulsions from the Old Guard would have granted to anyone who wished to make a new start.[189] Only after the Congress had declared the Opposition's views as incompatible with party membership did the Zinovievites, without renouncing their views, promise to abstain from their propagation, while the Trotskyites promised to defend their views within the framework of party discipline: this was a contradiction in terms since the party had just described these views as anti-communist.

On December 18, the Oppositionists were expelled from the party. On the following day, the Zinovievites submitted, as a group, to all the demands made upon them. The Congress, however, authorised the new CC to re-admit them to the party only as individuals, and not less than half a year after the submission of declarations renouncing the Opposition platform. Of the hard core of four thousand who had voted for the Opposition in the discussion preceding the XV Congress, 1,500 were expelled from the party and exiled ; 2,500, most of them Zinovievites, immediately submitted statements of repudiation.[190] The exiled Trotskyites returned, as individuals, one or two years later under the impact of Stalin's policy of industrialisation and agricultural collectivisation. Many of the former oppositionists again played important parts in economic reconstruction and even became

members of the Central Committee before they fell as victims
to Stalin's 'great purge', together with so many of his supporters in
the earlier discussions.   They were innocent of the crimes of
which they were accused.   Still, their fanatical struggle during
the years 1926-27 provided evidence in favour of Stalin's thesis
that every opposition against his policies was bound to under-
mine party and state.   Thereby they made a major contribution
to that silencing of frank argument which turned all future opposition underground, resulting in their own destruction and promoting that very growth of bureaucratic dictatorship they had
feared.

(d) THE CRISIS OF NEP, THE DEFEAT OF THE RIGHT-WING
OPPOSITION, AND THE LEVY ON THE VILLAGE

When Stalin settled accounts with the left-wing opposition he
added a few remarks about the dangers involved in party leaders
who ignored the existence of different classes with contradictory
interests within the country, who disliked self-criticism and
believed that the current of life would carry them and the country
easily forward.   Yet 'the struggle between the old and the new,
between that which is dying away and that which is being born
is the basis of our development'.[191]   In his report to the Congress
he had argued against unnamed opponents who had suggested
delaying the development of industry because it had outrun that
of agriculture.   This, he said, was a reactionary Utopia, industrial
development should be accelerated further so as to prepare the
eventual industrialisation of agriculture.   Stalin saw amongst the
party's immediate tasks 'the gradual transition of the dissipated
peasant farmsteads to large-scale . . . . socialised, collectivised
cultivation of the land on the basis of the intensification and
mechanisation of agriculture . . . . so as to accelerate the development of agriculture and to overcome the capitalist elements in the
villages'.[192]

These general considerations had been provoked by a crisis
in grain collections.   Although the harvest had not been below
average, by the end of 1927 grain collections were 2.1 million
tons below the level of the preceding year.   By a CC directive

of January 6, 1928, regional party organisers were made personally responsible for speeding up collections. Party leaders went
to the most difficult points to supervise the work of the regional
organisations (Stalin went to Siberia). In order to force the
kulaks to deliver their stocks, article 107 of the Criminal Code,
which threatens speculators in articles of mass-consumption with
confiscation of their stocks, was put into operation against those
who refused to sell. In order to find them out and to preserve some
good-will in the village, 25 per cent of the confiscated stocks were
earmarked for long-term credits to the poor peasants, who otherwise would have bought them from the *kulak* on usurious terms
before the new harvest. During the preceding years, however,
many party and state officials had become used to regarding good
relations with the most prosperous peasants as a token of success.
Stalin noticed on his Siberian tour that many attorneys and judges,
being on terms of familiarity with kulaks, were unwilling to prose-
cute them. Already in spring, party members in the villages who
opposed the offensive against the kulaks had to be expelled.[193]
Stalin's conclusions from his Siberian experiences went far beyond
the problems of the present emergency. In order to make the
industrial population and the army independent of the kulaks'
whims, state and collective farms had to be developed so that
within three or four years they might supply a third of the marketed grain (according to statistics upon which he founded his
further analysis, these farms supplied at present a mere 6 per cent;
20 per cent were supplied by the kulaks, 74 per cent by the poor
and medium farmers: the latter, however, were very much inclined
to follow the kulaks' lead). Even this was a mere short-term
target. In the long run, the Soviet regime could not rest on two
foundations so different as a socialised industry and an agriculture
dominated by private enterprise. Already at present crystallisation points should be created for a mass collectivisation movement which would eventually secure the supply of agricultural
products and destroy all chances of a capitalist restoration.[194]

A show-down was unavoidable. As long as the kulak's
influence in the village was strong it was impossible to tackle the
grain-problem by simply by-passing him. Either the marketing
of grain had to be made attractive to him and those under his

influence, or alternative ways of getting grain from the country-side had to be found. In order to achieve Stalin's short-term target, the major half of the non-kulak farmers would have to be immediately collectivised. This was clearly impossible on the voluntary basis to which the party still clung. Hence some additional expropriation of kulaks was needed, but as soon as this started, even the following strata of the peasantry would withdraw from the market. In order to shorten the unavoidable transition crisis, the expansion of industry had to be accelerated. The drive against the kulaks was paired with one against those specialists in industry who emphasised the difficulties of industrial expansion and tried to preserve existing routine. In March a group of old-standing engineers of the Shakhty group of mines were convicted for having, in conspiracy with the former mine-owners (foreigners) sabotaged the execution of the orders of the Government. The District Party Committee was dissolved because it had expelled from the party workers who had criticised the treacherous specialists, for appointments made according to family connections, etc. The Plenary Meeting of the CC and CCC in April 1928, on a report by Rykov, adopted a special decision on the case. The majority of the old specialists were described as loyal, but the party organisations were reproached for insufficient vigilance against those who were not, as well as for a failure to encourage the workers' criticism of specialist routine, and to promote young specialists from amongst the working class. Stalin appealed to the communist specialists—most of them former workers from the bench—to master complicated scientific problems. In this connection he said that there were no fortresses which communists could not storm. It was, however, necessary to create conditions in which the communist engineer or manager could have his full say in the factory. Hence the Plenary Meeting demanded the repeal of the factory regulations (of 1926) which enhanced the rights of the technical manager (in those days, as a rule a non-party specialist) as against the general manager (usually a communist).[195]

Consultation of the broad strata of the workers on suggested promotions was recommended.[196] Even workers who fairly recently had come from the countryside were to be recruited for the party. In some major works, indeed, the percentage of unskilled workers amongst party members rose to a level roughly corresponding to their share in the total staff.[197] (This was, of course, for a short time only, as the non-party people promoted to posts of responsibility were expected in due course to become party members, the unskilled worker recruited for the party was expected to acquire some trade: by the mere fact of joining the party he had bound his future to industry.) Criticism of administration by the workers was encouraged. Stalin deemed it helpful even if a mere five or ten per cent of the criticisms made proved to be justified.[198] Instances of corruption noticed in the Smolensk Provincial party organisation offered the occasion for CCC decisions intended as a warning against similar phenomena elsewhere.[199] The communist youths were advised to organise mass criticism from below, especially against communist bureaucrats who were far more dangerous than that popular target of the caricaturist, the *chinovnik* with a civil service record dating from Tsarist days. Stalin appealed not only to the young communists' enthusiasm but also to their industry and ambitions. They should start a mass-movement to master science so as to create a new generation of Bolsheviks who were technical specialists as well.[200] Sixty years after Pisarev's days, in a very different setting, his old advice was thus revived.

Even without Stalin's explicit appeal to criticism and self-criticism as a means of placing the leaders under the control of working-class opinion, the leaders of the party's right-wing were bound to sense the direction of his attacks. Already in February, organised opposition started in Moscow against a circular letter of the CC which appears to have reflected Stalin's Siberian observations.[201] On the whole, however, the right-wing leaders kept their powder dry. During the discussions with the left-wing opposition Stalin had stated that its mistakes appealed more to the existing intellectual climate within the party than did those of the right-wingers, while the opposition had noticed the strong positions held by the right-wing in public administration. Both statements may have been true. Now that its turn had come, the right-wing let Stalin have some run until he landed in such blind alleys as the skilled administrator and the student of agricultural economics could easily foresee. In July, a Plenary Session of the CC and CCC adopted a compromise decision[202] on the experiences of the grain-collection campaign. The excesses committed during that campaign were condemned and Stalin agreed to an increase in grain purchase prices.[203] Three Weeks after having dispensed a sound beating to a theorist who had read a paper on the limitations, rather than on the tasks, of self-criticism, Stalin emphasised in *Pravda* the purposes and limitations of criticism from below. Only such criticism was desirable as strengthened work discipline and the authority of party and state.[204] As part of the compromise, it had been agreed in the Politburo not to mention the disagreements existing in its midst to the full CC, and even to deny their existence to the non-Soviet delegations to the VI Comintern Congress which was then in session. This effort to blur the differences on fundamentals was bound to fail. Bukharin put forward his views—in tactful terms which, however, made the substance of the conflict perceptible enough[205]—in his *Notes of an Economist*. He also used the opportunity of the Comintern Congress to approach Kamenev with a view to forging an alliance of the old with the new Opposition.[206] From the fact that even after Trotsky's indiscretions about these negotiations no disciplinary measures were taken against Kamenev, it appears that Bukharin did not get an encouraging reply. To the average supporter of the left-wing opposition it would have seemed rather favourable argument when he learned that Stalin was now fighting those who had advised the kulaks to enrich themselves.

As frank argument about domestic policy was prohibited, the right-wingers resorted to arguments on the diverse interpretations of the decisions of the VI Comintern Congress on the economic conditions in the capitalist world, and the imminence of 'a new period of wars and revolutions'. While the Moscow Committee elaborated Bukharin's interpretation of these decisions, the German sympathisers among the right-wingers opened an attack against Thaelmann.[207] When Bukharin backed them against the German party's reactions, which after some hesitation were supported by a majority of the Politburo,[208] he gave his opponents the first opportunity for more outspoken argument, although internal Russian issues were still carefully avoided. On October 2, 1928—the day

of crisis—a majority of the Moscow Committee revised the
attitude maintained by it as late as mid-September. A letter of
the CC to the Moscow organisation opened a campaign for re-
election of the party committees. As the right-wing members of
the Politburo had not voted against the communication, the existence of right-wingers within the Politburo was again denied and
criticism restricted to 'individual members of the Moscow Committee'.[209] By now, the augurs must have begun to laugh if not
at the spontaneity of the Moscow workers[210] then at the denial of
obvious facts. Such denial, indeed, made no sense unless it was
silently taken for granted that a professed disagreement on major
points of political practice meant the removal of the minority
from the leading bodies of the party.

Such removal, however, had two sides. After what had
happened a year before, Stalin could not be too eager formally
to break with another group of famous names, least of all on an
issue where they appeared as the defenders of the interests of the
most numerous class in the country. On the eve of the Plenary
Meeting of the CC in November, the opposition leaders offered
their resignation in protest against the degradation of agriculture
threatening from excess taxation of the more wealthy peasants and
from the encouragement of the poor peasants' class struggle
against them. A compromise was found in a comparatively
moderate formulation of the party majority's policy. The Opposition agreed to an increase of industrial investments by 330 million
rubles against the level of the preceding year and withdrew its
resignations. On its ultimatum, the Politburo members again agreed
to deny the existence of disagreements amongst them at the Plenary
Meeting and in public speeches.[211] Frumkin, who in his capacity
as finance minister tried to keep allocations for investments down,
served as the whipping boy for his more illustrious friends. Stalin
made the point that non-interference with the development of the
productive resources, as suggested by Frumkin, would strengthen
the hostile capitalist forces in the village. Being technically and
economically backward in comparison with the leading capitalist
countries, the USSR could not afford a slow pace of industrialisation as long as she was the only socialist country in the world.
Her whole future and national independence depended on the

maximum speed of industrialisation.[212] This, indeed, was the strong side of Stalin's case. It was so strong that he had to explain to his own followers why the right-wing Opposition was still tolerated in the party's leading bodies. Stalin answered with a reference to Trotsky against whose views an ideological struggle was waged from 1918 to 1923. In 1924 they were described as in essence lower-middle-class and still he was left on the Politburo till he broke party discipline.[213] The implications were obvious.

The next stage of the drama opened in the trade union field. Up to the autumn, the dispute with the right-wingers was in terms of a defence of the workers' interest in quick industrialisation (with the consequent abolition of unemployment) against the peasants' interest in preservation of the market. We have seen how Stalin operated upon an appeal to the very broadest strata of the workers. But as soon as industrialisation assumed a quicker step a conception of trade union politics as representing the workers' particular interests within the general equilibrium aimed at by communist policies became problematic. Tomski, who headed *UTsSPS,* kept to the accepted standpoint that it was the manager's task to lead the production drive, and the trade union's task to defend the workers' sectional interest (surely, aiming at its reconciliation with the public interest in a success of the production drive). Yet a fully planned economy could not allow its wages fund to be determined by the outcome of negotiations on the level of the factory, or even of the individual industry. With the formation of a new working-class mainly interested in industrial progress as such, traditional trade unionism lost much of its appeal. At the VIII Trade Union Congress, in December 1928, the old trade union leadership offered resistance only to party interference in trade union autonomy, in particular to the introduction of Kaganovich (whose part was clearly envisaged as that of a supervisor) into the Presidium of *UTsSPS.* Tomski even denied the existence of disagreements about the party line in the trade unions.[214] It appears that an argument on principles was regarded as impolitic, yet it must have been obvious already at that time that a policy of industrialisation was incompatible with a wage structure in which the first five places were occupied by engineering, printing, electric power-stations, shoemaking and furriery.

A key industry such as coal-mining occupied the fifth place as late as 1935.[215] An industrialisation which required a rise in the labour force far exceeding the increase in the output of consumers' goods (and in particular of foods) excluded an increase in real wages. Hence the desired wages differentials could not be established without serious sacrifices to the workers of the industries with lower priorities. Those workers even lacked the moral compensation of quick expansion which, to the workers of the key industries made the necessary sacrifices appear as merely temporary.

The fact that with the end of NEP traditional trade unionism came to an end should not be misinterpreted as an ascendency of the managerial interest. At this time, the party made the greatest efforts to assume the leadership of the workers' struggle against bureaucratism and lack of understanding on the side of existing management. Failure of party organisations to lead that struggle —not to speak of palliation of existing shortcomings—was described as the main cause of unsatisfactory recruitment results, while good results rewarded those organisations which approached the task of directing production, even though such 'direction' might be as modest as the Dnepropetrovsk meetings of workers at three months' intervals to discuss production problems.[216] The problems discussed under party guidance would differ from those predominant in the traditional trade union sense, and different strata of the workers would be most active in either setting.

At the top, matters came to a head after Bukharin's secret negotiations had been published by a Trotskyist journal abroad. On January 30 the incident was discussed in a joint meeting of the Politburo and the Presidium of the CCC. Apparently, Stalin wanted to use the incident to chastise the Opposition leaders without going to the length of removing them from high office (with possible repercussions in the village). Bukharin, Tomski and Rykov (the latter eventually withdrawing) reacted with declarations of resignation unless their views were considered in formulating the party line, and the attacks against Bukharin's *Notes of an Economist* as well as on Tomski's policies in the trade unions were stopped. Stalin replied that the existence of a right-wing faction was evidenced in the negotiations with Kamenev but insisted upon the oppositionists' remaining at their posts. The representatives of the CCC thought that the loss of the three right-wing leaders, after the exit of Zinoviev, Kamenev and Trotsky, might compromise the party. After one week of mutual reproaches they suggested that Bukharin's attacks against the party majority as well as the resignations should be withdrawn and that the speeches made in the discussion (evidently including that of Stalin) should be removed from circulation. Some crudeness of the majority's side is indicated by the CCC's suggestion that care should be taken to ensure for Bukharin normal conditions of work in Comintern as well as in *Pravda*. With the growth of the fiction of Politburo homogeneity the position of a dissenting party leader became untenable whether he continued in office (with his juniors believing that he no longer represented the party line), or whether he resigned (which would be interpreted as an appeal to non-party opinion).

As Bukharin rejected the compromise, on February 9 the meeting condemned the Opposition's views but rejected the resignations. The disagreements were brought to the notice of the Plenary Session of the CC and CCC which met on April 1, concurrently with the XVI Party Conference.[217] That meeting adopted a motion condemning the right-wingers' views and circulated it (together with their own declarations) amongst the party organisations. Special precautions for keeping the secret of internal disagreements were required.[218] Bukharin and Tomski remained on the Politburo but were removed from their offices. 93 members of the communist group of the Trade Union Congress, however, opposed Tomski's removal.[219] Rykov made the report to the Party Conference on the Five Year Plan, i.e. on the very item on the order paper in which the main policy decisions were summarised. All the decisions of the Conference were adopted unanimously. But within the CC Stalin found elements of factionalism in the very existence of a group defending certain views on a joint platform. The right-wingers' use of a local peasant insurrection in Adzharia as an argument for its views, he said, differed unfavourably from Trotsky's behaviour at the time of the Kronstadt mutiny which he had helped to suppress though being in opposition at the time.[220] The strength of Stalin's case lay not in its formal aspects (the right-wing communists took great care to avoid breaks of formal discipline as had been current with the Trotskyists) but in the character of the social forces bound to be encouraged by the very existence of a group within the ruling party which claimed to defend the peasants' interests.

Behind the closed doors of the CC, Stalin now frankly faced the implications of a large-scale collectivisation drive. As Bukharin had reproached the majority with burdening the peasants with a tribute (*dan*) in the form of compulsory deliveries at insufficient prices, Stalin regarded the levying of such a tribute as necessary and bearable for the peasants who had their private households to fall back upon. (This argument excludes any complicity of Stalin in the currently popular arguments about direct transition to the agricultural commune, which would have deprived the peasants of that very support which was supposed to make the 'tribute' bearable.) Stalin regarded increased social tensions, and even local peasant insurrections, as unavoidable.[221] Being reproached for having now adopted the standpoint of the former left-wing opposition, Stalin explained that, because of the possible repercussions, the ruling party could make no statements on issues concerning the peasants which it could not carry out immediately. Collectivisation would have been clearly impossible two or three years ago.[222]

NOTES AND REFERENCES

1. Cf. the data compiled in M. M. Vasser's article on the Workers' Opposition, in *Vestnik Moskovskovo universiteta*, 1957, No. 4, p. 162.
2. *Sochineniya*, vol. XXX, p. 472.
3. Ibid., vol. XXXI, p. 397.
4. *VKP(b) v rezolyutsiyakh*, pp. 375-76.
5. Ibid., p. 377.
6. See above, p. 162.
7. *Sochineniya*, vol. XXXII, p. 190 and point 5 of the Congress resolution on Party Unity (Lenin's original draft, ibid., pp. 217-20).
8. *VKP(b) v rezolyutsiyakh*, p. 362. The two CC members—Preobrazhenski and Dzerzhinski—had a Left Communist record from 1918, and hence may have been acceptable to the opposition. Still, the inclusion of a party secretary and of the head of Cheka even in a provisional CCC was strange enough.

9. Ibid., pp. 377-78.

10. At the XII Congress (*Otchet* pp. 225-26) it was stated that the results of the division given in the *Otchet* of the XI Congress (p. 186) were incorrect.

11. *VKP(b) v rezolyutsiyakh*, p. 512.

12. *Sochineniya*, vol. XXXIII, (Sel. Works, vol. IX). In September 1921 Lenin addressed to Stalin (who since 1919 headed the PC of Workers, and Peasants' Inspection), critical notes on its work. He emphasised the need to concentrate on a few investigations of some characteristic institutions, carried out with a highly qualified staff and with the intention to suggest definite improvements in the work of the institutions. Stalin's reply contains the interesting point that the two engineers who carried out one of the investigations criticised by Lenin, received together less salary than one messenger boy in one of the institutions investigated. Cf. ibid., p. 21 ff., 441-42 and 404.

Like everything connected with Stalin's career, Lenin's article 'Better Fewer but Better' has been interpreted, particularly in publications influenced by Trotsky's writings, as part of a struggle allegedly waged by Lenin against Stalin's ascendancy. In fact, Stalin had already left the PC of Workers' and Peasants' Inspection in connection with his appointment as Secretary General. Whatever misgivings he may have felt about Lenin's article would have been not those of the victim of an attack but those of a politician who still feels himself associated with a machine built under his supervision in an earlier stage of his career. Opposition within the Politburo against Lenin's criticism, was more likely to originate from Bukharin or Zinoviev, who were greatly enamoured of the more Utopian aspects of the institution's origin than from Stalin who for years had shown a tendency to emphasise the administrative aspects.

13. *Otchet*, pp. 221-22.

14. *VKP(b) v rezolyutsiyakh*, p. 368.

15. As in the earlier efforts which, though inspired by similar concepts, were far less systematic and thorough, the term *chistka* ('purge') was used only informally (in the West, it has acquired a completely different meaning by confusion with the political repressions of 1936-38, which were carried out through the Political Police or through the Courts).

16. Cf. Lenin's *Sochineniya*, vol. XXXIII, p. 328.

17. *Otchet*, p. 114.

18. *Sochineniya*, vol. XXXIII, pp. 18 ff. (Sel. Works, vol. IX, p. 253).

19. Shkiryatov, *Otchet* XI Congress, pp. 336-38. A not very flattering picture of the way in which the directives were carried out is given in F. Gladkov's novel *Cement*.

20. *Otchet* XI Congress, pp. 336 ff.; see also Zinoviev's speech, ibid., p. 358.

21. Medvedev (ibid. pp. 173-74) claimed as a merit of the 'Workers' Opposition' the efforts to prevent good workers from leaving the party in despair; solemn condemnations of the opposition would drive these elements away from the party, as had already the resolutions adopted by the Congress.

22. *VKP(b) v rezolyutsiyakh*, pp. 420 ff. and 447.

23. Ibid., p. 448.

24. *Sochineniya*, vol. XXXIII, pp. 227-29 (*Selected Works*, vol. IX pp. 320 ff.).

25. *VKP(b) v rezolyutsiyakh*, p. 441. See also Schapiro, op. cit. p. 341. As we have seen, and soon shall see again, it is incorrect to say that overrulings of Lenin even in fairly serious matters did not occur as long as he was in good health.

26. *VKP(b) v rezolyutsiyakh*, pp. 438 and 434.

27. Lenin was conscious of this opposition : *Sochineniya*, vol. XXXIII, pp. 453-54.

28. Text in Lenin's *Sochineniya*, vol. XXXIII, pp. 159 ff. ; the final text as adopted by the XI Party Congress is in *VKP(b) v rezolyutsiyakh*, pp. 427 ff.

29. Cf. Dobb, op. cit. p. 152, and M. Farbman (*After Lenin*, Leonard Parsons, 1924, pp. 111-12). From the end of 1921 on wages increased again.

30. See above, pp. 167-8.

31. Cf. point 10 of the CC resolution of January 12th, 1922 (see note 28, and note 57 of the same item in vol. XXXII of the 3rd ed. of Lenin's *Sochineniya*, pp. 515-16).

32. Ibid. note 121 on p. 538. See also the motion of the XI party Congress On some Members of the Former Workers' Opposition, *VKP(b) v rezolyutsiyakh*, pp. 459-60.

33. See above, p. 181.

34. *Otchet* XI Congress, p. 155.

35. Ibid. p. 47. Vasser (as quoted in note 1) gives details from which it is evident that in Omsk a re-registration of the Omsk city organisation was carried out in May 1922 (i.e. *after* the general 'purge', which had been carried out in Omsk, too). The three local leaders of the Workers' Opposition were expelled from the party. Other opposition strongholds mentioned by Vasser are the Motovilikhinsk organisation in Perm which was Myasnikov's special stronghold and the Ukrainian organisations of Shakhty and Lugansk. By the time of the XI Congress, however, these two had dissociated themselves from the Opposition, as had also the miners' leader, Kiselev.

36. Shlyapnikov at the XI Congress, *Otchet*, p. 169, Popov, op. cit. vol. II, p. 155 ; even Vasser, loc. cit. is quite frank about the methods of command applied on the occasion. The irregularity of the procedure applied by the CC is indirectly admitted by the demand of the XI Party

17

Congress that the necessary renewal of leading trade union bodies should be carried out in strict conformity with trade union Rules— *VKP(b) v rezolyutsiyakh*, p. 433).

37. *Otchet*, XI Congress, p. 114, Popov, op. cit. vol. II, p. 164.

38. *Sochineniya*, vol. XXXII, pp. 479 ff. Molotov (*Otchet* XI Congress, p. 40) stated that the negotiations of the CC with Myasnikov continued for six months.

39. Lenin's *Sochineniya*, 3rd ed., vol. XXVII, pp. 269-70, 539 and 583, Ruth Fischer, *Stalin and German Communism*, Harvard, 1948, pp. 246-47.

40. Carr, op. cit. vol. IV, pp. 79 ff.

41. Vasser reports that Shlyapnikov and Medvedev were expelled from the party as late as during the 1933 purge for their alleged 'double-dealing' (i.e. for their keeping to their old views notwithstanding the lip-service they had to pay to party decisions). This long delay of the inevitable shows that even during their support of the United Opposition of 1926-27, they were careful in the choice of their means, so as to avoid breaks of party discipline.

42. *VKP(b) v rezolyutsiyakh*, p. 432.

43. See above, pp. 195-6.

44. Molotov at the XI Party Congress, *Otchet*, pp. 44 and 46.

45. See above, p. 164.

46. Glazyrin, op. cit. pp. 14-15. For more details of these developments, see Carr, op. cit. (1959), pp. 190 ff.

47. Ibid. pp. 44 ff.

48. This has been discussed later on.

49. *VKP(b) v rezolyutsiyakh*, pp. 448-49.

50. Ibid. pp. 478 ff.

51. Stalin's *Sochineniya*, vol. VI, p. 198.

52. Ibid. p. 10.

53. *VKP(b) v rezolyutsiyakh*, pp. 442 ff.

54. At the XIII Congress Stalin (*Sochineniya*, vol. VI, p. 228) mentioned critically the existence of party members with incomes of 1000-2000 rubles. Kuibyshev (*Otchet*, p. 297) spoke of a communist who earned 1200 rubles as a specialist—'of course, we (the CCC) called him to account and he was fittingly punished'. Earnings exceeding the *partmaximum* mentioned below in the text, if based upon appropriate achievements, might reach quite considerable proportions even with many of those Communists who earned less than the *partmaximum* (though, of course, rarely more than one or two extra hundreds of rubles). To have made such contributions was well to the credit of a party member. From my first stay in Russia (1926-27) I do not remember any protests against such differentiations on the basis of extra work.

55. Up to the present day, comparisons between Soviet and western

incomes depend on the way in which they are spent : he who enjoys
books, the arts and interesting holiday travel is better off than he
who cannot live without fashionable clothing; housing conditions in
the twenties were for most people very bad.

56. See above, p. 154.
57. *Sochineniya,* vol. V, p. 390.
58. See above, pp. 149-53.
59. Stalin's *Sochineniya,* vol. VI, pp. 196-200.
60. Ibid., vol. V, p. 199, *VKP(b) v rezolyutsiyakh,* p. 421.
61. *My Life,* p. 409.
62. Preobrazhenski (*Otchet,* p. 75) reproached both of them for assuming more organisational responsibilities than their health would stand.
As Politburo, Orgburo and Secretariat were organs of the CC, their
composition was formally decided in the first meeting of the newly
elected CC after a party Congress, yet lists of the envisaged appointments were circulated amongst the delegates so that they knew what
they were voting for when electing the new Central Committee.
Preobrazhenski may have voiced Trotsky's disagreement (according
to accepted standards of corporative discipline, no member of the
Politburo should show disagreement with a decision arrived at in its
midst).

63. See Ch. VIII.
64. *Sochineniya,* vol. XXXIII, pp. 186 ff., *Selected Works,* vol. IX,
pp. 305 ff.
65. Letter to Kurski in February 20th, 1920, Ibid. vol. XXXVI, p. 518.
66. Ibid. vol. XXXIII, pp. 240 ff., (*Selected Works,* vol. IX, pp. 332 ff.).
67. Ibid., pp. 428 and 433 (403 ff.).
68. See above, p. 193.
69. *Sochineniya,* vol. XXXIII, pp. 457 ff. (*Sel. Works,* pp. 398 ff.).
70. Ibid., pp. 273-74.
71. See above, pp. 197-9.
72. *Otchet,* pp. 359-60 and 362.
73. *Sochineniya,* vol. V, pp. 219 and 226.
74. Ibid., p. 104.
75. *Otchet,* XIV Congress, pp. 398-99 and 455-56.
76. *Sochineniya,* vol. V, pp. 216-17.
77. Cf. Stalin's *Sochineniya,* vol. V, pp. 361 (the example of a Ukrainian
Gubkom which had had to nominate 80 of the 130 secretaries of its
party cells) and p. 365.
78. *Sochineniya,* vol. XXXVI, pp. 543 ff.
79. Ibid. p. 546. There is no reference to political disagreements ; so far
as these were evident in the nationalities question (ibid. pp. 555 ff.)
they must have contributed to Lenin's judgement mainly by illustrat-
ing Stalin's method of dealing with political opponents, whom Lenin
himself could hardly regard as being politically right. Lenin had

characterised Trotsky as 'possessing excessive self-confidence and unduly attracted by the purely administrative approach' (ibid. p. 544). There was little to choose, in these respects, between the two potential successors of Lenin. It appears that these very qualities, abhorrent though they might appear to many Bolsheviks, were required in any successor of Lenin.

80. See above, pp. 121-3.

81. This has been discussed later on.

82. The number had been increased to 40 already at the XII Congress on Stalin's motion.

83. Cf. Dobb, op. cit. pp. 171-72 and 181 ff. An English translation of Preobrazhenski's *New Economics* (by Brian Pearce, introduced by A. Nove) has been published in 1965 at the Clarendon Press, Oxford.

84. *VKP(b) v rezolyutsiyakh*, pp. 488 ff.

85. Dobb, op. cit. pp. 174-76.

86. Cf. Stalin's *Sochineniya*, vol. V, p. 356 and Eastman, op. cit. p. 33.

87. Carr, op. cit. vol. IV, pp. 75 ff.

88. Ibid., pp. 270 and 277.

89. Eastman, op. cit. pp. 36 and 142-43.

90. First published as an Appendix to Carr's, op. cit. vol. IV. I cannot agree with Carr's interpretation (ibid. p. 297) of Trotsky's failure to join the platform as a sign of his lack of resolution. Such an attitude was evident in later stages of the dispute but signature of an opposition platform by a Politburo member, jointly with persons who were not CC members, would have invited the sanctions of the resolution On Party Unity. See also Eastman, op. cit. p. 154.

91. This point was made by Zinoviev at the 13th Party Conference with reference to Lenin whose offer of an investigation commission to go into the causes of the Warsaw defeat had been rejected by the X Congress (*Otchet* XIII Congress, p. 269).

92. At the XIII Party Congress Manuilski (*Otchet*, pp. 364-65) stated that without the defeat of the German communists the discussion in the Russain party would have been kept within the CC and would have been overtaken by the new revolutionary wave, for the support of which the Russian party made the appropriate preparation (ibid. p. 367). I heard the same argument from Russian communists in Germany during the weeks following our October defeat. At least in the interpretation given at the time by Comintern, the German crisis reached its culmination with the Federal intervention against the left-wing governments in Saxony and Thuringia, and the failure of the German CP to react upon it by armed resistance, i.e. on October 22, 1923 (cf. my *Central European Democracy*, pp. 244 ff.). Some wishful thinking continued for weeks. It is possible that the real state of things was realised in Moscow just when the party discussion was opened on November 7th.

93. *VKP(b) v rezolyutsiyakh*, pp. 542-43. Of those who had voting rights, 102 voted in favour of the resolution, two against and ten abstained.

94. *Sochineniya*, vol. V, pp. 356 ff.

95. *VKP(b) v rezolyutsiyakh*, p. 548.

96. Trotsky agreed only to a condemnation of factions, i.e. groups with a stable organisation and with a discipline of their own. Cf. Stalin's *Sochineniya*, vol. VI, p. 224.

97. Ibid. vol. V, pp. 368-70.

98. Ibid., pp. 12-13.

99. Text in Annex VI to Eastman's, op. cit., pp. 175 ff.

100. *Sochineniya*, vol. V, pp. 383 ff.

101. Cf. Eastman, op. cit., p. 128.

102. Deutscher, op. cit., p. 277.

103. Cf. ibid., pp. 264 and 275 ff.

104. Pressure brought to bear upon Trotsky by his leftist allies, with whom Ruth Fischer had connections, may be indicated by her occasional complaints (as quoted in note 39, pp. 356 and 358) about his intentional abstention in critical moments of the struggle. Such pressure might enforce upon him the use of sharp formulae but could not force him to fight it out.

105. Carr, op. cit. vol. IV, p. 325.

106. *Sochineniya*, vol. VI, pp. 42-44.

107. *Otchet* XIII Congress, pp. 202-03, 280 and 284-85.

108. *Sochineniya*, vol. VI, pp. 22-23 and 39-40.

109. Ibid., pp. 8-9.

110. Ibid., pp. 226-27.

111. February 1st 1924.

112. Glazyrin, op. cit. pp. 21-23.

113. *Sochineniya*, vol. VI, pp. 255-56.

114. See above, p. 211.

115. Glazyrin, op. cit. p. 48.

116. P. 11 in the Gosizdat edition of 1925.

117. See above, pp. 173-4.

118. *Sochineniya*, vol. VI, p. 71 ; *Leninism*, p. 14 (my italics).

119. Stalin makes this point in a very definite way : 'The theory is the generalised experience of the labour movement of all the countries' ; *Sochineniya*, vol. VI, p. 88 ; *Leninism*, p. 26.

120. See above, pp. 217-8.

121. Stalin's *Sochineniya*, vol. VI, pp. 257-58. See also Zinoviev's and Sokolnikov's speeches at the XIV Party Congress, *Otchet*, pp. 333 and 454.

122. Stalin's *Sochineniya*, vol. VI, pp. 308-09 and 315 ff.

123. A. Piontkovski, *Sovetskoye ugolovnoye pravo*, vol. II (Special Part), Moscow 1928, p. 287.

124. Molotov's report to the XIV Congress, *Otchet*, p. 71. M. Khatayevich

in *Na agrarnom fronte,* 1925, No. 2 ; the figures given by Khatayevich from 15 Gubernia of the RSFSR for the number of villages and non-party peasants served by the average party nucleus are about three times as high as Molotov's general figures.

125. Stalin's *Sochineniya,* vol. VI, pp. 306-07. The outstanding presentation of the campaign for Revitalising the Soviets is now Chapter 22 of Carr's, op. cit. (1959).

126. Three years before, after the condemnation of the views of the Workers' Opposition as non-Marxist, the discussion in literary publications not intended for the current information of party members had been permitted. The point, of course, was that Trotsky was not another Shlyapnikov or Kollontay. A book of his which dealt with the party's attitude during the October revolution could not be regarded as a mere historical study.

127. *Sochineniya,* vol. VI, p. 357, vol. VII, pp. 9-10 and 379-80. For the formation of the majority caucus cf. Carr, op. cit. 1959, p. 6, note 6.

128. See, for example, pp. 120-1 above.

129. Ja. Jakovlev, in his *Leninism* (2nd ed. with N. N. Popov, *Krasnaya,* November 1924, p. 155), implicitly arguing against Trotsky, treats the readiness for the CPSU to help in 1923 the supposedly growing German revolution, notwithstanding the latter's immediate failure, as evidence of its continuing proletarian character. Of Trotsky's vacillations in the assessment of the retreat of the German communist leadership in October 1923 from approval in his theses of January 1924 to sharpest condemnation in the *Lessons of October,* September 1924, which can hardly be explained otherwise than by factional considerations, the most has been made by Zinoviev (as quoted in note 116) note 2 on pp. 26-27.

130. Stalin's *Sochineniya,* vol. VIII, pp. 282 and 348.

131. Ibid. vol. VII, p. 132.

132. Two years later he devoted the three hours of his last address to Comintern (at the VII Plenary Meeting of its Executive Committee) nearly exclusively to quotations from Marx and Engels, to demonstrate the unorthodox character of 'socialism in one country'.

133. *Otchet* XIV Conference, pp. 125 and 139, XIV Congress, pp. 65-66.

134. *VKP(b) v rezolyutsiyakh,* pp. 658 ff., and *Izvestiya,* April 23, 1925.

135. Glazyrin, op. cit. pp. 29 and 31. See also Carr, op. cit. (1959), pp. 335 ff.

136. *Otchet* XIV Congress, p. 270.

137. The full text (Stalin's *Sochineniya,* vol. VII, p. 153) shows that the authors regarded Bukharin's *enrichissez-vous* as a potential matter of discussion, but not in the youth's organisation. Mikoyan stated at the XIV Congress (*Otchet,* p. 187) that he, and presumably also other members of Stalin's group, had explicitly rejected Bukharin's slogan.

138. *Sochineniya,* vol. VII, pp. 382-84.

139. The Path to Socialism, quoted by Popov, op. cit., vol. II, pp. 241-42.

140. *Sochineniya,* vol. VII, pp. 116-17 and 126.

141. Ibid. pp. 381-82.

142. *Otchet,* XIV Congress, p. 168.

143. Ibid. p. 179.

144. Zinoviev pronounced the formula even in his co-report to the XIV Congress (ibid. p. 244). Shortly before Trotsky, whose attitude towards the Leningrad opposition was not yet decided, had published in *Izvestiya* (November 15th, 1925) the Preface to his book *Towards Socialism or towards Capitalism?* The question was answered in the affirmative, provided the party pursued policies which would protect the state industry from dangers threatening from the social differentiation in the village. Kaganovich, speaking during the preparation of the XIV Congress at the Ukrainian Party Conference explicitly expressed the hope that Trotsky be allowed closer participation in party leadership (ibid. December 10th, 1925). As to Kamenev, Stalin (*Sochineniya,* vol. VIII, p. 273) agreed that he *formally* supported 'socialism in one country'. Such support, however, was a mere formality because of his continued support of the Opposition. In this way of thinking, the theoretical formulae are evidently regarded, not as the foundations but as the symbols of political attitudes.

145. Sochineniya, vol. VII, p. 337 ; *VKP(b) v rezolyutsiyakh,* vol. II, p. 38.

146. *Otchet* XIV Congress, p. 109.

147. Stalin's *Sochineniya,* vol. VII, pp. 344 ff.

148. *Izvestiya,* December 17, 1925.

149. *Izvestiya,* December, 1925. *Neposredstveno* is italicised in original.

150. This was actually done but Evdokimov resigned three months later as was unavoidable in view of the further development of the opposition.

151. In fact passages of the Moscow draft which referred to the opposition in deprecatory terms were eliminated and the desire to overcome the differences within the party leadership was emphasised but the opposition's amendments (which contained all its main tenets) were rejected. *Otchet,* pp. 521 ff. ; *VKP(b) v rezolyutsiyakh,* vol. II, pp. 50-52.

152. *Otchet,* pp. 283, 297 and 423.

153. But even Tomski, who made the main speech for the right-wing, sharply disclaimed any desire to remove the oppositionists from the party leadership. Ibid. p. 288.

154. See above, p. 193.

155. *Otchet* XIV Congress, pp. 575, 600 ff., 612-13, 623-24 and 629. Solts, one of the majority representatives on the CCC, still attempted to clear it of the reproach that it operated upon denunciations (ibid. p. 615). Before, the representation of oppositionists in the CC had been regarded as a guarantee of its objectivity. Now, Krupskaya,

when defending this view within the CCC, ran into difficulties (ibid. pp. 531, 673 and 619-20).

156. Cf. her book (quoted in note 39), pp. 544 ff.

157. *Sochineniya*, vol. XII, p. 342.

158. *VKP(b) v rezolyutsiyakh*, vol. II, pp. 48-49.

159. Stalin's *Sochineniya*, vol. VIII, pp. 119 ff. and *VKP(b) v rezolyutsiyakh*, vol. II, p. 148.

160. Cf. A. I. Rykov and N. N. Bukharin, *Partiya i oppozitsionny blok* (their reports in Moscow and Leningrad on the Plenary Meeting of the CC and CCC of July 14th-23rd, 1926, with an Annex including the party documents on the Lashevich affair), Gosizdat, 1926.

These statements, like Stalin's 'the party (i.e. the party majority) cannot be a faction' appear to have been caused by the awkward situation in which the party majority was placed by Zinoviev's disclosure, at the July 1926 meeting of the CC, that, two years before, the party majority (including himself, of course) had established some kind of Politburo of its own so as to confront Trotsky within the official Politburo with a compact bloc (see note 127 above, p. 262).

161. Stalin's *Sochineniya*, vol. VIII, pp. 145-46.

162. From the Trotskyite side, the purely tactical character of Trotsky's conciliatory statements of 1926-27 is stated by Eastman, in his note on p. 181 of the translation of Trotsky's *The Real Situation in Russia* (New York, 1928). On the Zinovievite side, I heard in the days of the events from some of their leaders, explanations of the strange alliance such as 'there are situations in which the working-class (i.e. the Leningrad opposition) must join hands with the lower-middle-class (the definition of the social background of Trotskyism by the party majority) against the peasants (i.e. the Stalin-Bukharin combination)'.

163. Popov's statement (op. cit. vol. II, p. 274) fits with what I heard at the time of the events. There is no evidence than that of Ruth Fischer herself to support her assertion (loc. cit. 546 and 564) that direct military action was being contemplated. Stalin's omission, in 1948, from vol. VIII of his *Sochineniya* of the speech made by him on the discussion of the Lashevich affair (cf. ibid. p. 397) may indicate that he regarded that speech as too mild according to 1948 standards. But Popov's interpretation of the events would account for such an attitude of Stalin.

164. *VKP(b) v rezolyutsiyakh*, pp. 114 ff.

165. *Izvestiya*, October 22nd, 1926.

166. Trotsky (*My Life*, p. 445) later quoted this statement as a characteristic expression of Kamenev's 'bureaucratic optimism'. But unless he expected something similar at the time of the events, and even of the street demonstration in November 1927, it is difficult to see for what purposes he entered the *bloc*. Some of his supporters had,

indeed, suggested an alliance with Stalin (ibid. pp. 444-45), which would not have been inconsistent if industrialisation was regarded as the central issue.

167. Trotsky's statement in *The Real Situation in Russia*, p. 194 is directed against these tendencies. As, in autumn 1927, the idea was not considered practical by 'certain elements of the party machine'; the argument appears to be directed only against the despair of oppositionists of winning a majority within the party.

168. *Izvestiya*, October 5th, 1926.

169. *Sochineniya*, vol. VIII, pp. 209 ff.

170. *Izvestiya*, October 17th, 1926.

171. Ibid. October 29th. The Workers' Opposition within Russia had never gone so far in its attacks as did Ruth Fischer who was abroad. From her own record about the subsequent negotiations before the International Control Commission (loc. cit. pp. 571-72) one gets the impression that her group, too, might have been re-admitted if ready to make a fitting declaration. The point, however, was that at the time of negotiations the Opposition was taking a new stand in the Enlarged Plenum of ECCI. In combination with Ruth Fischer's refusal to submit this was bound to be regarded by the majority as evidence that Ruth Fischer said abroad what the Opposition continued to think.

172. Deutscher (op. cit. 1959, pp. 295 ff.) suggests that the publication, by Eastman in USA, of Lenin's 'will' on October 18th, i.e. two days after the Opposition's submission, may have caused Stalin's sharper approach since it made him doubt the sincerity of that submission. Since the Opposition's decision to compromise was taken as early as October 4th (the Leningrad effort was merely intended as a means of pressure to improve the conditions) there should have been time to recall Eastman, if Trotsky so desired or, in the case of his refusal, to delimit the Russian Opposition so sharply from his diehard tactics that misunderstandings were excluded.

173. Stalin's *Sochineniya*, vol. VIII, pp. 233 and 294-95; *VKP(b) v rezolyutsiyakh*, p. 161.

174. Stalin's *Sochineniya*, vol. VIII, pp. 351 ff.

175. Ibid. p. 227, *VKP(b) v rezolyutsiyakh*, p. 159.

176. Trotsky, *My Life*, p. 451.

176a. Already at the 15th Party Conference Stalin hinted at that possibility when he compared his alliance with Bukharin with that once concluded between Lenin and Plekhanov, *Sochineniya*, vol. VII, pp. 240-41.

177. Popov, op. cit. vol. II, p. 310.

178. *Izvestiya*, October 5th and December 9th, 1926.

179. Glazyrin, op. cit. pp. 47 ff.

180. Ibid. pp. 56-57.

181. Trotsky, *My Life*, pp. 452-53, Popov, op. cit. p. 313, Ruth Fischer, op. cit. p. 582. The text of the explanation given by Trotsky to the

Chairman of the CCC, Ordzhonikidze, is quoted in Stalin's *Sochineniya*, vol. X, p. 52.

182. Ibid. pp. 85 ff. ; *VKP(b) v rezolyutsiyakh*, pp. 197 ff.

183. Eastman's publication of that platform, *The Real Situation in Russia*, as Trotsky's work is not refuted by its adoption in meetings in which 200 delegates of Opposition branches were said to have participated. When it was submitted to the CC on September 3rd, it was signed by 83 well-known Old Bolsheviks ; another 3000 party members added their signatures (*Otchet*, XV Congress, pp. 237 and 255). If, in the adoption process, Trotsky's original draft was modified at all, it was surely not in points of substance. Such concessions as resulted from Trotsky's combination with the Zinoviev group had been already in his own draft.

184. Trotsky, *My Life*, p. 453, Ruth Fischer, op. cit. p. 604.

185. Ordzhonikidze at the XV Congress, *Otchet*, pp. 393-94.

186. Stalin's *Sochineniya*, vol. X, pp. 263 ff.

187. Ibid. p. 349.

188. Cf. Kamenev, *Otchet*, XV Congress, pp. 255-56.

189. Cf. Kalinin's speech, ibid. p. 1251, and even Kirov, ibid. p. 240.

190. Popov, op. cit. p. 327 (note), ibid. p. 323. The total number of votes polled in the primary party organisations for the Opposition is given as 6000 against 725,000 voting for the platform of the CC. Stalin usually used the lower figure but in November 1928 did not object when even the figure of 10,000 Oppositionists was mentioned. He added that twice as many opposition sympathisers might have abstained (*Sochineniya*, vol. XI, p. 277).

191. *Sochineniya*, vol. X, pp. 329 ; see also Popov, op. cit. vol. II, pp. 353-54.

192. Ibid. pp. 304-09.

193. Stalin's *Sochineniya*, vol. XI, pp. 4, 13 and 235.

194. Ibid. pp. 5 ff., 12-13 and 85. Nemchinov's statistics (published in *Pravda*, June 2nd, 1928) upon which Stalin's last-quoted analysis of conditions on the grain-market were based, were themselves open to criticism : in 1925 the Left-wing Opposition had given even higher assessments of the kulaks' influence (cf. Rykov's report to the XIV Moscow Gubernial Conference in December 1925), since then, the differentiation in the village had made further progress.

195. *VKP(b) v rezolyutsiyakh*, pp. 277 ff. ; Stalin's *Sochineniya*, vol. XI, pp. 58-59.

196. *Izvestiya Ts.K. VKP(b)*, 1928, No. 26.

197. Ibid. p. 13.

198. Stalin's *Sochineniya*, vol. XI, pp. 31-33.

199. *Izvestiya Ts.K. VKP(b)*, 1928, Nos. 16-17, 21 and 28.

200. Stalin's *Sochineniya*, vol. XI, pp. 70-71.

201. Cf. Penkov's speech at the XVI Party Congress, *Otchet*, p. 363.

202. In such terms it was described in the Politburo decision of February 9th, 1929, on the history of the disagreements, *VKP(b) v rezolyutsiyakh*, p. 329.

203. Ibid. pp. 274 and 286 ff., and Stalin's *Sochineniya*, vol. XI, pp. 117 ff.

204. Ibid. pp. 99 and 131 ff.

205. The present author, for example, used in those days a juxtaposition of Stalin's articles—mainly *On the Grain Front*—and Bukharin's *Notes of an Economist*—as the basis for an explanation, in an article in the German *Internationale,* of the substance of the dispute. Its exact nature was not known at the time and, even if known, could not be divulged by anyone interested in preserving his party membership. The restrictions put by conventions on Politburo homogeneity and the expression of controversial views worked just to the extent that they prevented such demagogic and brutal expressions of the conflicting views as had become current during the struggle against the Left-wing Opposition: precisely for this purpose they had been adopted.

206. The comparatively moderate terms in which the incident eventually was dealt with (*VKP(b) v rezolyutsiyakh*, p. 323) makes it unlikely that Bukharin's statements to Kamenev were quite correctly reported by the Trotskyite source (the revelations which eventually led to the explosion). The content of the information received by Trotsky is now available in Deutscher's op. cit. (1959), pp. 440-43. Exaggerations, or distortions of certain aspects of the discussion are not excluded. The CCC, of course, was bound to base its disciplinary measures on the terms of the interview as established by a confrontation of Bukharin with Kamenev, in which the sharpness of Bukharin's remarks was bound to be denied.

207. I have discussed this incident in my *Central European Democracy,* Routledge-Kegan Paul, 1952, pp. 376-79.

208. This is in obvious contrast to the behaviour of Zinoviev who in August 1925, when his struggle with the Politburo majority was developing, loyally carried out its decisions about the demotion of Ruth Fischer whose support he was eventually to seek. Yet quite apart from Zinoviev's personal attitude to her group (from this standpoint, the demotion rather than the subsequent rapproachment was consistent) it was comparatively easy for him to voice disagreements on internal Soviet policy but difficult to dissociate himself within Comintern from the prestige of the USSR. Bukharin, on the other hand, was handicapped in outspoken discussion of Soviet internal politics but quite ready to voice, on the international stage, some rapproachment with the Social Democrats. If mishandling of international factionalism should result in the removal of Comintern's Chairman by a Politburo majority (as eventually happened in any case) this would be a catastrophe in Zinoviev's political career which he tried to avoid as

long as possible. For Bukharin it was a minor incident not worse than any other loss of prestige.

209. *Izvestiya Ts.K. VKP(b)*, 1928, No. 31 ; Stalin's *Sochineniya*, vol. XI, pp. 236 and 241 ; F. M. Baganov's article in *Voprosy Istorii/KPSS*, 1960, No. 4.

210. At the XVI Congress the leading part played by the CC in these events was made quite explicit: *Otchet*, pp. 90 and 363-64.

211. *VKP(b) v rezolyutsiyakh*, pp. 297 and 329-30 ; Ordzhonikidze at the XVI Party Congress, *Otchet*, p. 326. The Opposition's concession was enacted so modestly that Stalin (*Sochineniya*, vol. XI, p. 257) found it necessary specially to draw attention to this as the most important passage in the resolution.

212. *Sochineniya*, vol. XI, pp. 249-51 and 274-77. As late as in April 1929 the point about the undesirability of further development of *kulak* economy was still so far in the background that Kaganovich, speaking at the Urals Regional Party Conference, to a suggestion about the kulak's readiness to deliver grain if they were supplied with tractors, merely replied that the State industry could not produce enough tractors to supply both the kulaks and the kolkhozy, and that the latter were more important (*Izvestiya*, April 10, 1929).

213. Ibid. pp. 286-87.

214. Cf. the resolution adopted by the Meeting of the Politburo and the Presidium of the CCC on February 9th, 1929 (*VKP(b) v rezolyut-siyakh*, vol. II, p. 328). The resolution adopted by the Plenary Meeting of the CC and CCC which met at the time of the XVI Party Conference mentions the organisational tensions as 'a dangerous opposition of the party-leadership to that of the trade unions...... a *de facto* course towards weakening the party's leadership in the union field'. Tomski is said to have 'covered craft trends and tendencies to bureaucratic ossification in parts of the trade union machine' (he is not yet mentioned as their representative) and presented the party's struggle against these defects as a Trotskyist 'shaking up of the trade unions' (ibid. p. 321). The presentation given above in the text is based upon the explanations given by the participants at the XVI Party Congress.

215. Cf. V. Maier's and V. Markov's article in *Sotsialisticheski trud*, 1958, No. 2.

216. *Izvestiya Ts.K. VKP(b)*, 1928, Nos. 28, 32 and 36.

217. Stalin's speech was published in his *Sochineniya* (vol. XI, pp. 318 ff) in a short summary without indication of the dates at which its diverse parts were made (the meeting lasted nine days, and Stalin's initial approach was bound to be temporarily overshadowed by the CCC's intervention on February 7th ; see Ordzhonikidze's report to the XVI Party Congress, *Otchet*, pp. 325-26). The text of the adopted resolution, as printed in the quoted edition of *VKP(b) v rezolyutsi-*

yakh, pp. 323 ff., has a gap which was filled only in the 1954 edition. It concerns a recognition of Rudzutak's being right against Bukharin in issues of currency policies, the publication of which was apparently regarded as impolitic as long as the myth of the 'great purge' had to be maintained.

218. *VKP(b) v rezolyutsiyakh,* pp. 318 ff.; *Otchet* XVI Congress, pp. 263 ff.

219. In the 1938 trial (Proceedings, p. 161) Vyshinski asserted in the appropriate terminology, that most of them eventually joined the secret organisation of the right-wingers.

220. Stalin's *Sochineniya,* vol. XII, pp. 97-98. The comparison was not quite fitting as the Kronstadt mutineers opposed aspects of Soviet policy which Trotsky had represented even more energetically than the party majority. A comparison, not with Trotsky's but with the Workers' Opposition's behaviour in the 1921 crisis would have been legitimate if the right-wingers of 1928-30 had failed to repress peasant insurrections which exaggerated the criticism made by them within the party caucus. Such failure was not alleged at the time, though it may form part of the rational kernel in some accusations levelled later at the right-wingers.

221. *Sochineniya,* vol. XII, pp. 49 ff., 59 and 98. In a footnote (p. 1) the readers' attention is drawn to the incompleteness of the earlier report of that speech.

222. Ibid. pp. 65 ff. (and vol. X, pp. 155-57).

CHAPTER VI

THE SECOND REVOLUTION AND ITS AFTERMATH

(a) THE FIVE YEAR PLAN AND COLLECTIVISATION OF AGRICULTURE: THEIR IMPACT ON PARTY ORGANISATION

THE DEFEAT of the right-wing cleared the way for the reconstruction of the Soviet economy on a planned basis. Most of the concepts underlying that reconstruction were as old as the revolution itself: collaboration of the Academy of Sciences in the reconstruction of Russia's economic resources was offered and accepted as early as in January 1918. Immediately after the Brest Litovsk treaty, when the loss of Russia's old industrial centres had to be envisaged, plans for a development of the Kuznetz coal basin in connection with the metallurgy of the Urals were elaborated and approved by VTsIK. Plans to carry out the reconstruction on a mixed basis were overruled by the decision for full nationalisation.[1] In early 1920 these projects, like so many others, were integrated in the plan for the electrification and re-organisation of Russian industry (GOELRO-plan) which was adopted on Krzhizhanovski's suggestion and served Lenin as the handle to explain the long-term prospects of the revolution. As the following table[2] shows, the targets envisaged by the GOELRO-Plan remained far below the actual achievements not only of the post-war period but even of the first two Five Year Plans. Still they were important as symbols which only for a time were overshadowed by the more immediate needs of the war economy and then of.the New Economic Policy.

During NEP, Gosplan served as a place where non-communist specialists could exchange views with their communist colleagues and thereby influence Government decisions.[3] In accordance with the political trend predominant during the first period of NEP the 'genetic' school of planners interpreted Soviet planning

PRODUCTION

Commodity and unit of measurement	1913	1920	GOELRO plan	1935	1941 operative plan	1955	1958	1965
Coal mill. tons	29.1	8.6	62.3	108.9	190.8	391	496	
Crude Oil ,,	9.2	3.8	11.8–16.4	25.1	38.04	71	113	243
Peat* ,,	1.7	1.4	16.4	18.5	38.8	50	54***	
Iron ore ,,	9.2	0.16	19.6	27.1	34.03		88.8	66.2
Manganese ,,	1.25	—	1.64	2.37	3.1			
Pig Iron ,,	4.2	0.12	8.2	12.5	18.0	33	39.6	
Steel ,,	4.2	0.19	6.5	12.5	22.4	45	54.9	9.40
Copper thousand tons	31.1	0.3	81.9	75.2	—			
Aluminium ,,	—	—	9.8	25.0	—			
Paper ,,	197.0	30.0	688.5	—	969.8		2,200	
Bricks (in milliards)	2.1	0.2	9.8	—	9.1*	20	535	
Cement mill. tons	1.8		10.0		5.7**	22.5	33.3	

*without kolkhoz production
**actual production in 1940
***last column figure for 1957

	1913	1920	GOELRO plan	1935	1941 operative plan	1955	1958	1965
Capacity of regional power stations (in 1000 kw)	177	—	1,750	4,540				
Electricity output (in milliards kw hours)	1.9				54	170	233	

as the anticipation of the 'natural' exchange conditions between town and countryside, to be derived from pre-War experience.[4] As opposed to such an extrapolation of trends already observable, the 'teleological' school of planners aimed at the modification of existing trends by a suitable economic policy.[5]   The decisions of the XIV Party Congress on industrialisation tipped the balance within Gosplan in favour of the teleologists.   Still the PC of Finance reproached the planners with promoting inflation.[6]   In the conditions of NEP emphasis was bound to be laid on the elaboration of control figures for each successive year but a draft five-year plan, covering the period from 1925-26 to 1929-30, was drawn up by a commission headed by Strumilin, an outstanding representative of the 'teleological' school.   It was discussed in March 1926 (the five-year period was originally intended as an intermediate link between 'general plans' of the GOELRO-pattern which were to include large-scale transformations not only of technique but also of society, and the annual 'control figures' which had to be calculated every year by addition of the appropriate increase rate to last year's output figures).   As early as in the autumn of 1925 Strumilin defined the difference in approaches as one between 'state plan' and 'peasants' plan', i.e. such concessions to the elemental forces of the market as were demanded by Bukharin.

The choice of a section of five years was conditioned by the consideration that, during that period, new plants projected at its start could come into operation and that, on the average, amongst five harvests in Russia one complete crop-failure occurred.   This would reduce one of the main elements of insecurity in a peasant country.[7]   During the struggle against the right-wingers, Stalin treated the Five Year Period, undiluted by any parallel plans for shorter periods, as the very symbol of the party's devotion to long-term reconstruction.[8]   Such an approach was not incompatible with the encouragement of 'counter-plans' to be drafted from the factory floor to check the supposed underestimates of potentialities by over-cautious specialists, nor with the decision of the XVI Party Congress 'to complete the Five Year Plan in four years' (in consequence of changes in timing, it was actually four years and three months), however strange such changes might appear if planning is interpreted as conscious coordination of production efforts in various fields. Yet such coordination was hardly possible in those days, particularly if everywhere maximum speed of development was regarded as the decisive issue.

In August 1928, Gosplan had elaborated two variants of the Five Year Plan. The optimum variant, adopted in November 1928 for the first year and as a whole by the XVI Party Conference,[9] was based upon a number of assumptions. These included an uninterrupted chain of satisfactory harvests, long-term credits by foreign suppliers and doubling of the productivity of labour within the five years.[10] None of the assumptions was actually realised, least of all the planned increase in the productivity of labour. In order to carry out the planned investments, the labour force had to be increased far more than had been planned.[11] The increased demands upon an already insufficient food supply enforced the speeding up the collectivisation of agriculture. What modest contribution the new tractor-building industry could make at that stage to the productivity of agricultural labour was lost by the mass-slaughter of cattle with which the kulaks and all those who followed their lead reacted to collectivisation. An inordinately quick increase in a labour force insufficiently productive and supplied with insufficient amounts of consumers' goods was bound to result in wages increased in terms of money but reduced in purchasing power. The poor peasant drawn into industry might feel his lot improved even on a reduced industrial worker's wage. On the other hand he might have become an efficient worker more quickly had slower and more selective recruitment been accompanied by increasing material incentives for professional training and efficiency. Yet the speed of industrialisation was not with the range of the Soviet leaders' free decision. It was dictated by the international position of the USSR. The margin with which World War II was eventually won was narrow enough: success would have been unlikely if industrial reconstruction in the decisive sections had been slower. Equilibrium between the diverse sections of the national economy had to wait for another quarter of a century.

As new masses were drawn into industry, the human factor provided the central problem in industrial expansion. The re-

18

print, in January 1929, of Lenin's old articles on socialist competition opened a campaign to popularise it in the factories. Appeals were launched from selected factories and from the youth organisations to form groups of 'shock-workers' who challenged each other for competition in fulfilment and overfulfilment of the plans. Occasionally, the shock-workers met violent resistance from their more backward fellows who preferred to go slow.[12] The tardy encouragement which they got from a trade union machine still strongly dominated by the skilled workers' traditional outlook led to the removal of that leadership.

Mere enthusiasm, however, could not overcome the shortage of educated workers. During the last years of NEP, the absolute number of school children had increased annually by about five per cent. Increase in relation to total population was minimal (from 62 per 1000 inhabitants in 1925-26 to 64 in 1927-28). In 1929-30, however, the number of elementary school pupils was increased against the preceding year by 12 per cent (21 in the villages, 6 per cent in the towns) so that a total of 7.9 million school children was reached. On a decision of the XVI Party Congress obligatory elementary education was introduced by the decree of July 25, 1930. 40,000 new schools were opened in that autumn and the number of school children increased by another 1.7 million—still only 83 per cent of the children of school age went to school. In 1931-32, at last, a coverage of 94 per cent of all the children was achieved (this meant an increase against the preceding year of 15 per cent in the RSFSR as a whole, but of 29 per cent in the national republics).[13] While general elementary education thus became reality, the suggestions of the decree regarding adaptation of the methods of schooling to the needs of industry ('polytechnization') became a practical issue only in our days.

Only moderate progress was made in the schooling of skilled workers. The diverse institutions training them graduated about 80,000 pupils in 1929-30, another 40,000 were trained through the labour organisations (including apprenticeship in factories).[14] 167,000 students attended the *tekhnikums,* i.e. institutions training specialists of middle qualification from the nurse to the technician, and 124,500 the institutions of higher education: the increase against the academic year 1927-28 amounted to 38,000 and 17,000 respectively. In 1931, 45,000 specialists graduated from *tekhnikums,* 19,100 from institutions of higher education.[15] In every field except elementary education the major achievements still lay ahead but what had already been achieved initiated a cultural revolution hardly less important than the new factories and railways.

The party's slogan 'all eyes on production' implied its assuming direct leadership in the production drive. At the top, the CC adopted decisions on investment and production problems of major industrial combines. Primary organisations were concerned, not only with production propaganda but also with problems of the rationalisation of production, piece-work rates, savings in administrative machinery etc.[16] The adaptation of the central party machine to the new tasks took some time. In February 1930 the *Uchrazpred* Department, which had originally been concerned with the posting of communists to diverse jobs, was divided into a cadres department (which continued its original functions) and an industrial department, wth the appropriate sub-departments for various industries, to instruct communists working in those industries.[17]

93 per cent of all the managers, and all the managers of the major factories, were now communists.[18] Party and trade union representatives, who traditionally, together with the management, formed the 'treugolnik' ('triangle') controlling factory life, were now admonished not to interfere with managerial responsibilities, particularly at the shop level where trade union representatives used to intervene whenever a worker found his interests impaired by the foreman's rulings, and even to supervise the appointment of foremen.[19] The manager's status within the party might increase his, and his seniors', opportunities for repressing criticism. In one instance the secretary of a Provincial Committee caused the workers who were members of the city committee to be arrested as alleged oppositionists because they had criticised the Provincial Committee. The secretary was expelled from the party, his committee dissolved and his colleagues prohibited from occupying posts of responsibility for two years.[20]

The party tried to improve its ranks by a dual effort: a

prolonged recruitment drive intended to raise the percentage of party members who worked at the bench to half of the total and another 'purge' intended to cleanse it from bureaucratic and class-alien elements.[21] Neither of these aims was fully achieved. On July 1, 1928, 36.7 per cent of the party members had been industrial workers (and another 1.7 per cent agricultural labourers), 9 per cent peasants working on their own land and another 2.4 per cent peasants combining their production work with part-time work in the public service. 32.6 per cent were salaried employees (including junior officials), 7 per cent served in the army (of the total strength of which they now formed 13.5 per cent as against a mere 10.3 per cent in 1925). The 9.5 per cent 'others' included the higher officials of party and state as well as students.[22] From January 1929 onwards percentages of workers and peasants were calculated from party organisations other than those of the army. Now workers actually engaged in production numbered 44.3 per cent of the total party membership (as against 40.8 per cent one year before); there were 12.8 (12.3) peasants and 42.8 (46.9) per cent salaried employees and 'others'.[23] Some progress in the desired direction was evident, yet the new calculating method decreased the specific weight of the civil servants etc. in whose numbers obviously the professional army officers were included. In January 1929 the CC elaborated directives for the regulation of new admissions to the party: the share of manual workers amongst those admitted should amount to no less than 90 per cent in the industrial Provinces, 70 per cent in the agricultural Provinces, and about 60 per cent in the national republics. Naturally enough, some of the workers recruited in the chase for 'achieving the target' were not interested in party work while quite suitable candidates of non-working-class origin had to wait a long time till their place on the quota was reached.[24] In July 1930, with a proportion of 48.8 per cent production workers amongst the party membership (which might have meant some 45 per cent if the army organisations had still been included) the culmination of the drive for a workers' majority within the party was reached. After that numbers fell, even in absolute terms. During 1931, 152,000 workers who were communists were promoted to salaried offices or sent to institutions of higher education. The number of manual workers who were party members decreased by 182,000; their percentage in total party membership fell to 43.5 per cent[25] (probably less than 40 if the army membership had been included). No further figures were published but there can be no doubt that the end of preferential treatment of manual workers in admission to the party eventually resulted in a decrease of their share. The recent restoration of that share to some forty per cent represents a major achievement.

The directives for the 'purge' issued by the XVI Party Conference[26] warned against a repetition of the mistakes committed during the preceding one, eight years before. In particular they warned against the misuse of the public purge meetings for the settling of personal accounts and against the raising of irrelevant issues of the private life of party members. Bureaucratism, careerism, corruption and infestation of party members by class-alien influences, including anti-Semitism and religious prejudices, were described as the main evils to be fought. Of political offences, only clandestine support of the leftist groups expelled from the party was mentioned as a reason for expulsion from the party. In the circumstances, however, a purge directed against party members too friendly to the local *kulak* or too devoted to bureaucratic red-tape was bound to deprive the right-wing opposition of many supporters. A total of 116,000 party members—10.4 per cent of the total figure—were expelled (if those who left the party voluntarily during the purge are included, the number rises to 131,500, or 11.7 per cent of the total). The absolute figure —though not, of course, the percentage—comes near to that of the first 'purge', which included quite a lot of questionable decisions. Another 15 per cent of the party members who went through the 'purge' received reprimands. 17.2 per cent of the expulsions concerned 'class-alien elements' or party members too closely associated with these; 16.4 per cent misuse of officials' powers or violations of labour discipline; 15 per cent drunkenness (on the whole, demoralisation in everyday life, including anti-Semitism, practising religion and failure to support one's children caused 22 per cent, and violation of party discipline, which included factionalism, 21 per cent of the expulsions).[27]

The 'purge' thus had two aspects, different in their impact upon the party's social structure. It might have hit the ordinary manual worker who had been recruited in the chase for figures, though his attitude to labour discipline, alcohol and religion was not quite up to party standards,[28] or it might have eliminated the peasant whose growing prosperity had turned him into a *kulak,* or the official too closely connected with his kind. The party lost 7.5 per cent of those members who were workers according to present occupation, 9.6 per cent of the salaried employees, 4.6 per cent of those members who were students (their conformity with party standards had, of course, been scrutinised already before admission to university) and 17.6 per cent of its peasant members. Amongst the latter, the incidence of expulsions was in clear correspondence to their economic prosperity. A mere 14.4 per cent of those who paid no tax, but 68.3 per cent of those party members who paid more than 150 rubles annual agricultural tax, were expelled (in the ordinary small-holder income groups expulsions amounted to about 27 per cent of visiting members, while in the more prosperous middle peasant income groups 43 per cent).[29] The conception of the purge as aiming in substance at the removal of party members affected by NEP is also evident from the fact that a mere 2.4 per cent of party members of pre-revolutionary standing were expelled. Already for the next group of entrants, (of 1917-22) the percentage rises to 9.6 per cent and remains at that level until it falls again to 7.6 per cent of those who joined in 1928 (i.e. when strong preference was given to working-class recruits who had not had much opportunity to be exposed to the temptations of office).[30]

In substance, the purge of 1929-30 was still an elimination of persons not conforming to communist standards rather than of political dissenters. But the loss of a sixth of the party's support amongst the peasants made its weakness still more obvious. Much of this weakness was due to a refusal of peasant party members to support collectivisation. In early 1929 a number of discussion articles published in *Izvestiya Ts.K.VKP(b)* had dealt with the question whether peasants who were party members should be faced with the alternative of joining the collective farms or leaving the party. An author had advised against such a procedure excepted in cases where the party member concerned had already become an employer of labour who should be forced to choose between his entrepreneurial status and that of a party member (assuming that he had not become *kulak*ised to such an extent that it might be better to get rid of him in any case). The ordinary peasant party member should not be faced with ultimata but be allowed some time to convince himself of the superiority of collective farming. Other contributors to the discussion replied that if the party were to wait till collectivised farming became' an inviting prospect from the individual entrant's point of view, it would get no collective farms whatever.

By the beginning of 1930 the party had 51,000 primary organisations, 30,000 of them in the villages (many of these mere probationers' groups). Of the one and a half million party members 400,000 were peasants; of these 115,000 party members and probationers (i.e. 52.2 per cent of all those peasants who were party members) belonged to collective farms (another 26,000 communists worked in state farms and Machine Tractor Stations). In the Ukraine, 174 of the 4,037 existing collective farms had party groups (with a total of 1,800 members); 2,634 communists belonged to the 222 party groups existing in the 1,250 state farms[31]—even this was a mere fraction of what was needed to ensure party leadership even in the directly nationalised section of agriculture. During the three years 1928-30 one hundred thousand party members and ten thousand members of the *komsomol* were sent to the villages, notably in late 1929 when a large-scale campaign was developed for the posting of 'highly qualified and politically tested workers', on a voluntary basis, for leading work in collective farms, Machine Tractor Stations and village Soviets. 90 per cent of 'the twenty-five thousand', as they were known after the decision of the Plenary Meeting of the CC in mid-November, came from the main industrial centres, 80 per cent were already members of party or *komsomol*. Most of the rest joined during the preparatory courses.[32]

This injection of new blood had been decided upon because it proved impossible to advance collectivization on the earlier, voluntary basis. In 1929 the sowing area of the collective farms had more than trebled against the preceding year, while the state farms (originally regarded as no less important a source of marketed grain) had advanced by a mere quarter. Yet both together produced about 2.1 million tons marketed grain, i.e. a quarter of what then was regarded as the subsistence minimum for the towns and the army, not including the increase in the original plans of industrial development which became necessary for defence reasons. By the end of 1929, Stalin noticed that the smallholder's husbandry was in some cases unable to keep up even the existing reproduction level. It was impossible any longer to base the Soviet regime and socialist reconstruction on two foundations as different as large-scale socialist industry and dissipated smallholders' husbandry which produced little for the market. In Stalin's view, the conditions had grown for a change of policy from the mere limitation of the kulaks' exploitatory activities, as hitherto pursued, to a policy of liquidating the *kulak* class. Being deadly enemies of the kolkhozy, the kulaks should not be allowed to join them. Violent 'de-Kulakisation' measures, involving the deportation of 240,000 peasant families, not all of them *kulaks,* with perhaps a million members, followed.[33] By a Politburo decision of January 5, 1930, targets for the achievement of full collectivization were set for the diverse regions, varying between spring 1931 for the most advanced of the grain producing regions till 1933 for regions with inconsiderable grain production. By a TsIK decree of February 1, 1930, for the regions of full collectivization, those parts of the Land Code which dealt with hiring labour and renting land (i.e. admitted capitalist enterprises in agriculture) were repealed. Provincial Executive Committees were authorised 'to take all the necessary measures for combating the kulaks up to complete confiscation of their property and their deportation from the confines of the Region in which they live' (kulaks who had violated the existing laws fared worse). The credits granted to collective farms in 1929-30 were nearly doubled, at the expense of individual farming. Moreover, the former received all the help of the Machine Tractor Stations.[34]

In his December speech Stalin had to argue not only against the traditional right-wing theories about a possible and desirable equilibrium between the socialist and the private sectors, but also against unnamed opponents who denied the socialist character of the kolkhozy because the class struggle was still continuing within them.[35] The January decision of the CC emphasised the central importance of the agricultural *artel,* i.e. that type of kolkhoz in which the main means of production were socialised, as opposed to the hitherto predominant Societies for Joint Cultivation of the Land where means of production still remained private property and the distribution of the product depended as much on every member's stock as on his participation in the joint labour effort. On the other side, the Commune, i.e. a kolkhoz whose members had no longer any private husbandry of their own, was not recommended for the time being. Model statutes for the *Artel* were to be elaborated by the new Union PC of Agriculture with the participation of kolkhoz members. It was described as a transitory stage to the future Commune.

Now the collectivisation drive got into full swing. Targets had to be 'fulfilled and overfulfilled', as was the current phraseology where not social organization but coal and steel output targets were concerned. Whoever hesitated to apply full pressure against peasants unwilling to join the kolkhoz was liable to be regarded as an opportunist. In the given setting occasional excesses were inevitable. In some places they assumed a violent character, sometimes leading to the complete abolition of individual enterprise. Regional organisations such as Moscow and Transcaucasia which, according to the plan of January 5, 1930, had three years at their disposal, aspired to full collectivization by spring 1930. In some regions up to 15 per cent of the peasants were expropriated as alleged kulaks. Some districts showed a sudden 'progress' from 10 to 90 per cent collectivization. The *artel,* leaving some scope for private husbandry, was in many places replaced by the Commune. In some places even the chickens were collectivized: the PC of Agriculture itself issued Model Statutes for the *artels,* in which the private plot was not mentioned. Moscow made an extra contribution of its own by suggesting the immediate elimination not only of the *kulak* in the countryside, but also of the NEP-man in the towns (this mistake was corrected by the CC).[36] In other places collectivization was regarded as an opportunity to close down the churches.[37]

Peasant unrest found its main expression in demonstratively

leaving the Kolkhozes. When it assumed threatening dimensions, Stalin reacted, on March 2, with his famous article "Dizzy with Success". As some extremists still continued on the lines initiated by Stalin himself,[38] the Politburo issued, on March 15, a special decision on the mistakes committed. But especially in Moscow attempts were still made to explain the peasant disorders as the unavoidable vacillations of the lower middle-class.[39] eventually the Party Committees of Moscow and Transcaucasia had to be replaced. The peasants forced into the kolkhozy now left them in masses : for a moment it looked as if the party's policy had suffered a major defeat.[40] In his 'Reply to the Kolkhazniki'[41] Stalin explained the situation. Consolidation of the real achievements (as distinct from those artificial kolkhozy who owed their existence to mere administrative pressure) was the immediate task. Every middle peasant who wished to continue outside the kolkhoz was in his rights, though, in the party's opinion, mistaken. But the drive against the kulaks would continue and those peasants who continued to work on collective lines would be granted facilities and advantages not available to the individual peasant. A decree of April 2 established these privileges, for kolkhozy and their members, mainly as regards taxation. Another, of April 12, explained that Societies for Joint Cultivation of the Land (i.e. the type of kolkhozy which the right-wingers preferred) would enjoy these privileges fully only if their Rules regarding collectivization of means of production were practically identical with those of *Artels*.

By the end of the year, 24 per cent of all the peasant households (48 per cent in the main grain producing regions) were members of the kolkhozy.[42] This was less than was expected at the time of the publication of "Dizzy with Success" but more than Stalin, in his "Reply to the Kolkhozniki", took for granted.[43] In the following year the number of collectivized households as well as the sowing area of the collective farms more than doubled. In early 1934 two-thirds of the households and three-quarters of the whole sowing area were controlled by collectives, another 10 per cent of the sowing area by state farms. Only a third of the peasant households, with 15 per cent of the total area, remained on an individual basis. The change, executed by methods which Stalin a few years later himself described as a revolution from above carried out with such support as the party could find in the village, was accompanied by mass-killing of cattle and even by local famines. These could have been avoided if the peasants, from the very start, had tried to make the best of the new order.

During the first stage of 'de-kulakisation', the lower strata of the peasantry had profited and the standard of the agricultural labourers had improved even though the village as a whole fared worse. This was because the village had to meet public demands for deliveries the increase of which exceeded any increase in production possible before the new organisation and the new technique could be made to work. The grain harvest increased from 80 million tons in 1926-27 to 85 million in 1934, yet its marketed part increased from slightly over 10 to 24 million.[44] Even though in 1926-27, 7.5 million tons had been used in kulak's farms and perhaps 5 per cent of the rural population had migrated to the towns, it is obvious that at the conclusion of the crisis what remained for consumption per head of villages was less than before. Two-thirds of the sheep, half of the horses and two-fifths each of the horses, cows and pigs available before collectivization were lost by 1933. As late as 1952 only the losses of pigs had been made good ; only three-quarters of the pre-collectivization number of cows were available.[45]

The collectivisation crisis within the party caucus cannot be completely followed as, with the Plenary Session of April 1929, frank accounts on the disagreements came to an end. Eventually a mixture of truth and fiction was produced, *post eventum,* at the 'purge trials'. The only authentic contemporary documents which we have are the Oppositionists' statements at the XVI and XVII Party Congresses, carefully worded so as to deny the existence of the basic disagreements (which, at that time, would already have been regarded as incompatible with continuing party membership) and the published denunciations of opposition groups by the party majority (which, at that time, were still kept within limits so as to preserve some proportion between the crime alleged and its punishment by some demotion). An overt struggle during the summer of 1929 (documentation on which is unhappily absent) was followed, at the Plenary Session of the CC in November 1929 (the same which decided upon the full-scale offensive against private economy in the countryside), by a conciliatory declaration of the Opposition leaders which, however, was regarded as unsatisfactory. Bukharin was removed from the Politburo[46], and after the XVI Congress only Rykov was re-elected to it while Bukharin and Tomski remained ordinary members of the CC. The right-wing leaders asserted that the disagreements had concerned merely the speed of development and had thus lost their practical importance. The XVI Congress, on its part, declared defence of right-wing views as incompatible with party membership and emphasised the speed of reconstruction. Those very speakers of the majority who wished to keep the right-wingers as fully-righted members of the party leadership demanded from them a declaration of the detrimental implications of the policy formerly advocated by them.[47] But just this they would not admit notwithstanding their submission to party discipline. Naturally they were suspected of keeping in store for future crises of collectivization their claim of having been right against Stalin's majority. Any reference by themselves to their character as a group[48] was bound to strengthen such suspicion.

Rykov himself admitted that, in the circumstances, the formal observation of party discipline by an opposition group could not prevent it from becoming the crystallisation centre for all latent forces of counter-revolution.[49] The party majority used suitable quotations from illegal groups to show how they hoped to replace the existing regime by the Right-wing leaders, if necessary, even by armed force. In the Ukraine, a 'Popular-Revolutionary Socialist Party' circulated excerpts from party documents as propaganda material. In the North Caucasus a self-styled Buro of the Right-wing Deviationists described 'the right-wing deviation' as the most acceptable policy because the monarchy, anarchism and the existing Soviet regime had all proved to be either obsolete or oppressive.[50] There was no suggestion that the right-wing leaders in any way except by their mere voicing of disagreements had encouraged such use of their attitude. But the subsequent tragedy could be anticipated when one of the speakers drew the conclusion that 'conditions have to be created in which not a single member of the Politburo or the CC can serve even for a single counter-revolutionary, or vacillating party member, as a reference and as a potential leader for a counter-revolutionary groupment'.[51]

No choice was left to the right-wing leaders other than either simply to defend the policy which had been adopted against their warnings, and if they should prove right, share in their party's defeat without even attempting to provide an alternative to the existing regime, or to prepare now for such an alternative, preferably in combination with other dissatisfied groups. Since late 1928 a group, headed by Syrtsov, Lominadze and Shatzkin and based upon the Komsomol, had criticised Stalin because of his compromises with the right-wing, and later suggested the establishment of organisations of the village poor to fight for control of the kolkhozy. When its views were rejected by the leading group of the Politburo, it raised, as all previous oppositions had done, the issue of the internal party regime.[52] The factional struggle had its implications. On December 1, 1930, the three were excluded from the CC and the CCC respectively, as leaders of a clandestine 'leftist' factional group which had, however, entered a political alliance with the right-wingers and announced a platform which largely coincided with the latters' views.[53] In autumn 1931 Stalin published his article "On Some Problems of the History of Bolshevism" the implications of which went beyond what was indicated in the title. Fighting against an interpretation of Lenin's attitude before 1914 in terms of the left of the Second International in general (which included Rosa Luxemburg and Trotsky), Stalin defended the claim of Leninism (as developed by himself) to be the sole representative of revolutionary Marxism since Engels' death. The application of any standard other than the inherent needs of the Russian revolution to any developments in Bolshevik theory and practice was contrary to the spirit of Marxism. It must have been directed against opponents more important than some individuals who might, indeed, have used their position in research institutions as opportunities for a revival of some Trotskyist tenets. Moreover, Stalin's intervention marked a further step in the development of party historiography as an institutional device to strengthen the position of the leading group.

From this time onwards the record of internal disagreements within the party is a record of conspiracy available only in the presentation of the victorious side. In the spring of 1932 Ryutin, a less-known member of the right-wing Opposition, allegedly after consultation with its leaders[54] announced a platform on which a combination of all the oppositional forces was sought. In the 1937 trial[55] Sokolnikov stated that this platform enabled a rapprochement between the Zinovievists and Trotskyists (who had parted ways in 1927) though the alliance with the right-wingers was only later concluded. On this Ryutin and his immediate followers were expelled from the party and arrested for having formed a counter-revolutionary group. Zinoviev, Kamenev and two leading right-wingers (Petrovski and Uglanov) were expelled (but later re-admitted) because of their failure to denounce before the authorities the platform they were aware of.[56] This comparatively mild treatment contradicts the assertion, made in the trial of 1938, that on that platform the question of armed insurrection had been raised. The probable intention was the creation of a political combination which might serve as the alternative leadership once Stalin was removed by a majority decision of the CC. At the end of 1932, an underground group led by two of the less prominent right-wingers— Eismont and Tolmachev—was expelled from the party and arrested. At the time of the events (as distinct, of course, from the 1938 trials) nothing worse than anti-party propaganda was asserted and the right-wing leaders who had had some contacts with the culprits escaped with a reprimand.[57] Ciliga,[58] in his concentration camp, learned that Eismont and Tolmachev had prepared a 'palace revolution', whatever this might mean. Stalin had demanded their execution but this demand had been turned down by the CC majority. If this story is correct, the incident may have contributed to Stalin's later behaviour to the CC majority, but it is possible that the wishful thinking of political prisoners produced exaggerations of the facts similar to those in which Vyshinski later indulged in order to prove treason where there had been mere sharp political conflict. The new *History of the CPSU* (1959) mentions neither the Ryutin nor the Eismont-Tolmachev incident. This does not suggest that they were mere inventions, but may indicate that their actual content so grossly differed from what Stalin and Vyshinski made of them that silence on these events is preferable in the interests of the state's authority.

In any case, Stalin found it necessary to argue in February 1933 against 'some comrades' who suggested a return to private peasant enterprise, including kulaks. This, he said, was not a third alternative to collectivization and capitalism, but merely a round-about way to the latter.[59] Yet since the majority of peasants had been collectivized, resistance now had been transferred to the internal life of the farms. At the Plenary Session of the CC in January 1933 Stalin mentioned the activities of *kulak* inspired saboteurs as well as the surviving property instincts of the collectivized peasants.[60] The existing Machine Tractor Stations were criticised for having conceived their function as predominantly one of offering technical help rather than political guidance to the farms. The conception of their function as a means to collect additional grain was illustrated by the ruling (repealed only in our days) that those collective farms which did not use the MTS' services, and therefore not under an obligation to pay in kind for their services, had to deliver more grain by way of compulsory deliveries. To ensure the fulfilment of the political and food-collecting functions of the MTS and State farms, Political Departments were attached to them.[61] These were headed by directors who (like the Political Commissaries in the army, the heads of the Political Departments in the railways, etc.) were not elected by the party members but nominated by the superior authorities. These directors did not only head the ordinary party work in their farms but were also responsible for the struggle against hostile elements within the kolkhozy, the fulfilment of the delivery obligations, the apprehension of plunderers of socialised property, etc. The extra-ordinary character of the institution was recognised by another Plenary Meeting of the CC in November 1934, when three-quarters of the peasants were collectivized and the abolition of bread rationing had become possible. Now the Political Departments of the MTS were transformed into ordinary party organisations subject to the District Committees, but the institution of special Political Deputies of the

MTS managers, subject to the CC, was preserved to support the managers' activities as well as those of the Communists working in the kolkhozy.[62]

In the circumstances, the party's capacity to carry out its policy in the village depended to a large extent on its ability to supplement its rural strength by new cadres (even from the towns) and to make up the educational shortcomings of those peasant communists who supported collectivization. Another 25,000 communists were sent to work in the Political Departments. The whole party-educational system was reformed with a tendency to supply technically competent and politically reliable organisers of agriculture. By a CC decision of September 21, 1932, the 'communist universities' were turned into 'communist agricultural high schools', the Sverdlov University becoming the Highest Communist Agricultural University.[63] By these efforts, it was possible to staff the 3,368 Political Departments of the MTS, and the 2,021 Political Departments of the state farms with reliable and fairly efficient workers. At the kolkhoz level, however, the party organisation remained weak. By the end of 1933, only 30,000 of the 224,000 existing collective farms had normal primary party organisations; 20,000 had *nuclei* consisting of probationers for party membership, 22,000 farm *nuclei* were composed of Komsomol and party members (or at least probationers). In 38,000 collective farms there were only individual communists and in half the existing farms none at all.[64] The 'great purge' brought setbacks also in the countryside. At the XVIII Congress Andreyev[65] spoke of 12,000 existing primary organisations in kolkhozy, with a total of 153,000 party members. A fairly complete coverage of the kolkhozy by primary party organisations was achieved, after the mass-recruitment during the war, only in our days as a result of the amalgamation of the small farms.

(b) SOCIAL STABILISATION AND POLITICAL CRISIS

Fairly soon, the enthusiastic drive for industrialisation, with its emphasis on control from below and on promotion of the worker from the bench over the heads of the old specialists, gave way to

greater emphasis on managerial authority and working discipline.[66] The quick recruitment of newcomers from the countryside
into an industry which both needed them but was unable to
provide them with the most elementary amenities produced a
strong fluctuation of labour.   It was at its worst when expansion
was as its quickest and the cadres of old workers smallest.[67]
Counter-measures such as the refusal of labour exchanges to
assign new jobs to those who had left their old ones without
sufficient reason were bound to fail when managers, in order to
fulfil their plans, made desparate attempts to entice each other's
skilled workers.   The newcomers from the countryside on their
part, would find all dormitories equally bad.   The problem, which
eventually was tackled by Draconian measures, dominated the
situation in June 1931 when Stalin's speech "New Conditions—
New Tasks"[68] explained the six conditions of successful management : overcoming the labour shortage by systematic recruitment
of additional labour by contracts with the kolkhozy and by
mechanization of the labour processes ; re-organisation of the
wages system so as to overcome egalitarianism and to give the
worker an incentive to improve his qualifications by staying at
his job ; individual responsibility of the manager ; creating a new
technical intelligentsia from the ranks of the working-class; a
more tactful approach to the existing, pre-revolutionary specialists; and strict cost-accounting so as to get the means for additional investments.   These principles were soon elaborated in
special legislation.   The reforms of the last years have affected
them only insofar as extreme wage differentials were reduced and,
in the interest of quicker development of agriculture, recruitment
of industrial workers from the countryside was stopped.

At the time when the 'six conditions' were formulated some
of them were regarded as contrary to traditional tenets of the
labour movement.   Stalin's effort at establishing his firm authority
on matters of party history may have been directed against a
leftist trend, which opposed his attacks on 'lower-middle-class
egalitarianism' as much as his realistic approach to the *kolkhoz*
problem.   The drive for general education, one of the greatest
achievements of the period, further contributed to tension within
the party as (together with the Hitlerite threat) it encouraged a

19

more positive approach to the national history. The critical observations drafted by Stalin, Kirov and Zhdanov on history textbooks date from August 8 and 9, 1934, though they were published as late as January 26, 1936, when the country was already drifting into the 'great purge'. Whatever benefits for Soviet historiography may have resulted from the dropping of its original schemes,[69] in the given party setting this no less than Stalin's claim to be the supreme judge in historical questions was bound to strengthen the opposition against a regime which only by extreme centralisation managed to get through the collectivization crisis.

The external dangers arising in East and West and internal tension as illustrated by the Eismont-Tolmachev case contributed to the CC decision of January 1933 to open a new purge less than three years after the conclusion of the last. Iron discipline should be secured and all unreliable or vacillating elements should be eliminated.[70] The new purge was more severe than that of 1930. Of the 1.15 million members and probationers who had passed it by January 1, 1934 (i.e., 40 per cent of the total), 17 per cent were expelled.[71] A large proportion of the expulsions concerned 'passive' elements, who were more likely than not to be ordinary workers. 40 per cent of those who cared to appeal against their expulsion were successful.[72] The 'purge' appears to have raised doubts about the expediency of similar measures. By the XVII Party Congress it was allowed to fade until it was absorbed, in mid-1935, by the even more brutal 'check of party documents.' It can hardly have affected the position of political oppositionists who had already been expelled on a mass-scale.[73] As late as July 1929 oppositionists with outstanding records such as Radek, Smilga and Preobrazhenski, had been allowed to return to the party as long as they without fully identifying themselves with the party regime recognised that Stalin's policy of industrialisation and agricultural collectivization refuted Trotsky's charge of 'Thermidorian degeneration', and believed that it would eventually result in a restoration of democracy within the party.[74] They were allowed to collaborate on this basis (at the XVI Party Congress Pyatakov was even elected to the Central Committee as a full member, Sokolnikov as a candidate member) until they fell victim to the 'great purge'. (There is no indication of their having participated in the intrigues of 1932-33, in particular those connected with Ryutin platform. Ordzhonikidze's enforced suicide in January 1937 appears to have been connected with his effort to protect Pyatakov and other former oppositionists who actively participated in economic administration. It is inconceivable that this old supporter of the Stalin line would have done so had he regarded them as capable of sabotaging the Five Year Plans, of which they were fond.)

From the XVII Party Congress, in 1934, we enter the period, in which the fragmented, biased and partly falsified documentation allows only for guesswork. The gaps in our knowledge concern not only important details (such as the actual extent of Ryutin's and Rismont's conspiracies or the vacillations in the Central Committee which preceded its plenary session in January 1933), but even the main line of development. At the 1938 trials it was asserted that on the very eve of the XVII Congress the opposition leaders rejected the suggestion, made by Enukidze and Tomski, that things might be settled by the arrest of all the Congress delegates.[75] Enukidze and Tomski were amongst the first to be rehabilitated at the time of the XX Party Congress in 1956. Surely they would not have been if the statements of 1938 were true. These statements may have been invented by defendants confessing under duress and selecting as victims of their denunciation persons who had already died. Yet they may also refer, in the particular language dictated by Stalin and Vyshinski, to an actual suggestion to protect an effort at frank speaking at the Congress and the conciliation policy eventually attempted by it, against interference by GPU troops. In other words, the reference may have been to an attempt to defend party legality, be it even by extraordinary means, against the Secretary General. Certainly the XVII Congress of 1,966 delegates, from whom, according to Khrushchev's secret session speech, eventually 1,108 were arrested, needed no coercion for its attempt at reconciliation. It is possible that the alleged plots arose from fears lest Stalin coerce it in the opposite direction, and collapsed when (for a time) he had agreed to a compromise.

The 'Congress of the Conquerors', as it was called, served as

the platform from which the leaders of all the defeated oppositions pronounced their declarations of loyalty. Stalin's success
in accomplishing the 'second revolution' against apparently overwhelming odds as well as the danger threatening from abroad
provided the golden bridge for submission. On that basis, the
former Oppositionists got their full opportunity for collaboration.
Of the old Trotskyists, Rozengolts now became a candidate member
of the CC ; of the old Zinovievists, Evdokimov and Nikolayeva
(who, before had been a candidate member) became full members.
The right-wing leaders were demoted to candidate members' status
—but in between the Congresses they might have fared worse.
Certainly it was not easy to undo all that had happened. The
coming tragedy was foreshadowed when Lominadze stated that
duplicity within the party was not an issue of the personal character of the individuals concerned but an implication of continuing
opposition after the party's consolidation,[76] and when Preobrazhenski stated that he would follow Stalin's lead even if he did not
understand why it was correct. The first statement was little
noticed, but the second provoked a woman delegate to interrupt
Preobrazhenski with the remark that the party needed him if he
understood its line and therefore supported it, but not if he said
something and thought something else.[77] The Congress decisions
emphasised discipline and ideological homogeneity. In Article 57
of the Rules as adopted by the Congress, the party members'
right to 'free and businesslike discussion of questions of party
policies' was emphasised, but so also were the limitations set since
1926 on general policy discussions. The combination of the
Central Control Commission and Workers' and Peasants' Inspection, which since Lenin's days was intended to combine reconciliation between trends in the party with the workers' opportunity
to learn by supervising administration, was replaced by two control
commissions. One was for the party, now subordinated to the CC
and organizationally bound to fulfil its directives, and the other
for the state, on the line of a centralised check on administration.
In favour of the abolition of the CCC it was stated that the party's
unity was no longer threatened. This argument was refuted by
the events of the following years, unless it is supposed that dissent
with Stalin's group implied, by definition, not intra-party disagree-

ment but treason. Yet while, by the CCC's subordination to the CC, dissenting members of the latter lost some protection against its majority, the latter itself could use the Control Commissions as its arm. If constitutional guarantees had functioned, Stalin would have been unable to execute 70 per cent of the members and candidates of the CC elected by the XVII Congress, as he eventually did.

In order to strengthen its authority, the Central Party Control Commission like the earlier CCC was elected directly by the Party Congress.[78] But instead of operating upon Control Commissions elected by the lower organisations, it now had a machine of its own (The XVIII Congress, in 1939, abolished the election of the Central Commission of Party Control by the Congress, making it merely nominated by the CC; during the pre-Congress discussion there were suggestions to have the Provincial and Republican Control Commissions elected by the corresponding party committees.[79] These suggestions, however, found no expression in the Rules adopted by the Congress.) The XVII Congress strengthened the party's control of economic reconstruction by the replacement of the functional departments of higher party committees (for organization, propaganda, etc.) by departments delimitated according to various fields of economic, political and cultural life.[80] This line, however, was reversed when the XVIII Congress, on Zhdanov's report, rejected the industrial departments as an unnecessary duplication of the work of the industrial ministries. Functional departments were retained only for the supervision of agriculture, in view of its special problems and of the weakness of the work of the two Ministries concerned, and, at the highest level, for schools, in view of the absence of an all-Union Ministry of Education.[81]

The hopes for reconciliation and gradual development were defeated on December 1, 1934, when Kirov, upon whose election as Stalin's adjunct much of those hopes had been based, was assassinated shortly before his leaving Leningrad for his new appointment. The murderer was a former member of the Provincial Komsomol Committee which Kirov had removed nine years before. The new *History of the CPSU*[82] describes him as an outcast, full of hatred against the party leaders, and associated with 'some former participants in the Zinovievite group', i.e.,. apparently with its lunatic fringe.   (This official statement implies the withdrawal of all accusations of complicity in the murder on the basis of which the Zinovievite leaders were executed, and which also played a large part in the indictments against opposition leaders of the most diverse outlooks.) After the speeches made by Khrushchev at the secret session of the XX and, in greater detail at the XXII party Congress it is evident that the murderer acted with the connivance of the Leningrad GPU, and difficult to doubt that Stalin himself encouraged that connivance.[83] In the interpretation most favourable to Stalin, such encouragement was intended to produce, even at the risk of his colleague's life, evidence of the length to which the opposition might go and thereby to produce that atmosphere of terror in which it might be overlooked that Nikolayev's circle was a group of fanatics who despised the Zinovievite leaders because of their compromises with the regime, and that Zinovievism as a whole was the least influential of the opposition trends.   On the very evening of the day of Kirov's assassination, on Stalin's personal order and anticipating the decision of the Politburo, a decree was issued.   This ordered speedy investigation into all cases of terror and the immediate execution of those sentenced without giving them the opportunity to petition for a reprieve.   A few days later, special procedures were enacted which practically deprived defendants accused of counter-revolutionary crimes of the ordinary judicial guarantees.[84]

Zinoviev and Kamenev were tried, at first (as distinct from their later trials) under the moderate accusation of having permitted the growth of terrorist tendencies amongst their supporters.   On January 18, 1935, an internal circular letter to party members appealed for vigilance against hidden terrorists. A decision of the plenary session of the CC on February 1, 1935, envisaged constitutional reform.   The introduction of equal, secret and direct suffrage was envisaged.[85] Bukharin and Radek were amongst the members of the Committee which had to prepare the draft.   Such broadening of the institutional basis of the regime was, however, combined with a further narrowing down of the scope for potential dissent within the party which controlled that broader framework.   A circular letter of the CC of May 13, 1935, which was read in all the party organisations, but only fragments of which have since been published,[86] emphasized that hidden enemies of the party, in particular former oppositionists, were applying underground methods and were helped by the existing disorder in the maintenance of party records. Even foreign intelligence services had succeeded in sending their agents into the party in the guise of political refugees and members of fraternal parties as these were frequently admitted to the VKP(b) without the prescribed procedure. For these reasons the resumption of admissions to the party which had been envisaged by the XVI Congress[87] was to be delayed until the party had put its own house in order. Whatever incidents may have given an excuse for this decision, its carrying out, quite apart from starting the 'amalgam' of political opposition and at least suspected treason, exceeded its alleged purpose. The check of individual party members' records was carried out in such a way as to eliminate not only the oppositionist who, after having been expelled in one place appeared in another, and because of the prevailing disorder, was recognised as a party member (he was, when discovered, arrested), or the person who had found an easy way round the prescribed procedure of admission. It also eliminated those whose submissions were deemed not to be fully supported by their subsequent behaviour. The very fact that a party member had formerly belonged to another party, even if he had joined the VKP(b) many years ago in quite a straightforward way, was regarded as ground for suspicion lest he show some particular propensity for opposition views.[88]

In December 1935 a Plenary Session of the CC, or a report of Ezhov's, adopted a special decision on the results of the check of party documents.[89] A new procedure of exchanging old party tickets against new ones was opened. According to point 3 of that decision, the opportunity was to be used to get rid of indifferent members who, although their papers were in order, did not come up to required standards. The mass-expulsions for 'passivity' characteristic of this purge tended to estrange honest workers from the party[90] but it is difficult to ascribe this result to a thwarting of the Central Committee's intentions by the lower organisers. Shcherbatov criticised party organisations which had shown insufficient eagerness to expel sub-standard members.   In particular, he referred to the East Siberian organisation which, after its initial percentage of expulsions had been disapproved by the CC as insufficient, succeeded in expelling 15, in some district organisations even 32 per cent of its members.[91]   In the party as a whole, 9.1 per cent of the members were expelled during the check of their records, 13.4 per cent in those organisations which had not carried out the preceding purge so that it was absorbed into the new procedure.[92] When what in the West is usually described as 'the great purge', i.e. the mass-trials of oppositionists, had started, admission to the party, on a strictly individual basis, was reopened by CC decision of September 29, 1936.   A warning against the possible infiltration of hostile, class-alien, or even simply unsuitable, elements into the party was added.   In the prevailing atmosphere of terror it was hardly astonishing that few party members dared to sponsor new members.   A particular party member who knew an applicant well and even made favourable statements about her, might refrain from giving the required recommendation 'because I am afraid that, later, you might become an enemy of the people'.[93]   Both the women concerned knew how easily one could 'become an enemy of the people', and that party members had suffered expulsion, if not worse, for connections with such enemies.

In the outcome, total party membership (including probationers) fell from 3,555,000 on January 1, 1933, to 2,350,000 on January 1, 1935 (i.e. after the official purge), 2,077,000 on January 1, 1936 (in consequence of the 'check of party documents'), and gradually to the minimum of 1,920,000 on January 1, 1938.   During the last-mentioned period, which includes the 'great purge', there had been a mere 33,000 new admissions.[94]   The net loss, including natural death, for that period amounts to 190,000—much less, but at least in a considerable section much more tragic, than during the preceding ordinary 'purges'.

It is difficult to interpret Stalin's intentions.   Like many of his moves of those years, the effort to remove potential opponents of his policies may have gone out of hand. The result was the party's loss, not just of the hidden oppositionist or at least of the Belorussian Old Bolshevik (with a far-away past in the *Bund* and an ensuing propensity to behave as a critic)[95] but also of the average worker with a modest interest in preserving a status which had become increasingly dangerous when many traditional associations of the party were breaking down (the manager or official, though even more exposed to the dangers of the 'great purge', could not leave the party without exposing his civic loyalty to doubt). Presumably Stalin wished to create an atmosphere of terror within the *body politic* so as to prevent criticism of the methods of collectivization and opposition against the enlisting of non-communist support for the defence of the fatherland. The prospect of war may have caused him to aim, from the very start, at the annihilation of oppositionists who might use military setbacks as an opportunity for assuming power.[96] From the last-mentioned point of view, only the dead oppositionist was safe. Stalin can hardly have intended at any stage to restrict the annihilation process to the Zinovievists, a completely uninfluential group though the only one which was involved in the only major terrorist act which had occurred. On the other hand, Stalin hardly intended from the start to go as far as the annihilation of a majority of the new Central Committee and of nearly all the army high command. That things went so far as they did may be due to acts of self-preservation (not necessarily illegal insofar as the CC members were concerned) taken by high officials in party, state and army as soon as it became clear that the terror would not stop at the punishment of those involved in Kirov's assassination.[97]

By the very nature of things, more evidence about the terror aspects of Stalin's policy is available than about the conciliatory ones. Still we would like to know much more about the different stages of the preparation of the new constitution and the reactions to it by the diverse strata of the population. The public discussion carried out in the summer of 1936 (some glances at which are made possible by Stalin's concluding remarks) brought the still available forces of counter-revolution to the fore. Only some of them, such as those which attempted to use the enfranchisement of the priests for the formation of an alternative political

party, with private property as its main plank and local Church
choirs, cooperatives, etc., as the local basis, were publicly denounced
in the Soviet Press.[98]   The tensions brought to the fore in the
attempt to open the valves appear to have been sufficient to discourage the use of the general and secret elections in a more
liberal way than the eventually applied lists of the *bloc* of the
Communists and non-party members'.   The different reactions
in various quarters to these phenomena may have contributed
to the explosion of early 1937.   Long before these events, some
strengthening of party discipline was necessitated by the very
unorthodox character (in traditional Marxist terms) of the social
phenomena encouraged by the party—from Stakhanovites encouraged to increase output norms (which would be resented by the
average worker) and wives of managers whose readiness to accept
jobs far away from Moscow had to be stimulated by recognition
of the merits of lady welfare workers, to epaulettes for army
officers, and from reprimands for historians who failed to pay
due tribute to the past of the Russian nation, to the abolition of
the freedom of abortion.[99]

The public trials against the opposition leaders started with
the Zinovievite group, on August 19-24, 1936.   Presumably
because the defendants made quite a lot of their opportunity, the
published record of the trial is incomplete.   Their statements
about their acceptance, *in principle,* of terrorist methods (whatever this might mean) were fairly straightforward, but their statements about the organisation of particular terrorist actions other
than that against Kirov were extremely vague.   Practically all the
Trotskyist and right-wing leaders were mentioned—Trotsky himself, of course served as the villain in the party—in connections
which need not indicate more than the intrigues which during the
crises of 1931-34 were undoubtedly spun between the diverse
opposition factions.   From Smirnov's statements it is fairly clear
that the alleged 'centre' was a loose connection between political
friends.   There was yet no suggestion that the defendants had
acted for purposes other than to bring about a change within
the existing regime (presumably connected with the physical
annihilation of Stalin).   As for foreign connections (other than
with their old fellow-oppositionist Trotsky), Zinoviev regarded the

very appearance, together with himself, in the dock of German secret service agents (who may have traced their way into a dissatisfied faction as agents of secret services try to do), as the worst punishment which could befall him.

Yagoda's failure to induce the defendants to confess treason in the service of foreign powers was regarded as the main shortcoming of that first trial.[100] Stalin and Zhdanov deemed that the NKVD was four years behind in that matter (i.e. it treated the Zinovievites in the same way as he had done with the Ryutin and Eismont groups). Hence, in a wire of September 25, 1936, they demanded Yagoda's replacement by Ezhov. This was duly carried out by the Politburo but a group of CC members tried a counter-action. Enukidze and his closest friends were tried and executed during the first days of 1937, in secret as they were unwilling to confess what was now required, and perhaps also because the actions of which they might plead guilty were not illegal unless the Soviet policy was indentified with Stalin's whims. (According to Khrushchev's secret session report, the confessions eventually extorted from a former CC member might include decisions of the CC and of the Council of People's Commissars which were not even made on his suggestion, but this happened in 1939-40, and even then it was preferred to try Eikhe in secret.) In late January the Trotskyist leaders were tried. Their confessions included the organisation of sabotage, unofficial diplomacy in order to save in the case of war some revolutionary achievements (Radek stated that this orientation came to an end in 1935, when the country's capacity to defend herself had become evident), and an intention to withdraw state subsidies from those collective farms which could not support themselves. At the Plenary Session of the CC in February-March 1937, Bukharin and Rykov were expelled from the party, still on political grounds (E. Yaroslavski, writing in *Partiinoye Stroitelstvo,* 1937, No. 6, explained the expulsion only in terms of *objectively* counter-revolutionary implications of their attitude and of their having known of the counter-revolutionary activities of the Trotskyists and Zinovievists as well as of some of their own followers). By the end of April the military crisis reached its culmination ; in early May the generals were shot.

In his secret session report Khrushchev states that most of the members of the CC elected by the XVII Congress were shot in 1937-38.[101] The possible culmination of the terror (as distinct from the political crisis, which apparently fell into the first half of the year) is indicated by Ezhov's inclusion, as a candidate member, in the Politburo by the Plenary Session of the CC held in October 1937. We do not know the date and mode of his fall. When the right-wing leaders, and the NKVD officials said to be associated with them, were brought to trial in March 1938, alleged efforts to poison Ezhov led to the indictment and sentence. At that trial, Yagoda made mechanical confessions of the type he had so frequently required from others (still, he rejected some personal reproaches), and the worst possible explanation was put on some acts of unofficial diplomacy. Bukharin did not confess to being guilty of crimes other than of having aimed at Stalin's overthrow by the promotion of peasant insurrections and of the so-called 'palace revolution' in the years 1932-34 (which, in fact, might have been an entirely legal meeting of the full CC). The way in which he disposed of the accusation of having aimed, in 1918, at Lenin's assassination, or the way he dealt with the confusion in the indictment of a plan to attack Gorki in the press with an alleged plan to assassinate him, undermined the prosecution's stand perhaps even more than did Krestinski's short-lived withdrawal of an extorted confession. By now, no person in his senses could have believed all the stories recorded by the defendants. The fact remained that old Bolsheviks who had sacrificed everything in an effort to overthrow Stalin, had arrived at the conclusion that his Russia should be defended against the Hitlerite threat by every means, including the acceptance of false accusations.

In the decisions of the Plenary Session of February-March 1937 Stalin had his theory of the NKVD's being late by four years officially enacted. To what was happening all over the country he provided a rationalisation by the statement that the very victory of socialism implied a sharpening of the class-struggle. The outside opponents of the USSR now turned the remaining internal opposition into traitors and saboteurs. Indeed, what would have been the purpose of extorting from the Trotskyists confessions of sabotage (as distinct from political intrigue) unless it was intended to 'purge', after the deputy ministers and heads of departments, the ranks of factory managers and higher officials ? According to Khrushchev's secret session report, during the years 1937-38 Ezhov sent 383 lists, containing the names of many thousands of party, Soviet, Komsomol, Army and economic workers earmarked for imprisonment or execution, to Stalin for advance approval of the proposed sentences. In 1954 and 1955 alone, 7,679 persons were rehabilitated, "many of them posthumously", by the Military Collegium of the Supreme Court which had passed the earlier sentences. The Military Collegium dealt only with the most serious cases, passing sentences of death or long imprisonment. The ordinary person accused by the NKVD of 'counter-revolutionary activities' was sent by one of its *troikas* for five or ten years to the labour camp—bad enough, in particular since sentences expiring during the war were automatically prolonged. Even of those who had been properly convicted—so far as one can speak of propriety under the 'Kirov-law'—not every person who had died (before the squad or in the camp) had anyone to care about his rehabilitation, nor was the revision procedure concluded at the time of the XX Congress. Khrushchev's figure would suggest a total number of victims, imprisoned or executed, high in the region of five figures.

Certainly the extent of the 'purge' exceeded Stalin's original intentions. Personal intrigue and denunciation (including those by real enemies of the regime who thus found an easy way to harm it)[102] as well as competition among ambitious police officials for 'good' results played their part in increasing the number of victims. Cautious people were afraid lest any attempt to protect a person suspected by the NKVD expose themselves to suspicion. Any kind of association with any person described (without appeal) as an 'enemy of the people' might result in sanctions ranging from the loss of one's party ticket to arrest as an accomplice[103]—there were special concentration camps for the wives of the main victims of the 'purge'. We do not know the actual number of the victims of the 'purge'. Khrushchev's above-quoted statements indicate the lower limit, while the upper limit is given by Stalin's[104] estimate of a total figure of 270,000 expulsions

from the party, the majority of whom were expelled for mere
'passivity' during the preceding purge.   Even amongst those expelled for political reasons, for everyone arrested as an 'enemy of
the people', some more must have got off with mere expulsion
from the party for 'insufficient vigilance' towards him (on the
other hand, there were also non-party victims of the 'purge';
presumably, they formed a minority amongst the total number
of victims).   The danger of excesses appears to have been realised
fairly soon.   Already the CC decision of March 5, 1937, adopted on Stalin's report, condemned party leaders who expelled
communists by the tens of thousands, as individuals apparently
did not matter to them.   This practice, Stalin said, supplied the
conspirators with a reserve of desperate people to whom to appeal.
Two months later Molotov[105] warned against wholesale dismissal
from their jobs (which in any case was less severe a measure than
arrest) of former Trotskyists who had recognised their error.
Yet the mass-terror continued until the replacement, in the following year, of Ezhov by Beria (from Khrushchev's secret session
report it is evident that some of the worst repression measures
against individuals continued until the very eve of the war).

It was not Stalin's intention to stop the internal life of the
party completely.   In his speech at the Plenary Session of the
CC, on March 3, 1937, he treated issues of party life as a
struggle of sound elements, whose work required a permanent
check by close contact with the masses of the people, against
cliques who were incapable of moving with the times.   By cliques
he understood, not only the oppositionists—(in his opinion, completely incapable organisers who merely by their possession of
the party ticket had been admitted to the posts of responsibility)—
but also some of his own political friends who, as he said, could
not move from one post to another without taking a retinue of
thirty or forty personal supporters with them.   Stalin's supporters,
the Lenin recruits from 1924 whom, in 1928, he had invited to
'master technique' so that they could supplant the old specialists
were now invited to 'master Bolshevism' so that they could replace the Old Bolsheviks, those 'party-ticket holders' whose only
strength lay in their mastery of the party terminology.   As a
safeguard against isolation of the party cadres from the rank and

file, the Plenary Session introduced the secret ballot for the election of all party committees and party secretaries.[106] As a safeguard against the use of the opportunity by hidden oppositionists, the secret ballot was to be preceded by a discussion and an open vote on nominations of the candidates submitted to the ballot. Of course, the higher party committees retained their right to refuse confirmation of those elected. The change was clearly directed against the entrenchment of individuals who might use managerial power to prevent criticism. In his report to the Plenary Session, on which the decision was based, Zhdanov had noticed that for some years in most party organizations elections had been avoided and vacancies been filled by co-optation. Higher party committees, not satisfied with their right to confirm changes in the leadership of lower ones, had high-handedly carried out the changes by nomination. Even where elections were held they were a mere formality as, under the existing procedure, the adoption of prepared lists of candidates in an open ballot was a foregone conclusion. The eagerness of party leaders to end such a state of things may have been prompted by the ease with which an oppositionally minded party secretary, or factory manager, might place his supporters in a place where critical eyes were least desirable. But certainly Stalin was sincere when, in the very speech which asked the young generation to 'master Bolshevism', he compared the party with mythical gaint Antaeus who, whenever thrown down, drew new strength from the contact with his mother Earth (in Stalin's parable, the masses).

By another comparison, Stalin revealed the contradictions inherent in his own position. He treated the party as a military body, headed by 3,000 leading officials, comparable to the generals in an army (since the figure far exceeded the membership of the Central Committee plus the secretaries of the Provincial and Republican party organisations, it is clear that Stalin included in it also the higher officials and managers—all the occupants of posts whose holders, according to existing regulations, are selected by the CC's Cadres Department). Under these 'generals' served 30-40,000 leaders of middle rank—in Stalin's simile 'commissioned officers' of the communist 'army' (apparently, those on the *nomenklatura* of the Provincial Committees). Under these were the 100-150,000 'non-commissioned officers', i.e. the junior party commanders (all of them, apparently, full-time workers in the offices of party and state). The rank and file played the part of private soldiers, whose confidence in their leaders, however, had to be tested by the secret ballot. The function of the secretarial hierarchy was conceived as that of a check on administration and management. Hence the 'triangle', the traditional framework for the settlement of disagreements on the factory and shop level, was abolished. With apparent naivety, Stalin made the point that it had no basis in existing legislation. He must have known as well as anyone that it offered the only check on managerial power short of a complaint to the manager's seniors or to the higher party authorities. His interest lay just in that latter remedy. If it was not very efficient in settling the individual workers' grievances it would result in the managers pursuing their factory's if not their private, interests to the detriment of the general interest as established in existing directives. It would work better if party (and trade union) secretaries ceased to be part of a body the members of which shared responsibility for managerial decisions (and might bargain for the conditions on which support for such decisions was granted).[107]

Even the supervisory—not to speak of the democratic—functions of the party machine, were undermined by the 'purge' which submitted it (in fact, though not in form) to the control of a more powerful institution, the political police. It had been Stalin's intention to disrupt some links in the upper strata of the machine. By its own dynamics, the surgery went further than he had intended. In many places scores of communists whom even the NKVD found not necessary to arrest, were expelled from the party as alleged 'enemies of the people'. The technical leader of a minor enterprise (who some time before had got a reprimand because of some incorrect expression used in a study group) might fall under that sinister description because some suggestions of his for rationalization of production were regarded as unsound. Moreover, as on one occasion he had asked the Chairman of the Factory Committee for permission to continue work overtime, the latter, too, was expelled from the party because of his 'connection with an enemy of the people'. The secretary of a Kharkov factory committee who had been called by the NKVD as a witness in the proceedings against an arrested Trotsky-ist was not only dismissed herself, because of her alleged 'connec-tion' with him, but also saw her brother lose his job as a newspaper-editor because of his failure to denounce that connec-tion. In some Ukrainian villages teaching came to a near stand-still because of the mass-dismissal of teachers (one of them was not only dismissed herself, but found her husband dismissed as well, because in the local newspaper her brother—incorrectly—had been denounced as a nationalist). Of approximately 40,000 members of the Azerbaibhan party organisation, 13,000 were expelled (6,000 of these were reinstated during the consideration of their appeals). The Kuibyshev Provincial Committee dissolved thirty-four District Committees.[108] In January 1938 the Plenary Session of the CC denounced these excesses, and in particular the type of careerist who advanced by the denunciation of innocent party members. He should be unmasked and expelled from the party. Extreme carefulness in expulsions from the party and quick consideration of appeals by the higher party committees was demanded. Even those whose expulsions had to stand (but who were not arrested) were not to lose their jobs unless this was really required by the nature of their positions ; and even in those cases they should not be sacked before other jobs suitable for non-party members were found. By February 15, 1938, jobs were to be found for all those expelled from the party. Some higher party committees proved slow in consideration of the appeals of those expelled in 1937. A CC decision of March 15 had to draw their attention to the inadmissibility of giving priority to the consideration of those expelled at an earlier stage, during the 'revision of party documents', and thus to delay the correction of the mistakes committed in 1937-38.[109] As late as September of 1939 it was found necessary to reprimand the Kursk Provincial Committee for its failure to decide upon all the appeals of 1937-38.[110] A high proportion of the expulsions was unfounded. In Kiev Province 57 per cent, in Belorussia 60, in Archangelsk Province 63, in Kursk 70 and in Yaroslavl Province even 72 per cent of the appeals were successful, in the army organizations 50 per cent.[111] Still hundreds of thousands remained in force ; there was practi-

20

cally no remedy for him whom the NKVD had arrested. Outside that particular sphere normality returned, and so also some readiness to join the party (and to support applications). During the first half of 1938, a quarter of a million persons applied for party membership ; 109,000 (many of them, of course, earlier applicants), were admitted as probationers.[112]

It would be a mistake to regard the decisions of January 1938 as the conclusion of the 'purge'. Postyshev's tragedy may date from that time (he was, though still on honourable terms, replaced as a candidate member of the Politburo by Khrushchev).[113] The last, and largest, of the 'purge' trials took place some months later. Stalin later conceded that mistakes had been committed in the course of the 'purge', even more than could be foreseen. Still, quite apart from the elimination of conspirators and foreign agents, he regarded the improvement of the quality of the remaining party members as an achievement. In his position he could hardly say less. Some after-thoughts may be indicated by the slight difference between his approach to the renewal of cadres and that of Zhdanov. While the latter hailed the opening of the way for the promotion of cadres grown during the last period as a great achievement, Stalin demanded attention for the old as well as the new cadres and a proper combination of both with their different merits.[114]

A new generation had moved into the foreground. Amongst the party members there were still 20,000 who had joined the party in or before 1917 (1.3 per cent of the total). Malenkov, making Stalin's case for the combination of the old and new cadres, noticed that their share amongst delegates to the XVIII Party Congress was as high as 5 per cent (yet nearly a third of the delegates to the XVII Party Congress had had a similar record). The percentage of persons who had joined the party in the years of the civil war decreased from nearly half of the delegates of the XVII to a seventh of those of the XVIII Congress (twice their share in the total membership). 70 per cent of the existing party members had joined the party in 1929 and later (i.e. had known no conditions of party life other than those under Stalin's sole leadership). They provided 43 per cent of the delegates of the XVIII Congress.[115] Of the 71 members of the Central Committee elected by the XVIII Congress, a mere

16 had been members of the preceding one (another six had been candidates of the CC and five had been members of the Control Commission). The destruction the old CC by the 'purge' must have provided one of the main reasons for Stalin's convening the Congress (another one was the imminent danger of war). The membership of the Politburo elected after the XVIII Congress already contains the names familiar up to the Khrushchev era: apart from Kalinin and Zhdanov, who died before Stalin, Andreyev, Voroshilov, Kaganovich, Mikoyan, Molotov, and Khrushchev were full members ; Beria and Shevernisk became candidates of the Politburo, Malenkov sat on the Orgburo but was already one of the party secretaries. One year later—on the occasion of the reorganisation of the Economic Council attached to Sovnarkom—we find also the names of the leading organisers of Soviet economics who, with one tragic exception, have remained in the foreground in the following twenty years : Bulganin, Malyshev, Voznesenski (who also kept his post as Chairman of Gosplan), Pervukhin and Kosygin.[116]

As the 'purge' had most strongly affected the higher strata of the party hierarchy, the renewal was more moderate—though still considerable—at the lower levels (where it should have been strongest in the natural process of absorption of a new generation). According to Zhdanov's statement at the XVIII Conress,[117] 35 per cent of the members of the committees of the primary party organisations, 41 per cent of the members of district committees, 46 per cent of those of city committees and 60 per cent of the members of Provincial and Republican Committees were elected for the first time. 53 per cent of the responsible party secretaries and nearly 50 per cent of the delegates to the XVIII Congress were not older than thirty-five years, more than 90 per cent of the secretaries and 82 per cent of the Congress delegates not older than forty. Less than 7 per cent of the responsible secretaries of districts and cities, less than 20 per cent of the Provincial and Republican secretaries had joined the party before 1924, and 29 and 59 per cent respectively had at least full secondary education. Amongst the Congress delegates, 26.5 per cent had higher education—nearly half of them a technical one—another 22.5 per cent a complete secondary education, characteristic of those black-coated strata which, at the same Congress were included in Molotov's definition of the 'Soviet Intelligentsia'.

For the benefit of the new party generation whom Stalin had invited to 'master Bolshevism' a commission, headed by himself,[118] produced of *Short History of the CPSU* which up to his death served as the basis of all political education. In the Decision adopted by the CC at that occasion[119] it was described as 'a single guidance.... representing an official interpretation of the basic problems of the history of the *VKP(b)* ...preventing any arbitrary interpretations'. Emphasis was laid on the basic importance of the *Soviet intelligentsia* which, grown from the ranks of the workers and peasants, formed the cadres of the Soviet regime. The former contempt of the *intelligentsia* was said to have resulted in a neglect of its political education. In its description of historical events, the *Short History* represents a typical example of political mythology. This does not exclude its being franker and more realistic in its presentation of events whenever it suited the leaders, in particular when the collectivisation of agriculture was now honestly described as a revolution from above, carried out with such support as the party could find in the countryside. (The fact that it had had to carry out, and was still carrying out, a 'revolution from above' formed, indeed, the only possible Marxist justification of the authoritarian regime which has developed, and was still developing.) The presentation of Marxist dialectics—the only part of the book in which Stalin's personal authorship is evident— was the first popular treatment of the subject which gave the essentials without unnecessarily burdening it with Hegelian terminology. (It is hardly necessary to note that the simplifications, some of them perhaps not unconnected with Stalin's approach to politics, were subject to criticism after the end of his 'cult'.)

But whatever the historian may think about the correctness of the record, and the theoretician about the fullness with which some aspects of the Marxist theory have survived this popularization, it provided the sort of Marxism which finally reached the political cadres with the responsibility of leading one-third of mankind. Its authors regarded unified indoctrination as the guarantee of unity of action. Appropriate measures, including a reorganisation of the Marx-Engles-Lenin Institute and the preparation of a new edition of Lenin's work 'purged' of all undesirable contents,[120] were taken to ensure that no presentation of facts different from the authorised version could reach the faithful. Naturally enough, the falsification of party history eventually provoked an elementary reaction against the 'cult', in particular since the destruction of reputations had been so closely associated with the judicial murder of so many Old Bolsheviks. The application of party authority to all fields of knowledge reached its climax in events which we shall discuss in the next chapter of this book. In the field of party history, however, after the correction of Stalin's extremes, the principle of applying such authority, with no other than self-imposed restrictions, has survived. The party no longer believes that successes won after such indoctrination · necessarily prove its correctness. It takes it for granted that even greater successes may be achieved if past tactics are subjected to critical scrutiny. Still, the self-assertion of its machine sets limits to such scrutiny. However, obvious it may be that new conditions will first be realised by individual people and that these are likely to be in a minority then, the machine still likes to believe that, as a rule, such suggestions would be premature before the date when they are actually adopted by a majority! Moreover, the machine will not easily accept the responsibility for grave errors and injustice unless it is definitely forced to do so, i.e. only when certain of its leaders and the traditions associated with them are dropped. Immediately after the XX Congress one hoped that the study of the history of the CPSU would be freed of organisational limitations. The Political implications of such critical review meant slightly detached disputes on the problems of the present. But this would imply a dropping of the party's claim to give a final evaluation of the different trends from the struggle between which it arose. Moreover it would have meant its conscious reduction to an institutional framework within which these trends could continue to compete, within such limits as were necessary to defend the new society. Such prospects are just appearing on the horizon, with all kinds of setbacks. Thirty years ago, when the 'great purge' had been completed and the authorised version of party tradition just proclaimed, it would have appeared fantastic even to dream of them.

(c) THE PARTY ON THE EVE OF THE SECOND WORLD WAR

When addressing the economists in February 1932, Stalin had spoken of Russia's backwardness which had allowed every enemy to beat her.   Ten years, he said, were given to the country to make good the backwardness of a hundred and fifty years.[121]   A feeling that such evaluation of the situation was correct had carried Stalin through all the difficulties, horrors and atrocities of the second revolution and of the 'great purge'. When in March 1939 the XVIII Party Congress met, it was obvious that the contingency for which the country had prepared was approaching. Stalin explained that the Second World War had already started. From an international standpoint this statement, made two years after the start of the Sino-Japanese war, was more plausible than it may appear to those who suppose that a major war starts only after the Governments of Britain and France issue declarations of war.   That war, Stalin deemed, was conducted by the fascist aggressors against the Western powers which, however, still attempted to direct the storm in the direction desirable from their point of view, namely against the USSR.   The USSR's refusal to pull other people's chestnuts out of the fire called for a statement meant more for foreign rather than for internal consumption.   Still, it contributed to the party's ideological preparation for such diplomatic manoeuvres as were required to prevent the war from being fought out solely between the USSR on the one hand and Germany and her allies on the other, the Western powers waiting for the appropriate exhaustion of the belligerents in order to dictate a settlement fitting their own interests.

All legislative and organisational measures during that three years preceding the Hitlerite attack were dictated by the need to make the USSR ready for war.   In this they found their real justification.   The phraseology sometimes applied in order to avoid a straightforward description of emergency measures as such, and to confuse them with long-term communist aims, however, its own implications which fitted the concepts of a one-side managerial interest. Only since Stalin's death has a clearer balance been drawn between society's permanent interest in the production drive and the sacrifice of working-class achievements, which was justifiable only by the needs of the war and the social services for workers who had recently changed employment (and also of maternity leaves for women) as well as by a prescription dismissal for those workers who were late by more than twenty minutes (decree of December 28, 1938). For kolkhoz members on May 12, 1939, minimum performance (still very modest in comparison with what since has become current)[122] were established : failure to comply was to be penalised by expulsion from the kolkhoz and loss of the tax privileges associated with kolkhoz membership. On June 26th, 1940, i.e. after the fall of France, the eight-hour day and seven-day week were restored without increase in earnings : workers were prohibited from leaving their places of employment without permission, which was to be granted only in certain defined cases. As under the decree of 1938 dismissal could easily be enforced by a worker's failure to appear at work ; its sanctions were now replaced by criminal sanctions, amounting to the retention of up to 20 per cent of the wages earned during six months. By the decree of July 10, 1940, managers were subject to imprisonment from 5 to 8 years for delivery of sub-standard output— it may be assumed that the law was applied mainly in those cases where the output was essential for national defence. On the other hand, the manager's authority within the factory was increased by every means at the government's disposal. Familiar relations to subordinates, and the latter's resort to objections otherwise than by direct submission to their seniors, were strongly disapproved.[123] The decrees of October 2nd, 1940, did not only establish Industrial Schools of Labour Reserves, the pupils of which could be recruited by conscription (for many village lads such conscription opened up the career of a skilled worker, and the way to material improvement); they also abolished the privilege of secondary and higher education except for pupils with excellent school records. This measure, if continued over any prolonged period,[124] would have granted the better-paid strata of the Soviet population a privileged position insofar as children of average gifts from such families could aspire to a position within the Soviet *intelligentsia*.

After the severe setback of the 'purge', the party resumed its numerical growth : from 1.92 million members and probationers on January 1st, 1938, to 2.3 million one year later and just under 4 million on January 1st, 1941 (the latter included 1.42 million probationers, i.e. fairly recent recruits). The party's social structure underwent a further shift towards the *intelligentsia*. At the XVIII Congress Stalin did not only re-emphasise his arguments against the formerly current reservations: the Rules were also changed so as to eliminate any differentiation in admissions according to social status and origin.[125] From the standpoint of the *intelligentsia* which had supplied so many victims of the 'purges', the Congress decision to end these periodical upheavals must have been particularly gratifying. We have no comprehensive statistics of the party's social structure for any date later than 1932 but by January 1st, 1941, the 600,000 party members who were specialists with higher or secondary education[126] formed 15 per cent of the party's total strength, and many persons in managerial and similar positions had not had even secondary or professional education. The 600,000 communists formed just a quarter of all the professionally schooled specialists existing at a time when the party's share in the total of 31.5 million workers and salaried employees[127] cannot have amounted to more than 10 per cent. If some allowance is made for self-educated managers and officials amongst the party members (and most of these 'practicians' were communists) it is unlikely that more than eight per cent of the manual workers and junior employees were communists (of course, this percentage differed greatly from industry to industry, or from other branches, of employment).

Party organisations in industry, being deprived of such organisational handles as might involve them in co-responsibility for management enjoyed, according to Article 61 of the Rules adopted by the XVIII Party Congress, the right to supervise (*kontrol*) it. The question of co-responsibility has remained controversial up to the present day. Extension of the right of supervision by the party organiser to administrative institutions (where it would clearly threaten the institution's subordination to the higher administrative hierarchy), and even to research institutions have been repeatedly demanded. These suggestions are still rejected by the party authorities.[128] At the time of which we are speaking, under the pressure of the preparation for war, the party organisations' function of supervising economic management was extended so as to involve the assumption of supra-managerial functions at least by the higher party committees. Reversing the decision of the XVIII Congress, the XVIII Party Conference, in February 1941, required the city Provincial and Republican Committees of industrial regions to have more than one secretary for industrial affairs, and, where necessary, special secretaries as well for railway transport and for waterways. Party organisations were required to be familiar with the leading managerial and technical staff, in order to suggest the removal of the unit and also new promotions (including from the ranks of non-party members).[129] The need for secrecy set limits to the information of party committees about the decisions taken in the next senior link hierarchy. It might happen (though as an abuse, criticised in *Partiinoye stroitelstvo*)[130] that the decisions of a District Committee were withheld from its instructors who had to supervise their execution! In its desire to secure the strict observance of party discipline, the CC not only took, but even published, decisions on all kinds of individual issues. For example, it took reasonably important decisions such as the rejection of the right of the editor of a provincial newspaper to criticise in its columns the provincial Committee on whose behalf it was published,[131] or the restriction on the celebration of jubilees of all kinds,[132] down to the settlement of individual personnel questions such as the public denunciation of District and Provincial Committees which kept a secretary on their staff though the CC wished to send him to a factory, or, *vice versa*, appointed a jurist to a party job[133] without the Central Committee's preliminary agreement. The need for strict discipline on the eve of the coming trial was obvious but already some people may have asked whether, at that very trial, it would be advisable to take all the required

decisions at the centre and to discourage the exercise of personal
judgement by those who had to work on the spot.

NOTES AND REFERENCES

1. The first detailed record of these attempts has been given by V. S.
   Golubtsov in *Vestnik Moskovskovo universiteta*, Historical-Philogical
   Series, 1957, No. 4. See also Carr, op. cit. vol. II, p. 366. On the
   negotiations with the Academy of Sciences, see Gorodetsky's book.
   Rotheniye Sovetskovo Gossudavtoa 1911-18.

2. Sources : T. A. Gladkov, *Voprosy planirovaniya sovetskovo khozyaistva 1918-20* (Gospolitizdat 1951), *State Plan for the Development
   of the National Economy of the USSR* in 1941 (a secret document,
   a copy of which fell into German hands, and was eventually reproduced by the American Council of Learned Societies, Baltimore, 1951)
   and recent annual progress reports, published in the Soviet press.

3. G. M. Krzhizhanovski, *Problemy planirovaniya* (vol. II of his
   Collected Works, Moscow Academy of Sciences, 1934), p. 11. Of
   the thirty-four economists and technical specialists originally employed
   by Gosplan, only seven were party members.

4. Ibid. pp. 27 ff., and cf. the article by Groman (a leader of the 'geneticist'
   school) published in *Planovoye khozyaistvo*, 1925, No. 1.

5. Cf. Dobb, op. cit. pp. 327-28 ; R. E. Vaisberg, *Problemy perspektiv-
   novo pyatiletnevo plana*, Gosizdat, 1928, pp. 56 ff. ; and A. Kaufman
   in *Soviet Studies*, vol. IV, pp. 266-67. I have discussed these and the
   subsequent developments in *Soviet Studies*, vol. XVI, No. 1 (July
   1964).

6. Krzhizhanovski, op. cit. p. 289. See Carr, *Socialism in One Country*,
   vol. I, pp. 508 ff.

7. Vaisberg, loc. cit. p. 33.

8. Stalin's *Sochineniya*, vol. XII, pp. 81-82 (*Leninism*, pp. 278 ff.).

9. See my article on *Soviet Studies*, July, 1964.

10. Krzhizhanovski, loc. cit. pp. 403-04 and 420.

11. Dobb, op. cit. pp. 237 ff.

12. Cf. Kaganovich's report to the XVI Party Congress, *Otchet*, p. 61.

13. *Ot s'ezda k s'ezdu* (Materials of the Goverment Report to the XIV
    Soviet Congress of the RSFSR, Moscow, 1929), p. 132 ; *Dva goda
    raboty* (Two years of Work, 1931-32, Moscow), pp. 91 ff. By way of
    comparison it may be noted that in 1913-14 there were five school
    children per 1,000 inhabitants of Tsarist Russia.

14. *Dva goda raboty*, pp. 99 and 123. The actual demands of industry
    are characterised by the input of a quarter of a million pupils planned
    for 1931 ; nothing of that order of magnitude was achieved before
    the formation of Labour Reserves in 1940.

15. Ibid. p. 100.

16. *Izvestiya Ts.K. VKP(b)*, 1929, Nos. 25 and 28 ; Kaganovich's report to the XVI Party Congress, *Otchet*, p. 65.

17. Kaganovich's speech in the Orgburo, *Partiinoye stroitelstvo*, 1930, No. 2.

18. Kaganovich's report to XVI Party Congress, *Otchet*, p. 79. In 1923 a mere 29, on January 1, 1924, 48 per cent of all the managers had been communists.

19. *Partiinoye stroitelstva*, 1929, No. 1.

20. Kaganovich's report to XVI Congress, *Otchet*, p. 88.

21. *VKP(b) rezolyutsiyakh*, pp. 308 ff. and 357 ff. According to *Izvestiya Ts.K.*, 1929, No. 11/12, the 'purge' was at first intended to be accomplished by May 15, 1929. In fact it just opened about that time, and was completed one year later.

22. *Izvestiya Ts.K. VKP(b)*, 1928, Nos. 31 and 37-38.

23. Ibid. 1929, No. 10.

24. Ibid. 1929, No. 4, and Glazyrin, op. cit. pp. 64 ff.

25. Glazyrin, op. cit. pp. 85-86.

26. See n. 21 above.

27. *Partiinoye stroitelstvo*, 1930, No. 10, *Otchet* XVI Congress, p. 340.

28. Locally it might happen that the percentage of expulsions from factory organisations was higher than in state institutions. This was criticised as a misunderstanding of the basic purposes of the 'purge' (*Izvestiya Ts.K. VKP(b)*, 1929, No. 26).

29. *Partiinoye stroitelstvo*, 1930, No. 12, p. 45.

30. See n. 27 above.

31. Glazyrin, op. cit. pp. 69 ff. ; Kaganovich at the XVII Party Congress, *Otchet*, p. 557.

32. Cf. V. M. Selunskaya's article in *Voprosy istorii*, 1954, No. 3.

33. Stalin's *Sochineniya*, vol. XII, pp. 125-26, 145-46 and 167 ff. ; Voroshilov at the XVI Party Congress, *Otchet*, p. 285. Since June 1962, in the course of the de-Stalinisation campaign, the facts about the enforced collectivisation of 1929-30 have been revealed in a number of articles published by F. N. A. Ivnisky, M. L. Bogdenkov and I. E. Edenin in *Istoiveliskii Aaktivo* (1962, No. 2), *Voprosy istorii* (1962, No. 4, 1963, No. 5), and *Istoriya SSSR*, 1962, No. 4. I have discussed the historical setting of 'de-Kulakisation' in my article 'On the Scope of Necessity and Error', published in *Soviet Studies*, vol. XVII, No. 3 (January 1966).

34. As a decision of the Politburo (cf. Stalin, *Sochineniya*, vol. XII, p. 289) the document of January 5, 1930 is given only in the Appendix (pp. 661-62) of *VKP(b) v rezolyutsiyakh*. The text of the decree of February 1, 1930 is reprinted in *The Slavonic Review*, vol. X (1930), pp. 209 ff.

35. *Sochineniya*, vol. XII, pp. 161 ff. ; *Leninism*, pp. 315-16. The argu-

ment is directed against 'leftist phrasemongers', but there is no indication of identity with the 'leftist' group mentioned below, p. 285.

36. Bauman at the XVI Party Congress, *Otchet*, pp. 214-15.

37. *VKP(b) v rezolyutsiyakh*, pp. 662-63; cf. my *Soviet Legal Theory*, 170-74.

38. Cf. Stalin, *Sochineniya*, vol. XIII, p. 213, and *Leninism*, p. 339; and the articles cited in n. 33 above.

39. Bauman XVI Party Congress, *Otchet*, pp. 214-15; Leonov, pp. 114-15.

40. Three months later Stalin had still to argue against comparisons of that 'retreat' with Brest Litovsk or the introduction of NEP (*Sochineniya*, vol. XII, p. 231).

41. Ibid. pp. 202 ff. (*Leninism*, pp. 332 ff.).

42. *Otchet* XVII Party Congress, p. 20. Virtually the same figure (23.6 per cent for the whole USSR, as against 21.6 per cent in January 1930) is mentioned by P. N. Sharova (in *Voprosy istorii*, 1953, No. 10, p. 5) for 'spring 1930': the artificial rise against which Stalin's article was directed, is thus simply discounted but so also is any possible recovery during the second half of 1930.

43. *Sochineniya*, vol. XII, pp. 219-20; *Leninism*, p. 344.

44. Cf. Levin's article in *Na agrarnom fronte*, 1935, No. 2-3, p. 36, and Dobb, op. cit. p. 285.

45. Cf. Stalin's report to the XVII Congress (*Otchet*, pp. 19 ff.); Khrushchev's speech at the Plenary Session of the CC in September 1953, and *Soviet Studies*, vol. V, p. 242.

46. *VKP(b) v rezolyutsiyakh*, p. 396.

47. Cf. Solts' statement (*Otchet*, p. 361) that the party was interested in Tomski and Rykov not as subjects of amnesty. Precisely in order to qualify for leading positions they should recognise that they had been wrong. See also Kirov's speech, ibid. pp. 156-57.

48. Cf. ibid. p. 130.

49. Ibid. p. 150 Kirov was not satisfied with such a general admission of the consequences of open dissent. He found in the very specific views advocated by the opposition the reason for its use by the kulaks (ibid. pp. 156-57).

50. Ibid. pp. 135 and 337.

51. Sheboldayev, ibid. p. 136.

52. Cf. Knorin, op. cit. pp. 432-33 and 459-60; Lominadze's speech at the XVII Congress, *Otchet*, pp. 118-19. The only indication of the earlier disagreements in the Proceedings of the XVI Congress was the fact that the statement of the new Komsomol leader, Kossarev, that his organisation had no political line different from that of the party was greeted with applause (p. 134), while the (quite conventional) speech of Lominadze immediately afterwards was not. (In fact, all speakers who defended the party line were applauded).

53. *VKP(b) v rezolyutsiyakh*, pp. 668-69.

54. Court Proceedings 1938, pp. 132, 162-63 and 388-90.
55. Proceedings, pp. 150-51.
56. *VKP(b) v rezolyutsiyakh*, pp. 669-70.
57. Ibid. pp. 531-32.
58. Op. cit. pp. 279-80.
59. *Sochineniya*, vol. XIII, pp. 241-43 ; *Leninism*, pp. 443-44.
60. *Sochineniya*, vol. XIII, pp. 207-08 ; *Leninism*, pp. 422-23.
61. *VKP(b) v rezolyutsiyakh*, pp. 524 ff.
62. Ibid. pp. 623 ff.
63. Cf. M. P. Filchenkov's article in *Voprosy istorii KPSS*, 1958, No. 1, p. 117.
64. Glazyrin, op. cit. pp. 89-90, Kaganovich at the XVII Congress, *Otchet*, p. 557. According to Kossarev's statement (ibid. p. 123) in the most important grain producing areas up to 70 per cent of the farms existing within an MTS area had Komsomol *nuclei* (presumably these were farms with individual party members, too).
55. *Otchet*, p. 109.
66. It was unavoidable that some of the promotions overtaxed the abilities of those promoted. An honourable come-back to the factory bench may have been provided for such communists by the CC decision of April 7, 1929 (*Izvestiya Ts.K. VKP(b)*, 1929, No. 7) on the posting of leading party and state officials at the factory bench and in lower organisational work, preferably in those enterprises from which they had come, with a prospect of eventual new promotion.
67. According to the data given in *Dva goda raboty* (as cited in note 13 above, p. 121) of each hundred workers employed in 1929-30 in mining 42.1 left their jobs during the year, as against 26.7 in 1928-29. The figures for metallurgy were 31.5 and 22.6 respectively, those for engineering (which was quickly expanding but had an old labour force) 19.8 and 15.6. In transport, the fluctuation of labour remained nearly stationary (24.1 as against 23.8).
68. *Sochineniya*, vol. XIII, pp. 51 ff. ; *Leninism*, pp. 359 ff.
69. I have discussed these issues in *Zeitschrift fuer Sozialforschung*, Paris 1938, No. 1-2, and in *Soviet Studies*, vol. I (1949) pp. 298 ff.
70. *VKP(b) v rezolyutsiyakh*, p. 531.
71. Rudzutak at the XVII Party Congress, *Otchet*, p. 287. According to Yaroslavski's statement (ibid. p. 299), 9.8 per cent of the party members investigated were reduced to probationer's status.
72. E. Shvarts in *Partiinoye stroitelstvo*, 1939, No. 5, p. 34.
73. At the XVII Congress, Yaroslavski (*Otchet*, p. 297) reported that between January 1931 and June 1933, in Provincial organisations which comprised two-thirds of the party members, 40,000 disciplinary investigations for alleged association with the condemned opposition groups were opened. 15,400 of the involved party members were expelled

(there were another 2,100 investigations, followed by 800 expulsions, for nationalist deviations).

74. *Court Proceedings*, 1937, pp. 82-83.

75. *Court Proceedings*, 1938, pp. 178, 570 and 575.

76. *Otchet*, XVII Congress, p. 119.

77. Ibid. p. 239, and also Radek, p. 628.

78. Stalin's *Sochineniya*, vol. XIII, pp. 373 ff. (*Leninism*, pp. 515-18) : *Otchet* XVII Congress, pp. 35 and 600 (Shkiryatov's speech).

79. *Partiinoye stroitelstvo*, 1939, No. 5, p. 49.

80. Kaganovich, *Otchet*, XVII Congress, pp. 561-62.

81. Zhdanov, *Otchet*, XVIII Congress, p. 532.

82. *Istoriya kommunisticheskoi partii Sovetskovo Soyuza*, Moscow 1959, p. 463. A few years before, J. A. Tokaev (*Betrayal of an Ideal*, London, 1954, espec., pp. 214 and 241) had stated that the assassination was prepared as early as 1933 by a Leningrad opposition group but denied the existence of any association between that group and the Opposition leaders, who were regarded by the young oppositionists as capitulators.

83. This is also a possible explanation of the strange way in which Yagoda (*Court Proceedings* 1938, p. 376) talked about what had happened.

84. In the formulation of December 10, 1934 (Article 468 of the additions to the Code of Criminal Procedure of the RSFSR), the trial of terrorists was to be conducted even in the absence of the defendants. Hence it was technically possible to give 'judicial' sanction to an execution even after it had been carried out.

85. The short published communique (*VKP(b) v rezolyutsiyakh*, p. 627) refers to equal, secret and direct, but not to general suffrage, i.e. to the abolition of the traditional Soviet structure but not necessarily to the granting of civic rights to those hitherto disfranchised.

86. In the decision of the December 1935 Plenary Session "On the Results of the Check of Party Documents" (ibid. pp. 646 ff.). The failure of all the authors who since have 'chosen freedom', and some of whom must have been present when the document was read in the primary party organisations, to give a fuller text illustrates the discrepancy between the actual events of 1935-36 and the accounts of those events current in the West. Khrushchev, too, in his secret session report remained silent on this all-important phase of developments.

87. *VKP(b) v rezolyutsiyakh*, p. 592.

88. Cf. for example *Partiiyone stroitelstvo* 1936, No. 5, where failure to apply such standards is disapproved.

89. See n. 86 above.

90. Zhdanov at the XVIII Congress, *Otchet*, pp. 519-20. The points had been made by Stalin already in his speech at the Plenary Session of the CC, on March 3, 1937 (*Partiiyone stroitelstvo*, 1937, No. 7).

91. *Partiinoye stroitelstvo*, 1936, No. 1. Already at that time we find warnings against light-handed expulsions of workers (e.g. ibid. No. 14, p. 52, and No. 15, p. 14). In those days, however, they could not affect the general trend.

92. Ibid. No. 2.

93. Ibid. 1938, No. 13, pp. 39 and 41.

94. Cf. *Partiinaya zhizn*, 1947, No. 20, p. 80, *Partiinoye stroitelstvo*, 1938, No. 15, p. 68.

95. Ibid. 1946, No. 5.

96. Similar explanations are suggested by Bukharin's and Rykov's statements at their trial (the public one, as distinct from certain formulae, the signature to which may have been extorted from them in the preliminary examination) about the Tukhachevski group's 'opening the front to the Germans', etc., with consideration for the language required from anyone who wished to have the opportunities of a public trial. There is no reason to assume that Tukhachevski and his friends wished the USSR to be defeated (usually, only victorious generals qualify for Bonaparte's role) but setbacks during the first stages of a war could be easily foreseen, and it was not unnatural for cliques of oppositionists to discuss what they would do in such an event.

97. Trotsky had this in mind when he spoke of a 'conspiracy of bureaucrats' (*Stalin*, p. 420).

98. Cf. A. Yurin's articles in *Izvestiya*, November 21 and 22, 1937. Another aspect of these underground discussions—intended as organised influence upon the public—may have been hinted at in T. G. Tokaev's report (*Kavkaz*, Munich, October 1952, p. 11) about a 'Balaklava Conference' held on July 28, 1936 by the 'Democrats —Decentralists' apparently a group of non-Russian right-wing oppositionists which resumed the old 'Democratic Centralist' slogan about the admission of non-Communist parties. In statements of this character, exaggerations (at least of the importance of the group reported) can be taken for granted, but Stalin, in his speech on the Constitution, in fact defended the preservation of a strong RSFSR as the nucleus of the USSR against suggestions such as those described by Tokaev as having been forwarded by his fellow-oppositionists.

99. Materials on these discussions are translated in my *Changing Attitudes in Soviet Russia ; The Family*, London, 1949.

100. Its 'correction' started with the Novo-Sibirsk trial on November 19-22, 1936, where the defendants had to confess intentional production sabotage. Hence the 'bridge' to leading officials in the PC of Heavy Industries, in particular Pyatakov, was established.

101. Naturally these persons, and others who were shot merely because of their association with earlier oppositions from which they had dissociated themselves long since, such as Antonov-Ovseyenko, Kossior

and the Polish communists, occupied a prominent place amongst those rehabilitated at, or immediately after, the XX Party Congress. Some reluctance formally to disown the published court proceedings may also play its part. Otherwise it would be difficult to understand why historians might be criticised for not paying tribute to Gamarnik's merits while mention of Krestinski's name was still avoided. Cf. *Soviet Studies,* vol. VIII, p. 192.

102. Cf. *VKP(b) v rezolyutsiyakh,* 1941, ed., pp. 671 ff.; see also A. Weisberg, *Conspiracy of Silence,* London, 1952, p. 305.

103. Weisberg (ibid. p. 149) reports that when he denied belonging to any illegal organisation, his examiner said that he might have a mistaken conception of the kind of illegal organisations which existed in the USSR and explained to the prisoner : 'if three of you are in a room talking about something or the other and a fourth man comes in and then you change the subject, you three belong to the organisation and he doesn't'. Certainly, whatever political conspiracy existed in the USSR must have worked according to this rule. There are, however, many harmless 'conspiracies' which fit it too—for example if colleagues speak about something which they would not like their seniors to hear (in an atmosphere such as existed during the 'great purge' the senior might easily regard any distrust of him as an act of treacherous conspiracy).

104. *Otchet,* XVIII Congress, p. 28. The statement is made in a polemic against the excesses of expulsion. According to our calculation above, no more than 150,000 expulsions from the party can have occurred during the 'purge' period proper, but many of those deprived of their party membership during the earlier 'check of party documents' were potential candidates for arrest.

105. At the Plenary Session of the CC in May 1937, cf. *Bolshevik,* May, 1937, *Partiinoye stroitelstvo,* 1937, No. 8, p. 17.

106. Decision of February 27, 1937, *VKP(b) v rezolyutsiyakh,* 1941 ed., pp. 654-55. This first decision on the secret ballot in the election of party officials was explained by the introduction of general and secret elections to the Soviet (i.e. by the need to avoid circumstances in which pressure within the party would keep bureaucrats in office who, later, might be struck out from the ballot paper to the Soviet, to the obvious detriment of the party's authority). This explanation, however, is irrelevant for elections of officials of primary party organisations (i.e. that very link in the party hierarchy where guarantees against managerial arbitrariness were most needed) and of the ordinary members of the higher party committees, i.e. those people who had to check the activities of the higher party secretaries. Yet precisely for the election of ordinary committee members—in all links of the hierarchy—the secret ballot was subsequently preserved. In the instructions for the 1938 elections it was abolished for the

elections of party secretaries of all ranks. (*Partiinoye stroitelstvo,* 1938, p. 62. Extensive applications of the open ballot were, however, disapproved. Elections of junior party officials carried out in that way were annulled. Cf. ibid. No. 10, p. 15). In the instructions for party elections in 1940 (ibid. 1940, No. 3, pp. 37 ff.) and in 1941 (ibid. 1941, No. 7, pp. 40 ff.) it was made clear that in small primary units which had no *buro* the secretary and his deputy were to be elected by secret ballot, and that the delegates to the party conferences electing the higher committees had the right to eliminate names from the submitted lists and to replace them by any other names.

107. A lucid picture of the interrelations of management with party organisations and staff had been given in D. Granick's *Management of the Industrial Firm in the USSR,* Columbia University Press, 1954.

108. *VKP(b) v rezolyutsiyakh,* 1941 ed., pp. 671 ff. ; *Partiinoye stroitelstvo,* No. 3, p. 46 and No. 5, p. 30 ; *Otchet* XVIII Congress, pp. 147 and 548-49.

109. *Partiinoye Stroitelstvo,* 1938, No. 1, p. 54.

110. Ibid. 1939, No. 19, p. 63.

111. E. Shvarts, ibid. 1939, No. 5, p. 34 ; Mekhlis, at the XVIII Congress, *Otchet,* p. 326.

112. CC decision of July 14, 1938 ; *Partiinoye stroitelstvo,* 1938, No. 15, p. 63.

113. In his secret session speech, Khrushchev reports a speech, fairly moderate in form, which Postyshev made at the February-March session of 1937 against Stalin's concept of increasing subversion.

114. *Otchet,* XVIII Congress, pp. 28-30 and 529.

115. *Otchet,* XVII Congress, p. 303, XVIII Congress, p. 148.

116. *Partiinoye stroitelstvo,* 1940, No. 9, p. 54.

117. *Otchet,* p. 256.

118. A letter of his to the commission indicating the desirable periodisation of party history, was published in *Bolshevik* as well as in *Partiinoye stroitelstvo* (1937, No. 10). No one in the USSR can have regarded the later descriptions of Stalin as the chief editor of the book as anything other than established protocol (some sections, in particular that on 'Dialectical and Historical Materialism', which is close to his early work of 1909, show, however, the traces of his pen). The attention devoted in the West to this 'discovery' of the obvious illustrates how the necessary study of the growth of the myth was frequently replaced by the mere statement that it was a myth.

119. *VKP(b) v rezolyutsiyakh* (1941 ed.), pp. 680 ff. ; *Partiinoye stroitelstvo* and *Bolshevik,* November 1938.

120. English ed. of 1948, p. 376.

121. *Sachineniya,* vol. XIII, pp. 38 ff. ; *Leninism,* pp. 356-57.

122. The minimum amounted to 100 Labour Days for the cotton growing regions, 80 for the main grain-growing regions and 60 Labour Days

for the North, Centre and East. It was about half as high as the one in force before, in 1954, farms were allowed to set their own minima, and also about half the average performance of collective farmers in the days when it was enacted. (According to *Narodnoye khoz-yaistvo SSSR*, pp. 128-29, the members of the 18.7 millions collective farm households—perhaps some 40 million people of working age—worked a total of 9,319 million Labour Days. This would lead to an average of more than 200 Labour Days per worker). In 1953, i.e. before the new incentives introduced in September of that year could become effective, just over 9 milliard Labour Days were worked by something over 30 million active farmers, belonging, after the heavy war losses and migration to the towns, to the 19.7 million kolkhoz households existing. The figures of 1940 reflect already the effects of the 1939 decree. As they so much exceed the prescribed minimum, there is no reason to question the assertion of the authors of the decree that its pressure was applied only against people whose activities remained far below the standard current on the earlier voluntary basis (certainly, there were weak farms which existed almost only on paper).

123. Cf. for example *Partiinoye stroitelstvo*, 1940, No. 15-16, p. 28.
124. It was abolished only after Stalin's death.
125. Zhdanov's argument (*Otchet*, XVIII Congress, pp. 515-16) centered on the irrationality of making a Stakhanovist worker's admission to the party more difficult if he had qualified for a managerial position. In this he was obviously right, though the Stakhanovist was more likely than not to have joined the party in an earlier stage of his career. The person most likely to profit from the change was the member of the old *intelligentsia* or the child of a worker's family who immediately went to university without having a factory record of his own. The amendments to Zhdanov's theses submitted during the pre-Congress discussion included suggestions to preserve the earlier admission privileges either for workers only, or for workers and peasants, or to retain a more complicated admission procedure only for members of the old *intelligentsia*. There were a few such suggestions. (*Partiinoye stroitelstvo*, 1939, No. 45).
126. *Partiinaya zhizn*, 1957, No. 20, pp. 88-89.
127. *Narodnoye khozyaistvo SSSR*, pp. 189 and 193.
128. Cf. *Voprosy partiinoi raboty*, p. 157, and *Soviet Studies*, Vol. IV, p. 300. ('Preparation of the XIX Party Congress'). But see M. Ivanov's correspondence to *Partiinaya zhizn*, 1958, No. 23.
129. *Partiinoye stroitelstvo*, 1941, No. 4-5, p. 151.
130. 1941, No. 9, p. 32.
131. Ibid. 1934, No. 14, p. 61; this decision was referred to again, though in different circumstances, in *Partiinaya zhizn*, 1956, No. 22, p. 68.
1323. *Partiinoye stroitelstvo*, 1941, No. 8, pp. 49-50.
133. Ibid. 1940, No. 8, pp. 40-41.

WAR AND RECONSTRUCTION

(a) THE PARTY ORGANIZATION DURING AND AFTER THE WAR

A COMPARISON of the impact on the party's life of the Second
World War with the impact of that other great struggle for
survival, namely the civil war nearly a quarter of a century before,
reveals similarities as well as contrasts.   In both, the war-emer-
gency promoted a fusion of the functions of party and state.   But
while during the civil war the party was about the only organized
body and thus, at least in the beginning, had to assume most of
the defence functions of the state, the USSR entered the Second
World War with a well-developed state machine.   And however
heavily the 'great purge' had hit the army, it had hit the party's
internal life even more.   Already during the preceding years, all
important measures had been decreed jointly on behalf of party
and government.   The assumption of the premiership by Stalin
when the danger of war became imminent only emphasized the
preceding fusion of party and state.   During the war, the Committee of Defence served as the apex of the party as well as of
the state organization.   Further down, the high party officials
acting as 'members of the war councils' of the operating armies
as well as the party organizations in the rear could be regarded
as specialized institutions for handling the human factor in the
war effort.

Relations between party and state were different in the rear
of the German advance where state organs were destroyed.   Here
all the initiative in organizing the guerilla movement ((in Leningrad
Province this began just two days after the German attack) lay
with the party organizations.   The extent to which they could fulfil
that function depended, of course, on their capacity to adapt

themselves to the new conditions. The CC of the Belorussian
party organisation, for example, as early as June 28th, 1941,
decided to turn to underground work; three days later it issued
directives on the organisation of guerillas. Subsequently 9
provincial committees, 174 city and district committees and
1,113 primary organisations functioned in the underground.
During the three years of work under Hitlerite terror, party
membership increased from 8,500 to 25,150 members and probationers. The much larger Ukraine, the party organisations of
which, however, appear to have been surprised by the depth of
the German penetration, by October 1941 had twenty-three
underground provincial committees, 63 city and 546 district
committees; 14,875 party members (most of them presumably
soldiers whose retreat had been cut) fought in the ranks of the
guerillas.[1]

Similarities as well as differences may be noticed in the development of the party's social structure. During both wars the
fact that civic faithfulness could best be shown by soldierly virtues
resulted in a reduction of the specific weight of the working-class
element within the party. As the party meanwhile had abandoned
the preferential admission of working-class recruits, the change
during World War II proceeded unchecked. The party's numerical development during the Second World War is shown by the
following figures:[2]

by the end of	total membership (in millions)	of these in the Armed Forces
1940	3.9	1.1 (mid-1941)
1941	3.1	1.3
1942	3.9	2.5
the war	5.8	3.3

These figures, however, show only the balance between new
admissions and losses. The former amounted in 1942 to 1.4, in
1943 to 1.8 million: it follows that loss of party members
mainly on the battle fronts amounted to no less than 600,000
in either year.[3] The main channel of admissions was through
the fighting forces, as in the days of the civil war. Joining the

party on the eve of some decisive operation, likely to demand extreme sacrifices, became a recognised expression of a soldier's civic consciousness. By the CC decisions of August 19, and December 9, 1941, the admission of soldiers who distinguished themselves on the battlefield was facilitated and the probationer's stage reduced to three months'. During the second half of 1941, when, as in Denikin's time, the party ticket might secure a place on the gallows, 126,000 probationers and 50,000 full members were admitted to the army organisations. During the first half of 1942, 432,000 members, and during the second half of the year—i.e. at the time of the Stalingrad battles—another 640,000 members were admitted by the army organisations. In August and September 1943, 280,000 soldiers were admitted as full members (most of these, presumably, had been probationers during the preceding year) and 460,000 as probationers. Three-quarters of those admitted were private soldiers and non-commissioned officers. During 1942 a mere 280,000 members were admitted in the rear. The number of party members sent to the front during the war amounted to one million. Nearly a third of these must have been sent during the first six months of the war, to make good the losses of party members in battle. Another third of a million followed during 1942; the rest between January 1st, 1943 and the end of the war.[4] During this last period, membership in the rear organizations increased by about 400,000 ; since some losses in civilian membership were still unavoidable, it follows that during the last period at least one and a half million civilians, most of them workers and technicians in the war industries, were admitted, as against not much less than two million (accounting for the losses of communists even during the victorious stage of the war) admitted in the army organisations. Total admissions in the army organisations during the war must have amounted to about three million, and in the civilian organizations to nearly two million, but more than half of the admissions were required to make good for the war losses. Many of these, of course, were newly admitted party members in the armed forces. The army admissions should have strengthened the party's position in the village, but for many peasant soldiers with some mechanical training, a party ticket and military promotion, the war may have formed a bridge to an urban or administrative job after demobilization.

After the war, recruitment was almost stopped so as to facilitate the assimilation of the new party members. By May 1st, 1946, the party had 4.6 million members and 1.4 million probationers.[5] This total of six million increased by a mere 900,000 up to mid-1952, the time of the preparation of the XIX Party Congress (during the three and half years from the XIX to the XX Congress it increased by a mere 333,000). Allowing for the losses on the front and in the rear, more than half of the total membership on May 1st, 1946, appears to have been recruited during the war. Of the three million new party members, no more than 600,000 had been recruited in the rear, i.e. from factories (including, of course, their engineers and technicians) and collective farms, (often women who, when the men had gone to the front, assumed leadership). Of the more than six million party members and probationers on January 1, 1947, 400,000 had higher, and another 1.3 million full secondary education.[6] At that time both these qualifications were characteristic of the salaried and professional groups (to speak in Western terms). Although the figures are not quite comparable[7] it appears that the share of these groups in total membership had at least not decreased as a result of the war-time admissions. It was bound to increase further in consequence of the post-war academic opportunities for veterans and the successful civilian careers of party members who had obtained commissions during the war. In post-war recruitment—as distinct from that following the conclusion of the civil war—no attention was devoted to 'regulating the party's social structure' (to use a term resumed in our days). Party organisers aimed at enlisting those people whose efforts were particularly important for the fulfilment of the Five Year Plan. These people might be engineers and agricultural scientists as well as manual workers in key positions. In the army, admission to the party had become a regular step in an officer's senior career.

If the party was in substance an association of patriotic and active citizens, and the war hero the prominent figure amongst its members, how could its continuing leadership be assured in the face of the warrior's attachment to his victorious leaders (who, as distinct from the party leaders, were not compromised by an enforced collectivisation and a 'great purge') ? During and after the civil war the problem had been solved by warnings to generals, or some party leader relying upon the generals, about repeating Napoleon Bonaparte's feats. Things were not so easy this time since the ideology on the basis of which Trotsky had been defeated had been abandoned and the party's triumphant leader himself had taken quite a few leaves out of Cromwell's and Bonaparte's books. The first effort to solve the problem proceeded by his taking a few more leaves, exalting his share in the victorious conduct of the war, considerable though it was, to a near-monopoly and thus raising himself upon a pedestal from which none of those who now appeared as his mere assistants could remove him. The tasks facing the party propagandists in this connection were not too inviting. That very aspect of Stalin's leadership which made it preferable to that of a Zhukov, i.e. the desirability of *political* leadership during a war, had also caused some of the worst blunders. On the eve of the war, a justified desire to let the peasant soldier fight only when he clearly saw that the fatherland was attacked and an understandable distrust of western governments (whose records included Munich and the efforts to switch the war against the USSR in the winter of 1939-40), had led to complete disregard of all warnings about Hitler's intentions (including some from communists who had sacrificed their lives in order to supply that information). Even such measures of concentration in the rear as could easily be carried out without offering Hitler some pretext for his aggression against the USSR were avoided. In his report to the secret session of the XX Party Congress, Khrushchev made the most of these shortcomings of Stalin. However, he was no more capable of frankly facing the main difficulty than Stalin. The soldiers resented not only the loss of hundreds of thousands of their comrades in positions which could not be defended except by a preventive attack (which Stalin refused for good political reasons) but also the loss of hundreds of thousands of square miles of territory in the initial stage of the war, a loss that was a necessary implication of a defensive strategy.

Stalin's major strategic mistakes—in particular his refusal to allow the Kiev army group to avoid encirclement by a timely retreat—were caused by concessions to public opinion, as were analogous mistakes in other lands.[8]

During the civil war, party life—including even discussions on the methods of waging the war—had preserved its liveliness. In contrast, the Great Patriotic War (as it was called from the very start) completed the concentration of all decisive power at the top, and within the top in the hands of an individual leader. In the period which separates the beginning of the war from the preparation for the XIX Party Congress (i.e. from a period of eleven years) we know of only one plenary session of the Central Committee. It met in February 1947, and its published decisions concerned the targets to be set for the restoration of agricultural production after the destructions of the war and the bad harvest of 1946. (The politically important decisions on the restoration of the kolkhoz structure against the tendencies to enlarge the private plots and to waste Labour Days for all kinds of administrative and unproductive activities, had been published already on September 1946, over the joint signatures of the Chairman of the Council of Ministers, Stalin, and the Secretary of the CC Zhdanov.)[9] There is no reason to assume that this published decision was the only one taken by the Plenary Meeting in February 1947[10] nor even that that plenary meeting was the only one which met during those eleven years. But certainly the failure to publish any decision of the party's supposedly guiding body other than one about a technical problem indicates the extent to which its authority had come into abeyance. We need not take Khrushchev's later complaints about Stalin's replacing the Politburo by committees managing individual fields of activity (appointed by himself) too literally implying that the Politburo itself had come into abeyance. (If it had, Voroshilov need not have had to ask for Stalin's kind permission to attend Politburo meetings). But it is obvious that the 'cult of the individual' had destroyed its authority. Khrushchev could not have said, in the presence of many of Stalin's old friends, what he said about the fate of Kuznetsov and Voznesenski if Stalin had not actually been capable of arresting and executing

Politburo members without a preliminary hearing in the body to which they belonged. Such a hearing had been granted even to Bukharin in the full CC, and later to Beria in the Presidium of the CC. Conditions in at least some of the Republican party organisations came nearer to normality. In the Ukraine, Khrushchev's domain, six Party Congresses took place between 1938 and 1956, and the Central Committee met regularly four times a year.[11] The Ukraine may have operated more normally than some other Republics, but we have annual reports in *Partiinaya zhizn* about the 'regular' full meetings of the Provincial and Republican Committees (which thus appear to have met just once a year). No delegates' conferences, however, were convened between 1940 and 1947.[12] Vacancies in many of the committees appear to have been filled by co-option.

According to the available data on the election of the new district committees in early 1948,[13] 31 per cent of the secretaries, 28.3 per cent of the members of the *buro* and 20.2 per cent of the committee members had joined the party before 1930; 54.4, 49.4 and 39.2 per cent, respectively between 1931 and 1940. It follows that the war-recruits formed mere minorities on the committees and fairly insignificant ones amongst those who did the actual organising work. It was noted with satisfaction that nearly three-quarters of the district secretaries elected had higher or complete secondary education. Further down in the hierarchy, demands on educational standards and to some extent, even the party experience had to be relaxed. The decisions of the Plenary Meeting of the CC in February had established Political Deputies of the Directors of the Machine Tractor Stations to head the work of the party organisations of those stations (as distinct from the Political Departments established in 1933); however, they had no formal powers to direct party work in the farms and villages. Of the 6,780 Deputies thus appointed, 55.3 per cent had joined the party before 1940 (24.4 per cent even before 1930); 57 per cent had higher, or complete secondary education (there were still 10 per cent with mere elementary schooling).[14] It was natural in the circumstances that much attention was devoted to the schooling of party members, with emphasis on private homework for those who could not attend the current elementary classes. Recommendations for such homework were restricted to the works of Stalin and current party documents.

The war, and the need to extract out of a disrupted agricultural system a maximum of food supplies for the towns, promoted the application of methods which in those days were criticised as fitting an institution working according to the rules of administrative discipline rather than one with an internal life of its own. District secretaries bombarded factories and farms with orders of all kinds, bypassing the primary party organisations and assuming functions which properly belonged to the economic and administrative hierarchy. On their part, they were pressed by the Provincial Secretaries who themselves worked under pressure from the Ministries (which regarded the party machine as the only means of getting things done quickly).[15] Ovechkin's sketch *District Routine*,[16] written five years later when the system of managing party affairs by order and command had become untenable, illustrates the way in which an agricultural district was managed, and the type of party official produced by that method of management. In order to give Ovechkin's Borzov his due, it may be mentioned that he terrorised his district in order to feed the towns. Khrushchev, writing in 1948,[17] however, gives examples of wires issued by provincial committees which cannot be regarded as having been prompted by extreme necessity: boxers were to be sent in time by the district committees so as not to disrupt a provincial sports festival; telephones which had just arrived at provincial headquarters should be collected by district committees, etc.

The CC Plenary Meeting of February 1947 condemned suggestions to make food deliveries dependent on the acreage actually sown (instead of on the farms' total acreage) as this would destroy the incentive to good cultivation. It opened, however, a loophole by permitting 'under present conditions' the establishment of different delivery norms for groups of farms formed within every district 'in accordance with the degree to which they have managed to cultivate the acreage assigned to them'.[18] There is nothing surprising in Ovechkin's Borzov's using this loophole in order to collect from those farms which had worked well the grain which their less efficient neighbours had failed to harvest so that the district might complete its planned deliveries in time. It is also not surprising that the members of the good farms were thereby discouraged from further efforts. It was only natural that district organisers tended to nominate the secretaries of primary organizations even if the latter explicitly refused to elect the suggested candidate. Already in those days such methods of 'leadership' were denounced in party periodicals[19] just as they are denounced in our days, with the difference that then, criticism was restricted to admonitions. At no stage of its development did the party will the methods by which its machine worked. Even Stalin, whose 'cult' made the position of the little Stalins in district and city secure, apparently approved of the criticism to which their methods were being subjected in official party publications. The nature of administrative methods depended on the character of the policies which had to be pursued. There was the objective need to accelerate reconstruction in a devastated country facing a hostile world and needing an atom bomb of its own. Also, no one in those days, could envisage an approach to the village basically different from Stalin's *dan*.

The conditions of internal party life which developed during the thirties have not been fully revealed even now. What we know does not allow for more than occasional glimpse at the political disputes which went on during the post-war period. Most of that information concerns problems of agricultural organization where disagreements were of emphasis only, and which accordingly have been solved in a civilised way. Reconstruction immediately after the war started with the link as the typical organisational unit of labour : a small group of kolkhozniki (as a rule friends, in many cases relatives) who could be relied upon to combine their efforts and to be influenced by incentives rewarding their joint effort. From the technical point of view, the link discouraged mechanisation. There was, thus, a need for large production units (brigades) subject to a common discipline and to a professional leader. When in 1949-50, the party decided to amalgamate the 235,000 collective farms existing from pre-war days into some 80,000 larger units (for mechanisation, and also in order to have enough party members to form a workable primary organization), this implied abandonment of the link (except in some special cases) in favour of the brigade as most suitable for mechanised grain production (an approach to brigade organization had been made in the Ukraine already on the eve of the war). Those who continued to defend the link including Andreyev who during the immediate post-war period had been the party's spokesman on agricultural questions, were publicly rebuked without suffering any fate worse than slight demotion (in 1952, Andreyev was re-elected only as an ordinary member of the CC).[20] When, on the other side, Khrushchev became slightly enthusiastic in his advertisement of the amenities to be expected from the new 'agro-towns' and announced a resettlement programme (without any time-table), *Pravda* and two Republican party congresses dissociated themselves from this forecast. They wanted to allay the fears of peasants regarding interference with their traditional way of life, and perhaps also to alleviate the Exchequer's fears of being burdened with a huge rural reconstruction programme. Khrushchev's enthusiastic announcement as well as the rebuke—moderate in form though it was— led to another of those bugbears the construction of which has become a favourite pastime of some Western students of Soviet conditions.[21] The amalgamation of the collective farms proceeded smoothly—by the end of 1935 there were only 91,200 of them; by the end of 1955 85,700; in 1958, at the time of their absorption of the Machine Tractor Stations, 70,000; in 1964 a mere 44,000 (the absorption of some very weak collective farms by state farms contributed to the more recent decreases in the number of collective farms). Khrushchev had to wait for a few more years before he could put large-scale construction programmes for the collective farms, now by their own efforts, on the order paper.

Disagreements in fields other than that of agriculture, however, were settled by the barbaric methods developed during the 'great purge'. About the reasons of Voznesenski's fall, in 1949, we do not know more than a post-eventum statement that he held 'voluntarist views of the parts played by the Plan and the state in Soviet society', i.e. believed that the social structure could be changed by State intervention even ahead of the objective conditions of the economy[22] and Khrushchev's statement that the 'Leningrad case' (as the victims of which Kuznetsov and

Voznesnski died) was an intentional effort of Beria's clique 'to denigrate the Leningrad organisation'. More positively Walter Ulbricht, explaining to the East German communists the liquidation of the Stalin cult, described Voznesenski's fate as due to his 'opposition to Stalin's tyranny'.[23] These interpretations do not necessarily contradict each other. It would have been grossly unfair for Khrushchev, when rehabilitating one of Stalin's victims, to remember theoretical errors, which in no case would have been more than an explicit expression of a trend represented in official party documents of those days. Nor could he, being involved in juridical rehabilitation, enter the dangerous field of speculation about which form of 'opposition to Stalin's tyranny' deserved the description as 'treason', and which belonged to actions which are honoured by history whatever the juridical servants of some oppressive regime may think about them.

(b) THE CULMINATION OF IDEOLOGICAL CENTRALISATION

Because of the paucity of political information proper, much of our knowledge of the development of the Soviet polity in the late forties and early fifties derives from the chain of party interventions in diverse fields of intellectual life. By their very nature, these interventions could not be carried out in secret. The increased weight of the intelligentsia within the party[24] and a realization of the fact that unless it worked as a group of 'engineers of the soul'[25] in the service of the regime, it might weaken it by providing an outlet for less easily controllable opposition, led to the intensity with which the party decisions on ideological issues were advertised. (A perusal of *Partiinaya zhizn* of those years gives the impression, misleading if aspects of party policy other than those advertised are considered, that kolkhoz reconstruction was the only issue which might compete with decisions on intellectual activities.) In cases such as Stalin's interest in Ivan IV's *Oprichina,* the inter-connection between Lysenko's theories on heredity and the introduction of grass-rotations all over the union, or in the drive against 'cosmopolitans', it is possible to see, at the bottom of the ideological waters, quite real issues of politics. Even the struggle of personalities for power is apparent, usually in issues on which Stalin eventually proved wrong. All these points were made within a framework of renewed emphasis on the general social responsibilities of the artist and the scientist implicit in the Marxist outlook. This resulted in a confusion, firstly among intellectual critics who attacked the decisions of 1946-49 from an unacknowledgedly individualist standpoint, and also on the part of the party bureaucracy which defended, if not concrete Stalinist policies, then at least the framework established for the defence of any adopted party policies against intellectual criticism.

The ideological campaign, which in the West has been associated with Zhdanov's name, although it reached its extreme only after his death, started in the summer in 1946. At intervals of twelve days, three decisions on artistic subjects were adopted. These deal with the literary journals *Zvezda* and *Leningrad*, with theatre repertories, and with the film 'The Great Life'.[26] In a manner since well established in the treatment of organizational problems, each decision starts from a critical analysis of the individual production, the shortcomings of which are said to have provoked the intervention. But the very first decision makes the basic point that artists had bypassed the political needs of Soviet society 'by neglecting the life essence of the Soviet system, its politics'. The Soviet system, however, 'could not tolerate an education of its young generation in spirit of indifference towards Soviet politics, of swimming on the waves and lack of principles (*bezideinost*)'. Very much depends here on the interpretation of 'politics'. Identification with Western concepts of party politics would be mistaken, but within the Soviet system of ideas there is a fair range of interpretation, from more emphasis on the author's social responsibilities, which was a feature of Russian progressive literature since the days of the classic, up to the popularisation of production targets and denunciation of those external foes who happened to be in the news, which had been characteristic of much of the Five Year Plan literature and, for some years, was to dominate the practical application of the 'Zhdanov line'.

'A-politicism' as attacked in the decrees has found in verses expressing pessimism and despair (as allegedly produced by the poetess Akhmatova); kowtowing (*nizkopoklonstvo*) before the alleged superiority of foreign countries, and 'offering the Soviet stage as a platform for the propaganda of the reactionary bourgeois ideology and morals', by the staging, for example, of love and detection stories by contemporary foreign authors. Everyone familiar with Soviet life in the twenties and thirties will remember the Soviet public's interest in Western dramas and films (usually second-rate). In view of the high artistic level especially of Soviet film production, that interest can only show a desire to escape from the propagandist content even of the best Soviet art and to find, at least on the stage or the screen, a picture of the quiet life of plenty which, rightly or wrongly, was associated with the West. Not unnaturally, the party leaders found such inclinations of the public particularly dangerous when the USSR, after enormous exertions in the course of the war, had still to make additional ones in order to face an increasingly hostile world. Through the occupation of Central Europe contacts with the West had increased. It was all-important to indoctrinate the soldier who was about to meet ordinary women who wore what in the USSR would be described as rare luxury goods, and to see houses much superior to those offered at home even to the Stakhanovite, with a spirit of contempt for this aspect of the *bourgeois* world—or at least to let him feel more strongly the superiority of his own one. Yet the reproaches were not confined to 'a-politicism' in this verbal sense. One of their main victims was Zoshchenko, an outstanding Soviet satirist who certainly had performed what others might regard as a useful social service by criticising shortcomings and misuses of all kinds. The shortcomings of the Soviet citizens depicted in Zoshchenko's *Adventures of a Monkey* (1946), which offered the main excuse for Zhdanov's attack, could be well observed in any other society with housing shortage, rationing and queues. Zhdanov overstated his case by describing them as 'idlers and monsters, stupid and primitive'. But, surely, they do not include such model examples of the genus *homo sapiens* as Soviet society should. Zhdanov could reproach Zoshchenko for having 'deliberately caricatured the life of Soviet people as unattractive and cheap' so that the monkey, having escaped from the zoo and been chased along the street, comes to

the conclusion that living in the zoo is better than being at liberty.[27]
The adjectives applied in that connection to Zoshchenko could not
have been meant seriously—otherwise it would have been
Zhdanov's duty, not just to have Zoshchenko expelled from the
Writers' Union and put into oblivion for a few years as an author
but to have him sent to the labour camp. In fact, he knew very
well that Zoshchenko regarded Soviet society as superior to any
other, yet did not take a very optimistic view even of this best of
all existing worlds.

Zoshchenko might be rightly reproached for a tendency to
introspection and an absence of fervour for improvement which
is characteristic of even the most sharply criticised authors of the
post-Stalin period. Yet the party decision on the film 'The Great
Life' makes it abundantly clear that the party objected to the very
drawing of attention to the shortcomings of Soviet life. Patriotic
enthusiasm might be impaired by the showing of wounded soldiers
who lie on the battlefield while the battle line is moving forward,
without the passers-by helping them (though in 1946 plenty of returned war-veterans could say that such things *do* happen).
But to reproach, as the CC decision did, a Soviet film producer
for having shown that coal production in the Donets basin
was resumed with very primitive means, that the cultural level
of the workers was low, that their housing conditions were bad
and that the bureaucrat (perhaps even an ex-collaborator) did
not attempt to improve them—this implied a demand to embellish reality, as against the producer's clear intention to move
society forward by denouncing bureaucratism and emphasising what
was achieved in spite of all those handicaps. Not 'a-politicism' in
the sense of aloofness from politics, but a certain supposedly wrong
kind of politics was under attack. Script-writer and producer were
criticised for having shown officials who counteracted the workers' creative initiative and for having described with sympathy
the mass-promotion of little educated workers to positions of
responsibility. In the present conditions of the Soviet State, the
decision said, as distinct from those of the civil war period with
which the producers appeared enamoured, cultivated and well-
educated members of the Soviet intelligentsia were promoted to
posts of responsibility. Even in the treatment of the past, authors

were prevented from describing the contradictory aspects of phenomena which Stalin regarded as necessary. This was the meaning of the criticism of Eisenstein's presentation in the second part of his film on Ivan the Terrible (which only in our days was publicly shown) of Ivan's *oprichniki,* as not appropriate to the historically progressive part allegedly played by them in Russian history. Stalin made no secret of his motivations. During his lifetime and presumably with his agreement, the film-producer N. K. Cherkassov published his recollections of a talk which he and Eisenstein had had with Stalin on February 9th, 1947, on the problems facing them with the completion of the second part of the film on Ivan IV. Stalin gave a very positive assessment of Ivan. Only his premature death, which prevented him from extinguishing the last five families of big *boyars,* involved Russia in the time of troubles in the early 17th century.[28]

The organisational prescriptions on the three decisions on the arts ranged from the solemn proclamation that the second part of the film 'The Great Life' should not be shown on the screen (similar things had happened before a hundred times without the whole publicity machine of the CC being put in motion) to the opening of a competition for dramas of the desired content, from changes in the editorial board of the two Leningrad journals to hints for the benefit of the organizations of artists. Akhmatova and Zoshchenko as well as Eisenstein had belonged to the 'fellow-travelling' groups formed in the twenties. Their civic loyalty and subjective intention to serve Soviet society was beyond question. But it was now regarded as intolerable that a man such as Zoshchenko could play an important part in the management of the Union of Soviet Writers in Leningrad and on the editorial boards of its Leningrad publication. All positions of influence should be reserved for reliable supporters of whatever the Secretariat of the CC deemed to be in accordance with 'the life essence of Soviet society, its politics'. For some time Akhmatova and Zoshchenko were even prevented from publishing. This ban, however, 'was soon removed by life itself—to speak more precisely, by the demands of the Soviet reader'.[29]

Music had to wait another year and a half for its integration into the new party line. Again, Zhdanov acted as the party's main spokesman, and again the conflict started with the performance of a piece of more particular importance. The first performance of Muradeli's opera 'The Great Fellowship' before an invited audience of party and State officials shocked those present. Nevertheless, under pressure from the Art Committee of the Composer's Union, the opera was accepted for performance in the *Bolshoi* Theatre.[30] The domination of that committee and of the Composers' Union in general by reliable supporters of a few outstanding composers—Shostakovich, Prokofiev, Miaskovski, Khachaturian—came under attack. Yet, because of the particularities of the musical form of expression no outright condemnation, as in the case of Zoshchenko and Akhmatova, was possible. Zhdanov addressed a meeting of the musicians concerned in order to strengthen the opposition against the leading group of composers. The more moderate of the critics who tried to differentiate in the leaders' work between healthy and unhealthy ('formalist') elements,[31] differed only in degree from the qualified self-criticism expressed by Shostakovich and Khachaturian (Prokofiev and Miaskovski did not take the rostrum, perhaps because they were not prepared to express even qualified self-criticism. After this discussion, the CC adopted a resolution straightforwardly denouncing the trend hitherto predominant in Soviet music. Notwithstanding Zhdanov's warnings against excesses of this kind,[32] for a few months the best-known Soviet composers went into eclipse, and a trend opposite to their standards had its run. The CC decision condemned 'abstract' music—intended only for a minority of connoisseurs (a real problem not only in the USSR) and stressed the national roots of art, which had been characteristic of the pre-revolutionary school of Russian composers. The decision was expressed in terms likely to discourage any quest for novel forms of expression. From here it was not a long way to that narrow-minded nationalism which characterised much of Soviet compositions during the last years of the Stalin era. On this occasion—as distinct from later interferences with biology and art criticism—the party intervention was not directed towards nationalist self-restriction. The merits of the Western as well as of the Russian classics were emphasised. The 'anti-cosmopolitan' element came in only insofar as Soviet composers were reproached for seeking the approval, which they could not get from Soviet wireless audiences or even any concert audience larger than that of the Small Hall of the Moscow *Conservatoire*[33] of like-minded connoisseurs in other lands. Zhdanov made the point that true internationalism in the field 'of music consisted, not in the impoverishment of one's own national art and a blind imitation of foreign styles but in the flourishing of all national cultures. 'It is impossible to be an internationalist in music or in anything else unless one loves and respects one's own people; only a people that has a highly developed musical culture of its own can appreciate the musical riches of other nations'.[34]

Between the discussion on music in February 1948 and the first days of July, when the party intervention in the biological dispute was decided upon, something must have happened within the Secretariat of the CC, the importance of which far exceeds that of interventions in intellectual activities. The party statement on music becomes relevant once the existence of a guardian of the social interest in intellectual activities is taken for granted. In itself (as distinct from its exaggerations in administrative practice, unavoidable though they were in the atmosphere of Stalin's Russia), it merely expresses a preference for a certain trend, telling the dissenters that they must not expect their symphonies and operas to be performed unless they come up to certain standards of accessibility. In his just-quoted statement,[35] Zhdanov spoke of the danger of someone's becoming a 'root-less (*bezrodny*) cosmopolitan', but only as an alternative to sound internationalism based upon recognition of the individualities of the diverse nations. There was no suggestion that the supporters of any school of musicians were more patriotic than the others.

It was different in the biology discussion. The party interfered in a dispute between academic schools the co-existence and competition of which had been regarded as a normal thing before (and was again so regarded after Stalin's death).[36] Both schools tried to make their case with reference to the services which they could render to practical farmers.[37] But neither of them— certainly not the one eventually supported—could make a strong case for a necessary coincidence of its views with the basic principles of Marxist philosophy.[38] Yet this was done in terms which implied a questioning of the civic loyalty of Lysenko's opponents. Unless intervention was indulged in for its own sake (that is, in order to teach too independent researchers a lesson), Lysenko's theory disposed of no political asset other than its association with Williams' theory, according to which soil qualities could be everywhere improved by the introduction of the *travopolye* system (alternation of field cultivation and grass). This theory was popular with the authorities as a means of providing increased stocks of fodder. Eventually, at the meeting of the CC in February 1954, Khrushchev stated that Williams, in his eagerness to change soil conditions, had concentrated his attention on Central Russia where certain atmospheric conditions could be taken for granted. The indiscriminate application of the *travopolye* system to all parts of Russia, however, could do no good and resulted in a mere restriction of grain cultivation. By the end of 1961 Khrushchev had rejected the *travopolye* system and Williams' concepts even for the non-blackearth regions of Russia. It was said to do great harm by restricting the cultivation not only of grain but also of high-value fodders such as corn (maize) and fodder-beans.[39] It is hardly necessary to state that, after Khrushchev's fall this extreme anti-Williams attitude, too, was described as one of his 'voluntarist' excesses. The relevant point here is not when, and how far, Khrushchev was right from the standpoint of agricultural techniques. Things were bound to seem different when, because of industrial progress, Russia became capable of tackling agricultural difficulties by mechanisation and, eventually, by large-scale application of fertilisers. What is important is the fact that a technological controversy, completely legitimate within its limits, had been transformed into part of the basic state ideology. Moreover, one element of the latter, Marxist Dialectics, had been re-interpreted so as to turn into basic heresy a mere failure of the scientist to deliver the desired 'justification' for the technological measures preferred by the Politburo. At the Biology Conference in August 1948 a supporter of Lysenko had argued that the introduction of the new rotation systems being 'extremely important measures of State significance', would be 'retarded and disrupted' if the disagreements amongst the specialists were allowed to continue.[40]

Biological theory had thus become a rationalisation of temporary industrial shortcomings, and the partisanship of Marxism a canonisation of its misuse for delaying scientific progress, whenever the latter did not fit Russia's alleged possibilities and needs.

The struggle against concepts of limitation was waged even outside the agricultural sciences. Lysenko denounced statistical approaches in general. The statistician Nemchinov found the chromosome theory of heredity acceptable, yet Lysenko said, 'Science is the enemy of chance'.[41] It was not an issue of philosophical determinism (Schmalhausen had opened the prospect that, eventually, the progress of knowledge would allow the forecast of the definite mutations provoked by definite agencies) but rather the contrary. Statistics were unpopular because they showed the working of objective and natural laws rather than selected favourable examples which could be held up to the rest of the country as a model. Surely there was a difference between the model kolkhoz which, by enormous efforts on the part of all those concerned, showed what was possible if similar efforts were made elsewhere and, on the other side, some experiment of Lysenko's pupils in which a useful variation made its appearance and encouraged the experimenters' hope that by creating similar conditions of growth (usually such ones as would in any case involve good farming) all the progeny might belong to the more useful variety. The first one, i.e. the model kolkhoz was a reality, even if a limited one. The second might be a delusion which would do positive harm if the monopoly of the experimenting school, backed by the party's authority, prevented checking of the experiments and a search for more fruitful approaches. To quote Yury Zhdanov,[42] those who granted Lysenko party support accepted short-term losses by the interruption of the orthodox geneticists' activities in order to direct Soviet science against all limitation concepts and thereby to influence the mood of Soviet society. This might appear necessary in view of the great difficulties posed by the post-war reconstruction of the kolkhoz system and the race for the hydrogen bomb, in conditions where any accident might throw the USSR into a war against an enemy still superior from the technical point of view. Yet while it is possible to understand the reason for the party support granted to Lysenko, the way in which it was granted, with the implied denunciation of his opponents as representatives of an approach alien to Soviet thought, demands political explanation.

Up to the middle thirties Soviet genetics did not differ from others, except by an aversion, natural for socialists, to philosophical generalisations such as the alleged 'eternity of the germplasma', not to speak of the misuse of neo-Mendelian genetics by the Nazis to demonstrate the superiority of their alleged 'Nordic master-race'.[43] The party greatly advertised the achievements of Michurin, an autodidact horticulturist who had produced plant varieties of great practical value by grafting. Following Darwin's line of thought, Michurin took some general concept of inheritance of acquired characteristics as well as natural selection for granted. Since 1936, these concepts were developed by Lysenko, a peasant-born agriculturist with considerable practical achievements, into a system of neo-Lamarchism sharply opposed to orthodox genetics. His views gained popularity because of the failure of genetic theory, in the USSR as in Western countries,[44] visibly to influence the practical methods of plant breeding. Notwithstanding conflict between the two schools of biologists, their co-existence continued until 1948. Lysenko was eventually elected to Presidency of the Lenin Academy of Agricultural Sciences and gained control of most of the institutions for practical breeding while the supporters of academic genetics were strongly entrenched in some research institutions and in Universities of Leningrad and Moscow. It was not easy to maintain this parallelism where one school enjoyed the sympathies of practical farmers and of the biologists directly connected with them, while the other was prominent in academic education and research. In any case, Lysenko was not prepared to play the game. In 1946 he prevented the Presidium of the Academy of Sciences from establishing two parallel Institutes of Genetics so that the two schools might compete. He also refused to contribute to the publication of the Academy, reserving his and his friends' contributions for his own journal *Agrobiology* (and afterwards, complaining of the resulting monopoly of orthodox genetics in the official academic publications).

In November 1947 Professors Zhebrak and Dubinin were attacked by *Pravda* for having criticised the Lysenko group in articles published by them in the American Journal *Science*. This was interpreted as an appeal of Soviet scientists to foreign academic opinion against possible intervention by non-academicians in their own country.[45] Zhebrak and Dubinin believed that they had strengthened the international prestige of the USSR by showing how insignificant a section of academic Soviet geneticists supported Lysenko. They were, indeed, supported by the Cytological Institute of the Academy of Sciences. (In current conditions such support was possible only on the assumption that a struggle was going on behind the closed doors of the Politburo, and that the *Pravda* article had expressed only one of the conflicting trends.) Lysenko reacted by an interview with the *Literary Gazette*. Now he even denied the existence of selection by competition within the species, i.e. the basic element of classical Darwinism which explains evolution even by non-directed mutations. When the Genetics Department of Moscow University invited the Department of Dialectical and Historical Materialism to a joint discussion of Lysenko's new approach, the latter refused. Now the Council of the Faculty of Biology of the University demanded a change in the personnel of the Dialectical Materialism Department. The terms used by the academic opponents of Lysenko as late as May 7th suggest that they relied upon powerful support. Lysenko, indeed, had gone very far by raising as his standard, in a non-academic publication, the most controversial aspect of his views, on which even in the hour of his triumph he never got full support.[46] Apparently he took it for granted that political considerations would swerve the balance in his favour.

Within a few weeks Lysensko's supporters became a majority in the Lenin Academy of Agricultural Sciences by additional nominations, which as Lysenko admitted, resulted from the personal intervention of Stalin.[47] The since famous meeting of the Academy was convened on short notice and in such a way as to exclude proper and well-prepared presentation of the views of

Lysenko's opponents.[48] The latter took the floor only after they had been told, in *Pravda,* that failure to do so would be an act of cowardice. Speaking in a setting dominated by practical agriculturists, high officials and journalists, they attempted to demonstrate the practical service rendered by their abstract science to agriculture. Only a small minority of the Soviet academic geneticists were orthodox neo-Mendelians. The anti-Lysenko speakers at the Conference rejected the dogma of the impossibility of the inheritance of properties acquired during the life of an organism (which even in the West has since lost much of its former support). On the other hand, moderate supporters of Lysenko emphasised the fact that while phenomena of heredity cannot be reduced to the continuity only of the chromosomes in the germ cell, other ways of alteration should be regarded as supplementary. Lysenko's experimental data were already known for years. With the interruption caused by the party authorities' effort to protect them from criticism they have always remained controversial. In no case can they be regarded as unambiguous support for his philosophy. In the Soviet setting of those years, the decision on how the accumulated data should be generalised was a policy of decision on the character of academic life as well as on the prospects of Soviet agriculture. The centralised direction of the latter was supplemented by a conception of the former as the supplier of arguments in favour of those directives which the political leadership found necessary, rather than giving the leadership advice which might easily be controversial. This was more so as few problems of applied science (least of all the problems of agriculture in country which is more a continent) allow for generally valid solutions.

On August 7, Yury Zhdanov's letter (dated July 10, the latest possible date of the party decision) was published. On the same day Lysenko asserted in his concluding remarks that his opening report had been approved by the Party's Central Committee (i.e. in fact by the Secretariat). Thereby submission was made an obligation for all those who wished to continue in academic teaching and research. It was made easier as Zhdanov's letter contained most unfavourable judgement about Lysenko as a theorist and research worker, and even about the practical help given by his school to agriculture. Those who submitted, i.e. the majority of academic biologists, were thus assured that they submitted to a general philosophy which was to inspire biological research, not to an individual. The next meeting of the Presidium of the Academy of Sciences drew the practical implications. Research institutions too much 'infected' by academic genetic were closed down. Schmalhausen, the leading geneticist who had failed to recant, was dismissed. In all boards awarding academic degrees etc., a majority of safe supporters of Lysenko was assured. The leaders of the Academy of Sciences now exercised self-criticism for the mistake of having regarded the two trends in biology as equally legitimate scientific schools from which truth would emerge. Six years were to pass before this truism was to be frankly professed again.

It is remarkable that at the very time when the party prescribed to the members of fairly non-political professions the way in which they should guide public opinion and questioned the dissenting intellectual's civic loyalty, discussions amongst communists on Marxist theory were conducted in a spirit which favourably differed from conditions around 1930. Then 'deviations' on the philosophical or economic 'fronts' were denounced as camouflaged manifestations of the right-wing or left-wing oppositions. In May 1947 an academic discussion started on State capitalism in the western countries and on the characteristics of the economics of the people's Democracies expressed in E. Varga's book *Changes in the Economics of Capitalism in the Outcome of the Second World War.*[49] On January 26, 1948, *Pravda* criticised Varga for allowing an intermediate stage between State-supported monopoly, capitalism and socialism. In the autumn of that year, the attacks concentrated upon his alleged over-estimate of the staying power of capitalism. While modifying his statements on some details, Varga refused to submit to the decisive point of the criticism; to do so would mean to betray the party which needed a sober assessment of the USSR's international environment. Only in March 1949, when all kinds of dissent were being brought under the official label of 'cosmopolitanism', did Varga withdraw from his interpretation of nationalisation measures carried out by a bourgeois state as a progress towards a new type of democracy. He recognised that his purely economic investigation

of the role of the State in war and post-war economics obscured
the decisive role of the working class in the struggle for power.
Notwithstanding the attacks, he upheld his interpretation of the
emancipation of India and other former colonies as a progress
to real independence. His standpoint in this question was eventually approved by the XX Party Congress.

Zhdanov himself took the lead in a philosophical discussion
which, though it hardly went beyond the establishment of a new
philosophical journal, may have formed part of political developments which resulted in the biology intervention and in even more
dramatic events of the following year. During the war a textbook of the history of philosophy had been written by a group
of authors (ed by G. Alexandrov, at the time one of the party's
leading spokesmen on general ideological problems). The Stalin
Prize awarded for this work was withdrawn soon after the publication of the third volume because of the conventional tribute paid
in this volume to the importance of the German classical philosophers as forerunners of Marx[50] and its underestimation of Russian
progresssive philosophy. Alexandrov attempted to draw the appropriate lessons from that criticism by writing, single-handed, a one-
volume *History of West European Philosophy* which was favourably received. This very reception, however, caused the CC to
convene in June 1947 a special conference of the philosophers
at which they were reproved by Zhdanov for their failure to notice
Alexandrov's basic shortcomings.[51] By his emphasis on the
positive contributions made by the diverse non-Marxist philosophers to the further development of philosophy, and eventually
to the formation of Marxism, Alexandrov had obscured the
qualitative difference between Marxism as a fighting philosophy
and all the earlier philosophies. Soviet Philosophers were criticised for their failure to draw from the party decision on literature the appropriate conclusions for their own field of activity.
Soviet philosophy should form an active element in the evolution
of Soviet society which not being class-divided, could move
forward only through an ideological form of the 'struggle of
opposites', i.e. through the dynamics of criticism and self-criticism.
This statement was made in explicit opposition to stagnation and
dogma. Although the line of attack is directed against conti-

nuation of sympathetic approach to western developments as had prospered in the days of the Great Alliance, it is difficult to see how the man who made it could be in sympathy with the party intervention in Lysenko's favour (except in the most general sense that Lysenko, too, emphasised the active and creative role in man).

The next fairly violent disputes in Soviet intellectual life concerned the relation between 'the new', to be promoted according to Zhdanov's advice, and Russian national tradition. Michurin, the Lysenkoists' hero, had made his contribution to Soviet reconstruction. In other fields, the desire to break with western tradition promoted the emphasis on the achievements of pre-revolutionary Russian scientists who had been rejected by western science and public opinion. Most of such re-assertions formed legitimate corrections of that arrogant western tradition according to which any discovery made by a Russian must necessarily be inferior to a parallel one made at the same time—or even slightly later—by a western colleague of his. In some cases, however, Russian national pride might serve as a cover for opposition to progress in science if it had originated in the West, and for the tendency to submit modern physical theories to the test of compatibility with that type of primitive materialism which is regarded by the popular propagandist of adult education as the essence of Dialectical Materialism.[52] Maximov, an old representative of that tendency, sharply attacked in the *Literary Gazette* of May 1948, a paper published in the new journal, *Problems of Philosophy* by M. A. Markov, the former defended modern physical theories (though not the philosophical interpretations given by their western authors) against attacks from the standpoint of materialist orthodoxy. Kedrov, the editor of *Problems of Philosophy,* who had refused to publish Maximov's article except as a contribution to the discussion, condemned the tendency to replace the former cult of Hegelian dialectics by materialism. Furthermore, he attacked the ridiculous extremes to which Maximov had gone in emphasising the contribution made by Russian (non-Marxist) philosophers to the development of Russian natural science. This would replace the Marxist appreciation of the class content of ideas by

a narrowly nationalist outlook. Although Kedrov had acknowledged the merits of the pre-revolutionary Russian scientists, and
even conceded that the philosophical inspirators of the early stage
of the Russian revolutionary movement relied on Russian rather
than on foreign science, he was now attacked in party official
publications for his alleged attempt to halt the struggle against
servility to alien culture. In a letter to the Editors of the journal
of the party's Propaganda Department he had to recant.[53] Leadership of the philosophical profession passed again into Alexandrov's
hands. It appears that during the nine months which had passed
since the decision on the party intervention in Lysenko's favour
much of Zhdanov's approach, rather than this preference for a
particular philosophical school, had been dropped. His death
was only a secondary factor in these developments (more important facts may eventually be known in connection with the real
background of the 'Leningrad case' of 1949).

The new trend soon made its appearance in a witch-hunt
against the 'un-patriotic' art critics who failed to appreciate that
type of novel and drama which was encouraged by the decisions
of 1946 and by the ample rewards offered in consequence of
those decisions.[54] Unless it is assumed that only under foreign
influence the nation of Chernyshevski, Tolstoi and Gorki reaches
proper literary standards, the issue could have been defined in
simple terms of whether a critic's interest lies in the improvement
of artistic standards, or in ensuring a large public for novels and
plays of the desired propaganda content. True, in that case the
'cosmopolitan' critics could have asked whether propaganda so
poor that no good works of art were inspired by it could serve
the public interest from a long-term point of view. For example,
whether a presentation of the real difficulties and conflicts facing
Soviet reconstruction—which certainly would encourage capable
authors to give their best—rendered less service to the nation's
cause than the usual embellishment of actual Soviet conditions
(with the Stakhanovite boy marrying the Stakhanovite girl after
they had improved upon their records and slight disagreements
about the best technical methods had been happily settled) or
the caricatures on foreign conditions which provoked in every
Soviet citizen who occasionally went abroad the question of how

much of what he had been told by domestic propaganda was a lie. To avoid such awkward questions, the critics' civic loyalty and patriotism were questioned, with anti-Semitic overtones in the more popular aspects of the campaign against the 'cosmopolitans'. In the atmosphere created by the biology intervention and the drive against 'cosmopolitans', demands of all kinds of schools for official recognition as part of the party creed rose like mushrooms. Among them was Olga Lepeshinskaya whose controversial experiments alleged to prove the organisation of new cells from living albumen of a non-cellular structure (an observation which, if correct, would have supported Lysenko's ideas on the possibilities of influencing inheritance by changing the organism's general conditions of life).[55] Then Pavlov was defended against some of his pupils' alleged reliance on Freudian psycho-analysis and even against some of them devoting excessive attention to research on the functions of the lower parts of the nervous system, the spinal cord and the sympathetic nerves, at the expense of the study of cortical functions.[56] In the latter case, the very name of the founder of the school should have satisfied national pride in a field where no honest westerner disputes Pavlov's greatness. The incompatibility of Marxism with psycho-analysis as a philosophy (as distinct, of course, from methods of treatment, applied in the USSR as anywhere else) may be taken as recognised by every Soviet scholar. Of practical applications of the Pavlovian theory, today as at the time of the 1950 Conference, emphasis on therapy of all kinds of disorders by artificial sleep (so as to give the forces in the cortex their opportunity of action) and a sound denunciation of psychiatric treatment by lobotomy (so popular in US) are evident. It is difficult to imagine that a major crisis in Soviet Research Institute occurred before these things were accepted. We are forced to the conclusion that the struggle of academic cliques (which goes on in the USSR as elsewhere) offered ample opportunities to party leaders to demonstrate that the party's philosophy as well as national pride required some definite solution to every major problem arising in any field of knowledge.

But such eagerness was bound to over-reach itself. The brutality with which the Lysenko school purged the academic

institutions of its opponents, may have invited comparisons with
the regime of Arakcheyev under Tsar Alexander 1. Although
Stalin coupled his intervention against the Marr school in linguistics with the just-mentioned establishment of a standard of
orthodoxy in the psychological field, he found it convenient to
use the Arakcheyev argument against the Marxists. The eagerness
with which the protagonists of the 'anti-cosmopolitan' drive chose
nuclear physics of all fields of knowledge as a suitable stage for
witch-hunting may have convinced the Politburo that the price to
be paid for ideological encouragement might be too high. If
there is any truth in the *post eventum* explanations of Voznesenski's fall because of his voluntarist deviations, the party leaders
might easily find that the necessary correction could best be carried
out by the denunciation of voluntarist speculation in some field
where it could be done without undermining the authority of
scientists who had just received official party backing, or the trend
towards stronger national self-assertion.

If this interpretation is correct, the field of linguistics offered
an ideal opportunity for correction. Not by mere accident was
this intervention (apart from the statement of his standpoint in
the economics discussion two years later, which was the party
leader's normal business) the only one directly carried out by
Stalin. The field was sufficiently removed from practical politics
and production efforts to allow for a frank discussion without
undesirable implications, yet near enough to history and general
sociology to attract general interest (and to allow for such genera-
lising statements as Stalin would wish to make). An attack
upon this particular brand of innovators would encourage sound
learning in general yet, because of the particular kinds of mistake
made by them, also strengthen national pride.

The immediate issue of the linguistics discussion[57] were the
teaching of the late Academician Marr, one of the very few
Russian scholars of first rank who from the very start collaborated with the Soviet regime and tried to apply Marxism to their
specific field. Starting with application of the traditional methods
of comparative linguistics to an ever-increasing number of new
languages, recent and extinct, Marr at first tried to solve difficulties by the construction of a new 'Japhetic' group of languages

spoken by the pre-Indo-European population. The similarities as well as the differences between modern languages were said to have arisen from the process of fusion between conquerors and conquered. Since 1924, however, he replaced this concept by one of parallel 'Stadial' developments, the similarities existing between the so-called Indo-European languages being explained by the similarity of the social structures of the peoples who had arrived at that stage of development, at least by the fact that they were class-divided. (Marr never attempted any explanation of how definite changes in language would follow from those in socio-economic structure nor of the occurrence within certain language families of societies representing very different stages of social development). According to Marr, observable affinities of languages result not from the divergence of peoples originally speaking one, or kindred languages but from the *convergence* of the original tribal languages as a result of the fusion of tribes into larger peoples and the development of their societies according to certain universal economic laws. Marr's further speculations about the origin of tribal languages from certain elements common to all mankind were so vague that he himself later abandoned them. After his death, they were upheld only by the most fanatical of his pupils (in particular when they aspired to introduce Marrism as the standard of political orthodoxy and, following Lysenko's example, tried to provoke their opponents by exaggerations).

Notwithstanding the early efforts of Marr's students to proclaim his theory as the Marxist and 'proletarian' one, ever before Stalin's intervention Marr's School of Linguists never attained a status of equilibrium with the traditional, 'comparative' one. Still, in spite of its obvious shortcomings it appealed to Marxists as an alternative to the well-known nationalist, and even racialist, associations of the Indo-European theory. It replaced assumptions of migrations and conquest as shapers of history by emphasis on the internal development of diverse societies. For the orthodox, Marrism—even in some modified form—had the merit of clearly placing language amongst those phenomena which were regarded as 'superstructures' resting on the socio-economic basis and being shaped by it. As it is clearly impossible to place it directly amongst economic phenomena this appeared, indeed, as the only way to give it a place in the Marxist scheme of society. True, modern Russians have experienced the transition from feudalism to capitalism and from capitalism to socialism without its being accompanied by any major change in the system and vocabulary of their language. In the party setting existing before Stalin's death, however, nothing of his personal intervention would have destroyed the Marrist's claim to Marxist orthodoxy.

Marxism would probably have gone on as one leftist trend existing in the field of cultural activity unless the party intervention in Lysenko's favour had encouraged its supporters to seek a monopoly in *their field*. During the first half of 1949 leading party periodicals, including *Pravda,* and the Presidium of the Academy of Sciences of the USSR indeed condemned their opponents.[58] The encouragement which they received behind the scenes is shown by the fact that quite a few of them took the platform when, on May 9th, 1950, *Pravda* opened its columns for discussions. The strength of Marrism in the accepted dogmatic framework was illustrated by the fact that even its opponents hesitated to criticise the description of language as a superstructure, bound to develop in leaps. Stalin was the only person who had the authority to re-interpret party ideology. There was something unrealistic in Bolshevik's criticism (in June, i.e. shortly before Stalin's intervention) of 'certain professors who did not find the courage to maintain their point of view in questions concerning their speciality, simply because in some newspaper a review or article on these subjects had appeared, and what is more not always a sufficiently qualified one....'. (Similarly Zhdanov, three years before, had criticised the philosophers for their cowardice shown in not criticising a book apparently written with official approval. In either case, the reproach amounted either to not having made a heroic stand on behalf of science against the party machine—this, presumably, neither Zhdanov nor Stalin would have desired—or to not having correctly guessed which of the conflicting cliques in the machine would get the upper hand). In his intervention in the linguistic dispute, on June 20th, Stalin did something to undo that harm by criticising the 'Arakcheyev' regime (true, in a field where its establishment was aimed at by people with whom he disagreed), by recognising Marr's merits in his specialised field, as distinct from his generalisation, and by avoiding repressive measures against the defeated school. After submitting to Stalin's criticism, the leading Marrists retained leading academic posts, including leadership of those research institutions which were devoted to their special fields in linguistic research.

In the substance of his intervention, Stalin cut the ideological knot by defining superstructures as institutions created by ruling classes for the purpose of the preservation of the existing social order. It follows that language, being created by the whole of society and serving all classes of society, can be no superstructure. Nor is it a means of production, as it serves purposes much broader than the production process. It follows that at least this social institution is created not by the particular classes of society but by society as a whole. This last conclusion may be upheld independently of Stalin's teleological definition of superstructure (which was influenced by his own efforts to create such ideological superstructures as he deemed useful for society and, because of its contradiction to the classical Marxist approach, came under criticism as soon as Stalin's 'cult' was denounced).[59] It has been obvious for Marx and Engels that the class-struggle takes place within nations. All the earlier pre-occupation of Marxists—including Stalin himself—with the problem of nation would have been senseless unless it was supposed that the classes co-existing, and opposing each other, within one society formed a unit in that sense.[60] Quite apart from the overtones of national pride, which were evident whenever Stalin spoke of the Slavonic languages' capacity to absorb different national cultures, it was politically important that in the summer of 1950 Stalin explained that for the duration of capitalism, the bourgeois and the proletarians of a capitalist country 'will be bound together by every economic thread as parts of one capitalist society'. He intended this statement to be distributed and thoroughly propagated by all means at the disposal of the State party. In the field of domestic politics, Stalin stated the obvious fact that languages do not develop by leaps but in a prolonged gradual development. He added 'in general for the benefit of comrades who have an infatuation for explosions' that, even for the economic basis and the superstructure, 'the law of transition from an old quality to a new by means of explosion....does not necessarily apply for a society which has no hostile classes'. He illustrated his concept of gradual transition by the collectivisation of agriculture, which in 1938 he had described in a more realistic way.

In intellectual life, the most evident follow-up of Stalin's intervention in the linguistic dispute was a general search for other intellectual phenomena of a non-class-bound, and therefore non-superstructural character, however inconsistent that search, is bound to appear from a Marxist point of view. (Stalin's case for the interpretation of language as an institution belonging to society as a whole rests precisely upon its character as a means of intercommunication serving equally all the members of the national society, while the Marxist case for expressing law, the arts, or religion in terms of class rests upon their enforcing the interests of a certain class against the others, or expressing ideas grown in the course of social conflict). In the particular climate of Stalinist Russia, however, conservative educationists would defend separate education of boys and girls. One of the 'achievements' of the conservative trend of the war-period which was already coming under attack, was a natural implication of the different functions of men and women in the social division of labour, originating in primitive society.[61] Stalin's peculiar reinterpretation of the social conditioning of 'superstructure' as not being *caused* by class-divisions but *serving* the interests of the ruling class also presented those who wished to emphasise the merits of the Russian classics (most of them obviously shaped by the social conflicts in Tsarist Russia but few of them contributing directly to the formation of the ideology of the socialist state to come) with the alternative of either accepting the alleged ideology of Tsarist Russia as a treasure of socialist civilisation, or to assert the non-class character of outstanding works of arts. Most preferred the latter. These disputes[62]—interesting, in their days, as an outlet for disagreement the straightforward expression of which was not yet possible—went on for a year or two until the artificial character of Stalin's definition became obvious. Of course, it was formally dropped only after his death.

(c) THE CRISIS OF THE STALIN SYSTEM

In the address to the economists, on February 4th 1932, Stalin had correctly stated that Russia was given ten years to make good for the backwardness of a hundred and fifty years. When on November 22nd, 1942, the prongs of the counter-attacking Soviet armies closed round Hitler's Stalingrad troops, the fate of the world was decided. Ten more years were given to Stalin to prove that he could not only enable his nation to win a decisive war but also make sure that its fruits would mature. At first, there was no choice. American credits for reconstruction were available to the USSR only on condition of withdrawal to her pre-war frontiers, with the implication that the rest of the world would be organised by a power in control of the atom bomb and basically hostile to all that the USSR stood for, and that new *cordons sanitaires* would be established in East Central Europe. In order to restore the economy disrupted by the war, efforts not inferior to those of the pre-war period and a corresponding degree of social discipline were required.

In 1948, however, the pre-war output of coal and steel, and about two years later (the date varies for the different groups of workers) the pre-war level of real wages was reached.[63] The number of workers and salaried employees in 1950 reached the figure of 38.9 million, as against 31.2 million in 1940 (in industry alone it had increased by nearly 60 per cent). It had already exceeded that of the collective farmers plus the remaining individual craftsmen.[64] Even in the villages seven years' education now became fairly general[65] and it could be taken for granted at least amongst those skilled workers who entered industry after the war. The penal sanctions against absenteeism, the enforcement of which had been difficult, went into abeyance. By a decree of June 14, 1951, they were restricted to cases of repeated and prolonged absence from work without excuses (in the typical case, this meant attempts of workers to enforce their dismissal). On November 13th, 1952, they were withdrawn from the decrees which prohibited tractorists and combine drivers to leave the MTS without permission and which obliged engineers, technicians and skilled workers to accept transfer to other enter-

prises where they were needed.[66] As, in view of the continuing
emphasis on the production of producers' goods, absolute wage
increases were bound to have inflationary effects, since 1950 it
became the government's policy to let the workers share in the
country's increased prosperity by annual reductions of retail
prices. But since the workers' general standard of life still caused
them to spend by far the larger part of their incomes on food
or industrial goods the output of which depended on that of
agricultural raw-materials, the state of agriculture formed the
main obstacle to the development of industrial incentives. Efforts
to increase agricultural output by general campaigns for the introduction of improved cultivation methods failed because of the
lack of sufficient incentives within agriculture itself (even if the
cultivation methods recommended were of less questionable
character than the introduction of the *travopolye* system all over
Russia). The introduction of more differentiated methods of
remuneration within agriculture which was resumed in pursuance
of pre-war efforts[67] failed. This was partly because the total
rewards available for the collective farms were too low to allow
for better payments to the efficient workers lest the inefficient
be reduced to zero, and partly because the existing methods of
agricultural administration required party secretaries to squeeze
out every hundredweight of product from the efficient farms to
make good for the failure of the inefficient ones. It was the merit
of Valentin Ovechkin's sketch *District Routine*[68] that this wrong
method of approaching agriculture was not only noted—this
the government had done long ago—but also associated with
the very method of managing agriculture by order and command
in which the party had indulged since the early days of collectivisation. It was a shortcoming of Ovechkin and of the whole
first period of the 'thaw', that the solution to the difficulties was
envisaged essentially as a replacement of the methods of coercion
indulged in by the great and little Stalins by more civilised ones !
What room could there be for persuasion if the very means of
persuasion was taken away from the farms ?

These practical and political issues stood in the background
of the discussion amongst the economists which opened in
November 1951 and was concluded by the formulation of Stalin's

observations published on the eve of the XIX Party Congress under the title *The Political Economy of Socialism*. This 'political testament' of Stalin had diverse aspects (to some of which we shall later have to return). Its central theme, however, was the question whether, and to what extent, the law of *value*—that is to say, production for a market—remained relevant under socialism. At that time, as distinct from discussion in our days, it was still taken for granted that the state could fix the prices paid between its own enterprises according to considerations of expediency. On the other hand, it was obvious that the external trade of the USSR, at least outside the 'socialist camp' (consciousness of the need to pay proper prices even to the allies of the USSR increased only after Stalin's death), had to be carried out at world market prices. It was also obvious that the prices paid by Soviet consumers depended upon the law of supply and demand. The real dispute hence concerned whether (a) the prices paid to collective farms for their output need be in proper relations to production costs, and (b) whether this being confirmed, such a state of things was compatible with the socialist character of the Soviet economy. Two 'deviations'—both possibly reflections of policy arguments proceeding in higher places—were advocated in the discussion amongst the economists. Yaroshenko described the very continuation of exchange relations as incompatible with socialism (i.e. he advocated, in substance, the nationalisation of the kolkhozy). Venzher and Sanina, on the other hand, suggested that the farms should be allowed to purchase the machinery from the MTS, i.e. from those very institutions which had been established in order not only to help them in their production effort, but also under the title of payment in kind, to collect a large part of the obligatory deliveries. The interesting fact about the Venzher-Sanina suggestion, which was realised six years later, is that its rejection by Stalin (who had had Bukharin executed for similar suggestions) was moderate in tone. Yaroshenko's standpoint, on the other hand, was rejected in very sharp terms, though it hardly exceeded the repetition of an old-standing dogmatic argument. Stalin formulated the party line in the dispute by stating, on the one hand, that the existence of collective-farm property alongside State property was 'already beginning to hamper the powerful development of our productive forces' since it created obstacles to the inclusion of agriculture in centralised planning. He argued against Venzher and Sanina on the ground that the realisation of their proposal would greatly increase the sphere of market operations (he also questioned the collective farms' capacity properly to replace obsolete machinery ; in 1958 this argument was rejected on the ground that, meanwhile, the farms had become economically stronger). On the other hand, Stalin regarded the preservation of market relations for a considerable time as compatible with the socialist character of Soviet society. Since objective economic laws could not be overruled by party decision the eventual replacement of commodity exchange by exchange of products (i.e. the abolition of the market) must be a gradual process. In the outcome, agricultural policy remained unchanged. Even after Stalin's death increased taxation of the kolkhoznik's private plot was regarded as fair. During 1952 total livestock and the index of total agricultural output decreased even in comparison with 1950. In Moscow Province, the number of auxiliary economies with an income of more than 4000 rubles decreased between June 15th, 1952 and June 12th, 1953, by 11 per cent.[69]

In the international field, too, Stalin's very triumph involved his system in a deep contradiction. He had conquered the party under the slogan 'socialism in one country' yet the USSR was no longer the only country building socialism as defined in the course of its own development. In 1946 Varga described the 'democracies of the new type' as dominated by State capitalism, where the State was no longer an organ of the bourgeoisie even though private ownership of the means of production was preserved as a rule.[70] At the foundation Congress of Cominform the representatives of the 'People's Democracies' protested against such a description of their economies.[71] In 1947 Varga had described them as transition stages to socialism.[72] The hardening of international tensions during that year caused (on either side of what was soon known as the 'iron curtain') withdrawals from the ambivalent descriptions of transition stages based upon the forces which during the war had been in sympathy with the different partners in the 'Great Alliance'. In France and Italy,

under American pressure, the Communists were removed from
the coalition governments while the East European 'people's
democracies' were soon described as specific forms of the dictatorship of the proletariat.[73] The conflict with Yugoslavia
strengthened the Russians' desire to define that dictatorship as
rule by a Soviet-controlled party. Such insistence on strictness
of control (like so many aspects of Stalin's policies) restricted
the external popularity of the Soviet system. This was the price to
be paid—not too unwillingly by supporters of 'socialism in one
country'—for increased centralisation and homogeneity. In
any case, the weight of the People's Democracies was insufficient
to justify an interpretation of any differences in their system from
the Soviet pattern as more than local modifications.

The position changed fundamentally with the triumph of the
Chinese communists. At first, the Chinese revolution was still
treated as one of those bourgeois-democratic revolutions in backward countries in which, according to old-standing Leninist
tenets, hegemony had to be assumed by the proletariat. The
fact that it implied emancipation of a formerly semi-colonial
country brought it even nearer to the categories established by
the Comintern programme of 1928. But in 1952 the Chinese
communists, having solved the most elementary tasks of the
restoration of the destroyed national economy, proclaimed the
beginning of their country's transition to socialism while making
very serious efforts to integrate their national bourgeoisie
into the new society. They refrained from describing their
regime as a dictatorship of the proletariat. (They accepted the
formula as late as their Politburo statement of April 4th, 1956,
'On the historical experience concerning the Dictatorship of the
Proletariat', i.e. after the dropping, by the CPSU's reconciliation
with Tito and and by the decisions of the XX Party Congress,
of the. identification of 'proletarian dictatorship' with the
particular Soviet model). In this field, Stalin reacted to the
new data by half-hearted acceptance. In the *Economic Problems of Socialism* he spoke of the formation of a second, socialist
world-market but failed to draw any conclusions as to the future
of international politics from the great change in international
relations. One might even interpret his 'second world-market'

as a dispensation from the liberated to compete in the first one. In order to demonstrate that his country might escape the horrors of a new war, Stalin still argued that wars between the imperialists were unavoidable. If there was any sense in the argument it would have led, in the autumn of 1956, to emphasis on potential American backing for the Egyptian resistance against the Anglo-French invasion rather than on the anti-imperialist content of Arab nationalism.

Much attention has been given to the frictions which developed in the intellectual sphere during Stalin's last years. This is partly due to the greater opportunities for publicity available then and partly because of the conspicuous part played by writers and other artists (at least in those aspects of the post-Stalin 'Thaw' which have been most noticed in the west). Yet to anyone who does not start from the assumption that the Soviet intelligentsia was the main driving force in the post-Stalin changes (which is merely an inverted formulation of its description by Stalin as 'engineers of the soul') it should be clear that the writers were concerned about social issues of *general* importance rather than their own professional worries. One example is co-education. In the conservative atmosphere of the Great Patriotic War, separate education of boys and girls had been introduced for the senior forms of secondary schools in large towns. Notwithstanding its being backed by Stalin it never ceased to be a controversial issue. In 1950 it was openly discussed in the *Literaturnaya gazeta* and its implications as regards the position of women in society were firmly raised. When the discussion stopped in the press—presumably because it was regarded as inconvenient at party headquarters—it continued in city and county educational authorities on a more practical level, with the result that when it was re-opened in 1953, the system recommended by the central authorities had already been abolished at most places. By then, the 'development of particular feminine traits', praised in 1950 by conservative headmistresses, was denounced as 'inculcation of a parasitic way of life'.[74] Meanwhile the XIX Party Congress had envisaged the introduction of polytechnical education, i.e. the close association of teaching with preparation for practical work. Formal reintroduction of co-education in all the schools followed within a year. The example is interesting in that it shows the limitations of the ideology of the late Stalin period and also the beginning of its abolition even before Stalin's demise.

In the field of literary production, too, the changes started before the XIX Party Congress. The reactions of the public in the capital cities to indifferent plays after the 'cosmopolitan' critics were silenced were registered by low box-office returns. In March 1952 the semi-official pattern of 'conflictless drama' became the issue of a discussion in the periodical *Sovetskoye iskusstvo* (Soviet Art).[75] Truly ridiculous examples of regulating the respective number of positive and negative heroes, and the standing within the official hierarchy allowed to a hero, were quoted. This type of petty regulation had hardly originated higher up than in the minds of theatre directors afraid of the smallest risk of being involved in another 'anti-cosmopolitan' drive. But everyone knew that these minor sinners had been afraid of people *very* much higher up, including the very same people who now permitted and even encouraged criticism of the excesses committed in the application of what was still supposed to be a correct line. The inhibitions regarding the depiction of actual conflicts of Soviet life were due to a political restriction. Soviet literature was not allowed to exercise that very function of criticism which, according to Zhdanov, formed the lever of progress in a socialist society. When this restriction was lifted, the time-seeker who tried to save his position by explaining how he had been forced to write what was demanded from him, made his appearance, one and a half years before he was described by Pomerantsev and Ehrenburg as a typical figure on the stage of Soviet art. Of course he got his beating. When Surkov, writing in the *Bolshevik*[76] officially rejected the theory of 'conflictless drama' he denounced those authors 'who attempt to blame others for their faults' and warned against the danger of a revival of Zoshchenko's mistakes. But he also quoted Stalin's old warnings against fear of facing the truth 'however bitter it may be' and called for new Gogols and Shchedrins to show the shortcomings of Soviet society. This call was soon repeated by Malenkov from the platform of the XIX Party Congress.

The basic contradiction of Stalinsim, however, lay in its very mode of operation based upon, and finding its justification in, the rule of the party, i.e. a broad organisation which could not exist as a living body, and still less retain power against potential competitors, without discussing the urgent issues of national life. In circumstances where every disagreement on major policy issues might be treated as treason, Stalin's manoeuvrings and perhaps also the effect of arteriosclerosis on an ageing man (upon which Khrushchev naturally laid much emphasis when denouncing these developments), led to his narrowing down the leadership. Yet the approach of his end—about which his doctors appeared to have spoken frankly with him—demanded the settlement of the succession problem in a way which would secure continuity of the party's rule. A party Congress, duly convened and prepared by discussion and election in the party organisations, provided the legitimate setting in which prominence could be given to the successor elected by Stalin (it was Malenkov) under the old leader's very eyes. Also the people with whom he would have to work would get the authority of a Central Committee duly elected on a definite platform (this was provided by Stalin's *Economic Problems of Socialism*). Stalin also deemed the time ripe for a discussion preceding the Congress as the country's increased economic strength showed itself in the improvements of the people's conditions. Such improvement was described in the *Economic Problems of Socialism* as the basic law of development of a socialist society. The call for definite improvements, in particular in housing, together with the voicing of local demands for suitable investments, played a prominent part in the pre-Congress discussion.[77] Malenkov's report to the XIX Congress and the decision on the Fifth Five Year Plan adopted by it envisaged a reduced share of investments but an increased share of the output of consumer's goods in the national product. Rural conditions should improve in a step slightly quicker than urban standards of life.

Yet to turn economic activities towards greater satisfaction of consumer's needs demanded from the party organisations activities far broader than when they worked as mere propagandists for the fulfilment of plan targets. As in the days of the great purge, though in a more promising atmosphere, appeal to the individual communist sense of responsibility became the obvious check on the tendency of those in local authority not to preserve discipline towards the national authorities while demanding strict discipline. In the documents of the XIX Congress and in the articles published afterwards[78] great emphasis was laid on the necessity of fighting tendencies to put the local (or factory) interest before the national one in fulfilling plans, to mislead the central authorities as to plan fulfilment, to squander State property for the benefit of local organisations, or even worse, for that of individuals. Party members were invited to be vigilant against clique spirit, nepotism and the old-Russian evil of *votchina,* i.e. little kingdoms controlled by individual members of the higher bureaucracy. In some cases the party's unifying function was associated with definite efforts to repress local autonomy. In 1951-52 the alleged Mingrelian conspiracy caused Stalin, acting without Politburo assent, to have many Georgian party workers arrested, and some even shot. The party could not fulfil its function as the uniting agency in decentralised reconstruction unless it was revived from the lethargy caused by the purge and the military conception of party discipline practised by Ovechkin's Borzov in his master's image. On the eve of the XIX Congress, Ovechkin had left it open whether Borzov or his critic Martynov, who relied upon methods of persuasion and incentives, would get the higher party authorities' support. Notwithstanding all its shortcomings, the Congress made its contribution to the eventual decision in Martynov's favour.

Even more than at the XVIII Congress the shifts in the party's compositions and ideological attitude were recognised when the Rules adopted by the XIX Congress replaced the former (1934) definition of the Communist Party as 'the organised vanguard of the working class . . . exercising the leadership of the working class, peasantry, the intelligentsia, of the entire Soviet people' by its description as 'a voluntary militant union of like-minded communists, consisting of people from the working class, the working peasants and the working intelligentsia'. It removed the term 'Bolshevik' which, to speak with Khrushchev's theses for the Congress, was a mere synonym of 'Communist'.

But 1952 was not 1939. By the very convention of the Congress, and by the discussion preceding it, it was visibly demonstrated that the party organisations and their conference were the place where millions of people could discuss and voice their opinions. The Congress emphasised the point extending the rights of party members to discuss issues of party policy (this right had formerly been limited to practical questions only). Their duties were re-defined to include those 'to develop self-criticism from below, to report shortcomings in work to the leading party organs, up to and including the Central Committee of the party, irrespective of whom it may concern,' 'to permit no concealment or distortion of the truth', in particular towards the party organs, and 'daily to strengthen contact with the masses, to respond quickly to the requirements and needs of the working people'. The observation that the party had only one discipline valid for the leaders as well as for the rank and file helps to illustrate the background of the Congress.[79]

The Congress made its contribution towards solving the succession issue by getting the main report from Malenkov. Stalin's participation was restricted to a short speech on communist international solidarity and the prospects of eventual world-wide triumph by revolutions in the capitalist countries, promoted through the example of socialist construction in the USSR. The intellectual outlook of the dying man thus combined his youthful dreams with the unexpectedly great triumphs of his ripe age. His organisational suggestions, however, followed the pattern established by Lenin in an analogous situation. The party's leading organ was broadened by enlarging the Presidium of the CC (as the Politburo now was called) to twenty-five members and eleven alternates. Since the arrangement of 1923, against Lenin's violation, had led to the ascendancy of an individual leader (namely Stalin) Khrushchev may be right when stating, in his secret session report, that Stalin in 1952 wished eventually to eliminate 'old Politburo members' (i.e. competitors of Malenkov; as this implication could not be made explicit at the XX Congress, Khrushchev made the most of such attacks as Stalin directed at the first Plenary Meeting of the CC elected by the XIX Congress against Molotov and Mikoyan).

Whatever Stalin's intentions, the enlargement of the Presidium failed to achieve the supposed purpose, and the old Politburo members continued to work together as its 'executive committee'. Immediately after Stalin's death this smaller committee of ten members and four alternates resumed full responsibility as the Presidium of the CC, the other members of the enlarged Presidium being returned to ordinary CC, and in some cases ministerial status. More successful was another measure of the XIX Congress—the broadening of the full CC to 125 members and 111 alternates, a substitute for the Party Conferences (which, according to the Rules, were to be held every year but had not been convened since 1940). At the XX Party Congress it was further broadened to 133 members with 122 alternates. Because of the events following Stalin's death, the Beria crisis and the need to concentrate the country's attention upon the agricultural problems, Plenary Meeting of the CC were held even more frequently than required by the new Rules. Invitation of leading party, state and managerial officials from the Provinces to attend in an advisory capacity became the rule.[80] The Presidium of the CC proved to be a body just small enough to allow for its working as a collective leader and large enough to carry the party's authority against Beria's attempt to concentrate power in the hands of the political police. The broadened CC enables the participation in central decisions of more local leaders than ever before—not excluding the days of the civil war when the frequent congresses and conferences were attended by a comparatively small numbers of delegates.

NOTES AND REFERENCES

1. Cf. B. S. Telpukhovski's article in *Voprosy istorii KPSS*, 1958, No. 2, which is based on archive materials; S. M. Klyatskin in *Voprosy istorii*, 1958, No. 7.
2. Sources: ibid. *Partiinaya zhizn*, 1957, No. 20, p. 88; 1. Petrov, ibid. 1960, No. 4, pp. 52 ff.; *Kommunist Ukrainy*, 1958, No. 2, p. 8.
3. The *Istoriya velikoi otchesvennoi voini Sovetskovo Soyuza*, 1941-45, vol. III, p. 588 gives the figures of 1368 and 1787 million respectively of new admissions. Party losses during the first year of the war (which included the lost battles of 1941, the most critical stage of the siege

of Leningrad, and only semi-successful Soviet counter-offensives in early 1942) are assessed by Telpukhovski, as quoted in note 1 at 400,000. Losses in the two Stalingrad battles (in particular during the first, defensive one when there was no superiority in men—not to speak in material—to the invaders) can hardly have been smaller than during the first battles of the war ; in the second, offensive battle there was on the Soviet side a slight superiority in material, but not in men (on either side about a million man were involved.—ibid. p. 26). No figures for total party admission in 1944 are yet available, and admission policy may have changed during the last two and a half years of the war. The above estimate of losses in 1943 is purely tentative, based upon the assumption that losses as well as admissions slowed down during the last victorious stage of the war. If the difference between admissions and losses during the last eighteen months of the war should amount to less than 700,000, which is possible but not very likely, my estimate of 600,000 losses of party members in 1943 would prove exaggerated. Losses in party members include, of course, civilian death, which in places such as Leningrad, in particular in 1942, were high above the normal death rates, and expulsions from the party, the number of which was not negligible in the front or in the rear, in view of the vastly increased demands of the war economy upon civic discipline.

4. Ibid.

5. *Partiinaya zhizn,* 1946, No. 1, p. 24.

6. Ibid. 1947, No. 20, p. 83.

7. The figures for 1941 cited in the previous chapter refer to specialists with higher or secondary education, professional army officers being explicitly excluded. So were civil servants with non-socialised secondary education (only a few at the time) and party officials whose schooling in party schools was combined with the corresponding general educational level. According to the source quoted in the preceding note, by January 1st, 1947, 148,000 engineers, 24,000 agricultural specialists, nearly 40,000 doctors and 80,000 pedagogues were party members. Even if, particularly in the last-mentioned group, only teachers with high education are counted, this leaves still 100,000 party members with higher education outside the enumerated professional groups. The proportion amongst specialists with higher, and those with merely secondary education in 1941 was 3.5. If this proportion held true also amongst those specialists who were party members, communist specialists with higher education employed in the national economy on January 1st, 1941, numbered about 225,000, as against more than 300,000 six years later. Allowing for the fact that in the course of the war some civilian engineers became professional army officers, the increase in the numbers of party members with academic qualifications roughly corresponded to the increase in general

party membership (the increase in the number of party members with secondary education was much larger).

8. Western readers who are used to other criticisms of Stalin's strategy on the eve of the war should remember that his responsibility was to the peoples of the USSR, and that such broader loyalties as even the father of 'socialism in one country' realised surely contradicted any attempt to base the future of the USSR on the reliability of allies who were its opponents at the time, before, and after.

9. *Partiinaya zhizn,* 1946, No. 1, and 1947, No. 4.

10. On the occasion of his dismissal in December 1957, Zhukov remarked that this was the second time he was removed from the party's Central Committee. The first decision could have been taken only at the meeting in February 1947, or at some earlier one about which we do not know.

11. Cf. John A. Armstrong, *The Soviet Bureaucratic Elite,* New York, 1959.

12. *Voprosy istorii KPSS,* 1959, No. 1, p. 189.

13. *Partiinaya zhizn,* 1948, No. 5, p. 27. By that time, 60 per cent of the Districts had carried out their party conferences.

14. *Partiinaya zhizn,* 1947, No. 13, p. 37.

15. Khrushchev in *Partiinaya zhizn,* 1948, No. 5, p. 12 ; see also, ibid. No. 3, p. 31.

16. English Translation in *Soviet Studies,* vol. IV (1953), pp. 447 ff.

17. Op. cit.

18. *Partiinaya zhizn,* 1947, No. 4, p. 47.

19. Ibid. No. 17, p. 47.

20. Cf. the materials given in *Soviet Studies,* vol. II, pp. 70 ff. and 345 ff., and sources quoted here.

21. Cf. ibid. vol. III, pp. 298 ff.

22. Cf. *Soviet Studies,* vol. IV, p. 432 ; Suslov in *Pravda,* December 24th, 1952 ; editorial of *Kommunist,* 1953, No. 2. It is just possible that these mild reproaches—which, even if true, would clearly not justify anyone's execution for treason—implied some stage in the rehabilitation of Voznesenski, unavoidable already during the last months of Stalin's life.

23. Reported in *The Times,* March 19th, 1956.

24. Cf. the editorial of *Partiinaya zhizn,* 1947, No. 14.

25. The term had been coined by Stalin, in the autumn of 1932, in a talk with a group of writers to whom he pointed out the general purposes of 'Socialist realism'.

26. Their internal coherence is emphasised, for example, by their joint publication in the introductory part of the collection of decrees, *Direktivy VKP(b) i postanovleniye sovetskovo pravitelstva po narodnomu obrazovaniyu,* 1917-1947, Moscow, 1947, pp. 77 ff.

27. Zhdanov, op. cit. p. 20.

28. Cf. S. M. Dubrovski's article in *Voprosy istorii,* 1956, No. 8, where

the not very Marxist views on the role of the individual in history expressed by Stalin are emphasised. Some overtones of what Khrushchev had to say in his secret session speech about Stalin's intentions, if he had lived longer, are unmistakable.

29. *Kommunist,* 1957, No. 3.

30. Cf. Zhdanov and Gorodinski, as quoted in A. Werth's *Musical Uproar in Moscow,* London, 1949, pp. 47 and 65. In spite of some omissions, this book is the most extensive presentation of the discussion available to the English reader. Reviews, by J. Miller and K. E. Birkett, have been published in *Soviet Studies,* 1949, No. 2.

31. Cf. for example, Ivanov, Bely and Kabalevski, as partly translated in Werth, op. cit., pp. 66, 71-77 and 78.

32. Ibid. p. 69.

33. Cf. Nestiev (representative of Moscow Broadcasting House), ibid. p. 84. Nestiev, however, regarded the appeal of the 'formalist' Soviet composers upon a likeminded western public as an asset.

34. Zhdanov, op. cit. pp. 62-63.

35. Ibid.

36. Even at the 1948 Conference Nemchinov, head of the Timiryazev Academy of Agricultural Sciences, raised the question of his resignation because of his continuing defence of the freedom of competition between different schools (*The Situation in Biological Science,* Proceedings of the July-August 1948 session of the Lenin Academy of Agricultural Sciences of the USSR, Eng. ed., Moscow 1949, p. 559). In the survey of Soviet Science given in the last (post-Stalin) edition of the volume *SSR* of the *Great Soviet Encyclopaedia* the 'cytogenetic' school of biology and 'the school headed by Lysenko' are treated as equally right. Data about their main representatives and lines of research are given. After 1958, however, a tendency to protect Lysenko, on the ground of his practical achievements, against the danger of becoming a victim of 'de-Stalinisation', was evident. He was even allowed to address the XXI Party Congress in January 1959, though he was not a party member. Even in articles intended to destroy the authority of Williams' conceptions of *travopolye* rotations with which Lysenko's original triumph had been associated, tributes were paid to the less controversial of Lysenko's views. Cf. the article published by Pryasnikov and Sokolov in the memory of Academician D. N. Pryasnikov, one of the once condemned opponents of Williams, in *Pravda,* December 11, 1961. The moves and countermoves around the recognition, in Lysenko's views, not of a consistent application of Marxist dialectics to Biology (this, of course, had become impossible since the XX Party Congress) but still some useful contribution to the practice of agriculture continued right up to Khrushchev's fall : only then the defeat of Lysenkoism was completed by the establishment of the Genetics Institute of the Academy of Sciences and by the official investigation, by a joint Committee

of that academy, the ministry of agriculture and the Academy of Agricultural Sciences, of the achievements of Lysenko's allegedly model farm. A whole issue of the *Vestnik Akademii Nauk USSR* (November 1965) was devoted to the publication of the report of this investigation, plus Lysenko's not very impressive replies.

37. In Yury Zhdanov's letter of Stalin (of July 10th, 1948, published in *Pravda*, August 7th (English translation in *Soviet Studies*, vol. I, pp. 175 ff.), it is taken for granted that the balance of practical help given by the two competing schools—as distinct from moral encouragement—lay in favour of Lysenko's opponents.

38. Opinions about the fitting of either school into the socialist world-outlook differed even before the October Revolution. I personally learned in Vienna, 1916-17, about these implications from Dr. Kammerer, an enthusiastic neo-Lamarckist who went to Moscow in the twenties and committed suicide in 1926 after the discovery of what was described as a faked experiment. As Kammerer was since regarded by Soviet supporters of 'the school of inheritance of acquired characteristics', who included, for example, Lunacharski, as a victim of the persecution by the orthodox geneticists, it may be taken for granted that his experiments, if in any way promising, would have been repeated. But even the Lysenko school, in the days of its triumph, restricted itself to general tributes to his memory.

39. *Pravda*, December 16, 1911.

40. *The Situation* . . . , as quoted in note 39, pp. 308-9.

41. Ibid., p. 615.

42. Zhdanov's letter to Stalin, op. cit.

43. Even more harm was done to the standing of orthodox Western genetics in the USSR by Soviet sympathisers trying to convince its leaders of the desirability of the application of the methods of animal-breeding (including artificial insemination of women from a few superior fathers) in a class-less human society. Cf. Julian Huxley, *Soviet Genetics and World Science*, London, 1949, p. 184. Huxley's failure to understand the need for the USSR (with or without party dogma in science) to reject such views, is characteristic of that way of thinking of some Western scientists which provokes bitter resentment in the USSR.

44. This point was made even by Nemchinov, who defended Zhebark and Dubinin's freedom of argument. Cf. *The Situation* . . . , p. 557.

45. Ibid.

46. Cf. Yury Zhdanov's letter, op. cit. Polyakov insisted, in his very declaration of submission, that he would go on fighting Lysenko on this point (*The Situation* . . . , p. 623).

47. Ibid., pp. 602 and 30.

48. Ibid., p. 335. There was no reply to this reproach.

49. The book was published (in Russian) by the Academy of Sciences, 1946. The first stage of the discussion was by Varga himself in a

special Appendix to the November 1947 issue of the journal *Mirovaya khozyaistvo i mirovaya politika* which subsequently was closed down but resumed, under a slightly changed title, after the XX Party Congress (English translation in the *Current Soviet Thought* series published by the Russian Translations Project of the American Council of Learned Societies, comments by F. C. Barghorn in the *American Slavic and East European Review*, October 1948, and by me in *Soviet Studies*, vol. I, pp, 28 ff ; ibid., pp. 172 ff., a summary of Varga's eventual self-criticism, from *Voprosy ekonomiki*, 1949, No. 2).

50. Having read that volume before its being withdrawn from circulation I could find in it no more Hegelianism, and no less criticism of Hegel than was current in all Marxist books. After Stalin's death the traditional Marxist assessment of Hegel's contribution to the formation of Marxism was restored. Cf. T. Oizerman's article in *Kommunist*, 1955, No. 2.

51. A commentary, by J. & M. Miller, was published in *Soviet Studies*, vol. I, pp. 40 ff. See also G. Wetter's *Dialectical Materialism* : *A Historical and Systematic Survey of Philosophy in the Soviet Union*, English ed., London (Routledge & Kegan Paul), 1958.

52. I have discussed earlier stages of the struggle for the recognition of modern physics in the USSR in *Zeitschrift fuer Sozialforschung*, Paris-New York, 1939, No. 1-2.

53. For the materials of this discussion, cf. *Soviet Studies*, vol. I, pp. 84 ff. and 178 ff.

54. Cf. the materials published in *Soviet Studies*, vol. I, pp. 178 ff. Y. Lukin's article Soviet Dramaturgy and a certain Group of Critics, available in English in *Soviet Literature*, 1949, No. 5.

55. Cf. the collection *Sessii, konferentsii i zasedanii akademii meditsinskikh nauk*, 1950-52 gg., published by the Academy, 1953, pp. 51 ff.

56. Ibid., passim. The Proceedings of the Conference which met from June 28th to July 4th, 1950, have been published in a special volume (only in Russian). English translations of the fairly full *Pravda* reports are available in *The Current Digest of the Soviet Press*, August 5th to September 9th, 1950, an attempt at evaluation by W. W. Gordon in *Soviet Studies*, vol. III, pp. 34 ff.

57. The most extensive report on that discussion is by J. Ellis and R. W. Davies in *Soviet Studies*, vol. II, pp. 209 ff. A translation of Stalin's contributions was published in the Soviet Newsletter Series, 1950.

58. Ellis and Davies, loc. cit., pp. 230-1.

59. Cf. Kammari in *Kommunist*, 1956, No. 10, and the Editorial of *Voprosy filosofii*, 1956, No. 3.

60. Stalin's speaking of 'society' as the substratum carrying language—and possibly, other not class-conditioned forms of social life—follows from his having, since 1913, reserved the term 'nation' for particular (capitalist, and later socialist) stages in the development of the unit

which in Western sociology is usually described as 'nation' (using for its description vague terms such as 'nationalities'). Cf. my *Marx, his time and ours,* London, 1950, pp. 349 ff. The use of the term 'nation' for that historical continuum obscures the changes in its substance which have occurred with the growth of capitalism. On the other side, Stalin's terminology of 1950 by-passes the basic Marxist conception of society as class-divided.

61. Poznanski, writing against Korolev in *Sovetskaya pedagogika,* 1951, No. 7 ; in No. 9 he was answered by Goncharov.

62. Reports on them were published in *Voprosy filosofii,* 1951, No. 2 and in *Izvestiya akademii nauk, seria ekonomiki i prava,* 1951, No. 4 ; see also P. F. Yudin's article in *Vestnik akademii nauk,* 1951, No. 7, F. Konstantinov's article in *Bolshevik,* 1951, No. 11, and P. S. Trofimov in *Voprosy filosofii,* 1951, No. 2.

63. *Narodnoye khozyaistvo SSSR,* p. 37 gives only percentages from which, for 1950, a level of the real wages of *all* the workers and salaried employees at 125 per cent of the 1940 level (about 135 per cent for those employed in industry, railway transport etc., 115 for the rest) may be calculated. It is not clear whether the footnote which explicitly states how the real wages were calculated, refers to both the links of the necessary calculation or only to the comparison between real wages in 1950 and 1955. Even if the correctness of the whole statement is taken for granted, it follows from the policy of wages differentiation pursued in those years that an average of 115 per cent pre-War real levels for all groups of workers and salaried employees outside industry must have included considerable groups which were just attaining the pre-War level.

64. Ibid., p. 188.

65. Cf. ibid., p. 224. This statement is not intended to imply that 'incomplete secondary education', as the seven years' school had been called in pre-War days, became general by 1950. In Azerbaidzhan villages, even on the eve of Khrushchev's educational reform, it was still necessary to enforce it, in particular as far as girls were concerned. Cf. the decree of the Azerbaidzhan government published in *Bakinski rabochi,* April 9th, 1958.

66. The existence and content of those decrees, which before was a matter of guesswork amongst Western scholars, was confirmed by the decree of April 25th, 1956, which removed all violations of factory discipline from the competence of the courts. *Vedemosti Verkhovnovo Soveta SSSR,* No. 10(852), art. 203.

67. Cf. the materials translated in *Soviet Studies,* vol. I (1949), Nos. 1 and 2.

68. Published in *Novy mir,* September 1952 ; English translation in *Soviet Studies,* vol. IV, pp. 447 ff.

69. Cf. *Soviet Studies,* vol. V (1953), pp. 164, 229 and 236, and M. I.

Piskotin, *Nalogi s selskovo naseleniya v SSSR, Izdatelstvo akademii nauk SSSR*, 1957, p. 72.

70. *Izmeneniya v ekonomike kapitalizma v itoge vtoroi mirovoi voiny* (Changes in Capitalist Economy in the outcome of the Second World War) Moscow, Ogiz 1946, pp. 323 and 291-92.

71. Cf. the special Appendix to the November 1947 issue of *Mirovoye khozyaistvo i mirovaya politika* (see note 49, above) (Kuzminov's speech).

72. *Mirovoye khozyaistvo i mirovaya politika*, 1947, No. 3. The article was written before the attack against Varga's description of state capitalism (in the West) as something different from classical mono-poly capitalism, which I have reported in *Soviet Studies*, vol. I, No. 1 (1949).

73. Cf. B. Bierut's report to the foundation Congress of the United Workers' Party of Poland, in *For a Lasting Peace, for a People's Democracy*, 1949, No. 1.

74. *Soviet Studies*, vol. II, pp. 180 ff. and 322 ff., vol. V, pp. 316 ff. ; vol. VI, p. 316.

75. Reported by D. L. Meek, ibid. vol. V, pp. 188 ff. ; see also ibid., pp. 78 ff., 199 ff. and 445-46 (on films).

76. 1952, No. 9.

77. Cf. the materials on the preparation of the XIX Party Congress, collected in *Soviet Studies*, vol. IV, pp. 296 ff.

78. E.g. Zhukov's article in *Kommunist*, 1952, No. 20.

79. Khrushchev's Theses, p. 311 in the English translation in *Soviet Studies*, vol. V.

80. Struyev at the XX Congress, *Pravda*, February 19th, 1956. At the Plenary Meeting of the CC in December 1958, which dealt with agricultural problems (its full proceedings have since been published), even a number of non-party kolkhoz-chairmen and scientists were invited, and took the floor. This practice was maintained whenever practical tasks for industry or agriculture were discussed by the CC, though, since Khrushchev's fall, these greatly advertised mass-meetings have been pushed back by orderly, and confidential meetings of the CC proper, a few specialists being invited to the relevant meetings.

CHAPTER VIII

THE PARTY AFTER STALIN

(a) BERIA'S FALL, THE 'THAW' AND THE EMPHASIS ON AGRICULTURE

THE EVENTS described in the preceding section fit normal concepts of political life within a state party. There is another aspect of developments about which it is impossible to speak with the assurance required from the historian because we have no reliable evidence other than Khrushchev's speech at the secret session of the XX Congress, which incriminated one of the potential culprits, but exonerated others. During the last months of his life, even more than the compaign against 'cosmopolitans', Stalin played with the darkest force of traditional Russian nationalism, anti-semitism. In June 1952 he had a number of communists of Jewish extraction, amongst them Old Bolsheviks such as Lozovski who from boyhood had learned to despise Zionism and all its works, executed for treason. 'Treason' was found in their proposal to replace the Birobidzhan Soviet alternative to Palestine by a more inviting one in the Crimea, which was almost uninhabited since the Tartars—or what remained of them—had left with their German protectors. During the winter of 1952-53 'Doctors' case' was built up, with implications which can only be guessed at but which appear to have been in Khrushchev's mind when he said that Molotov and Mikoyan could hardly have attended the XX Party Congress if Stalin had survived a few more months. Whatever happened behind the walls of the Kremlin, Stalin's demise must have been regarded as a relaxation in a sense more literal than in the case of any statesman who does not vacate his place in time and hence proves an obstacle to the further development of trends which he himself has helped to start.

In any case, a three-member collective, composed of Malenkov, Beria and Molotov, was available when Stalin passed away. Their warning, in their first proclamation, against the danger of 'panicky disorientation' may have sprung from Beria's professional desire to demonstrate the need for his machine. Events during the following months suggest that the party and the country were riper for self-government than expected by those whose business was administration. Within fifteen days Malenkov found himself faced with opposition against his uniting in his own hands—presumably in accordance with Stalin's will—the leadership of the Government as well as of the party. Even if he had a choice, from his policies during the following year it appears that he was bound to choose the premiership, as with Stalin's demise the party was bound to recede into the background. In substance, though not in form, the main responsibility for the party machine was transferred to Khrushchev who at the XIX Congress had acted as the main spokesman on organisation questions. As distinct from Stalin at the corresponding stage of his career, Khrushchev's political record was not equal to that of some members of Stalin's old guard (yet, even of these, only Molotov was included in the narrowest circle of the 'collective leadership', and even he was regarded as junior to Malenkov and Beria whose own political experience was not superior to that of Khrushchev's). Like Stalin in 1923, Khrushchev in 1953 was one of the old leaders who was least associated with the dogmatism of the preceding period. As distinct from the brilliant speakers and journalists who had been Stalin's competitors for the leadership, however, Malenkov and Beria were just such machine men as was Khrushchev himself. The great difference was that they had won their spurs in activities which now were regarded with greater suspicion than the career of a successful Provincial Secretary.

The first acts of the new leadership demonstrated that the country had had enough of Stalin, but the amnesty of March 27th, 1953, showed a reluctance to undo precisely those works of Stalin's 'justice' which were resented. Apart from hundreds of thousands of peasants who had been imprisoned for long terms under the Draconian laws enacted in 1947 for the protection of socialist property, other hundreds of thousands of ordinary criminals were set free so that for years the courts were kept

busy with punishing their new crimes! The only clear directive
given to the jurists who had to amend the criminal code was
that the punishment of officials' offences (those in which the
manager might easily be involved) should be reduced. For a few
months Stalin's name was in complete eclipse, possibly because
of the influence of Beria. Then it made its reappearance in
public documents as one of the outstanding party leaders and
pupils of Lenin. In future, however, the part played by leading
personalities was linked to their function as servants and mouth-
pieces of organisations.[1] Since then, in Soviet historical writing
all importance is given to the statement that 'it is the people
who make history'.

In the last days of June, Beria was arrested and eventually
executed under the 'Kirov laws',[2] the same under which he had
sent so many, and better, people to their death. Certainly his
colleagues put more responsibilities on his shoulders than actually
were his, but there is no reason to doubt that he aimed at the
establishment of his personal dictatorship and thus forced his
colleagues to act lest Stalin be succeeded by a police chief and
the party be transformed into the propaganda machine of a police
state. Beria, with ample information about public opinion at his
disposal, knew that some dissociation from Stalin's deeds might
promote the popularity of a new regime. He failed to grasp that
even more popularity could be earned by disposing of himself
and of his police machine. The Plenary Meeting of the CC held
in July 1953 'approved of the resolute measures taken to liqui-
date the criminal activities of Beria and his associates'.[3] The
communique issued at Beria's trial[4] was a public repudiation of
GPU and its successors (put into even sharper light by the
tribute paid to Cheka, which had honestly served the revolutionary State in its gravest hours) and of the murder of officials
of which Beria now was accused. The mention of the Ordzhonikidze case in this connection and the revision of the 'Leningrad
affair' in the course of the trial of Beria's associates, showed that
the new leaders were not afraid of destroying the authority of
the 'purge'. The reduction of the police to the status of an
ordinary Government Department was marked by the appointment of a comparatively junior official as Minister of Internal

Affairs, without a seat in the Presidium of the CC in the inner cabinet, by the transfer of the MVD troops to the Ministry of Defence, and the concentration of counter-intelligence proper in a special Committee for State Security directly under the Government. On the very day when Beria's fall was announced, *Pravda* asked the party organisations closely to supervise every state institution and in particular the organs of State security.[5] However natural such relations are in communist ideology, they had been nearly inverted at the time of the 'great purge'. An unsuccessful attempt by Stalin to return the party machine to police control may have characterised the dark events of the winter 1952-53. On September 1st, 1953, the power of the Administrative Board of MVD (the 'Special Conference') to exile was abolished so that punishment could no longer be inflicted except by the normal judicial procedure.[6]

The disappearance of physical terror and the destruction of the myth of Stalin's infallibility (which, even though not explicit at the time, was implied in what was said in public about Beria and his works) led to an immediate weakening of intellectual controls for which no reasonable case in accepted party ideology could be found. Discussions on Lysenko's theory, in strictly specialist terms, had started in the *Botanicheski zhurnal* as early as 1952. Lysenko's general position was not in trouble before his close association with *travopole* propaganda in its most extremist applications, and the methods applied by him in patronising his followers, made him a target for the grain production drive. Scientific achievement was recognised even when it had come into conflict with the less formalised manifestations of party orthodoxy. In the autumn of 1953, Markov, as well as the main representatives of the reasonance theory (another victim of the dogmatics' attacks), were elected members of the Academy of Sciences. Since then no limits appear to have been put to the appreciation of new scientific theories even in the party's philosophical periodical though, of course, there are controversies about their interpretation (as exist amongst the scientists themselves).

Western appreciations of changes in the Soviet intellectual climate were most affected by literary publications, not by those which, like Ovechkin's *District Routine*, directly dealt with the country's organisational problems, but by those dealing with the artists' own professional problems. During the early autumn of 1953 the institutional setting of Soviet arts, as developed during the preceding quinquennium, was questioned in three articles, the most important parts of which are available in English translation.[7] Ilya Ehrenburg's article 'The Writer's Work' was published in the October issue of *Novy mir*. Pomerantsev's article 'Sincerity in Literature', which carried the point much further, appeared in the December issue of the same journal. The November issue of *Sovetskaya musyka* published Khachaturian's article 'On Creative Boldness and Inspiration', as the second leading article, along with a picture of the author. All three authors spoke in very frank terms about the unsatisfactory state of Soviet arts, though there are differences in emphasis. This varies from the statement of Ehrenburg's supposed correspondent that 'our artistic literature is weaker and paler than our life', to Khachaturian's description of the conventional type of music foisted by the machine of the Union of Soviet Composers upon the people as 'second-hand goods', to Pomerantsev's denunciation of the kind of literature officially encouraged during the last years. He calls it an artificial distortion of the truth, be it done crudely by fabrications or, more subtly, by a choice of subject in which the real difficulties and contradictions of Soviet life disappear. On the other hand, all three authors agree on the need for purposeful art and its close connection with the aims pursued by Soviet Society. Ehrenburg, who more than the others dealt with the achievements of the arts of all nations (at a time when the nationalism of the preceding period was not yet officially repudiated), regarded tendentiousness as a characteristic of all great art. Pomerantsev stated that a general communist world outlook could be taken for granted although differences of opinion were possible within that common framework. He saw writer's task precisely in raising controversial issues. It follows that the bureaucratic framework which controlled artistic production was the main (though not the only) culprit of the shortcomings of Soviet arts. The others were the artists themselves!

All three authors agreed that the artist should create only what he feels (and not what is put by the bureaucracy on the order paper of topical priorities). Khachaturian as well as Pomerantsev denounced the type of artist who wrote with a feeling of responsibility to the artistic bureaucracy rather than to the people. Ehrenburg positively emphasised the artist's duty to follow his creative impulse. If the artist is inspired by the ideals of his society, works of arts cementing that society will emanate only if light is thrown on its difficulties and growing pains. Here, however, the difference between the three authors starts. Ehrenburg (and, of course, Khachaturian who, being a musician, had to depict psychical experience) saw the artist's task as description of the inner life of the people in which the life of society is reflected. He denounced the former demand for 'production novels' which, bypassing the heroes' private lives, give information which every engineer writing a popular article can give much more competently. Pomerantsev, however, was afraid that, under the new dispensation, readers would get tired with love stories just as before they got tired with production achievements. His article ended with an illustration of the wealth of material which could be collected during the conversation in a railway compartment. Lawbreakers (including uncontroversial ones like illicit whisky-brewers) in the course of their effort to serve the common good are prominent amongst the heroes suggested by Pomerantsev as rewarding subjects for writers. He might be suspected of even condoning illegality committed with an honest intention to serve the common good, for instance managers' breach of existing regulations if committed with an intention to fulfil the plan. Even if the party could tolerate a description of those authors who had served it under the earlier dispensation as mere timeservers, it could not possibly leave to the publicists the right to decide which laws should be obeyed and which, pending their repeal, be disobeyed. Yet the way in which Pomerantsev was criticised implied a come-back of those who disliked writers criticising shortcomings of Soviet society before these had been denounced by the Central Committee; and even of those who found the former tendency to embellish Soviet conditions in accordance with the party line of those days as being essentially correct.[8] No wonder that students who were afraid of such a come-back defended Pomerantsev against his critics, though not without reservations.[9] When Surkov, secretary of the Writers' Union, defended in the columns of *Pravda* the traditional party-line in literature (though conceding individual mistakes committed in its application), *Komsomolskaya pravda,* which had first published the students' letter, made a complete turnabout.[10]

While these arguments were going on, some works representing the critics' efforts at using the novel and drama as a means of promoting progress made their appearance. As the party's attack against bureaucratism developed, Ovechkin's further instalments, though becoming sharper, found official approval as soon as they were published.[11] Before the year closed, Korneichuk's play *Wings*,[12] in which the party's past agricultural policies as well as the investigation methods of the political police were described in unmistakable terms, was greatly applauded, particularly by Khrushchev and other party leaders who attended the Moscow premiere. Some other literary products, however, raised more controversial questions.

In his novel *The Thaw*, published in *Znamya,* May, 1954, Ehrenburg depicted the most distasteful phenomena of the Stalin period—the persecution of the relatives of those 'purged', the anti-semitism of the period of the 'doctors' plot', and the time-serving manager who defends whatever policy he has just found explained in *Pravda* and greatly disapproves of the Jewish doctor who was disturbed by what has happened (he is also eager to find 'little stains' such as foreign relatives on the record of colleagues from whom he fears an attack). Such statements, and even the famous title of Ehrenburg's novel (with the mere limitation, in my opinion justified, that Ehernburg in that title promised more than he kept) were passed without objection by Ehrenburg's critic.[13] The trouble started with those parts of the story—most important from Ehrenburg's point of view—which deal with the position of art under the dispensation of the late Stalin period. Amongst Ehrenburg's heroes there are two painters : Volodya Pukhov, the time-server who produces what is demanded, knowing that it had no artistic value, and Saburov who paints for its own sake without caring whether anyone will purchase and exhibit his works. Saburov is right, but even Pukhov, the victim of forces stronger than himself, is sketched not without sympathy. The established management requires from him who wishes to swim against the current a strength of character which Volodya Pukhov, in contrast to his father, the old Bolshevik Andrey Pukhov, does not possess. And it is not only an issue concerning arts. Says Pukhov, at one occasion : 'The insulted are not liked in our country ; only successful people . . . are trusted'. Eventually, however, the 'successful' manager is demoted by intervention of the CC because in order to show greater successes he has spent funds earmarked for workers' housing in new factory investments resulting in a breakdown of emergency housing accommodation. Four years later, in a novel intended to attack *The Thaw*—the novel as well as the social phenomenon—Kochetov declared that the manager depicted so unfavourably by Ehrenburg had been right.[14]

The deterioration of standards is also treated in L. Zorin's play *The Guests*.[15] Three generations meet in the country home of an old Bolshevik who once served in Cheka. His son Peter is a very influential official in the Ministry of Justice who, knowingly supports injustice because he wishes to be on good terms with some officials in higher positions. The grand-children eventually pass judgement by leaving their father's home and joining the struggle for the vindication of justice (it finally becomes unnecessary as *Pravda,* the *deus ex machina,* is just coming out against the injustice committed). For our purposes, it is not the contents of very average play, but Zorin's interpretation of the situation existing in the USSR which is important. Says Peter: 'A post of responsibility is a dreadful thing: it has its own morals, its code. It does not allow you to be kind. The State machine is an orchestra ; if you wish to play in it, follow the baton and accept its rhythm.' His younger sister who strongly condemns the bureaucratic attitude explains it, however, in similar term: the enjoyment of power has corrupted those who wield it. The friend to whom she talks observes that power has not corrupted all those who exercise it—not her father, Alexey, for instance. But Alexey is an old Bolshevik. In Peter's opinion the standards which he represents do not fit the new times. Notwithstanding the timely intervention of the *deus ex machina* it is clear enough that Zorin expected relief from a revolt of the young against the Stalin generation. Tribute is paid to the merits of the Old Bolsheviks without the latter being regarded as very helpful in our days. No group within the CC was likely to accept the theory that power by itself corrupts those who wield it. Yet the bureaucracy's self-assertion caused Zorin's 'slanderous' work to be put out of bounds in terms so drastic that, as Korneichuk remarked in his report to the II Writers' Congress, experienced writers said: 'Tell us exactly how far we can go and then we can write satires'.[16]

More important for the future of Soviet society than the literary explosions of tensions long accumulated was the practical reversal of the former approach to agriculture as supplier of the 'dan'. The concessions made to the diverse strata of the population by the new collective leadership included a reform of agricultural taxation, introduced by Malenkov's speech to the Supreme Soviet on August 8, 1953. A change in basic policies was heralded by Khrushchev's report to the plenary session of the CC of September 3-7, 1953, and by the decisions adopted by that session.[17] The frankness with which Khrushchev spoke about the failure of the collectivised economy to restore the livestock destroyed in the collectivisation process both eliminated much of the Stalin myth and anticipated the arguments of those who preferred a conventional solution to the crisis. The reduction of obligatory deliveries of livestock products, and the increase in prices for obligatory deliveries as well as for excess state purchases (*zakupka*) reversed the former policy of skimming off a maximum of the agricultural surplus-product. In such a setting, the condemnation of the practice of collecting from the better working farms such deliveries as the weak farms failed to supply (and thereby destroying the good farms' incentive to work) was likely to be more effective than it had been at earlier occasions. But complaints about circumvention of the prohibition have continued till the very liquidation of the Machine Tractor Stations in 1958. The distribution of labour days to each farm now demanded greater attention since otherwise the increase in the delivery prices for livestock products and vegetables (i.e. the products of the private plots), might cause the peasants to devote extensive attention to the latter. (Safeguards against such developments were established by the ruling that if any member of a household failed to work the minimum number of labour days, the household would have its tax liabilities as well as its compulsory delivery norms, for example for meat, increased by 50 per cent.) The farms' organisation problems were tackled by strengthening both the technical help available from the Machine Tractor Stations and leadership within the farms themselves.

To achieve the first aim, and to counter the increased profitability of private plots under the improved marketing conditions, tractor drivers were made employees of the MTS as combine operators already were. Thus they got a guaranteed minimum pay and the benefits of social insurance and paid holidays. Factory schools analogous to those training skilled workers for industry were organised to train new tractor drivers and combine operators. Already in the spring of 1954, 100,000 agricultural specialists were to be relieved of their work in various administrative offices and directed to work in the farms as employees of the MTS. This implied a trebling of the number of agricultural specialists employed in collective farms and MTS (the goal was reached as late as September 1955).[18] Khrushchev suggested that 50,000 urban party workers should be sent to the villages where, though not specialists, they should permanently settle and apply their organisational experience. The suggestion had to wait for another one and a half years before adoption.

As late as 1953, only 80 per cent of the enlarged *kolkhozy* had primary party organisations. But party guidance was to be brought as close as possible to the farms, so that the bossy-bureaucratic approach to rural problems current in many places was avoided. The post of political deputy to the MTS director, which had played such an important part in earlier stages of collectivisation, was abolished, party guidance of the farms being exercised, not by the District committee but by special groups of instructors for each individual MTS zone, headed by a secretary of the district committee. Since many decisions could now be taken on the spot, the large number of formal meetings at District headquarters and conferences of all kinds were said to have been reduced.[19] The instructors' groups were of varying strength, in

some cases up to five farms being served by one permanent in-
structor. In one example which was evidently regarded as good,
a group of five instructors served the MTS and eleven farms.[20] The
need to strengthen the rural party organisations and the fact that
many district organisers moved to the farms to assume posts as
chairmen, necessitated the posting of Provincial (or Republican)
officials to the rural districts. In small Lithuania, 210 Republican and city officials were sent to the Districts. 57 of them
became District party secretaries, 16 became Chairmen of District
(Soviet) Executive Committees, 95 instructors, propagandists
and heads of departments in District party officies, 19 secretaries
of party organisations of Machine Tractor Stations.[21] A reduction in the senior staff of the Provincial and Republican party
organisations by 20-25 per cent was envisaged. The strengthening of the rural party organisations must have increased the weight
of the party as a whole as against the state apparatus. In personal terms, this strengthened the position of Khrushchev who had
realised the key position of agriculture, whereas his colleagues
still moved within the traditional framework, trying to satisfy as
much as possible the demands of the most vocal parts of the
people by price-reductions, increases in the output of consumers'
goods (so far as these could be produced by industry) and reduction of Stalin's ambitious investment schemes.[22]

A reversal of the last-mentioned policies was necessitated by
the very drive for agricultural reform which, in its turn, was a
necessity if the most urgent of consumers' needs were to be
satisfied. The decisions of the Plenary Session in September
1953, encouraged livestock-farming and vegetable-growing. In
order to restore the balance and to supply the feed necessary for
increased livestock, the Plenary Session of February-March 1954
devoted special attention to measures intended to increase grain
production.[23] The most spectacular of these measures was the
campaign to open new cultivation areas in the East (32 million
hectares—i.e. 80 million acres—were planned, and actually
cultivated during the first two years). Two-thirds of these virgin
lands were to be brought under cultivation by *kolkhozy,* the
other third by state farms (the question of the eventual lines of
development of Soviet agriculture was thus left open). The

labour force required was built up partly by encouragement of the migration from the old agricultural regions, and partly by an appeal to the *Komsomols*. 350,000 young men and women went to the new lands.[24] Leading officials, specialists and skilled workers were systematically directed from existing MTS and state farms as well as from industrial and other enterprises to the new MTS and state farms. The new farms received a priority on the assignment of young graduates of agriculture. In connection with these measures, and with the necessary strengthening of the existing Machine Tractor Stations, state investments in agriculture were increased from 12 million rubles in 1953 to 21 million in the 1954 plan—still a comparatively modest beginning in comparison with what was to follow.

Grain production in the existing farms received new attention. The technical measures suggested included a break with Williams' *travopole* system in the regions where its application had resulted in a reduction of grain production. Some supporters of that approach who had held high posts in agricultural administration were demoted, after frank criticism in public, to less senior posts. Lysenko himself was criticised in *Pravda* for the methods applied by him in promoting the careers of his supporters.[25] Positive measures included a campaign for the growing of suitable feeding grains, particularly maize, in the collective farms so as to increase their livestock and, even more important, their productivity. In June 1954 another Plenary Session of the CC supplemented the incentives created in September for livestock-farming and vegetable-growing by a reduction in the obligatory deliveries (at a still very low price) of grain, combined with an increase in the prices paid for excess (*zakupka*) deliveries. Increased stability of the farms which were properly managed created the conditions for increased demands on the *kolkhozniki's participation* in collective work, which now could be better rewarded.[26]

Meanwhile, power had shifted within the leading group. There is no reason to doubt that Malenkov's resignation, on February 9, 1955, was caused by his opposition to a renewed increased investment in heavy industry. Before and after Stalin's death he was a protagonist of meeting consumers' dissatisfaction by a re-orientation of industry towards the output of consumers' goods, agriculture (a basic re-organisation of which required huge long-term investments) being treated within the limits of the existing framework. These limits were narrow enough. Already at the September 1953 session of the CC Khrushchev stated (apparently against farmers' demands which went much further) that the concessions regarding potato and vegetable prices had gone so far that the state would have to sell at a loss. (This did not prevent the party from subsequently increasing these and other agricultural delivery prices even more.) The last general reduction in the prices of consumers' goods occurred in April 1954. It was also the smallest (with the emphasis on consumers' goods produced by industry). The common man, as distinct from the Stakhanovite or member of the intelligentsia who could afford nice clothing and a television set, needed good food in ample supply more than anything else. He could not get it unless agriculture was expanded, which was impossible without further investments. Malenkov and his friends apparently refrained from the risks involved in large-scale investments in opening the new lands. Unless, by definition, consumers' interests are described as opposed to investments, it is hardly proper to describe Khrushchev's approach as opposed to consumers' interests. In particular, he wished to relieve the housing shortage which, however, required further large-scale investments. It was necessary to secure maximum satisfaction of urgent needs. A builders' conference was devoted to the introduction of standardised industrial mass-building. It rejected the parade architecture characteristic of the Stalin period.[27] Investments in the industries producing consumer goods was further restricted by the dangers of the 'cold war', accelerated by the remilitarisation of West Germany. The Soviet warning to the Western powers, in December 1954, against the consequences of German re-armament foreshadowed further developments. An increase in Soviet defence expenditure in 1955 by 12 per cent as against its level both in 1953 and 1954 was announced in Zverev's budget speech at the very Supreme Soviet Session which accepted Malenkov's resignation.

Malenkov, whose capacity of holding the highest office had been questioned fairly soon after he had assumed it,[28] appears to have offered only limited resistance. As his resignation even-

25

tually had to be tendered in a form which allowed for his con-
nuation as a member of the supposedly homogeneous collective
leadership, such evidence on the actual argument as we possess
is based upon a discussion with a number of economists. They
asserted in the autumn of 1954, probably in reflection of arguments proceeding behind the closed doors of the Presidium, that
the predominant development of the heavy industries had been
necessitated merely by the initial needs of industrialisation.
According to these economists, emphasis on the industries producing consumers' goods since 1953, far from being a mere temporary correction of planning mistakes committed earlier in the
opposite direction, reflected the normal state of a society directed
towards the maximum satisfaction of the needs of its members.
The spokemen of the party majority, on their part, regarded an
expansion of the production of consumers' goods as necessary.
This was partly in order to enable the latter expansion to continue over long periods and partly to enable the continuous introduction of new techniques.[29] Very different interests were involved
in the dispute. Khrushchev's support of agricultural development
prevented it from appearing as a mere conflict between defence
and industrial interests on the one hand and the consumer's
interest on the other (the outcome of such a conflict might have
been uncertain in the post-Stalin climate of opinion). For an
assessment of historical developments, it is irrelevant to what
extent Khrushchev acted from a mere realisation that Soviet
agriculture, more than any other section of Soviet society, needed
quick reform and to what extent he realised that a consistent
representation of the interests of a near-half of the Soviet people
offered the safest basis for his eventual attainment of leadership
(just as it is irrelevant for the historian to what extent, thirty years
before, the Lenin recruitment was undertaken because Stalin
realised that it provided the only means of saving the party from
the danger of stagnation, and to what extent by his expectation
that the new recruits would strengthen his position within the
caucus).

(b) POLITICAL REASSESSMENT : THE XX PARTY CONGRESS AND ITS AFTERMATH

In appearance, the year 1955 was one of the least dramatic in Soviet history. The smoothness with which the replacement of Malenkov by Bulganin could be carried out even strengthened the impression that, at last, a stage of gradual evolution in politics, without those dramatic accelerations or setbacks in the careers of individual politicians, had been reached. A man whose career had been pursued mainly in the party's cadres department and in Stalin's secretariat (and who himself remarked, in his letter of resignation,[30] that he had never headed a ministry) was replaced by a typical administrator with a record of service in Cheka (during the civil war), in important managerial posts under NEP, as Mayor of Moscow (1931-37), head of the RSFSR Government, of the State Bank, member of the Military Councils of diverse army groups during the war, member of the State Defence Committee (in 1944), and, since 1947, Minister of Defence and Deputy Prime Minister. The preponderance of state administration in the party's leading body, as confirmed after Stalin's death, was strengthened. To the inner cabinet of 'First Deputy Prime Ministers' (Molotov and Kaganovich since 1953), the 'Deputy Prime Ministers' appointed that year (Mikoyan, Saburov and Pervukhin) were added. Malenkov became an ordinary Deputy Prime Minister. Of the members of the Presidium, only Khrushchev, the first party secretary, and Voroshilov, the President of the Republic, remained outside the Government, the nucleus of which also formed the nucleus of the Presidium.

The priority of investments having been reassessed, the party could return its attention to technical reconstruction. At the Plenary Session of the CC in July 1955, which had been prepared by a conference of managers and industrial organisers, Bulganin described the situation as 'the threshold of a new technological and industrial revolution, far exceeding in importance the industrial revolutions associated with the appearance of steam and electricity'.[31] The existing industrial structure had served the purpose of concentrating the country's efforts on a few key production branches working with an already known technology.

Now it was necessary to decentralise technical research and management and to overcome the conservative tendencies which threatened industry with stagnation. Apart from the centralised direction of industry and the managers' fear of new and risky ways, the ideological attitudes which had developed during the period of national self-assertion were mentioned in this connection. 'Great harm is caused to technical progress in our country by under-estimating the achievements of technology abroad'. The transfer of factories and whole industries from Union to Republican Government, which had started in 1954[32] was to be accelerated. To promote technical innovation and its systematic application, a State Committee on New Technology was established and Gos-plan concentrated on long-term planning (the elaboration of the current annual plans was transferred to a new agency, the State Economic Commission).

In the field of agriculture, Khrushchev now got his opportunity to carry out, though on a more modest scale than originally intended, his plan of transferring urban party members with organisational experience to collective farms. The figure of 30,000 such organisers required in the announcement of April 5, 1955, suggests that about a third of the existing 87,000 farms were regarded as backward and needing organisational improve-ment. In the accompanying propaganda, tribute was paid to earlier party drives to support the re-organisation of agriculture from outside.[33] The task of the new messengers from the town, however, was more hopeful than of earlier ones who had had to enforce deliveries distateful to the peasants. Now it was a matter of helping the peasants, by proper labour organisation, to make use of the incentives offered by the Government. As Khrushchev reported at the XX Party Congress, 20,000 such organisers were actually sent to the farms. If, as a rule,[34] the farms with the weakest party organisations were also the economically most backward ones, the new organisers were sent to farms which had either no party units (still 7,356 at the time of the XX Congress) or only very small ones (10,850 primary party organisations in collective farms had only 3-5 members). According to Khrush-chev's report to the XX Congress, the primary units engaged in agriculture—kolkhozy, state farms and MTS—had one and a half million members. The fact that this figure was regarded as insufficient, illustrates the extent to which party's rooting in agriculture had risen since the days when 115,000 party members working in collective farms was treated as an achievement. Further additions to the collective farm *nuclei*, important in quality though not in quantity, resulted from the transfer of the agricultural specialists attached to the farms from the payroll of the MTS to *kolkhoz* membership. As a rule, these additions concerned the more prosperous farms which could reasonably remunerate an agronomist or veterinary surgeon.

Major reforms in the field of justice had been prepared already during 1954. In pursuance of what was still officially described as 'the Beria affair', re-examination of the cases of those 'purged' under Stalin was started. The results were so appalling that, at the XX Congress, Khrushchev had to argue against unnamed comrades, apparently in high places, who had arrived at the conclusion that the organs of state security in general should be distrusted. The huge number of revision cases arising in this connection may have led to the establishment, by the decree of August 14, 1954, of Presidia of the Provincial Courts and of the Republican Supreme Courts to which the power of revision, hitherto reserved to the Supreme Court of the USSR, was transferred,[35] together with the transfer of factories, and even whole industries, to Republican management. This measure represented a major step in the decentralisation of government. In order to safeguard the observance of the law, the statute 'On the Supervisory Functions of the Public Procurator' was enacted on May 24, 1955. Already on April 12, *Pravda* had stated that no citizen could be arrested otherwise than by decision of the court or with the sanction of the Public Procurator, who has also to supervise police investigation, and to order the immediate discharge of anyone arrested without ground. 'Every case of unfounded prosecution', *Pravda* said 'should be followed by the punishment of those responsible for it'.[36]

In the diverse fields of science, the 'thaw' resulted in the destruction of the monopolist claims of definite schools encouraged by party intervention. In some cases[37] there was a denunciation of the methods by which a monopoly was maintained (the party interventions as such remained taboo up to and beyond Khrushchev's day). On January 11, 1955, the *Literary Gazette*—once the protagonist of least interference with scientific research—under the heading 'Schools in Science' published an article by Academicians K. Knunyants and L. Zubkov. The harmful consequences of monopoly positions of scientific schools range from the failure of the Lysenko school to take notice of 'many facts firmly established in science and a number of urgent tasks in this field' to the 'lack of experimental discipline under which the necessary strictness of experiments is lost'. Moreover, the theory, instead of being based upon data obtained in nature and in the laboratory, 'itself begins to distort the experimental data, causing it to be viewed quite differently from what it is in fact'. The article mentioned the harm done by the authoritarian claims of established Soviet schools to collaboration of Soviet scientists with their colleagues abroad, mentioning in this connection the orthodox philosophers' attacks against the quantum concept and the theory of resonance.[38] When *Kommunist,* the party's leading theoretical organ, wrote[39] about the philosophers' harmful attacks against the theory of relativity (which could be put right only by the intervention of the scientists in the philosophical discussions), it no longer mentioned the biology discussion of 1948 as one of the many fruitful discussions in the diverse fields of science. Now, competing scientific schools were mentioned on terms of equality, without preference to those who in 1948-51 received party backing.

On January 1, 1956, the party had more than 350,000 primary organisations—nearly twice as many as fiften years before. As we have already noticed, nearly half the increase was due to collective farm organisations, the number of which had increased from 12,000 in 1939 to 80,000 in 1955. There must have been also a considerable increase in the number of army organisations. Since the XIX Congress, the total number of members and probationers had increased by a mere third of a million. In view of the discouragement of prolongations of the probationer stage (by the decisions of the XIX Congress), the 450,000 probationers included in the total of 7.2 million might be no more than admissions during the year 1955. Khrushchev was not dissatisfied

with the increase but criticised the failure of lower party organisations, in their policy of admission, to strengthen the working-
class nucleus of the party. The current concept about the importance of education as a criterion for admission to the party was
obstacle to that drive. In Georgia, for example, it was so deeply
rooted that some workers and peasants found it futile even to
submit applications for admission since these were so likely to
be rejected.[40]

To overcome such traditions takes time. As Suslov pointed
out at the XX Congress, the results of the drive for increasing
working-class membership might differ even between provinces
with comparable social structure. 47.2 per cent of the 1955
admissions in Sverlovsk Province, but only 32.2 per cent of
admissions in Novosibirsk Province (which includes the Kuznetsk
combine), were workers from the bench. In Omsk Province
31.7 per cent of the new admissions were collective farmers as
against 11.4 per cent in Stalingrad Province. In Belorussia, 60.8
per cent of the admissions in 1954-55 were workers and peasants.
This would not compare unfavourably with the early part of the
Stalin period (apart from special drives such as the Lenin recruitment) except that the new admissions constituted only a moderate
section of the party's total membership. Within the existing
membership, promotion and acquisition of additional qualifications were bound to reduce the percentage of workers at the
bench. In the outcome, 14.7 per cent of the total membership
on January 1, 1956, had higher education, as against 11.8 per
cent at the XIX Party Congress and a mere 7 per cent on
January 1, 1947. Another 22 per cent, i.e. about as many as
in 1947, had full secondary education. The percentage of
members with seven-years education had increased from 25 per
cent in 1947, when such education was still characteristic of
the better educated manual workers, to nearly 30 per cent in 1955
when it could be regarded as common among the young generation. Still, a third of the membership in 1956 had only education
upto the age of 11 (which was predominant in pre-war days in
the countryside and among industrial workers who had come from
the village). The number of specialists with higher education
who were party members had increased from 600,000 in 1941

to 1.88 million in 1956, their share in the total number of such specialists in the country from a quarter to a third,[41] their share in total party-membership from 15 to 25 per cent—even more if army officers etc. are included. To these a large number of party members who are specialists—practicians without higher or even specialist, secondary education[42]—must be added. Hence it is not astonishing that in 1955 a mere 42.4 per cent of the members even of those party organisations which operated in industrial, building and transport enterprises worked on the bench. Because of the change in admission policy after the XX Party Congress their share in 1958 exceeded half the total membership of these organisations.[43] Since the party at large contained many organisations with few, or no, manual workers, it is obvious that only a minority of the party members performed manual work in factory or farm. The workers' share amongst party officials was even smaller than their share in total party membership.

In the re-elections of party committees which preceded the XX Congress, the CC insisted on more manual workers and quoted with approval a number of cases where four of eleven committee members elected in major works were workers (but there were also instances where only a single worker was elected). Amongst the voting delegates elected to the XX Party Congress, 56 per cent were graduates, 7 per cent had been students of higher education institutes without graduating, and only a 5th did not have full secondary education. As 506 of the 1,436 Congress delegates were full-time party officials (there were also 12 trade union and 8 *komsomol* officials), and this group presumably contained a majority of 'self-made-men', the chances of an ordinary worker or peasant being elected to the Party Congress cannot have been great. Conditions at the republican congresses were similar.[44] Yet, though there was no profound change in the social structure of the party, its internal life became livelier on the eve of the XX Congress. Attempts of district committees to enforce their candidates for secretary upon primary organisations were discouraged.[45]

The need to take decisions by the regular bodies, meeting at the prescribed times and offering themselves for re-election after the expiry of their term of office, was now taken for granted. The convention of the XX Congress even before its statutory date was an illustration. There was no reason for this except the desire, now that the general lines of industrial and agricultural policy had been clarified, to have the Sixth Five-Year Plan adopted by the competent authority at the start of its period (as distinct from earlier Five-Year Plans which were sanctioned after their start). Yet as soon as the constitutional machine, together with public discussion and re-election of all party bodies, had been set into motion, the urge for reform which had inspired the nation since Stalin's death, quickened. Every major policy move of the leadership, such as Bulganin's and Khrushchev's journeys to Yugoslavia, India and other lands, when carried out on the eve of a Party Congress, was bound to lead to theoretical discussions in which different opinions would be expressed.

But it is remarkable that in spite of the novelty of many policies now advocated, no overt division took place. This may have been due partly to a desire to avoid divisions on theoretical issues, the practical implications of which were no longer controversial. Examples are the orientation of Soviet foreign policies towards a peace bloc with the uncommitted nations and the use of the USSR's increased economic potential for economic competition with the West for the sympathies of those nations. Even reconciliation with Yugoslavia, which involved a loss of prestige, appears to have been opposed by Molotov only.[46] Those who felt that in the Cominform dispute with Tito not all the wrong was on Stalin's side may have, however, felt that there was so much wrong in the methods applied against Tito's sympathisers in the People's Democracies that it might be preferable to make a clean start. The position of Stalin's closest associates was definitely weak in view of what was already trickling out about the dark aspects of his regime. As Malenkov had avoided a life-and-death struggle on the popular issue of consumers' goods (true, on that issue he was bound to be opposed by old industrialisers such as Molotov and Kaganovich), it would have been impolitic to wage a struggle with them on the merits of the 'Leningrad case', not to speak of the 'great purge'. The ideological preparation for the Congress[47] proceeded. It was directed against the dogmatism which might harm appreciation of the new international situation and against the cult of the individual, the manifestations of which in educational and practical work had caused considerable harm. The terminology recognised the un-Marxist character of the dominance of one individual, however outstanding, and the consequent fettering of mass initiative. No special tenet of Stalin's came under direct attack at that stage. Only his statement that the productive forces of capitalism were bound to decline during the 'general crisis of capitalism' was indirectly rejected as incorrect (on the eve of the Congress, this statement was denounced, without naming Stalin, as 'alien to Marxist teaching'; at the Congress itself it was the only point where Stalin was explicitly criticised in open session—by Mikoyan).[48] The only sign of internal arguments during that preparation period was Molotov's withdrawal, in a letter to the *Kommunist*,[49] of the statement made by him in February 1955 that in the USSR the *foundations* of socialism only had been laid (and not socialism established in the main, as the party dogma said since 1936). In February, the statement may have been made against Malenkov. It is possible that in internal discussions, Molotov was pressed to withdraw it because of its possible implications regarding the compatibility of the *kolkhoz-market* with socialism (in the sense of Stalin's *Economic Problems of Socialism*). If this is correct, the contradiction between Molotov's statement and Stalin's position of 1936 offered the occasion for his formal withdrawal from Stalin's standpoint of 1952.

A prolonged struggle behind the scenes preceded the explicit disowning of much of Stalin's works and actions as part of party orthodoxy. Stalin's 76th birthday was celebrated in the conventional way in party publications and on the very day the Congress opened, a number of provincial party papers appeared with slogans referring to 'the banner of Marx-Engels-Lenin-Stalin' and corresponding pictures (the Moscow *Pravda* of that day carried only the picture of Lenin and marching workers and peasants, and an editorial which praised collective leadership without explicitly condemning the 'cult of the individual'). On the other side, the change in conventional attitudes to Russian and party history, which in the columns of *Voprosy istorii* had proceeded along with the 'thaw', was carried one step further at a readers' conference arranged on the eve of the Party Congress as a platform for Soviet historians. The falsification of party history current during the last decades was now denounced by the editors of the journal in terms which left no doubt that the whole ideological climate of these decades, and, by implication, its main inspirer were under attack. The editors and many speakers at the conference started the rehabilitation of innocent victims of the 'great purge'. This would have been impossible without strong backing within the Presidium of the CC.[50] The existence of disagreements within the Presidium is shown by variations of the terms in which the 'cult of the individual' was denounced by the diverse party leaders in the open sessions of the XX Congress. It ranged from Kaganovich's statement that the move, though necessary, was 'not an easy thing', to Mikoyan's explicitness which went as far as possible without depriving Khrushchev of much of his fire for the secret session speech. These differences, however, may have been reduced by a threat of Khrushchev's and his friend that the denunciation, if not carried out by unanimous decision, would have implications for the re-election to the party leadership of those who would defend Stalin.

The Plenary Session of the CC which met on the eve of the XX Congress decided to circulate amongst the delegates Lenin's 'will' of 1924[51] and other evidence of Lenin's critical attitude of some aspects of Stalin's character and policies. After the Congress, these documents and an edited version of Khrushchev's secret session speech were circulated amongst the party organisations. The documents were eventually published in the *Kommunist*.[52] Khrushchev's secret session speech was never officially published but eventually circulated even in the party organisations of the People's Democracies. From there the American State Department got it and, faithful as it is to the principle of non-intervention in the affairs of other countries, hurried to publish it before the Soviet leaders had time to carry out the intended piecemeal release of the bitter truth. The dropping of much of party tradition was explained by Khrushchev in secret session in a speech on the consequences of the 'cult of the individual'. Since more than enough had already been written about Stalin's merits, Khrushchev deemed that he had to concentrate on Stalin's

shortcomings and misdeeds. Even then, the speech was selective :
it dealt with only those actions of Stalin under which the very
communists who now wished to defend his memory might have
suffered, but omitted a clear explanation of the 'great purge'. In
parts it was unjust, as usually happens when a semi-god is reduced
to human status, particularly if the reduction is carried out by people
who shared in the responsibility and hence must make the most
of his individual shortcomings. Even without the American publication (which could have been foreseen by anyone who circulated
a document of that kind in the Polish and East German parties),
Khrushchev's secret session speech was bound to cause a great
stir. Its very justification was that 'shock-therapy' was needed
in order to secure Soviet society against any future repetition of
the 'purge' and to prevent any opponents of future reforms from
resorting to the orthodoxies of the Stalin period in the absence
of practical criticisms of such reforms. The first point dominated
Khrushchev's Secret Session speech and has since been made
explicit in all party documents. The second emerged only gradually, when, eventually, Stalin's old comrades-in-arms, who had
not been able to defend him, defended industrial centralisation.
When the most important and most unorthodox reforms in the
agricultural field matured, they were already removed from the
party's leading councils.

Nobody could deny the truth of what Khrushchev had said
about Stalin's deeds. Those who had opposed the 'shock-therapy'
could only point to the harm to party authority, as made evident
already by the events of June 1956 in Poznan and a series of
crises in Western communist parties. When, on June 30th, the
CC decision 'On Overcoming the Cult of the Individual and of
its Consequences' publicly declared as much as could be
said in public, it was pointed out that the party had denounced
the serious mistakes and misuses of 'the last period of Stalin's
life' by its own initiative and in full conscience of the partial
harm which would be done by such a declaration which might
be used by its enemies. Such temporary difficulties, however,
would be far outweighed by the long-term benefits to the communist cause, including clarification of principles as well as the
prevention of a repetition of what had happened in Stalin's days.

It is difficult to quarrel with this statement if communism is conceived as a historical process the hardships of which are justified precisely by their temporary character and by the party's capacity to outgrow its earlier stages. It is no use disputing whether the necessary clarification could have been carried out quicker and less painfully if it had started immediately after Stalin's death, or at least after Beria's execution, instead of still using the Stalin symbol during the first stages of 'de-Stalinisation'. Social institutions have dynamics of their own, and also some inherent conservatism. Leaders do not like to see policies with which they have been associated disowned in public. If the urge for reform is strong enough to enforce a change, that very conservatism will require a cure by 'shock-therapy'. There was a delay in 'de-Stalinisation' till the time when it could be carried out without overt dissent within the party leadership. This avoided changes in the leadership on what were, after all, historical issues. The elimination of the Malenkov-Molotov-Kaganovich group during the following year resulted from disagreements which immediately, notwithstanding the background explanations given at the XXII Congress, did concern the advisability of definite reforms. However sharp that dispute, it lacked that extreme severity which would have been unavoidable if the party leadership had split on the issue of the respective shares in responsibility for the horrible things that had happened under Stalin.

At the XX Congress the whole Presidium of the CC was re-elected. Of the 125 members of the CC elected at the XIX Congress, which had been managed by Malenkov under Stalin's eyes, a third failed to be re-elected. There had been a few natural deaths, five or six members had been involved in the Beria case, and there were some officials who, in Khrushchev's words, 'had not justified the confidence put in them by the party' (a term which might mean anything ; yet, even Stalin's Private Secretary, Poskribyshev, was allowed silently to retire into private life). Fifty of the 133 members of the new CC had not been members, and 37 of them not even candidate members, of the CC elected by the XIX Congress. Just over a fourth of the new CC, elected after three and a half eventful years, represented new promotions. We have no indication that the changes at the next-lower level were more extensive. Further down, quite a number of district and city Borzovs may have given way to elements more capable of dealing with people. The party leaders regarded such changes as one of the purposes for which the shock-therapy had been applied. 'Empty-headed careerists', *Partiinaya zhizn* said in its post-Congress issue,[53] 'who act only when ordered from above and who work not for the sake of the cause but in order to earn the approval of their superiors, are of no use for the party. The party needs intelligent and bold officials who show initiative and whose value increases as their knowledge increases, and as they assimilate the experiences of the masses.' As we have seen before, the vast majority of the delegates to the XX Party Congress were party officials, and even some who in major or minor positions had participated in the deeds of the past regime. Stalin's 'cult' rendered his party a last service, in that the necessary dissociation could be carried out by the mere disowning of the personality and some of the actions of a dead man. This was easier than changes in institutions the working of which had caused dissatisfaction. The general climate of opinion gradually changed and the programme of reform implicit in the act of dissociation could be carried out.

The demand for security of the law was one of the major driving forces with which the XX Congress had to reckon. The revision of individual miscarriages of justice and the creation of organisational safeguards against their repetition was well under way during 1955. By the time the Congress met, it must have been general knowledge that it was not a mere question of individual mistakes, but the person shot or sent to the labour camp for alleged counter-revolutionary activities in all likelihood had been innocent. What had happened was not just that the political police had had too much power, and the learned Procurator too little, but that the party machine had ordered the Procurator to sanction arrests and to demand convictions which he knew were founded not in the law but in the supposed undesirability of dissent. The only safe remedy was a declaration by the party itself that injustice had been done on a large scale and that it had harmed the country. When during the post-Congress discussion it was asked what the present leaders had done during

the events now condemned by them, they answered, in the CC
decision of June 30, 1956, that the people would not have understood an attempt at removing Stalin. Indeed, they would not
have. But a solemn condemnation of what had happened might
strengthen opposition against any future party leader who might
try to repeat Stalin's performance. It was not so much a question
of the remote past. After all, two-fifths of the delegates to the
XX Congress[54] had never heard the victims of the 'great purge'
referred to except as traitors during their party life. Three-
quarters of them knew no party setting other than that against
which those victims undoubtedly had offended (lies being con-
cocted in order to describe actions as criminal). The army felt
that its initial defeats in 1941 had to a considerable extent been
due to Stalin's mass-slaughter of capable officers. Khrushchev
paid tribute to this feeling by emphasising the point in his secret
session speech. Party opinion was bound to regard the tragedy
of 1936-38 as due to the less numerous (but, from the standpoint
of those concerned, not less tragic) instances of terror suffered
during Stalin's last years. Everyone knew that these victims of
oppression had not opposed the industrialisation of the country
or the collectivisation of agriculture, nor done anything else which,
retrospectively, could be described as a grave political error.
Those who had become victims of intrigue or denunciation had
made suggestions which, at least, had not been worse than the
officially adopted policy. A break with Stalinist terror appeared
to be a guarantee, not only of the citizen's personal security but
also of the party's ability to get different views on complicated
and controversial problems.

If so much of the party's recent past had to be denounced,
the heroic days of Lenin offered sufficient ground for self-
assertion. This was more so as they were sufficiently remote and
their hardships and problems, the very problems which Stalin had
solved in his brutal ways, lingered on as mere dim shadows. The
old Bolsheviks who had returned from the labour camp after 'the
long eighteen years', as Anna Bergholts sang, became a symbol of a
better past. Stalin's historical myth, which had obscured that
past, appeared to many as a force of evil which had to be
destroyed. Others even realised that not just that particular

myth but myths in general had proved harmful. Anna Pankratova,, the head of the History Institute of the Academy of Sciences, a member of the Central Committee in Stalin's days and, as the party's main spokesman on the 'historical front', responsible for much of its past, stated at the XX Congress that 'scientific problems cannot be decided by order or by majority decision : the party teaches us that science develops through discussion and free exchange of opinions'. Others simply enjoyed unearthing the enormous amount of historical data which had been buried in the service of the myth. The scholarly members of the party machine would enjoy any exaggeration committed in the course of the unearthing, in particular a rehabilitation of Trotsky, so that they might turn to a counter-attack. Many workers in the literary and historical fields attacked the time-servers, trying to demonstrate that the latter had served not the party but an idol now happily destroyed. The machine would have to wait for the day (eventually provided for by the Hungarian insurrection) when it could 'counter-attack the disruptive' forces, protecting the time-servers of yesterday against 'exaggerated' criticism since their deeds had been committed with the good intention to serve the party.

The struggle for security of the law led to some house-cleaning. By the decree of April 19, 1956, the 'Kirov law' was repealed. The new Statute on State Offences adopted by the Supreme Soviet in December 1958 clearly defined terrorism as murder of state officials for political reasons and excluded those vague definitions under which a great variety of activities had been brought under the heading of 'counter-revolutionary propaganda'. At the XXI Party Congress, in January 1959 Khrushchev could declare that not a single person was imprisoned in the USSR for political reasons (agents of foreign intelligence services being presumably not regarded as political prisoners). Shelepin, the new head of the State Security Service, assured the Congress and the people that 'this shameful experience, the violation of socialist legality' (during the 'purge') can never again be repeated. The transfer of codification to the Union Republics brought the endless committee work on the re-codification of Soviet law at least to a partial conclusion. In

December 1958 the Supreme Soviet of the USSR adopted the Basic Principles on Criminal Law and on Criminal Procedure so that the Union Republics now might issue their codes within the given framework. By that time, the emphases had changed slightly since the days of the XX Party Congress. The guarantees for security of the law were strengthened and the Draconic sanctions threatened during the Stalin period drastically reduced (less than three years later a decree of May 5, 1961, on the limitation of the remission of sentences withdrew part of this leniency so far as the professional criminal was concerned). But the interests of the defendant, which in reaction to the horrors of the past had dominated most of the earlier discussion, had to come to terms with an increased interest in efficient struggle against the professional criminal. On the other hand, the treatment of minor offences and of cases promising reformation of the offender were removed from the scope of the penal law to that of the moral influence of social organisations.[55]

The economic and social urges which had led to 'de-Stalinisation' were indicated by a series of reforms announced at the XX Congress, and enacted during the following year.[56] The decrees of March 6, 1956, encouraged the collective farms to amend their rules according to local conditions and to start monthly advance payments on the Labour Days earned. The latter measure, important though it was as a transitional step to regular payment of *kolkhoz* labour, could only be introduced on the most prosperous farms. A long list of important reforms shows care for the interests of the industrial worker. By the decree of April 25th, 1956, all penal sanctions for absenteeism and all restrictions on the right to change one's job other than the involved reductions of social benefits were abolished.[57] On March 8th the working week was reduced by two hours on each Saturday. On March 26th maternity leave was restored to its pre-1938 length. By the decree of May 26th the working day of juveniles of 16-18 was reduced to six hours without reduction of wages. (In December the employment of juveniles under 16, with the exception of apprentices of 15 for whom a working-day of four hours was established, was prohibited.) The return to the seven-hour day (six hours for underground or unhealthy work), which

26

was envisaged by the decisions of the XX Congress for the next five-year plan period, started in 1956 in the Donets mines. By April 1958 the most important branches of the heavy industries were included. By 1960, it became general. The wages of the lowest-paid groups of workers were increased, as from January 1, 1957, by about a third. The annual revision of output-norms (a current source of dissatisfaction) was replaced by a revision in only individual cases where conditions had changed because of improved techniques. By the decree of June 6, 1956, all fees for education, as introduced in 1940, were abolished. Internate schools (at first on an experimental scale) were established by the decree of September 15, 1956, to help childern from the poorest homes to get secondary education.[58] A system of social benefits and old age pensions, which compares favourably with the most advanced western systems, was introduced by the law of July 14, 1956.[59] These reforms, enacted within a few months, returned to the industrial worker the fruits of his prolonged efforts since the war. Their enumeration may help to explain both the pressures which backed the decisions of the XX Congress and the ease with which the party's authority survived the destruction of much of its former ideological symbols.

A number of measures taken at, or immediately after, the XX Congress reduced the inflated machine and gave greater scope to the initiative of the lower organisations. The Political Departments in transport establishments were abolished. (This method of managing party organisations from above survives only in the armed forces, where a sound case for it can be made.) No more organisers were sent by the CC to major enterprises and research institutions. The apparatus of the Central Committee, as well as of the Republican and provincial committees, was reduced (for the medium committees by 20-30 per cent).[60] Local organisers were assessed according to their initiative in tackling problems with a minimum of guidance from above. They were warned against the temptation of interfering with managerial tasks. Instead, they should study the basic economic problems of the industry concerned so that they could offer useful guidance. Party education, which already in September 1953 had been put on a voluntary basis,[61] was shifted to the study of economics (in particular those of the industry in which the party members worked). In any case it was difficult to continue with the former emphasis on party history, since the authority of the *Short Course* had been destroyed, while it took three years to produce the promised new textbook of party history.[62] Internal friction was kept within reasonable limits. The disowning of Stalin caused some students' demonstrations in Georgia.[63] On the other hand, 'demagogues' were said to pursue the critique of the 'cult of personalities' to the length of a general denial of authority and of individual management, to question the manager's right to transfer a worker to another job, to impose disciplinary penalties, etc.[64] Such phenomena were to be expected in view of the central place occupied by the Stalin cult in earlier party ideology and of the shock administered to any established authority by the revelation of the horrible things done by the highest authority in the country. The most remarkable fact is that in the USSR, as distinct from some of the satellite countries, they were not so numerous and local in character.

The destruction of the Stalin myth, however, had intellectual implications. Internally these were seen in an important trend amongst Soviet writers, externally in the communist parties outside the USSR, which could not rely on a general feeling of relaxation such as was produced by the XX Congress within the country but had to re-examine their former attitude. With the sole exception of party historiography where soon a near-Stalinist reaction set in, the lesson of the XX Congress was easily applied in the diverse fields of science and scholarship. The former search for 'orthodox' answers to all kinds of problems was replaced by competition of different schools and approaches, including Western ones, as the normal road to progress. The veil of secrecy which for so long had restricted statistical publications was withdrawn. Only legitimate security considerations of a state faced with opponents who walked 'on the brink of war' were considered. Many practical problems which were taboo during the Stalin period, and even immediately after Stalin's death,[65] were now frankly discussed in public. The works even of foreign authors who are clearly hostile to the USSR were published in translations, or at least reported in Soviet academic publications, provided they had something materially relevant to say.

The position of the artists differed from that of other intellectuals in that, since the 'thaw', their task was defined as that of describing people's psychic outlook and experiences. That these experiences were bad under the Stalin regime, could now be frankly admitted. Some critics indeed complained that no novel or drama dealing with the recent Soviet past was complete unless at least some person 'in regard to whom the principles of socialist legality were violated' (the official circumscription of the 'purge') appeared as a 'positive' hero. Some writers, however, who still had the sympathies of their colleagues arrived at the conclusion that their tasks included, not just the description of misuses already denounced by the party but the reasons for them. Naturally enough, the artist-author is inclined to give psychological rather than institutional explanations. For this reason he is unpopular with those party leaders who are not afraid of reforming institutions but who strongly dislike being told that the upper stratum of Soviet society is corrupted by power or 'lives by bread alone' (the title of Dudintsev's famous novel).[66] A strong alliance was concluded between Soviet leaders who interpreted writings like Dudintsev's as involving the threat of a repetition of the Hungarian events, and Western journalists who treated those authors as 'freedom-writers',[67] freedom presumably being defined in the 'Western' sense.

There is not the slightest indication of the correctness of such interpretations. Dudintsev himself regards his novel as recounting his experiences as a soldier when the make-belief of the Stalin period resulted in Soviet airmen having to face superior German fighters with insufficient arms. From the institutional standpoint, his novel gave the call for a dissolution of ministerial bureaucracy because of its tendency to form cliques which, on their part, obstruct technical process. These were the very changes which Khrushchev carried out six months after the publication of *Not by Bread Alone*. At the Writers' Congress in 1959, Khrushchev acknowledged Dudintsev's good intentions and condemned heresy hunts. But he would prefer authors who treated the positive experiences of reconstruction. The Dudintsev problem, even for those party leaders who are not afraid of criticism and radical reform, was his failure to treat the party as the *locus* where improvements can be achieved. Four years earlier, Ovechkin wrote a criticism where these institutional aspects went much deeper than in Dudintsev's novel. For the purposes of that novel the party does not exist at all, though the main figures are presumably its members, and one of the 'positive heroes' presumably an Old Bolshevik. What exists is the state machine. Most of its servants are careerists or people whose internal strength has been broken by futile efforts to overcome the careerists' resistance. Good people fight bad people ; eventually the good people succeed because their enthusiasm is backed by the military needs of the State. They are lonely individuals and have no delusions about the need to repeat the performance again and again, and always as individuals—whose number, they hope, will increase. In exoneration of Dudintsev, from the party standpoint, it may be said that his novel portrays the Stalin period where it would have been highly artificial to introduce the party organisation of a ministry as a factor fighting for improvement against ministerial bureaucracy. In other publications of the same period, however, particularly in some contributions to the anthology *Literaturnaya Moskva,* which was published by the Moscow branch of the Writers' Union,[68] the party organisations themselves are shown as subject to corruption. Good individuals behave insincerely and like machines as soon as they have to act in their party capacity. The most interesting fact about these writings is their very publication, by authoritative literary bodies, and the strong resistance put up by Soviet writers when, after the Hungarian tragedy, they were officially disowned,[69] though in a more civilised manner than in the Stalin period. The opposition against the party's literary machine by many influential Soviet authors, who wished to serve the party's cause by frank criticism, should not be confused with the attitude represented, for example, in Pasternak's *Dr. Zhivago,* which amounts to a denial of the importance of social reform and a retreat to private interests. Not only the hero but also the author and the book belong to the atmosphere of the Petersburg literary circles which flourished after the defeat of the 1905 revolution and experienced a short revival under NEP. The most serious literary criticism to which Pasternak's novel was subject came from the old Board of *Novy mir*,[70] i.e. those very people whom the machine superseded in early 1957 because of their independent attitude. The most efficient, though unintended, political criticism came from those Western circles who raised this book high and found it alone, of all the Soviet novels produced until then, worthy of a Nobel prize.

Politically more important than this new stir among writers were the reactions in the non-Soviet communist parties to the abandonment of the Stalinist tradition, particularly the Polish and Hungarian events which followed this ideological change. It emerged that the very triumph of Soviet industrialisation, which allowed the CPSU to draw a line under the hardships of the Stalin period, had caused a variety of patterns to emerge within the communist camp. On the one side, the Yugoslavs attempted at first a combination of economics patterned simultaneously on the old Workers' Opposition in the CPSU and the Bukharinites with a political structure closely resembling Stalinism (Milovan Djilas, an outsider of the Yugoslav leading group, wrote the book *The New Class* which to the revisionist ideology to its last extremities—he was promptly imprisoned). During the Hungarian crisis, the counter-revolutionary implications of which were felt in their own country,[71] the Yugoslav leaders accepted the necessity of the Soviet intervention. But at the same time they advertised their own brand of communism, not just as a national variety adapted to their local conditions (to this the Soviet leaders would agree, and concede that something might be learned even from the Yugoslav Workers' Councils), but as a far superior kind, free from any 'Stalinist' degeneration. This is certainly strange if the strength of the leaders' 'cult' in the diverse communist countries is compared. On the other side, there were the Chinese communists who were just in transition from the NEP stage of their revolution to full-scale industrialisation and agricultural collectivisation. Having the Soviet example before them and operating upon better acceptance of their national leadership than the Soviet communists could command at any time before the German invasion, they could manage without 'purges' on a scale comparable to the Soviet record. Moreover, being based upon a peasantry so destitute under former conditions that even the mere assurance of a subsistence minimum was bound to be accepted as major progress, they could proceed with collectivisation (eventually, it is true, driven to excesses not warranted by the Soviet example, and soon subject to correction) without having to apply repression as in the Soviet Union in 1929-32. To them, the phenomena now denounced by the CPSU were explicable by the backwardness of the countries in which socialism was being built, particularly by the peasants' demand for a father figure.[72] (This implied some exoneration for Russia's past and perhaps for China's present. In the heat of self-assertion involved in the Sino-Soviet dispute, the Chinese leaders did not realise that such exoneration of certain traits of their socialism also implied a demand for eventually overcoming them in the Soviet terms of de-Stalinisation.) A third approach was maintained by many Western communists who usually saw the USSR as a model of socialism (in general and not only for backward countries) and wished to see it attain these standards without granting extenuating circumstances to those responsible for what Togliatti, expressing their mood, described as a degeneration of the former standard. This attitude, though more disturbing from the standpoint of the party machine, fits well with the 'return to Lenin' call given at and after the XX Congress. Both the Chinese and Togliatti's explanations were available to Soviet communists when the American publication of Khrushchev's secret session speech disrupted its gradual spread after the XX Congress and when the effect of these disclosures first became evident in the Poznan riots. The importance of international communist opinion increased after the October crises in Poland and Hungary. In particular the latter showed signs of leaving the Soviet *bloc,* which necessitated Soviet armed intervention.

This distasteful operation had to be explained to Soviet opinion. Firstly, party officials who questioned Khrushchev's wisdom in breaking with the Stalinist tradition, had to be shown that the situation had originated precisely because the former Hungarian leaders had followed the Stalin model even after having been told by the Russians to drop it. Secondly, the broader strata of the Soviet peoples (including the army, which does not like having to storm barricades defended by workers) had to be convinced that the mutiny had outgrown any possible reforms *within* the communist system and that, in order to avoid similar catastrophes in other places, criticism had to be kept within sensible limits. The first course of action strengthened the position of the new Hungarian leaders against those who wanted a return to the Rakoszy system. It also made for collaboration with the new Polish leaders who, even though sharply dissociating themselves from the Stalin tradition as well as from Stalinists within the Polish party, recognised the bitter necessity of the intervention in Hungary. They vindicated the general approach of the XX Congress by developing a pattern of communism which was distinct from the Soviet pattern, yet still within the common framework. (Soviet-Polish relations were further strengthened during the following year when the new Polish leaders found it necessary to suppress the organ of the radical young writers whose role during the October events had been similar to that of their Hungarian colleagues. They also eventually reduced the position of the Worker's Councils formed in October in the Polish factories as organs of autonomous workers' self-management to that of an auxiliary of state management and of a link in the democratisation of trade union administration.)[73] Having deprived themselves of the claim to dogmatic authority inherent in the Stalin cult, the Russians could not restore the intellectual homogeneity of the communist movement except by appeal to international consensus. They were greatly relieved when a document published on behalf of the Chinese Politburo in *Jenmin jibao* on December 29th, 1956 (translated the following day in *Pravda*) appreciated the *generally* valid elements of the Soviet experience, which should be distinguished both from those which arose in the particular circumstances of the USSR, and from those which were mistakes even in these circumstances.[74]

(c) DECENTRALISATION IN INDUSTRY AND STATE :
      KHRUSHCHEV IN FULL CONTROL

When the Chinese Communists defined their attitude in the debate of 1956, they opposed the Yugoslav demand for a removal of the 'Stalinists' from the leadership of the communist parties. They appreciated the mistakes committed by Stalin 'and all those comrades who under his influence committed similar mistakes' in the historical context in which they were made. They were committed by communists, not by enemies of the working class. Any discrimination against these comrades would not only prevent them from learning lessons from past mistakes but would also confuse two types of contradictions, viz. those between correct and incorrect policies, and those between the camp of communism and its enemies. In his own statements, Khrushchev coupled recognition of Stalin's merits with the recognition of joint responsibility for his mistakes.[75] If already by then he regarded as unavoidable a split with those who (as he stated a few months later) had all the time opposed his agrarian policies and his measures to restore valid concepts of legality, it would have been very impolitic for it to occur on the issue of the distribution of responsibility for Stalin's mistakes. On the other hand, it might be said that even if Malenkov or Molotov had a great deal to do with a considerable part of those mistakes, it did the party no more harm than did Khrushchev's precipitate destruction of its mythology, with consequences in countries where communism still had more myths than practical achievements to rely upon. There was no reason to assume that the party, having learned the full truth about Stalin's policy of eliminating dissenting leaders, had any desire for further splits in the leadership. When these eventually occurred, the dissenters' moral position was harmed by their desire to attempt change through personal initiative probably as much as by the public's conviction of their political error.

Whatever Khrushchev's intentions, he could not raise new controversial issues of reform immediately after the Hungarian crisis. For his standpoint the Plenary Session of the CC which met in December 1956 was rather a setback. Plan fulfilment had run into difficulties because of the contradictions arising between the ambitious targets of the sixth Five-Year Plan and the increase in effective consumer demand as a result of the reforms of 1956 (perhaps also by reduced managerial resistance to demands for wage increases in an increasingly anti-authoritarian climate). These difficulties were solved, not by basic reforms in the management of the national economy but by a reduction in investments. A broadening of the powers of the Councils of Ministers of the

Union Republics was envisaged, but so also was a further broadening of the power of ministries and of their main administrations (*glavki*) as against those of the Council of Ministers. This meant some rationalisation of the central administration of the national economy but no general decentralisation. The State Economic Commission was even strengthened by the appointment of five senior economic ministers, so that it might carry out executive functions over the economy.

Less than three months later policies had changed—presumably because Khrushchev had succeeded at the plenary session of the CC meeting on February 13th and 14th, 1957, in rallying local opposition against the excesses of central planning. The decision taken on Khrushchev's report (which was published on February 16th) recognised the past merits of central administration as a means of concentrating resources upon the heavy industries in the interest of rapid industrialisation. These merits, however, had turned into shortcomings since the development and specialisation of industry had led to multiplication of economic ministries. Departmentalism now obstructed both natural connections between the diverse industries within areas and local decisions. It led to the existence of many uneconomic organisations and supply offices in each locality and to an accumulation in the ministries of highly trained technical staff who could be better applied in the immediate management of production. It hindered the participation of local party and trade union organisations as well as local Soviets in economic affairs. Hence the central ministries managing the national economy were to be replaced by Economic Councils (*Sovnarkhozy*) for individual regions under which all the enterprises hitherto belonging to the diverse ministries were to be concentrated (a few exceptions, mainly for industries of war-economic importance, were eventually agreed upon). Their coordination was to be worked out by the planning organisations, by the Ministry of State Auditing (*Goskontrol*), by the State Bank and by the Central Statistical Board.

On the basis of this general decision, a report by Khrushchev was elaborated and on March 30th, submitted for public discussion.[76] The delay suggests continuing friction within the Presidium. Emphasis was laid on the need to express controversial opinions and to discuss them frankly. In order to get a truly free decision, general workers' and trade union meetings were to precede the meetings of party groups.[77] Most managerial arguments during the discussion centred on the question of how the existing supply system, which worked sensibly for favoured key enterprises, could be replaced without disturbance of production. On the other side, the danger of a predominance of local interests under the new dispensation was emphasised. These two arguments were again prominent when the *Sovnarkhozy* were later abolished. But already in August 1958 the CC adopted a special decision on some officials who had expended funds assigned for industrial investment for the satisfaction of local housing, cultural and similar needs. Disciplinary measures were taken against the officials concerned.[78] A comparatively minor controversy concerned the number of *Sovnarkhozy* to be established. There was the question whether they should be established for large natural economic units (which would have meant a splitting up of the central government into fairly powerful sub-units) or for each of the existing administrative and party-organisational units. In favour of the second variant it was stated that only comparatively small *Sovnarkhozy* administrations could achieve the closeness to the local workers and organisations which was one of the aims of the reform. *Sovnarkhozy* were independent of local authorities other than the Government of the Union Republic concerned. In order to secure all-Union supervision of industry, in place of the abolished industrial ministries the chief officials of Gosplan as well as the Prime Ministers of the Union Republics were included in the Union Government.

The strengthening of the Union Republics was not restricted to the economic field. By a law adopted by the Supreme Soviet on February 12th, 1957 (i.e. a few days before the Plenary Session of the CC which decided on industrial decentralisation) the powers of codification of law (general principles to be established by the Union) and of court organisation was transferred to the Union Republics. Their Supreme Courts became the highest instance of law, apart from the right of supervision pertaining to the Supreme Court of the USSR.[79] To ensure homogeneity of jurisdiction, the Presidents of the Supreme Courts of the Union Republics became *ex-officio* members of the Supreme Court of the USSR—to be followed, as we have seen, within a few months by the Prime Ministers of the Union Republics as *ex-officio* members of Union Government. The changes in the party leadership which we shall soon discuss resulted in the secretaries of the most important Republican Communist Parties becoming—though only as individuals—members or candidate members of the Presidium of the CC, (while retaining their republican posts). Soviet federalism thus acquired a new meaning. It no longer implied mere devolution of certain administrative functions under Moscow, but also a share in the central power exercised in Moscow.[80] Yet the *party* remains centralised. Because this unity secures the exercise of devolved functions in a common spirit, decentralisation of government and management could go far without impairing their essential unity.

It would have been surprising if such a transformation could have been carried out without resistance from the representatives of the former set-up. The communique published after their expulsion from the CC mentions Malenkov, Molotov and Kaganovich, and Shepilov 'who had associated himself with them' as the representatives of the group which, after earlier disagreements on agrarian, legal and international policies opposed the decentralisation of industry and continued their opposition even after the popular discussion and legislation by the Supreme Soviet. Pervukhin and Saburov had opposed industrial decentralisation, but did not participate in the attempt to remove Khrushchev (hence they escaped with minor demotions). Bulganin declared at the December 1958 session of the CC that, though not the initiator, he had been the formal head of the group (i.e. presumably its candidate for Khrushchev's position). His status, however, could not be changed at the moment without destroying the concept of 'collective leadership'. In any case, he was comparatively free from co-responsibility for Stalin's deeds. As might be expected in view of his past, Voroshilov had defended at the June 1957 meeting his dead leader's memory and resisted, as long as possible, the rehabilitation of his victims. Notwithstanding the fact that Khrushchev, when preparing for the trial of strength, had tried to nail all four down as co-responsible for Stalin's terror[81] (a clearer issue for the party than controversial arguments on the merits of industrial decentralisation), Voroshilov was spared public mention of errors before the XXII Congress. This was presumably on the ground that already at the Plenary Meeting of the CC in June he had dissociated himself from the factional activities of the trio. Kaganovich and Malenkov then figured in the largely formal condemnation of its views, but not Molotov. The latter also appears to have been the only member of the 'anti-party group' who had opposed the 'new lands' campaign. All the three principals had opposed the abolition of obligatory deliveries from the kolkhoz households, certain (unspecified) measures 'for the liquidation of the personality cult' and (also unspecified) steps in the fields of foreign policies.[82] At the XXI Congress[83] Saburov mentioned in this connection the development of economic aid to the People's Democracies and, even more controversial, to non-communist underdeveloped countries of Asia. Dogmatism regarding the possibility of independent development of non-capitalist countries was linked with what Saburov described as 'narrow nationalism', i.e. concern only for socialism in the USSR.

On June 18th, 1957, the tension reached breaking point. According to Saburov, Khrushchev himself recognised his mistakes (presumably in carrying out the decentralisation of industry), though minor ones which should have been criticised in a full CC meeting. A majority of the Presidium members, however, used the occasion to try to remove Khrushchev from his post as First Secretary. Mikoyan and Suslov appear to have been his only supporter amongst the full members. Amongst the candidates Furtseva did her best to prolong the debates until, with the help of Zhukov who supplied the planes, a sufficient quorum of CC members had been assembled to demand an immediate plenary session. Here the opposition proved to be a group of officers without soldiers—more precisely, generals without colonels. In accordance with point seven of the decision of the X Congress, its leaders were expelled from the Central Committee and subsequently received minor managerial posts (Molotov a minor diplomatic one). In the process of re-election, Saburov was removed from the Presidium but retained his seat on the Central Committee. Zhukov and Furtseva were promoted to full membership of the Presidium, the strength of which was increased to fifteen full members plus nine candidates (Kosygin remaining amongst the latter). Most of the new places were filled by Provincial and Republican secretaries who retained their posts while sitting on the party's highest body.

Zhukov's ascendancy, which caused speculations in the Western press, remained ephemeral. In the summer, the CC secretariat issued directives to enliven the activities of the party organisations within the army, including criticism and self-criticism to be applied even to commanding officers.[84] Zhukov opposed such interference with the officers' commanding power and treated the educational activities of the military party organisations as a diversion from essential technical training. The Military Councils of the Army Districts (i.e. the bodies through which the cooperation of the civilian party organisations with the higher commands is organised) he saw at best as advisory bodies.[85] He was at the first opportunity relieved of his post as Minister of Defence. As he apparently refused to accept even the highest civilian appointment, he was expelled from the Presidium of the CC and from the CC itself.

With the changes in the Presidium of the CC and in the composition of the Council of Ministers, the relation between these two bodies changed fundamentally. In April 1958 Khrushchev replaced Bulganin as Prime Minister (Bulganin at first returned to his old job at the State Bank ; in August 1958 he was further demoted to the Chairmanship of a *Sovnarkhoz* and removed from the Presidium of the CC, remaining an ordinary CC member). Of the fifteen members of the Presidium, now nine (plus Pospelov, one of the candidates of the Presidium) were members of the CC Secretariat, which thus appeared as the actually leading body (a tenth, Shvernik, was President of the Party Control Commission). Only Khrushchev, and his 'First Deputies' Mikoyan and Koslov, occupied leading positions in the Government. The Plenary Session of the CC met on May 4, 1960, under the shadow of the U-2 incident. This may have raised doubts about the desirability of excessive control of the

Presidium by the Secretariat and its leader. The meeting dismissed five of the former members of the Secretariat, two of them who remained members of the Presidium in connection with their assuming Ministerial posts, two in order to transfer them to the Buro of the CC for affairs of the RSFSR; the fifth (Kirichenko) was regarded as a failure, and dismissed also from the Presidium. Kosygin now became a full member. The members of the CC Secretariat, even though for practical purposes the members of the RSFSR were added to their number, no longer formed an absolute majority in the Presidium.

In view of the increased importance of international relations, Khrushchev's occupation of the post of Prime Minister (without which Stalin could manage during the most critical years of his dictatorship) was no less significant than his party job. The same position had prevailed in Lenin's days. But then it was nearly a matter of course, as the party and its leader had established the state. Khrushchev as an individual had no comparable authority. But as a party man, he had succeeded in performing what Malenkov suspected as he was of subordinating the party to Stalin's state machine, had failed to accomplish.

The stabilisation of the party machine strengthened the campaign against 'revisionism' which was developing since the crisis of 1956. It got into full swing after the Yugoslavs' refusal to attend the conference of the communist state parties in November 1957 (at which the 'bloc' was re-asserted), followed by the adoption of the new programme of the Yugoslav Communist Party, reproaches and counter-reproaches. The interesting aspect of that campaign, which in 1958 occupied quite inordinate a share in the Soviet press, was its failure to raise topics other than the supposed 'main danger to international communism' from the embellishment, by the revisionists, of the prospects and development of world capitalism.

The sharpest reaction to ideological 'revisionism' occurred in the literary field. In May 1957 (i.e. before) and then in July (i.e. after the trial of strength with the 'anti-party' group), Khrushchev had talks with the writers, the contents of which were published in the *Kommunist*,[86] as an official document under the title 'For a Closer Connection of Literature with the People'.

Emphasis was laid on the social functions of literature, and criticism was directed against publications such as *Literaturnaya Moskva* and *Not by Bread Alone*. But even here, extreme denunciation was avoided. The party's official statements on literary and other artistic issues, while strictly upholding its claim to voice them, appeared fairly balanced. A CC decision 'On the Correction of the Erroneous Appraisal of the Operas "The Great Friendship", "Bogdan Khmelnitski" and "From a Full Heart",' adopted on May 28th, 1958, apparently after some internal disputes,[87] tried to establish 'the organic unity of party-inspiration of art and freedom of artistic creation'.[88] The tendency of the music decisions of 1948 to encourage closeness of musical creation to the people and to discourage the 'formalist' tendencies in modern music was re-emphasised. But the denunciation of individual musical creations due, as it is said, to Stalin's subjective approach to such things, was deplored (it is hardly necessary to say that the composers, when applauding the CC decision, stressed the second aspect).[89] In general the party demanded mere recognition as the inspirator of Soviet culture and left to the initiative of the artists the choice of the means by which they could best fulfil their accepted social function.

Some phenomena in the literary field, though not necessarily originating higher up than in the Writers' Union certainly represented an attack, not merely against some 'near-revisionist misuses' of the freedom of criticism, but against the line of the XX Party Congress itself. V. Kochetov's novel *The Yershov Brothers,* straightforwardly written as a retort (in parts very clumsy) to Dudintsev's and Ehrenburg's novels, attacks the whole 'thaw'— in small letters, not just the Ehrenburg novel.[90] Though reviewers differed in their appreciations of the novel, no one used the argument of Kochetov and his friends, namely that the object of their criticism is opposed to the party line. I. Abashidze, Secretary of the Georgian Writers' Union, stated at its Congress that although some elements of critical realism should be preserved and the dark aspects of Soviet life might be criticised, at the same time the bright socialist reality should be presented. On the whole, in every individual production and not just in the total picture given by Soviet authors, the bright aspects should properly overweigh the dark ones. This came very near to the old concepts regarding the admissible proportion of 'positive' to 'negative' heroes.[91] In any case, it restricted the function of literary productions as vehicles of reform. This is the very function whose importance, and the positive aspects of Dudintsev's novel, were recognised in Khrushchev's address to the all-Union Writers' Congress in May 1959.[92] At that time, a hard struggle was going on between those who supported the topically propagandist functions of Soviet literature (who themselves were divided between supporters and opponents of the new course of party politics) and those who upheld artistic quality. Kochetov and Surkov (for many years first secretary of the Writers' Union) were removed from their leading positions, but many statements made before and after the Writers' Congress continued their line. However, they no longer enjoyed a monopoly in representing the party interest in literature. Those who had helped the party in overcoming the 'cult' received public recognition when *Pravda* reprinted those parts of Tvardovsky's poem *Horizons beyond Horizons* which were devoted to these problems. He received in 1961 a Lenin prize for the poem. In the autumn he was elected to the Central Committee but failed to be re-elected at the XXIII (1966) Congress—so also were writers close to the Party's conservative wing. The prominent part played by literature in the first stage of the reform era— a corollary of Stalin's description of writers as the 'engineers of the Soul'—came to a natural end with the actual formulation of reform policies when all *practical* problems became open to frank argument.

(d) THE DISSOLUTION OF THE MTS AND THE ABOLITION OF THE 'LEVY' ON COLLECTIVE FARMS

With the organisational strengthening of the collective farms, the co-existence of 'two masters operating on the same ground' became controversial. 27,400 of the 83,100 kolkhoz chairmen had professional specialist education, another 20,000 had been sent from the towns because of their organisational capacities. The average annual money income per farm amounted to 1.15 million, average indivisible funds to 1.5 million roubles.[93] In

27

such conditions it could no longer be taken for granted that
the *kolkhozy* needed guidance and were incapable of applying and
renewing modern machinery, as had been argued by Stalin in
1951 when Venzher and Sanina suggested the transfer of the
MTS machines to the farms. The farms were dissatisfied with the
work of the MTS, performed according to regulations which
encouraged operations for which maximum payments in kind
could be claimed (not necessarily those in which the farms were
most interested, and not necessarily at the time when they were
most needed). To the state, in spite of increase in the prices
paid to the farms for their deliveries since September 1953, the
agricultural products obtained in that way (and those produced
in the state farms) came cheaper than those obtained as payments
in kind for the MTS-services to the farms.[94] During 1956-7,
experiments were made with both possible methods of overcoming
the problem. Some weak *kolkhozy* were replaced by state farms
operating on the basis of the existing MTS (those *kolkhoz-members*
who were ready to accept regular work being employed by
the new farms).[95] At other places the MTS were absorbed by the
farms, or MTS managers elected as chairmen of the enlarged
farms, which amounts to the same thing. A report in *Oktyabr,*
November 1957, on these experiments explicitly referred to Venzher and Sanina as the parents of the suggestion. When Khrushchev resumed it in his Minsk speech of January 22nd, 1958, he explained, however, that the suggestion had been premature in 1951.
Then the farms were not yet able to purchase the machines. This
argument is supported by the fact that even when the party made
the suggestion its own, at first more than a third of the farms
proved unable to buy the machines.[96] Under the impact of the
price-reform, this figure fell to 19 per cent by mid-December.

In December 1957, a conference of district party secretaries,
MTS managers and farm chairmen convened by the CC unanimously approved a transfer of the MTS machinery to the farms.
At that time the groups of instructors attached to the MTS since
1953 were taken out in the course of a general reduction of the
party machine. District committees (even those whose apparatus
was to be simplified) were directly to guide the farm organisations.[97] On January 22nd, 1958, Khrushchev raised the issue in

public in his Minsk speech. He enumerated the chief reasons for the uneconomic working of the MTS. They were, firstly, their high overhead costs and, secondly, a tendency to employ machinery allocated to them by the central organisations regardless of its usefulness (the collective farms, of course, would buy only such machinery as they needed). The function of the MTS of forcibly collecting cheap grain from the farms, though necessary in the past, could now be dispensed with. Further steps followed in quick sequence. The change was adopted on February 25-26, 1958, by a plenary session of the CC. Public discussion opened with the publication of Khrushchev's theses on March 1, and the law was enacted at the session of the Supreme Soviet at the end of March (the very same at which Bulganin was replaced by Khrushchev). Already during the discussion some farms had acquired the machinery used by them, though this was formally illegal before the amendment of the law. Warnings had to be issued against selling the MTS machinery below its value and also against the extension of purchase credits beyond five years.

From the dogmatic point of view, transfer of 'higher' state property to the 'lower' ones as represented by the collective farms, meant a setback. Even apart from all the economic difficulties the change could not have carried out as long as the 'dogmatists' kept important positions on the party's councils. From a practical point of view, however, Khrushchev argued that the legal forms of ownership do not matter as much as the way in which the title is used. In his report to the Supreme Soviet on March 27th, 1958, he advised the farms to aim at an investment of 30-35 per cent of gross income (twice as much as what was usual in productive assets and amenities including houses, schools, hospitals and roads)[98] rather than pay out large amounts to their members. He said that some were paying 40-50 roubles per labour day (this would mean that an unskilled worker in such a farm got as much as the average skilled worker in industry, and a skilled agricultural worker perhaps twice as much). Clearly, such payments were exceptional. Already in 1958 the collective farms, as a whole, invested more than what the whole stock of the MTS was worth and the better farms—about a sixth of the total—could buy the machines immediately. But about a fifth found even the five year period allotted by the government insufficient (the majority of the farms was ready to purchase the machines by instalments payable over 3-5 years).

Labour relations posed another problem. Some *kolkhoz* chairmen objected even to the tractorists' demand to transfer all the rewards of their former position—a guaranteed minimum wage, social security and pensions, sanitary regulations, etc.— to their renewed status as *kolkhoz* members. Only after a serious struggle was the mechanical workers' demand for the establishment of trade union groups on the farms (for themselves, for the agricultural specialists and for wage workers hired by the farms) satisfied.[99] They carried into the *kolkhoz* standards of labour and remuneration basically different from those of the glorified village community which was still the image in which the *kolkhoz* was viewed by many of its members. (There were others who regarded it as a deplorable way of managing the 'auxiliary economy' and for selling its output on the *kolkhoz* market ; this viewpoint was, however, unlikely to appeal to the farm chairmen who were foremost in opposing the machine workers' demands.) Two different approaches to work and remuneration cannot co-exist for long within one institution. By granting the machine workers' (and the trade unions') demand, the party envisaged the development of the *kolkhoz* into a socialised enterprise granting its members standards similar to those in industry. The special conditions of agriculture were being taken care of by a larger degree of autonomy in the framework of national planning and by linking earnings to results to an extent larger than what was usual in industry.[100] A start was made by the monthly money advances on labour-days earned. In 1956 these were paid in two-fifths of the farms.[101] Individual farms, which had to compete strongly with neighbouring industrial centres for their labour force, had already replaced remuneration by labour-days by normal wages paid on performance of the job. The farm's extra profit was then distributed by the end of the year as an extra-premium proportional to each member's earnings.[102]

The multiple price system, introduced in 1933, formed the main channel through which Stalin's *dan* was levied from the farms. It was also one of the main handicaps of collective work in comparison with work in the private plot, the fruits of which could be marketed by the kolkhoznik at favourable prices. Its reform, long regarded by specialists as overdue,[103] and in March described by Khrushchev as a subject of further investigation, was decided upon at a special Plenary Session of the CC on June 17th, 1958. Khrushchev denounced the injustice involved under former dispensation in different prices for identical products. The less productive farms were being penalised by getting much lower payments for such produce as they sold. (This, of course, had been the very concept of Stalin's incentive system; it could hardly be avoided as long as there were no proper rewards for the work of the average farm—where production costs were still inordinately high—but only the distribution of glittering prizes to those most advanced, which served as models for the rest.) By the decree of July 1, 1958, the farms' debts for incomplete compulsory deliveries, or payments in kind to the MTS for work performed before 1958, were remitted. Obligatory deliveries (or more precisely, the low prices paid for these deliveries) were abolished. In future all farm deliveries (which were to be planned so as to secure procurements at least equal to the former ones) were to be paid at the higher 'state purchase' (*zakupka*) prices. For those individual raw-materials the procurement prices of which had hitherto varied according to the farm's over-fulfilment of the plan, unified prices somewhere between the higher and the lower range of the former 'premium-prices' were introduced. Prices were subject to zonal and—in case of particularly good or bad harvests—annual variation. The new basic prices were calculated on the principle that the state should pay for the total output no more than it had cost it under the former dispensation, including the former losses of the Machine Tractor Stations. The published basic prices corresponded, indeed, to the level of traditional *zakupka* prices. They were to enable the normal farm to reward its members reasonably and, apart from the purchase of the MTS machines, to make those investments in the economic, educational and welfare field which Khrushchev had expected as a result of the economic progress of the farms. Those farms which hitherto had been unduly penalised for a moderately under-average productivity now moved into the ranks of those which could buy their machines. For backward ones, various remedies were considered at subsequent periods. An initial tendency towards amalgamations with more efficient ones, transformation into state farms or, at least, premature introduction of money wages, resulted in failures. At the Plenary Meeting of the CC held in January 1961 it was decided to seek, instead of overambitious attempts at the transforming the *kolkhoz* system, improvement by technical assistance (since 1963, apart from the desire for more and better machinery, the decision to supply fertilisers forms a main part of the 'chemicalisation' drive). The procurement demands were differentiated according to differences in regional possibilities and requirements. The new party programme, adopted in October 1961, envisaged the co-existence of the *kolkhoz* with the state farm for a prolonged period, and their eventual fusion, in the course of the twenty-year period, into some new form of socialist enterprise. This would combine the best features of both systems. The fusion is anticipated by the formation of district units of state and collective farms with attached local industries (the development of which may also solve the problem of agricultural overpopulation). Differentiation in procurements and taxation should ensure that, within the *kolkhoz* system, equal labour efforts applied in different farms and regions yield equal rewards until the level of state farm wages (to be increased in the meantime) is reached. The private plot can be dispensed with and the state social system can be extended to the collective farms. In 1963 a start was made with old-age pensions, still differentiated in accordance with the prosperity of the different collective farms. The XXIII Party Congress in April 1966, after Khrushchev's fall, made the system general.

(e) THE PARTY AND CLASSES IN SOVIET SOCIETY

At the time of the XXI Party Congress and the re-organisation of the collective farms, the party's influence on industry and state was beyond doubt. The development, however, of its organisation in the collective farms where it was needed most, still lagged behind. On the eve of the transfer of the MTS machinery to the farms, a Ukrainian Province which had primary groups in all its 584 farms (in 1953 party groups existed in a mere 239 farms), 125 of these groups having thirty to forty members each, was still regarded as fairly successful.[104] However, now in many farms brigade groups could be established. The transfer of the machine workers to *kolkhoz* membership further strengthened the farm organisations. In Stavropol Province, for example, in which all the 171 farms bought their machines and had party organisations, total party membership in the collective farms increased from 7,570 to 9,746.[105] Even more important than the quantitative is the qualitative change. By now, the typical member of the *kolkhoz* party organisation was not the holder of an office job, but a skilled worker interested in practical organisation of labour and labour discipline as well as in the remuneration of labour according to industrial standards.

The party's capacity to serve as the platform on which different interests can meet and be reconciled obviously depends on its social composition. Since the XX Party Congress, increased attention has been devoted to the share of factory workers and collective peasants in new admissions. Total party membership, including probationers, increased from 7,216,000 at the XX Congress to 8,239,000 at the XXI and 9,716,000 at the XXII, and 12,740,000 at the XXIII Congress in 1966. More than a third of those available at the XXII had joined since the XX Congress. It follows that total losses through death, failure of probationers to qualify for membership, and (200,000) expulsions of party members amounted to less than a million during five years of tremendous changes. Such stability was unheard of in earlier days. Amongst those admitted between the XX and the XXII Congress, 40.7 per cent were workers (in the period between the XXII and the XXIII Congress this percentage increased to 47.6 per cent), 22.7 per cent were collective farmers, 35.6 per cent salaried employees and professional workers, and one per cent students. In his report to the XXII Congress, Khrushchev emphasised that nearly two-thirds of the admitted non-manual workers were technical specialists employed in production. This leaves a mere twelve per cent of the total admissions for office employees, army officers, teachers, etc. Khrushchev also emphasised that in view of the all-national character of party and state, there would eventually be no need to divide party members into diverse social groups, yet he himself made the distinction between those employed in material production (including engineers, scientists, etc.) and the rest. A change in policy becomes evident from the fact that those not employed in material production still formed nearly 30 per cent recruited before 1956).[106] The change in admission policies to a definite broadening of the party appears to date from the XX Party Congress and, in particular, from Khrushchev's victory at the June 1957 Plenary Meeting of the CC. Total admission of candidates amounted in 1956 to 381,000, in 1957 to 424,000 and then rose steeply to 673,000 in 1960 and 527,000 during the first nine months of 1961. Admissions of probationers as full party members rose from 283,000 to 474,000 which shows an increasingly liberal approach. Still it appears that every fifth probationer failed to qualify as a full party member. With an evident intention to correct the former imbalance, during the first nine months of 1961 the workers' share in admissions in the RSFSR was increased to 55 per cent. Still, a considerable time is required for such corrections in *admission* policies to make their impact upon the structure of the *total* party membership, let alone the higher party committees. The mere fact that party membership operates as a factor of social mobility makes for a smaller percentage of workers in the existing membership than amongst newly, or recently admitted members. A mere 37.8 per cent of party members at the XXIII Congress were workers (to these were added 16.2 per cent collective farmers), as against 40.7 per cent amongst the admissions between the XX and XXII, and 47.6 per cent amongst those between the XXII and XXIII Congresses (i.e. between 1961 and 1965).

The share of women in new admissions and in total party membership may indicate the party's capacity to recruit members from strata where party membership is not a normal step in professional careers and may even require additional sacrifices of spare time. With the experience of Western labour movements in mind we shall not be unduly impressed by the fact that a mere seventh of admissions, in 1957, to the CP of Azerbaidzhan were women ; nor was, perhaps, Mr. Mustafayev who had to accompany the statement with an appropriate self-criticism lest further efforts in that difficult field would relax. In consideration of a Muslim country's background and the heavy demands put on the dairy maid's time, even the fact that a mere 8 per cent of the women working in collective livestock farming were party members is not as unsatisfactory as it appears. More difficulties are met in promoting women to posts of responsibility—not at the very top, where it is obviously possible to find a few women suitable for the very highest appointments (and thereby also to ease the position of their sisters who in less conspicuous posts have to fight against male prejudices) nor even on the Republican level, where Mr. Mustafayev could enumerate quite a few in important positions, but amongst the secretaries of districts and city committees and the chairmen and secretaries of village Soviets, not to speak of collective farms, where they form very insignificant minorities.[107] The problem arises even in an urban environment. At the Party Conference of Mari Region, a woman, herself a high official of a city committee, stated that, notwithstanding the achievements of women at the very top of the Union's political machine, their numbers in the Secretariat of the provincial committee and in the Government of the Autonomous Republic had decreased during recent years. Those who now were in high positions had started their careers during the war and in the first years of reconstruction when few suitable male candidates had been available, but very few women had been promoted during more recent years.[108] The problem is familiar in Britain too to those who in their youth fought for women's emancipation. The USSR, however, which acknowledges the permanent character of women's participation in production work and half of whose academically trained workers are women, should be expected to do better. Yet it is a fact that, for example, in the medical profession, three-quarters of whose members are women, nearly all the top positions are held by men. In industry women may fairly easily get into the second positions, where perhaps better scientific training is required than in top management, yet find access to the latter closed by male prejudices as well as by their own accommodation to them.[109] In the circumstances, the fact that women formed about a fifth of the total membership at the time of the XXIII Congress is not very satisfactory, though their percentage increase, since the XXII Congress, was slightly higher than that of male party members. What matters is the scope open to the thousands who do not aspire to top positions, yet whose encouragement greatly helps the progress of society. This problem is very much broader than the particular women's question, important though the latter is in itself as an indicator of social trends.

Many activities opened by recent developments allow the ordinary citizen without extraordinary ambitions to influence the fate of his factory or farm. In the collective farms, after some hesitations, 'brigade soviets' were formed as bodies supporting brigade leader in order to settle many problems which before had been dealt with by the farm's Board.[110] In industry and state farm, the trade union group was restored to the position envisaged by Lenin at the time of the introduction of NEP. *The Statute on the Settlement of Labour Disputes,* of January 31st, 1957,[111] gave the trade union organisations the decisive role in settling disputes in the factory, management being granted access to the courts only if existing laws were violated by the trade union decision (the employee can resort to the courts if he regards even a formally legal trade union decision as unjust).[112] In June 1957, the re-organisation of industry was followed by that of the unions (the member of which was now reduced to 23). Decision-making number was devolved from the Central Committees of the Unions to the *Sovprofy* in each *Sovnarkhoz,* which might be supposed to be nearer to the factory floor. Full-time trade union machinery above the factory level was greatly reduced.[113] On December 17th, 1957, a Plenary Session of the CC envisaged far-reaching extension of the rights of trade union factory committees, not only in defence of the workers' immediate interests (their consent is required for any dismissals of employees, for the fixing of wage groups and output norms, for the working of overtime) but also in advising management on all production problems. Permanent Production Meetings of employees' delegates were established for this purpose (more than six million workers and salaried employees were elected as members of these Meetings, which elect Presidia competent to supervise the carrying out of adopted decisions). According to the Statute of July 15th, 1958, by which these changes were enacted, trade union committees have to be heard on managerial appointments. They may suggest to the higher authorities the dismissal, or disciplinary punishment, of managers who fail to fulfil obligations entered in the collective agreement, who show bureaucratism or violate the rules of labour legislation. Full-time members of the trade union committees are secured of their former job in the event of a failure to be re-elected; part-time members are protected against managerial arbitrariness by the prohibition of disciplinary punishment, or transfer to another job, without the assent of the factory committee.[114] Managerial authority is now definitely subject to checks from the trade union as well as from the party side. This will be increasingly true if the recent economic forms succeed in making an increasing part of the workers' earnings dependent on factory performance. The 'constitutional factory' in the sense aimed at, for example, by the legislation of the Central European democracies of the period between the wars, with modifications as envisaged by Lenin in view of its functions in the production drive, is becoming a reality in the USSR. One of the most resented aspects of Stalin's policy is being undone. Certainly, there is a great difference between 1920 when management was either itself trade unionist in origin, or highly suspect because of its 'bourgeois' background, and 1958 in which a well-established and professionally trained managerial hierarchy is subject to checks (these are unlikely to go to extremes except in cases of gross misuse of powers). On the other hand, the trade union powers of 1958, as distinct from those of 1920 which were exercised by very small groups, are backed by a public of educated workers which is in no way bound to accept management's explanations at their face value, or alternatively to react with a purely negative distrust.

The party's decision to re-activate the trade unions as definite representations of the workers' sectional interests should not be explained simply by Khrushchev's need for popular support, nor by the desire to offer an alternative within the Soviet setting to the Revisionist suggestion of new Workers' Councils,[115] nor even by the need to check the 'managerial' tendencies evident in Soviet society before, and shortly after, Stalin's death. All these are factors; yet more important, and no more permanent, than any are the inherent needs of the 'second industrial revolution'.

Russia's need to keep the lead in industrial progress implies the need for an an educated working-class. Not because of a desire for social equality (important though it is in the mind of the Soviet communists) did the XX Party Congress envisage the general introduction of full secondary education, on the polytechnical basis envisaged by its predecessor. But the introduction of such education in the major towns resulted in a number of graduations from the secondary schools exceeding about four times the admissions to the universities. In these circumstances it was necessary to overcome the feeling of parents and pupils that failure of a graduate of the secondary school to enter university implies a failure in his career, and to end conditions in which influential parents can help their less deserving children to get university admission.[116] It was also necessary to organise secondary education in such a way that, without prejudicing the work of any of its graduates, it qualifies them both for skilled manual work in industry or agriculture and for subsequent higher education. After a prolonged period of discussion and experiment Khrushchev, in his memorandum of September 21st, 1958, suggested a radical solution. The obligatory basic school, prolonged, where possible, from seven to eight years, should be followed by an obligatory period of practical work in factory and farm, combined for those who desired it, with continuation of schooling, which would improve the workers' professional and general education and result in qualification for university entrance. This qualification would be less scholastic in character and depend, not on parental pressures but on a youth's readiness to make the extra effort required (notwithstanding the promised shortening of the working week for such students) for the combination of work and study, and on the recommendations of the social organisations in factory and farm. (This requirement would exclude those who did not take a serious approach to the practical work.) Khrushchev argued mainly with reference to the technical and managerial *intelligentsia* whose usefulness would clearly improve by such a preparation. It is obvious that the realisation of his suggestions would also result in the formation of an *intelligentsia* unlikely to aspire to a political role independent of, and potentially opposed to, that of the party (the fear of such developments led to the drive against 'Revisionism').

On the basis of Khrushchev's memorandum, but with some modifications, CC Theses were elaborated and published in November as a basis for a discussion, which proceeded with unprecedented participation of the public. At the December 1958 meeting it was concluded with the adoption, by the Supreme Soviet, of the law 'On Strengthening the Link between School and Life and the further Development of Public Education'.[117] Of Khrushchev's original scheme, the basic eight-year school was adopted without controversies other than those caused by a desire, particularly in the national republics (with their demands on language teaching) to have even two years added to the former seven-year basic course. This suggestion was rejected as exceeding present practical possibilities, but a large section of educational opinion accepted the replacement of the *promise* of the general ten-years education by the *actual and general* introduction of the eight-year school as a first instalment only. The new party programme, adopted in October 1961, envisaged for 1970 the introduction of universal eleven-years education and obligatory continuation schooling for all workers who, during the preceding period, had received less than eight-years schooling.

In fact, Khrushchev had overestimated the existing possibilities. A few weeks after his fall, the eleven-year school, where introduced, was returned to a ten-year course. The reasons are evident from the announcement[118] that, since a reduction of the academic programmes was impossible, and 'taking account of the needs of the universities as well as of industry' (i.e. of the reluctance of parent to let their children lose valuable time, as well as of general education which would be of little help in plan fulfilment), the costs of the reduction in school time should be borne by general training in some trade or manual work. This Khrushchev had saved from his original suggestion of a period of obligatory practical work between basic school and university. On the eve of the XXIII Congress, it was formally reduced to those schools 'where the necessary conditions are available'—i.e. presumably those where there is a good workshop, or a neighbouring factory willing to apprentice boys and girls in a trade regarded by them as helpful in their further careers. For the rest (which means the majority of schools) no more than general and polytechnical education (i.e. the use of subjects such as physics and chemistry to familiarise students with basic concepts of industry and agriculture) is required.[119] Khrushchev's effort to use educational reform for bridging the differences between mental and manual labour has thus failed, at least for the time being. Already in 1958 his suggestion to make continuation education the predominant channel of senior secondary education was rejected, under the pressure of angry parents. The universities also demanded early entrants, in particular in the mathematical and science faculties, with uninterrupted schooling. A storm of protest was caused in 1958 by a Khrushchevite suggestion (though only tentative) to compromise with that demand by the establishment of special schools 'for children with particular gifts'. Academician Nesmeyanov described the trend to establish such special schools as 'anti-democratic'.[120] Many years had passed since a suggestion submitted by the highest party authority, be it even in a merely tentative way, had been described in such terms.

The immediate failure, and even more the long-term one, of Khrushchev's effort to tackle the problem of social stratification by educational reform again demonstrated that the main shortage facing Soviet society of today is that of skilled labour in industry. This has been created by recent technological developments. In this field, the economic reforms to which we shall turn presently, make for even greater differentiation, according to individual and factory performance, including the hitherto neglected branches of the national economy, agriculture and the distributive and service trades. The improvements concerning these groups, envisaged by the party programme of 1961, have been carried out after Khrushchev's fall. The December 1964 session of the Supreme Soviet has advanced them—and the connected increase of the minimum wage paid by the state to 45 roubles per month—to the beginning of the following year. The XXIII Party Congress envisaged a close approximation of *kolkhoz* distribution to the level of state farm wages.

In the preparation of the 1961 programme, the party had

clearly envisaged the prospect of commodity exchange continuing through the whole period of socialism. It had thereby opened the discussion on the application of market incentives to increase the initiative of enterprises and the closer approximation of their output to social needs. It is only the self-assertion of the Western (or the doctrinarism of the Maoist) dogmatist which can confuse decentralisation, combined with incentives based upon the surplus ('profits') made by individual economic units (by far the largest part of the surplus product going, of course, to the state as the common owner of all its enterprises and subject to its planning), with a capitalist economy aiming at maximising profits in individual enterprises and allowing planning, if at all, only in the sense of forecasting what the entrepreneurs, if sufficiently interested, will do. Khrushchev aimed at a certain amount of decentralisation, but was afraid of locating it at the enterprise level, perhaps correctly since the existing managerial staff had grown up in conditions where nearly every detail of its work was prescribed. Hence he decentralised within the existing political machine, transferring the powers of the Ministries established for the guidance of individual branches of production to the *Sovnarkhozy*. But thereby he created the conditions for experiments with diverse possible modes of decentralisation and increasing autonomy. On September 9th, 1962, on the basis of a large-scale experiment carried out in the Lvov Sovnarkhoz, Professor Libermann published in *Pravda* his famous suggestions. A few days later Academician Nemchinov followed with the suggestion to burden the enterprises, in order to equalise the conditions for their competition, with a rate of interest for public funds invested in them. The suggestion was further elaborated by Ya. Kronrod and L. Mozhaiskova, writing in *Izvestiya*.[121] On July 1st, 1964, an important experiment, involving orders directly collected from the consumers, was started with two major fashion houses in Moscow and Gorky. With the second quarter of 1965, after Khrushchev's fall, this idea was introduced in 83 textile and 25 leather factories. Other 'experiments' followed.[122] At the September 1965 meeting of the CC these measures were generalised. The enterprises were to receive from the Ministries, which were restored after the dissolution of the *Sovnarkhozy*, definite instructions regarding their total sales and the share therein of the most important types of produce, their total wage fund (but not the number and remuneration of individual workers which were left to the individual factory), total profits and minimum rentability, and contributions to the state budget (or subsidies to be received from it). The central state organs also fix the amount of their investments in individual enterprises, the speed with which they expect these to come into operation and new techniques to be introduced, the supplies guaranteed to the enterprise as well as its obligations to supply others with their means of production (the freedom of state enterprises to choose their partners thus involves only products of second-rank importance).

In a system worked according to these, or similar rules many variations are possible and, indeed, are represented amongst the socialist countries basically operated on lines similar to the Soviet pattern. The social product created by the workers' effort falls into four parts : (*i*) that for himself, remunerated by tariff wages according to his individual efforts ; (*ii*) that distributed in form of premia ; (*iii*) that used for factory welfare services etc. (these two form his share in the performance of collective, not just his individual efforts) ; and (*iv*) the all-national surplus product, part of which feeds the national welfare services (it is this part upon which the programme of 1961 bases the expectation of a gradual transition to communism). These include investments, defence and insurance funds, i.e. that used by the community for purposes not immediately promoting personal welfare.[123] In the conditions of forced industrialisation and of defence against a hostile world, this last section had to be large. As far as defence is concerned, this part of the national product is fundamentally wasted, and the party's task consists in keeping it, by an intelligent policy of peace, as low as possible. As far as investments are concerned, it is an issue of the long-term versus the short-term interest of basically identical people. The party, being the most conscious section of the community, must help the nation in keeping the proper balance between short-term and long-term interests. It is the same question, but also that of differentiation between the interests of different groups of workers (e.g. semi-skilled women workers with many

children will prefer as large as possible a share in extra earnings
to be spent for crèches rather than for premia, different sizes
of which would mean for a highly paid engineer, a different type
of holiday but for themselves one dress more or less per annum).
As regards the relationship between the first two forms of
remuneration, it appears obvious that general standards of justice
(in the period of socialism this means that remuneration should
be proportional to the citizen's effort) demand maximum consideration for the first group of rewards (individual wages graded
according to individual performance) suitably mingled, from a welfare point of view, with the third and fourth ones so as to protect
the less efficient part of the community against need. Differentiation according to the collective's performance, with a tendency
to promote the interests of those members of the collective who,
often based upon educational advantage, perform the most
complicated and responsible work, is, in principle, justified only
as a means of increasing the national product and thereby every
citizen's share in it. It is a necessary evil mitigated, however,
by one fact. That is that this part of the national product (as
distinct from those which require large-scale policy decisions
before spending) is the most accessible to influence by smaller
groups and even by active individuals. It we concieve of
democracy as self-determination rather than as approval of
decisions taken elsewhere, a healthy development of that indivi-
dualised part of the national product provides a basis for an
active life of trade union groups in the factories etc., promoting
an increase in their surplus, and influencing its distribution. If
we regard the flourishing of democracy in that sense as an interest
of society as a whole, we may even accept its flourishing best
where there is most to distribute, provided the conditions for
competition are equal, i.e. it is within the powers of each collective to move into the ranks of the most prosperous ones.

For Khrushchev, and the authors of the party programme
adopted by the XXII Party Congress, it was self-evident that the
CPSU, being the organizer of industrial reconstruction, can
never again be a sectional party of labour. It must stand for some
higher form of social organization. In its new programme,
adopted by the XXII Congress, the creation of this type of social

28

organisation is conceived as an immediate task. By its very formulation in terms of reforms for the next decades, it loses many of the Utopian features hitherto associated with communism. It will be a society from which social differentiations will have disappeared, first by the fusion of the peasantry with the state-employed workers in a new united form of socialist ownership of the means of production. Eventually, major differentiations between workers and intelligentsia will disappear in consequence of universal higher education on the one hand and full automation of the production process on the other. There will be far-going equalisation of basic incomes, but for any foreseeable future incentive payments for good work and the use of money as a means of distribution will remain. Some steps will be taken, as envisaged already for the twenty-year period, to replace by unpaid social services the satisfaction of certain needs by purchases out of the wage incomes. For any foreseeable future there will be a state, though deprived of any association with the rule of any class over another. Hence, there will be also a state apparatus, consisting partly of professional officials, partly of voluntary associations of citizens who undertake many of the former state functions. Emphasis is laid on the encouragement of voluntary civic activities. The retention of the theoretical aim of an eventual 'withering away of the state' may be a Utopia. To put it differently, it is a mere expression of a healthy tendency to deprive such state machinery as will remain of any splendour and glamour and to put it in its proper place as the servant of the industrial organisation of the people from whose achievements further progress to higher forms of social organisation is expected.

Conclusion : The Party after Khrushchev

Khrushchev led the CPSU for eleven years, two-thirds for which formed the culmination of his work. These lasted from the XX Party Congress until the signing of the Test Ban Agreement, the culmination of the peace policies which soon after, with President Kennedy's assassination, ran into a crisis. This demonstrated that it is not enough for *one* side to an international dispute to pursue a policy of peace. Apart from these external limitations, Khrushchev's regime had its internal limitations too. He represented that first phase in the development of post-Stalin Russia when leaders who had matured under the Stalin regime were convinced that its terrorist and repressive policies had to be dropped (since the USSR was now wealthy and strong enough to function without terror). Yet, from their Leninist youth as well as from later days when terror had to be justified by Utopia, they had acquired a belief, and a capacity to make others believe, in realisations which appeared nearer than they were. Hence his tendency to what later was described as 'subjectivism', though it was nothing but belief in achieving by administrative means, without terror and major sacrifices in the standard of life, those things which communists had been used to see behind the horrors of the present : a class-less and free society. Sometimes, acting on that belief, he carried out reorganisations such as the establishment of the *Sovnarkhozy*, which were useful in that they prepared ground for later, and more effective, reorganisations. Sometimes—and it was these actions which led to the reproach of 'subjectivism'—he used his position to establish measures which, if feasible, might result in bringing the rulers and the ruled closer together. But these were impracticable. To this group of measures belongs the division, in the autumn of 1962, of the existing administrative units into two each, an industrial and agricultural one, a step which was simply impracticable (industrialisation had already proceeded too far for such a division). This was a main reason for his fall, two years later. Sometimes Khrushchev willed measures such as the educational reform of 1958, which kept to the socialist aim of overcoming the division between mental and physical labour, but for which the country, and perhaps the twentieth century in general, was not yet mature. To this group also belonged the decision of the XXII Party Congress, repealed by the XXIII, to introduce a rotation period in all higher, and in particular in junior, party offices so as to achieve the participation of a maximum number of party members in the exercise of these offices. Having lived so long outside the Soviet Union, I would hesitate to answer the question of whether the party was not yet, or no longer, mature for this, important though the answer may be. Khrushchev was trained to regard the word of the CC of the CEPSU—no longer an individual but a collective one, due to his efforts—as law for the international communist movement. Sometimes he spoke out his mind without sufficient tact. Those colleagues who had not enjoyed de-Stalinisation would reproach him for having thereby caused, or at least promoted, the break with the Chinese and the consequent weakening of the international position of the USSR. It took at least six months, and a quite efficient demonstration by the Chinese on their own part, to show that Khrushchev, whether good or overconscientious as a diplomat, had simply expressed objective facts of historical development. These were stronger than any individual—including, probably, Chairman Mao. But it should not be denied that his successors, indeed, have managed to make full use of the international situation largely created by Khrushchev's urge for clarity. They have replaced a situation in which even many West-European Communist Parties doubted whether his management of the Chinese situation had been very diligent, by that of the XXIII Party Congress at which all communist parties, with the sole exceptions of the Chinese and the Albanian, were represented, and hence a considerable degree of unity had been restored.

However, Khrushchev was dismissed by the CC on October 14th, 1964, in consequence of a combination of all these elements. In particular, there was his mistake of the division of the provinces which turned against him a fair section of the provincial organisers, his main supporters in 1957. There were also diplomatic setbacks, then factors which were beyond human control—two bad harvests in succession, followed, for his successors' benefit, by a fairly good one. There also existed a genuine fear of another personality cult—without terror, yet still burdened with the risk that the whole party be made to share in an individual's errors. A man whose grasp of the political machine was weakening must not be allowed to strengthen that grasp. The orderly manner of his dismissal in itself demonstrated one of the main achievements of his regime, the normalisation of the political life of the USSR. If Lenin, by tremendous will-power, had introduced the NEP, and thereby saved the Russian revolution from breaking at the point where the Jacobin dictatorship had fallen in 1795; if Stalin, by a combination of soberness and brutality, had given that decision a content which has turned the isolated Soviet Union into one of the 'big two', and what otherwise would have been a gigantic Paris Commune into the start of a new phase of human political and social organisation, then Khrushchev, surely less a genius but more lucky than either of those two, had turned the outcome of enormous efforts and sacrifices into a stable order in which people may enjoy normal lives. It may now be considered how much of the dreams of the start belongs to the realm of possibilities of the twentieth century, how much to that of the twenty-first, and perhaps, of a still remoter future. Whatever contribution the USSR has made to the solution of a most urgent international problem, that of the under-developed countries, was prepared under his predecessors, but Khrushchev has turned Lenin's genial idea, which in Stalin's realisation appeared tainted with horror, into a more or less realistic programme which people all over Asia can aim at. And he has shown that a world power with nuclear arms, intercontinental ballistic missiles, Sputniks and everything else, can be great by promoting peace.

When stating achievements which would stand even if every-one of Khrushchev's reforms should prove premature (which they are not) one must also emphasise his limitations. Being his party's child, Khrushchev shared in many acquired habits—with the exception of the terror, recognition of the obsoleteness and harmfulness of which was one of his chief merits. Yet another merit is shown in the fact that the man who probably assisted in Beria's execution lest the USSR be stabilised as a police state, himself retired like any Adenauer or Macmillan who has fallen out with his caucus. In all likelihood, he was the last Soviet leader at the occasion of whose dismissal the West German 'Sovietologists' could even try to produce the myth of a *'coup d'etat* in the Kremlin'. Khrushchev's recognition of the basic importance of the peasant problem and his concentrated efforts towards its solution has not only achieved for him the status of a great leader but probably saved the USSR from being turned into a major Hungary 1956. But the administrative habits acquired under Stalin had dominated his methods of reform. This holds true not only of the unhappy division of administrative units. He created a solution in which he, whom the Soviet peasants will always remember as a friend, had mishandled the issue of their private plots. It had to be corrected by his successors. (That the agricultural pension law prepared by him could be made efficient only by them is due to a comparatively speedy process: they, too, when their hour will come, will have to leave a lot of unfinished reforms on the completion of which their successors may prosper.) Having experienced the dead weight of intellectual Stalinism, Khrushchev probably felt about it more strongly than they do, at least judging by their former performance in the intellectual fields. But even here he, being the prisoner of his party's past, left them with some fairly elementary tasks such as the ending of Lysenkoism. Every active man, and in particular every leading politician, forms some kind of bridge between what has been before and what will be after. But of Nikita Khrushchev this holds particularly true, since he has saved the party from the contradictions of his predecessor's work, yet carried quite a lot of dead weight into the new environment.

It may be a little too early to attempt a definition of that dead weight. But we may safely state that, up to our day, three basic themes have dominated the growth of the CPSU: the struggle for industrialisation, the contest with the static element embodied in the state, and the conflict between centralising and decentralising tendencies. As regards the first, the party has maintained through all these decades an unambiguous and consistent line. Its triumph has been identical with that of industrialisation. In the competition of the groups of revolutionary intellectuals for leadership in the transformation of Russia, Social Democracy was selected because it set its prospect on the working class, small though it was in those days. In the factional struggle amongst the Bolsheviks, Lenin won because he advocated policies which the workers could understand. When fighting against left-wing communists for the employment of specialists, and when introducing NEP (to the disappointment of that minority of the workers who at the time were in employment) Lenin realised the workers' basic interest in industrial development. So did Stalin when he enforced an investment policy which granted to the consumer only a very modest share of the increase in production achieved by great efforts.

True, the party itself changed in this process. From its very formation it had delimitated itself against the Economists', and later the Mensheviks', emphasis on the workers' short-term sectional interests. The long-term interest of the working-class advocated by it was tied to a thorough democratic revolution, the eventual socialist transformation of society promoted by coordination with socialist revolutions in more advanced countries. Its discipline was that of revolution and civil war, a fair amount of internal freedom being enabled by the common interest of the workers and the more advanced strata of the peasantry in defeating counter-revolution. Yet when the party had to preserve its unity in a hostile environment, and eventually to start industrialisation by means which involved heavy pressure upon a large majority of the population, it became an extremely centralised and terrorist dictatorship, which had announced itself in the very first stages of the formation of the revolutionary 'elite'. That the party did not break down in the tensions of the Stalin period, and that in our days these tensions could be overcome by evolutionary means, was possible because industrialisation, based upon nationalisation of the means of production, became identified with the national interest. Such an obvious cause for working-class dissatisfaction as the existence of unearned incomes had been removed. Such differentiation of incomes as accompanied industrialisation was made acceptable by the increasing number of opportunities open to everyone who made the necessary efforts. By greatly increasing the national wealth in spite of the devastations of the Second World War, and by creating an educated working class, industrialisation has in our days allowed for a raising of the standards of life of the masses who had remained in the background during its first stages. The workers' interest in developing industry is identical with the national interest and the party is the embodiment of that interest. During the struggle for Stalin's succession, consciousness of this defeated all attempts to cash in on the consumers' justified complaints and made for a fairly easy triumph of Khrushchev's policy of further industrialisation of agriculture. By creating in agriculture conditions comparable with those in industry, and open to similar improvements, the party has made its membership attractive even to that type of peasant who has no managerial or administrative ambitions yet wishes to make an active contribution to his farm's prosperity. Moreover, the national interest in peace has been associated with positive help given to the industrialisation of under-developed countries. In this way, Stalin's concept of 'socialism in one country', which served as the intellectual skeleton for the earlier stages of the industrialisation process, was overcome. In the new party programme, it has been replaced by a concept of world revolution which differs from the original one. The emancipation of the under-developed countries is proceeding in an atmosphere of peaceful competition between the USSR and the USA, the world stronghold of monopoly capitalism. By winning this competition the USSR hopes to win leadership in the struggle for the orientation of the new nations and to encourage their choice of non-capitalist ways of development.

In the more realistic atmosphere of post-Khrushchevean days, this concept meets the objection that the level even of industrial productivity, not to speak of agriculture in the USSR, is obviously below that of its main competitor. This is not because it fails to grow (its tempo of rise is better than that of most capitalist countries, and quite understandably so unless one begins the comparison with the most absurd expectations, which is really the starting point of much of Western 'Sovietology') but because Western capitalism fails to stagnate. The prospect of the USSR really overtaking the West is bound to its capacity to use its form of social organisation for a quicker assimilation of the 'second industrial revolution' than the West is capable of. In the words of the *Kommunist*,[124] the party's task of leadership is conceived as 'scientific guidance of social processes'. It presupposes reliable and scientifically well-founded information on the internal state of the object of analysis as well as on external conditions. Otherwise subjectivism, project-making without preparation (the main shortcoming attributed to Khrushchev) and arbitrariness in administration become unavoidable. Guidance of social processes has its administrative as well as scientific sides. The first, though obviously necessary, has also its subjective aspects against which one has to be on one's guard by suitable selection of cadres and by the maintenance of close connection with the economic basis. All this appears simple enough but does *not* contain a clear answer to the question as to how the scientific element in the desired combination should be conceived. This implies assumptions regarding the existing level of development of the social sciences, the extent to which 'computorisation' is possible, and how much the party's cadres could be permeated with this, as opposed to the politico-administrative approach. At the time of the XXIII Congress 46.8 per cent of existing party members were between 26 and 40 years, the numbers of those with party records under ten (47.1 per cent) and 10-30 years, i.e. mostly dating from the culmination of the Stalin period (47.3 per cent), were nearly equal. The percentages of party members less than 25 years old (6.2 per cent) or with a party record of more than thirty years (i.e. before Stalin's 'great purge'—5.6 per cent), were insignificant. Amongst the delegates to the XXIII Congress, too, the 'middle-aged' generations of party members were predominant. 24.2 per cent had joined the party during the period between 1946 and 1955, slightly more during the War and 30.4 per cent after 1955. As regards their present social status two-thirds of the delegates belonged to the group of 'salaried employees' who form a mere 46 per cent of the total party membership, 1,141 delegates (i.e. 72 per cent of those working in industry) were workers, 554 (two-thirds of those who came from agriculture) *kolkhoz* members up to foreman's status. Nearly half of the delegates were intellectuals of different types : 1,484 technicians, economists etc., 493 agricultural specialists, 451 teachers, doctors and lawyers (55.1 per cent had completed higher education of some kind). But the professional party officials, who had been predominant at the time of the XX Congress now, ten years later, formed only the second largest group. Of 1,204 of them, 62 per cent were full-time party secretaries from the district level upwards; 82 trade union and 44 Komsomol workers have to be added. The state officials in the narrower sense of the word were represented by 539 delegates, 352 were army officers. Elections to Congresses are obviously affected by central directives, but if these reflect, to any extent, actual trends in social life, the prospects for the party's functioning as an agency for a thorough rejuvenation of society are not too propitious. But certainly it tends to become identical with society as it stands, neither a body opposed to it, nor propaganda agency of the state conceived as a power mechanism.

The party's relations to the state built and dominated by it have been continually changing. Short of an end to its dynamism, i.e. to its specific function, it is difficult to imagine these relations being finally stabilised. During both the major wars which the Soviet state had to wage, it absorbed much of the party, influenced its structure (in the sense of making it equally representative of all the enfranchised sections of the community). Its main activities were organisation of the home front and of the educational services in the armies. On the other hand, the party assumed direct control of the state functions during the 'second revolution' which clearly contradicted established routine. In quieter periods, the party kept some distance from the state machine, ready to check its potential deviations. This happened both during NEP, when the state machine was more exposed to the influence of hostile classes than the party which tried to keep its own ranks clean; and after Stalin's death when the party refused to be satisfied with a mere restoration of legality and to conclude the great drive by a stabilisation of the existing centralised structure of management. The ambitions of leaders and of organised bodies played their part in these events, but there is no reason to suppose that party officials are, *a priori*, more capable or cunning than those who have to manage the administration of a giant country, (or those who are popular victors in war). A feeling that the triumphant war-leader might be the most dangerous aspirant to dictatorship had led to the defeats of Trotsky, Tukhachevski and—in more civilised manner—Zhukov. But particularly in the last case, when experiences of party dictator are recent, such feelings are explicable only on the ground of a consciousness that the party stands for something superior to winning a war or even to restoring the country's normal life after a great upheaval. Partly in order to check potential army opposition, Stalin raised the least civilised section of the state apparatus to a position of strength superior even to that of the party machine itself. But the ease with which the party's internal life could be restored and the power of the political police broken may confirm Soviet people in the view that police rule was a tragic episode born out of particular circumstances and that the party represents the major check against any part of the state machine getting out of hand. In contrast since the XX Party Congress the 'withering away of the State' envisaged by Marxist theory is now conceived as an evolution of state administration into self-government by social organisations. It is obvious that in developments of this kind the party, being the guiding force of the mass-organisations, is bound to play the leading part. Some transfers of individual state functions to social organisations (as have taken place in the administration of labour law by trade union committees, or in the treatment of comparatively minor offences by the offender's work-mates) proceed, however, under the supervision of the courts. There is no reason to regard these changes as more than reforms in the operation of state organisation. Since the party programme expects the all-national state, free from class-associations as now achieved in the USSR, to continue for the whole period of communist construction, there may be very good reasons to reform but no urge to abolish it.

The ease with which the Stalinist form of government could be overcome may be explained largely by the fact that centralisation had over-reached itself. During the half-century which separated the foundation of *Iskra* from Stalin's death, it made nearly uninterrupted progress: first in order to secure the leadership of the consistent revolutionaries within the labour movement, then in order to conquer power and to win the civil war. Even the setback which centralisation within society as a whole experienced with the introduction of NEP was offset by increased centralisation *within the party*. The breaking of all resistance against Stalin's policy of industrialisation and collectivisation, the needs of war and, eventually, the drive of feverish reconstruction at a time when people demanded relaxation, drove centralisation to its climax in the postwar period when no aspect of intellectual life was exempt from direct party control. It is hardly surprising that opponents of planning all over the world have derived from events in Stalinist Russia the totalitarian nightmare depicted in this and many lesser expressions of the same idea.

In the USSR itself, the strain of over-centralisation carried its own remedy. The varied demands of complicated technique could not be satisfied with the simple emphasis on priorities which had enabled concentration of all efforts on elementary conditions of survival. The new generation which had been given an education superior to that provided in more developed countries could not be guided from a centre nor be intellectually fed with a mythology. It was useless to permit a few people to think at the centre according to typical patterns once hundreds of thousands had become capable of doing the job much better if allowed to modify general schemes according to local and changing needs. Likewise, it was futile to deny the quickest developing nation the use of experiences of other countries for the mere purpose of a self-assertion, which had in any case become unnecessary in view of obvious achievements. The need for some decentralisation was recognised by all the elements which competed for power after Stalin's death. Khrushchev and the party machine won the competition because they disposed of a unified framework which allowed for the preservation of unity of purpose even after a devolution of the choice of means. The Khrushchevean devolution within the existing political machine was overtaken by a further devolution down to the factory collective, the general planning functions being preserved in the restored ministries. But though this implies less power of the province as against the centre, it implies more, not less, autonomy at the lower level. This must be considered together with the recent efforts to increase the supervision of administrative and managerial organs by factory collectives and mass organisations, and to transfer to them even some judicial functions. To the Marxist, these developments are far more important than the fact that the party bureaucracy became afraid of too quick a 'thaw' in artistic and other intellectual fields. Nor do the basic conclusions of this study depend on the details of the process in which the surviving elements of orthodox conservatism, and the resistance of that part of the party machine which wants to lead intellectual life by its strings, will be overcome by the needs of industrial and scientific progress. Service to the latter ideal, indeed forms the party's *raison d'etre*. The end of Lysenkoism shows this clearly enough. The withdrawal of party controls from fields where they form an obstacle to scientific progress is bound in due course to be followed by their reduction in literary and similar fields. A socialist society cannot be indifferent to important aspects of its life. But there is no inherent reason for this kind of guidance being in any way repressive and promoting certain schools of artists, as distinct from general intellectual trends which may find expression in art, etc.

Decentralisation and increased participation of ordinary citizens in decision making obviously depend on developments *within the party*. An elite of thirteen million active citizens guiding two hundred million people is not the narrowest of oligarchies noticeable even in countries with longer traditions of broad political life. Conventional criticism of the one-party system can hardly be upheld if we keep in mind how many important policy decisions in our own society are removed from the check of party competition. This is itself most problematic in some acknowledgedly democratic Western countries. Democracy there is reduced to competition for that section of the electorate which is least interested in public affairs, yet most accessible to control by modern mass-communications. Sometimes decisions are taken even against the predominant trend of public opinion, by small groups in control of the caucus of the majority party, which itself may be supported by just half the electorate. Much of such democracy as exists in our society presupposes democracy within the existing party organisations, or in diverse sectional organisations cooperating with them. Few of us, and hardly those with clearly established views, are capable of choosing fields of our civic activities other than those to which we are bound by background and social position. There is little sense in denying the description of 'democratic' to a system within the framework of which intra-party democracy is *clearly* the essential one. In substance, Stalin was right when, in 1924, he described industrialisation of the country as a preliminary condition to democracy within the party. The correctness of the forecast is not impaired by the fact that, eventually, his own demise proved a milestone in the transformation of that potentiality into actual developments. It was certainly a prolonged process, perhaps with many setbacks. We are here interested not in general statements of a necessarily one-sided character, but in the assessment of trends of development.

How far are these likely to go? Any progress in the restoration of some type of factory democracy (certainly checked and coordinated in its work by the party organisation) would mean, not the realisation of some syndicalist utopia (which, indeed, would undo the main achievements of the planned economy), nor the denial of the hierarchy implicit in modern technique, but progress towards an equilibrium between suggestions going upwards from the factory floor and downwards from the managerial and technical councils. Any progress of citizen participation (at least in the lower links) in the struggle against criminality will strengthen, not only the professional jurists' struggle against the more serious types of criminality but also the ordinary citizen's feeling of being himself involved in an activity which, since time immemorial, he had regarded as the preserve of an organisation standing above himself. It is a long way from such progress to that 'withering away of the state' which is upheld as a goal in communist ideology. The party's own desire *not* to 'wither away' may be one reason for its encouraging all kinds of less formal civic activities. The inspiration of such activities would, indeed, offer ample scope for leadership even when the production drive would have lost its present urgency. Yet the

content of those activities itself would change. In such a hypothetical situation, the party's present role of emphasising the production interest—and, if international security should be achieved,
even that of emphasising the needs of national defence—would
cease to be overwhelmingly powerful. Still, the unity of the social
interest would need some institutional form of expression in the
very event of a transfer of the management of diverse economic
and social activities to social bodies. It may be more democratic
than anything existing in the world of today. But, surely, it would
be no glorified anarchy.

NOTES AND REFERENCES

1. Cf. *Pravda's* article of June 10th, 1953, translated in *Soviet Studies,*
   vol. V (1953), pp. 208 ff.
2. As an Appendix to his edition of Khrushchev's Secret Session Speech,
   Bertram D. Wolfe has translated, from the Menshevik *Sotsialisticheski
   vestnik* 1956, No. 7-8, an interview alleged to have been given by
   Khrushchev to Senator Pierre Commin, a member of the French
   Socialist Delegation which visited Moscow in March 1956. According
   to this record Beria was shot (presumably by his colleagues of the
   Presidium themselves) as soon as in a session of the Presidium
   the existence of his conspiracy became evident. Detailed evidence
   of his guilt was collected only after his death. The most recent
   authoritative statement (see footnote 3) does not contradict this
   version. In any case, the composition of the Extraordinary Court
   nominated to decide the Beria case was not judicial, but intended to
   represent public opinion.
3. *Istoriya KPSS* (1959), p. 629.
4. Of December 17th, 1953.
5. Editorial of July 10th, 1953.
6. *Sovetskoye gosudarstov i pravo,* 1956, No. 1, p. 3, and Alexandrov,
   ibid. No. 3. The atmosphere in which these events occurred is illustrated by the fact that the decree, popular though it certainly was,
   not published at the time. How they were treated by an influential
   section of Western public opinion is illustrated by the fact that Prof.
   H. Berman, when he brought the information to the USA from a
   visit paid to his Soviet colleagues in the autumn of 1955, was not
   entirely believed, in spite of the fact that the situation had been made
   fairly clear in an article of *Pravda,* April 12, 1955.

7. *Soviet Studies,* vol. V, pp. 422 ff. A full translation of Pomerantsev's article was published in *The Current Digest of the Soviet Press,* March 17th and 24th, 1954.

8. This is the substance of V. Vassilevski's disapproval of Pomerantsev's treatment of novels written in 1947, 1950 and 1952 'outside the historical conditions in which they were written and though they had all appeared at the same time'. Conditions in the village, the embellishment of which in novels written in 1947 and 1950 was denounced by Pomerantsev, were rather worse than in 1952 when Ovechkin wrote. What had changed was the party's attitude to criticism. Vassilevski's article, published in *Literaturnaya gazeta,* January 30, 1954, is translated in *The Current Digest of the Soviet Press,* March 24, 1954 ; another criticism of Pomerantsev (by L. Skorino, from *Znamya,* 1954, No. 2) is translated in *Soviet Studies,* vol. VI, pp. 91 ff.

9. Ibid., pp. 98 ff.

10. Cf. ibid., pp. 179 ff.

11. Translation ibid., pp. 77 ff.

12. Part translation (from *Novy mir,* 1954, No. 11), ibid., vol. VII, pp. 103 ff.

13. K. Simonov in *Literaturnaya gazeta,* July 17 and 20, 1954 ; part translation (together with Ehrenburg's reply, ibid., August 3, 1954) in *Soviet Studies,* vol. VI, pp. 290 ff.

14. *The Yershov Brothers,* English text in *Soviet Literature,* 1959, No. 2,

15. Published in *Teatr.* 1954, No. 2.

16. Cf. *Soviet Studies,* vol. VI, p. 415.

17. English translations in *The Current Digest of the Soviet Press,* October 24 and 31 and November 7, 1953 ; a discussion in *Soviet Studies,* vol. V, pp. 234 ff.

18. *Partiinaya zhizn,* 1955, No. 17, p. 28.

19. Cf. M. Efremov's report in *Kommunist,* 1954, No. 7, translated in *Soviet Studies,* vol. VI, pp. 173 ff.

20. *Partiinaya zhizn,* 1956, No. 5, p. 27.

21. *Partiinaya zhizn,* 1954, No. 4, p. 15 ; see also *Soviet Studies,* vol. V, p. 288.

22. On June 10, 1953, a programmatic article of *Pravda* spoke of a concentration of investments serving agriculture 'in the central thickly populated provinces of the country where capital investment can provide the most economic results in the shortest time'. Khrushchev's later attacks on Malenkov's original opposition to the 'new lands' campaign may date back to this period.

23. The decision, adopted on March 2, was published in *Pravda,* March 6, 1954 ; Khrushchev's report, delivered on February 24th, was published as late as March 21st (this delay may indicate disagreements on the sharpest statements in the report). Condensed translations in *The Current Digest of the Soviet Press,* April 14 and 21, and May 5, 1954 ; Cf. *Soviet Studies,* vol. VI, pp. 101 ff. and 109-10.

24. *Istoriya KPSS* 1959, p. 634.
25. Ibid., pp. 105 ff. The importance laid upon the issue in party organisational life is illustrated by the fact that when in April 1955 the secretary of the Saratov Provincial Committee was removed by decision of a Plenary Session of the Committee, his continuing application of the *travopole* system even after the decision of the Plenary Session of the CC in February-March 1954 played a prominent part in the criticism. (*Partiinaya zhizn*, 1955, No. 9, p. 46).
26. *Soviet Studies*, vol. VI, pp. 332 ff. In view of the enormous differences in local conditions, initiative was left to individual farms.
27. Reported in *Soviet Studies*, vol. VI, pp. 443 ff.
28. Even in the form of satire, which he could not stop as he himself had encouraged it, cf. *Soviet Studies*, vol. VI, p. 186.
29. A survey of these arguments and of their factual foundation has been given by R. W. Davies in *Soviet Studies*, vol VII, pp. 59 ff. For an illustration of how a party group's failure to oppose what eventually proved to be the minority view was still regarded as coming close to a disciplinary offence, see the Correspondence in *Partiinaya zhizn*, 1955, No. 5, pp. 53 ff.
30. Engl. translation in *Soviet Studies*, vol. VII, pp. 91 ff.
31. *Pravda*, July 17, 1955 (the CC decision is published, ibid., July 14). A report on the Industrial Conference of May 16-18 is published in *Soviet Studies*, vol. VII, pp. 201 ff.
32. *Soviet Studies*, vol. VII, pp. 118 and 316.
33. Materials on the 1955 drive are given in *Soviet Studies*, Vol. VII, pp. 230 ff.
34. Only as a rule. *Partiinaya zhizn* (1954, No. 11, p. 75, for example) gives cases of even comparatively large primary organisations which were distinguished mainly by their members having kept all kinds of administrative jobs on the farm but having had to be sacked because of their incompetence (usually these former officials retained a sound aversion to manual work).
35. Cf. *Soviet Studies*, vol. VII, pp. 170 and 180.
36. Ibid. pp. 166-67, and vol. VIII, pp. 203 ff. (slightly abridged text of the Statute on Procuratorial Functions).
37. Mainly those, of course, where the monopoly had caused direct practical harm.
38. English translation in *The Current Digest of the Soviet Press*, vol. VII, p. 2. The most scandalous case of 'discoveries' based, to put it mildly, upon wishful thinking concerned the alleged transition of antibiotics or viruses into microbes, and *vice versa* ('achievements' of the *Lysenko* era which had not received formal party sanction). It was investigated by a special commission, the findings of which were published, under the significant heading 'Against Scientific Truth', in *Meditsinski rabotnik*, February 22, 1955.
39. 1955, No. 7.

29

40. *Partiinaya zhizn,* 1955, No. 6, p. 51.

41. Cf. *Partiinaya zhizn,* 1957, No. 20, p. 28. See also F. Zanzolkov's article in *Kommunist,* 1958, No. 11.

42. According to *Partiinaya zhizn,* 1955, No. 19, p. 23, nearly 60 per cent of the 15.5 million members of the *Soviet intelligentsia* (in the current broad definition, which includes many of those described in other countries as white-collar workers) were such 'specialists-practicians'.

43. V. Okurayev in *Partiinaya zhizn,* 1958, No. 23, p. 18,

44. Cf. *Soviet Studies,* vol. VIII, pp. 19-20.

45. See, for example, *Partiinaya zhizn,* 1955, No. 15, p. 60 and No. 19, pp. 22-23.

46. Pervukin's speech at the XXI Party Congress, *Pravda,* February 4, 1959.

47. As expressed in the editorial of *Kommunist,* 1955, No. 14, summary in *Soviet Studies,* vol. VII, pp. 430 ff.

48. Ibid. and vol. VIII, No. 9 (and notes).

49. 1955, No. 14.

50. I have dealt with these, and later, developments in a report in *Soviet Studies,* vol. VIII, pp. 157 ff.

51. The publication, in Warsaw on February 19th (i.e. shortly after the XX Congress had started), of joint declaration of five Communist Parties, including the CPSU, to rehabilitate the Polish CP which during the 'great purge' had been dissolved by Comintern, shows that such far-reaching decisions had been taken already on the eve of the Congress.

52. 1958, No. 9.

53. 1956, No. 4, p. 7.

54. Only 4.5 per cent of them (as against 7.4 per cent at the XIX Congress) had joined the party upto 1920, 25 per cent (as against 36.4 per cent) between 1921 and 1930, 34 per cent (as against 36 per cent) between 1931 and 1940, 21.6 (16.6) per cent during the war, and 13.4 (4.6) per cent during the post-war period.

55. Cf. my report in *Soviet Studies,* vol. X, pp. 293 ff. (for the earlier stages of the discussion, cf. ibid. vol. IX, pp. 412 ff.) ; my article 'Social Law', ibid. vol. XII, pp. 56 ff. ; and on the new criminal code of the ISFSR, ibid. pp. 456 ff.).

56. Surveys are given in *Soviet Studies,* vol. VIII, pp. 106 ff. (for the time of the Congress) and in *Partiinaya zhizn,* 1956, No. 24 (for the whole year, with emphasis on economic and cultural measures).

57. By decree of January 25, 1960, the social insurance sanctions against a worker's changing his job on his own initiative were also repealed. (*Vichmosto Verkhovnovo Soveta SSSR,* 1960, No. 4, art. 56).

58. Cf. *Soviet Studies,* vol. VIII, pp. 213 ff.

59. Summary, ibid. pp. 307 ff.

60. *Partiinaya Zhizn,* 1956, No. 9, p. 6 ; 1957, No. 13, p. 12 ; *Spravochnik partiinovo rabotnika,* 1957, p. 429.

61. *Partiinazh Elion* 1954, No. 1, p. 35, and No. 2, p. 63.

62. *Istoriya KPSS,* published in 1959.

63. *Soviet Studies,* vol. VIII, pp. 111-2. In the following year, Stalin's death was commemorated in the Georgian Party paper by a dignified article which spoke of his mistakes in the now accepted terms.

64. Cf. *Partiinaya zhizn,* 1958, No. 6, p. 20 ; No. 7, pp. 5 and 8-9 ; and also the *konsultatsiya,* published ibid. No. 23 (i.e. after the Hungarian events), p. 56, which distinguishes between the legitimate, *partiinaya* critique which is of a practical character, and the illegitimate, destructive one.

65. Including, for example, the existence of the professional criminal in the USSR and the labour camp, from the standpoint of its educational effects upon him and others. Cf. *Soviet Studies,* vol. IX, pp. 423 ff.

66. Some foreign translations have been published. A summary, with a report on the early stages of the discussion of the novel, is available in *Soviet Studies,* vol. VIII, pp. 437 ff.

67. E.g. V. Zorza in the *Manchester Guardian,* August 30, 1957.

68. Very few copies of the book became available outside Russia. An extensive summary is published in *Soviet Studies,* vol. IX, pp. 322 ff.

69. For the earlier stages of that process (which after Shepilov's fall were regarded and still insufficient), cf. *Soviet Studies,* vol. IX, pp. 108 ff.

70. Published in *Literaturnaya gazeta,* October 25, 1958 ; English translation in *The Current Digest of the Soviet Press,* vol. X, No. 43.

71. Cf. the Choronological Survey given in *Osteuropa* (Stuttgart), 1957, No. 10, pp. 744 ff.

72. Cf. ibid. vol. VIII, pp. 165 ff. (with those passages of the *Jenmin Jibao* editorial of April 5, 1956, which were omitted when it was translated in *Pravda*).

73. A survey of the stages of that development has been given by O. Anweiler in *Osteuropa* (Stuttgart), 1958, No. 4.

74. I have summarised these arguments in *Soviet Studies,* vol. VIII, pp. 404 ff.

75. See ibid.

76. A survey of the discussion has been given by J. Miller in *Soviet Studies,* vol. IX, pp. 65 ff. ; an appreciation by R. W. Davies, ibid., pp. 353 ff.

77. *Partiinaya zhizn,* 1957, No. 7, p. 12.

78. *Partiinaya zhizn,* 1958, No. 15, p. 22.

79. Article 26 of the Basic Principles of the Constitution of the Courts, adopted by the Supreme Soviet Session in December 1958.

80. Cf. L. I. Mandelshtam and V. A. Kirin in *Sovetskoye gosuadarstvo i pravo,* 1958, No. 3.

81. *Pravda,* October 29, 1961.

82. This is the record given in *Istoriya KPSS* (pp. 654 ff.), i.e. after

the XXI Party Congress ended the tendency, noticeable in speeches of leading party officials at that Congress, if not to expel the members of the defeated group from the party then at least to exclude from the Central Committee those of its associates who had remained on it (Bulganin, Pervukhin and Saburov), i.e. to submit them to a disciplinary sanction. The fact that the Presidium of the CC had had an anti-Khrushchev majority before its correction by the CC Plenum was revealed as late as the XXII Congress. Perhaps sleeping dogs might have been allowed further rest had not Molotov's demonstrative stand against the new party programme, and the growing Sino-Soviet conflict encouraged Khrushchev to use his sharpest weapon, the charge against the 'dogmatists' of responsibility for the Stalinist terror. Shepilov, to whom this did not apply, was associated with the opposition to industrial decentralisation in Kusmin's speech at the XXI Party Congress (*Pravda,* February 5, 1959). Before, the only error for which he was reproached was his rather mild treatment of the artists' opposition (see note 70 above). This would have been no ground for demotion some months later, and would hardly have brought him into the neighbourhood of orthodox Stalinists such as Molotov and Kaganovich. We assume that the 'anti-party group' of June 1957, like so many earlier oppositions, was a conglomerate of persons dissenting for different reasons, united only in the demand for a change in the party leadership. Those to whom this demand was irrelevant, but who might have professional reasons for opposition to the particular point of conflict, i.e. Pervukhin and Saburov, were treated mildly. (Kosygin was the *only* one of the leading industrial managers who supported the change ; precisely for this reason he could eventually succeed Khrushchev, and partly repeal the change, without interrupting the continuity of party development.)

83. Contained in the published *Otchet* of the Congress, though not in the current press reports; summary in *Soviet Studies,* vol. XI, p. 220.

84. The text of these directives is only partially available in references in the army newspaper *Krasnaya zvezda,* September 26 and November 3, 1957. On the eve of Zhukov's fall, an article by V. Moskovski in *Partiinaya zhizn,* 1957, No. 20, warned against ascribing the victories of the Soviet armies to any individual, however gifted.

85. Cf. Zakharov's article in *Krasnaya zvezda,* March 26, 1958. Reports in this paper on party conferences in the army are summarised in *Soviet Studies,* vol. X, pp. 110.

86. 1957, No. 12.

87. *Kommunist Ukrainy,* May 1958 (which went to press before the adoption of the CC decision) had an article on the subject which upheld the supposed correctness of the 1948 decision, and on the supposedly continuing need to condemn 'formalistic' art. The July issue of the journal, however, published a decision of the Ukrainian CC (adopted on June 24, 1958) with the opposite emphasis, for which,

indeed, a good case could be made, as some Ukrainian writers and composers were amongst the worst sufferers.

88. A. Zis in *Izvestiya*, August 27, 1958.
89. *Pravda*, June 13, 1958.
90. An analysis of that novel, and its general setting, has been published by A. Dressler in *Soviet Studies*, vol. X, pp. 417 ff.
91. Cf. *Zarya Vostoka*, January 20, 1959.
92. A survey of the Congress has been given by A. Dressler in *Soviet Studies*, vol. XI, pp. 327 ff.
93. Figures for 1956, from *Dostizheniya sovetskoi vlasti za 40 let v tsifrakh*, Gosizdat 1957, pp. 165-6 and 192.
94. Cf. *Soviet Studies*, vol. IX, p. 446.
95. Such replacements were mentioned as a relatively frequent phenomenon (which helps to explain the reduction in the number of farms since the XX Party Congress) at the Conference of Statisticians which met in June 1957, reported in *Vestnik Statistiki*, 1957, No. 4.
96. Cf. *Soviet Studies*, vol. X, p. 92. Ya. Golyev (Chairman of the Agricultural Bank) stated in *Finansy SSSR*, 1958, No. 7, that by June 11th, 1958, 59 per cent of the farms had signed contracts for the purchase of MTS machinery; he was, however, greatly dissatisfied with the speed of payments even by those farms who had not required the credits offered.
97. *Partiinaya zhizn*, 1957, No. 3, summarised in *Soviet Studies*, vol. IX, pp. 447-8.
98. Apparently, Khrushchev regarded his old concept of 'agro-towns' as now coming into the scope of realisable aims ; at the Plenary Meeting of the CC in December 1959, he made quite a few observations on modern village buildings and amenities.
99. Cf. *Soviet Studies*, vol. X, pp. 89-90, 94, 186 and 239 ; report on the V Congress of the Kazakhstan trade unions, in *Kazakhstanskaya pravda*, May 24, 1958. Decision of the Presidium of VTsSPS, in *Trud*, June 1958 ; editorial of *Selskoye khozyaistvo*, August 22, 1958.
100. In his speech at the December 1959 Plenary Meeting of the CC (*Pravda*, December 26, 1959), V. V. Matskevich, USSR Minister of Agriculture, envisaged the acceptance of these two advantages of the *kolkhoz* system in an eventually unified system of socialist enterprise in agriculture.
101. Cf. N. Dyakonov's article in *Pravda*, August 19, 1957.
102. Cf. *Soviet Studies*, vol. X, pp. 237 ff. According to an article published in *Izvestiya*, August 21, 1960, in 1959 money wages had been introduced in about 6 per cent of the farms. The general introduction of money wages had to wait for the XXIII Party Congress, in April 1966.
103. Cf. *Soviet Studies*, vol. VIII, pp. 159-60 and vol. X, p. 81. I have dealt with the issues of the subsequent reform, ibid., vol. X, pp. 229 ff.
104. P. Yakovenko of the Volhynian Provincial Committee, writing in

Kommunist Ukrainy, 1958, No. 2. In 1953, 304 of the 585 *kolkhoz* chairmen were party members (65 of these had to manage without the support of a party group). The number of brigade leaders who were communists increased from a mere 104 to 658, that of party members in charge of livestock farms from 46 to 363 (if the kolkhozy of Volhynia maintain livestock farms in the prescribed numbers, this figure would indicate that one-fifth of all heads of livestock farms were communists.

105. I. Lebedev in *Kommunist*, 1958, No. 10. According to P. Zhukov's report from the same Province (in *Pravda*, June 13, 1958) individual *kolkhoz* party organisations were strengthened by 35 to 42 members coming from the MTS.

106. See also the report of the Credentials' Vertification Commission of the XXII Congress (*Pravda*, October 22, 1961). A report under the heading 'The Party in Figures' had been published in *Partiinaya thire*, 1962, No. 1 (English translation in *The Current Digest of the Soviet Press*, February 14, 1962) and the reports to the XXIII Congress : Ibid., March 30th and April 1st, 1966. The data for 1957 available from Georgia (*Zarya Vostoka*, January 29, 1958) and Azerbaidshan (*Bakinski rabochii*, January 29, 1958) show a remarkable co-incidence with the Union average, which is hardly explicable except by fairly firm directives issued for admission policy.

107. In the USSR as a whole, of the 83,100 *kolkhoz* chairmen existing on December 1, 1956, a mere 1,500 were women, *Dostizheniya sovetskoi vlasti za 40 let v tsifrakh*, p. 192.

108. *Partiinaya zhizn*, 1958, No. 5, p. 47.

109. A good illustration of the problems involved is given in A. Rekemchuk's novel *Summer Holiday Time*, English translation in *Soviet Literature*, 1959, No. 11.

110. I. Lebedev (Secretary of Stavropol Provincial Committee) in *Kommunist*, 1958, No. 10, p. 59. For earlier approaches maintained by agricultural economists cf. *Soviet Studies*, vol. X, p. 103.

111. Summary in *Soviet Studies*, vol. IX, pp. 99 ff.

112. Naturally enough, juridical representatives of the managerial interest attempted to interpret these rulings away. Their efforts, however, failed (ibid. pp. 406-7).

113. Cf. *Partiinaya zhizn*, 1957, No. 16, pp. 30 ff.

114. The Statute, and the materials of the developments leading to it, are reproduced, or summarised, in *Soviet Studies*, vol. X, pp. 176 ff.

115. In fact, while the Hungarian Workers' Councils ended in a catastrophe, the Polish, and in substance also the Yugoslav ones, have been co-ordinated with state management in a way which makes the difference from a straightforward democratisation of existing trade union machinery appear rather formal. Another solution was hardly possible

if party leadership, even of the 'Revisionist' Yugoslav pattern, was to be preserved.

116. This point was made with particular sharpness in Khrushchev's speech at the Komsomol Congress, April 18, 1958.

117. On these arguments cf. *Soviet Studies,* vol. IX, pp. 102 and 368, vol. X, pp. 104 and 432 ff.

118. *Pravda,* December 5, 1964.

119. *Vedomosti Verkhovnogo Soveta RSFSR,* No. 12 (March 24, 1966).

120. *Literaturnaya Gazeta,* December 20, 1958. The surveys of correspondence given in *Uchitelskaya gazeta,* December 5, and in *Pravda,* December 13, show overwhelming rejection of the suggestion which, indeed, had found few supporters other than some mathematicians looking for early recruits for their profession—and, of course, some ambitious parents. It did not appear in the law submitted to the Supreme Soviet, but one Kazakh woman deputy even at that stage found it necessary to protest against it.

121. August 24, 1964.

122. I have discussed the diverse stages of the reform, and also the processes which led to Khrushchev's fall, in my contributions to the *Annuaire de l'U.R.S.S.* published by the *Centre Nationale de la Recherche Scientifique,* 1965 and 1966. I restrict myself here to the reproduction of a few data, simply in order to show the continuity, in this and many other respects, with the Khrushchev period.

123. I. Sigov in *Sotsialicheskii Trud,* 1966, No. 2, p. 39.

124. 1965, No. 12.

LIST OF ABBREVIATIONS

CC—Central Committee (if no further description is added, of the party).

CCC—Central Control Commission (of the party).

CEC—Central Executive Committee (of the Soviets, before 1936).

CPSU—Communist Party of the Soviet Union (before 1952, the letter (b) indicating 'Bolsheviks' was added in brackets) ; see VKP (b).

Cheka—*Chrezvychainaya kommissiya*—Extraordinary Commission for the Struggle against the Counter-revolution and Speculation.

GPU—*Gosudarstvennoye politicheskoye upravleniye*—State Political Administration, Cheka's successor since 1922 ; eventually followed by the NKVD (People's Commissariat for Internal Affairs) and the MGB (Ministry for State Security).

Gosplan—State Plan Commission

Gubispolkomy—Gubernial (i.e. Provincial, before the re-organisation of the twenties) Executive Committees (of the Soviets).

MTS—Machine Tractor Stations.

NEP—New Economic Policy (introduced in 1921).

PC—People's Commissary, or Commissariat (since 1947 the terms 'Minister' and 'Ministry' were introduced).

Rabkrin—Workers' and Peasants' Inspection.

RSFSR—Russian Socialist Federal Soviet Republic; since 1922 the Russian member State of the USSR.

SNK, fuller *Sovnarkom*—Soviet of People's Commissaries—the Government, before its becoming, in 1946, the Soviet of Ministers.

SNKh—*Sovet narodnovo khozyaistva*—Economic Council during the period of War Communism.

Sovnarkhoz—Regional Economic Councils established in 1957.

VKP (b)—CPSU (b); since 1952 the Russian term is KPSS.

VTsIK—*Vserossiiski* (since 1923 *Vsesoyuzny*) *Tsentralny Ispolnitelny Komitet*—the All-Russian or All-Union, respectively, Central Executive Committee of the Soviets.

VTsSPS—*Vsesoyuzny Sovet Professionalnykh Soyuzov*—the All-Union Trade Union Council.

SELECT BIBLIOGRAPHY

Only those books are included which have been cited more than occasionally and the perusal of which is suggested as an introduction to further work on the subject. Books to which only occasional reference has been made are cited in footnotes only.

Congresses of the party are referred to by the first Russian word of the edition of the proceedings used, i.e. *Protokoly* for the earlier ones (which were published long after the event) and *Otchet* for the period since 1919 when they were published immediately after the conclusion of the Congress. Congresses of other bodies are simply referred to as 'Proceedings': no confusion regarding different editions is likely to arise on these materials, and the specialist interested will know where to find them. The distinction between the two kinds of party congress materials does not imply that the latter is more complete. Some of the *Protokoly* published in the Soviet periodicals provide the elaborate coverage expected of historical source of this kind, while, for example, the *Otchet* of the X Party Congress (1921) is hardly more than a compilation of newspaper reports.

O. V. Aptekman : *Obshchestvo zemlya i volya* (of the 1870s), Petrograd 1924 (on the basis of the first, 1906, edition).

Axelrod-Martov Correspondence : See correspondence.

A. Badayev : *The Bolsheviks in the Tsarist Duma,* English ed. (Moscow).

M. Balabanov : *Ocherki po istorii rabochevo klassa v Rossii* (Studies in the History of the Working Class in Russia). Quotations not marked otherwise refer to vol. II (Kiev 1924); vol. III was published in *Ekonomicheskaya zhizn,* Moscow 1926 ; vol. IV was published under the title *Ot 1905 g.k. 1917 : Massovoye rabocheye dvizheniye,* Moscow, Gosizdat 1927. These volumes are important as a collection of early source materials.

Guiseppe Boffa : *Inside the Khrushehev Era,* 1959.

J. Bunyan : *Intervention, Civil War and Communism in Russia, Documents and Materials.* Baltimore, Johns Hopkins University Press, 1936.

J. Bunyan and J. Fischer : *The Bolshevik Revolution* 1917-18 (Documents). Stanford University Press, 1934.

E. H. Carr : *A History of Soviet Russia : The Bolshevik Revolution,* vol. I (to which quotations, unless otherwise marked, refer), London 1950 ; vol. II, London 1952 ; vol. III, London 1953 (these three volumes deal with internal politics, the economics and the foreign politics of the 1917-22 period) ; vol. IV, *The Interregnum* (published 1955) deals with the year 1923. The following series *Socialism in One*

Country deals with the period 1924-28. Up to now ; vol. V (Economics) and vol. VI (Internal Policies) have been published.

A. Ciliga : *The Russian Enigma,* London 1940 (author's postwar publications, in French, contain no new material).

Correspondence between P. B. Axelrod and J. O. Martov (in Russian), ed. by F. Dan, *Russki revolyutsionny arkhiv,* vol. I.

Court Proceedings, of the trials of Pyatakov and Radek in 1937, and of Bukharin in 1938 ; the official English ed. with indications of the year of the trial are cited.

F. Dan : *Proiskhozhdeniye bolshevizma* (The Origins of Bolshevism), in Russian, New York, 1946. The best comprehensive study of the first period by a non-Bolshevik familiar with all the facts.

I. Deutscher : *Stalin, a Political Biography,* Oxford University Press 1949 (quotations refer to this book). *The Prophet Armed*: *Trotsky, 1879-1921,* OUP 1954. *The Prophet Unarmed*: *Trotsky, 1921-29,* OUP 1959. (This work is important because of its ample use of the Trotsky archives, which allows for a comparision with studies based upon the official documents).

M. Dobb : *Soviet Economic Development since 1917,* London 1948.

M. Eastman : *Since Lenin Died,* New York 1925, important as an early publication of Trotsky's documents, from a time when Trotsky himself was still restricted in his publications by party discipline.

J. Glazyrin : *Regulirovaniye sostava KPPS v period stroitelstva sotsializma* (The Regulation of the Social Composition of the CPSU—by the party itself—during the Period of Building Socialism), Gospolitizdat, Moscow 1957.

F. A. Golder : *Documents on Russian History* 1914-17, New York, 1927.

P. Gorin : *Ocherki po istorii sovetov rabochikh deputatov v 1905 g.* (Studies on the *History of the Soviets in* 1905), 2nd ed. Moscow, Kommakademiya, 1930.

S. I. Gusev : *The Lessons of the Civil War* (published by Comintern, 1921).

M. V. Nechkina, ed., *History of USSR,* University Textbook (in Russian), vol. II, 2nd ed., Moscow, 1949.

Istoriya kommunisticheskoi partii Sovetskovo Soyuza, Khrestomatiya, Gospolitizdat, Moscow 1959. Readings on the History of the Russian Revolution, especially of the Party, published by Istpart in seven successive volumes during the 1920s.

W. Knorin (ed.) : *Short History of the CPSU* (*b*), Moscow 1935 (the German ed. has been used).

KPSS v rezolyutsiyakh : see *VKP* (*b*) *v. rezolyutsiyakh.*

N. S. Khrushchev : Speech at the Secret Session of the XX Party Congress. (In the circumstances in which the text was published abroad, it is impossible to check the authenticity of the version available in most major western newspapers and, with some stylistic editing and in a propagandist framework, in B. D. Wolfe's *Khrushchev and Stalin's Ghost*, New York 1957. No more than the speech was made has been stated in Soviet publications. I used the document only in respects which are supported by internal evidence, or by the general attitude of other statements subsequently made in the Soviet press).

M. N. Lyadov : *Kak nachala skladyvatsya RKP (b)*. (The 1st ed. was published as *The History of the Russian Social Democratic Party* in 1906 ; the second, with little change of title, in Moscow 1925. The book is important as an early treatment of party history by a participant, without the later biases).

V. I. Lenin : *Sochineniya* (Collected Works). I have used the 4th Russian ed., which is more easily available, unless special reference is made to the 3rd ed., some important pieces of which as well as the interesting notes were omitted in the 4th ed. After the XX Party Congress, the items omitted in toto, and some important additional ones, were added as the XXXVI vol. of the 4th ed. (the XXXVII contains mainly personal correspondence, the XXXVIII Lenin's Philosophical Notes) which, of course, have been used and quoted. Publication of the new, complete, 5th edition started at a time when the present book was already half completed and did not in any case bring out any fundamentally new materials.

Where suitable, I have also quoted the English ed. (*Selected Works* or *Collected Works*—the latter a translation of a few volumes of the 3rd Russian edition), none of which even approaches comprehensiveness. In view of the quality of the translations, the specialist may be advised to use the Russian text.

V. Levitsky-Cederbaum : *Partiya 'Narodnaya Volya'*, Moscow 1928.

S. I. Liberman : *Dela i lyudi* (Facts and People), in Russian, New Democracy Books, New York 1944. Interesting as a reflection of the impressions received during the civil war period by a non-party specialist in a position of trust.

I. I. Mints : *Ob osveshchenii nekotorykh voprosov istorii velikoio Oktyabrskoio sotsialisticheskoi revolyutsii*, in *Voprosy istorii KPSS*, 1957, No. 2. I quote this article as an example of the more serious investigations of basic problems in recent party historiography.

M. Moskalev : *Russki byuro Ts. K. Bolshevistkoi Partii* (1912-March 1917), Moscow, Gospolitizdat, 1947.

Narodnoye Khozyaistvo SSSR (Statistical Handbook), Moscow 1956 (the first somewhat comprehensive publications of statistical data after the long eclipse of the late Stalin period).

Narodnaya Volya v dokumentakh i vospominaniyakh, Moscow, Society of former political prisoners, 1930 (most of the contributors were themselves former members of *Narodnaya Volya*).

V. Nevski : *Ocherki po istorii RKP* (Essays on the History of the Russian Communist Party), Ist part, vol. I, Petrograd 1923.

N. Nikitin : *Perviye rabochiye soyuzy i sotsialdemokraticheskiye organizatsii v Rossii* (The First Workers' Unions and Social Democrat Organisations in Russia), Gospolitizdat 1951 (like Moskalev's abovementioned book, a typical example of the more serious publications of the late Stalin period).

A. M. Pankratova : *Pervaya russkaya revolyutsiya 1905-07 gg.,* Moscow, Gospolitizdat, 1951.

Partiya v revolyutsii 1905 goda (collected documents), Partizdat, 1934.

Perepiska (Correspondence) of K. Marx and F. Engels with Russian political personalities (in Russian), Gospolitizdat 1947.

P. Pyatnitski : *Memoirs of a Bolshevik,* London, Martin Lawrence.

N. Popov : *Outline History of the C. P. of the Soviet Union,* 2 vols. ; London 1930 (most quotations are from vol. I and the vol. is indicated only where misunderstandings are possible).

L. Schapiro : *The Origin of the Communist Autocracy : Political Opposition in the Soviet State,* 1917-1922, London 1955 (quotations refer to this book).

———, *The Communist Party of the USSR,* London 1960.

E. Serebryakov : *Obshchestvo Zemlya i Volya,* in *Materialy dlva istorii russkovo sotsialno-revolyutsionnovo dvizheniya,* London, vol. XI.

A. G. Shlyapnikov :   1917 *god* (The year 1917), 2 vols. 2nd ed., Moscow 1923 (quotations, unless otherwise stated, refer to vol. 1).

Short History of the CPSU (*b*) : The official textbook of 1938, published under Stalin's personal supervision ; the English ed. is quoted.

I. V. Stalin : *Sochineniya* (Collected Works). In suitable places quotations from the 1947 English ed. of *Leninism* are added. No works dating later than 1933 are included in the published volumes; hence reference to periodicals or pamphlets has to be made.

S. Stepnyak : *Podpolnaya Rossiya* (Underground Russia, London 1893). With Serebryakov's above-mentioned work, published in the same collection, and also Aptekman's book, an example of writings of the pre-Marxist stage of the revolutionary movement, without hindsight.

N. Sukhanov : *Zapiski o revolyutsii* (Notes on the Revolution), 7 vols., Berlin-Petrograd-Moscow 1922 (this original edition, faithful to the author's original attitude to the events, and uninfluenced by the 'cold war', should be used).

I. Trotsky : *Sochineniya,* Moscow 1925-7. Eleven volumes were published.

M. Vetoshkin : *On the History of the Bolshevik Organisations and the Revolutionary Movement in Siberia* (1905-6, in Russia), Moscow, Gospolitizdat, 1947.

Franco Venturi : *Roots of Revolution,* London 1960.

VKP (*b*) *rezolyutsiyakh* : (The CPSU in Resolutions of its Congresses, Conferences, and Plenary Sessions of the CC). The main documentary source apart from Congress Proceedings, and supplementing the latter as it illustrates developments between Congresses.   I have generally used the 1936 ed. (in two vols. dealing with the years 1898-1925 and 1926-1935 respectively; the vol. is indicated only where misunderstandings are possible) since that edition gives some details which later were omitted, such as the composition of the CCs elected by the diverse Congresses. Where necessary, the 1941 ed. or the 1954 ed. (because of the changed title of the party : *KPSS v rezolyutsiyakh...*) are cited.

Voprosy partiinoi raboty : Questions of Party Work, Moscow, Gospolitizdat, 1957. A collection of relevant materials published in *Partiinaya zhizn* during the years 1954-57 but re-arranged so as to supply a handbook.

E. Yaroslavski : *History of the CPSU* (special reference—'1926'—are made to the first Russian ed. in three vols. ; the German ed. (of 1929) in two vols. has also been used. Comparison of the diverse editions of this standard textbook (before the publications of the *Short History* in the drafting of which, too, Yaroslavski took part) shows the development of the official version of party history.

A. A. Zhdanov : *On Literature, Music and Philosophy* (Collected speeches), London, Lawrence & Wishart, 1948.

INDEX

30

for the membership of, 195
Russian labour movement, 'agitation *vs* propaganda', 13
Russian Revolution, two stages of, 119
Russian Revolution (1905), the Bolsheviks in the, 60-70
Russian revolutionary movement : 3, 4, 15, 23, 35, 48, 219 ; prehistory and history of the, 2
Russian Social Democracy, Reunion and Defeat of, 71-82
Russian Social Democracy : 10, 26, 35, 48, 77 ; the first Congress of, 31 ; split of, 82, 88
Russian Social Democrats, members of the, 73
Ryazanov, F., 44, 112, 124
Rybinsk, insurrections at, 142
Rykov : 49, 125, 236, 239, 253, 299 ; arrest of, 82 ; expelled from the party, 299 ; on the Five Year Plan, 254 ; re-elected to the Politburo, 284 ; a special decision adopted by, 248
Ryutin : 299 ; expelled from the party & arrested, 286

Saburov, 387, 412, 413
Safarov, 232, 233
Saint Simon, 1
Samara, 141, 201
Sanina, 357, 358, 418
Sapronov, 168, 177
Saratov : 82 ; analysis of members re-registered in, 156-7
'saving-group for mutual aid', 11
Scherbatov, 94
Schmalhausen, 345
School children, increase in the number of, 274
Schooling of skilled workers, 274
'scissors' crisis, 214, 215
Second industrial revolution, 427
Second World War : 273, 310 ; the Party on the eve of the, 310-13 ;

31

Party's numerical development during the, 324 ; USSR entered the, 323
Secret session speech of Khrushchev, 291, 294, 299, 300, 301, 364, 373, 395, 396, 399, 407
Serebryakov : as secretary of the CC, 164 ; replaced by Molotov, 208
Shakhty group of mines, engineers of the, 248
Shatzkin, excluded from CC & CCC, 285
Shcherbatov, party organisation criticised by, 295
Shevernisk, candidate member of the Politburo, 307
Shkiryatov : and total party members on the eve of purge, 196-7 ; and trial of army personnel & state officials, 194
Shlyanikov : 76, 92, 96, 105, 177, 202 ; removal from the Central Purge Commission, 200
'shock-workers', 274
'shock-therapy', 396, 397
Short History of the CPSU, 79, 308
Siberian insurrections, 69
Sino-Soviet dispute, 407
Smilga, 196, 290
Smolensk Provincial party, corruption noted in the, 249
Social Democracy, 35, 36, 60, 61, 62, 63, 81
Social Democrat circles : and Narodnik, 27 ; and Narodovoltsy, 28
Social Democrat Duma, 88
Social Democrat factions, reunion of the two, 71
Social Democrat organisation, 70
Social Democrat party, 45, 46, 78, 79, 86
Social Democrat Workers' Party, 30